Pioneers in Forensic Science

Innovations and Issues in Practice

Pioneers in Forensic Science

Innovations and Issues in Practice

Kelly M. Pyrek

CRC Press
Taylor & Francis Group
Boca Raton London New York

CRC Press is an imprint of the
Taylor & Francis Group, an **informa** business

CRC Press
Taylor & Francis Group
6000 Broken Sound Parkway NW, Suite 300
Boca Raton, FL 33487-2742

First issued in paperback 2021

ISBN 13: 978-0-367-78400-3 (pbk)
ISBN 13: 978-1-4987-8529-7 (hbk)

Visit the Taylor & Francis Web site at
http://www.taylorandfrancis.com

and the CRC Press Web site at
http://www.crcpress.com

For Judi and Tony.

Contents

Preface

This book is a celebration of the expertise and contributions of leading members of the forensic science community, explored through the framework and context of the challenges faced by the profession. The inherent danger of such an endeavor is failing to be inclusive of every individual of merit; while no book can possibly include every practitioner, I have tried to include some of the more visible persons as a representation of the various disciplines and perspectives.

The pursuit of reform in forensic science has been an arduous journey. This book aims to refresh the reader on past attempts at course correction, present efforts at quality improvement, and future imperatives that require reconciliation of failures and triumphs within the medicolegal system.

While the old guard has practiced according to the techniques handed down by the masters, the next generation needs to synthesize the best of two worlds—the tried-and-true concepts and protocols, blended with the new agenda to improve reliability, raise standards, and enhance the field that drives the U.S. justice system.

The spirit of this book is unabashedly supportive of forensic science, tempered by the realistic understanding that every profession requires reexamination as science, technology, and techniques evolve, and that progress can only be made when past, present, and future coexist as teacher and student. I hope you'll join me on this journey of remembering all that makes forensic science an exceptional enterprise, and all that serves to provoke change and stimulate continued dialogue.

Acknowledgments

The author acknowledges the forensic science experts interviewed for this book. Their vision, passion, and dedication to their profession are an inspiration, and their quest to champion the truth and speak for the dead is essential to an effective justice system. The author also salutes forensic practitioners everywhere, and thanks them for their extraordinary service.

About the Author

Kelly M. Pyrek is an award-winning journalist who has served as editor of regional and national newspapers and magazines for more than 30 years. She holds established professional relationships with prominent members of the forensic science, legal, and healthcare communities. A graduate of the University of Southern California, she currently works in healthcare trade journal publishing. She is the author of three other books: *Forensic Nursing* (CRC Press, 2006), *Forensic Science under Siege* (Elsevier, 2007), and *Healthcare Crime: Investigating Abuse, Fraud, and Homicide by Caregivers* (CRC Press, 2011).

CHAPTER 1

The Forensic Science Experts: Pioneers, Masters, and Students

To understand modern forensic science, it is necessary to appreciate the origins of the field and understand that it is borne of some of the best (the quest for the truth) and the worst (crime, politics, adversarial adjudication) of humanity—and that it exists somewhere between an applied science and a technical science. Its birthright to pure science is denied by critics, while its proponents recognize that it shares the challenges inherent to any evolving enterprise. Its practitioners labor within this fractious environment, providing an essential service to the justice system while fending off criticisms of their intentions and their methodologies.

Forensic science operates within a realm of inherited processes from the masters and evolving techniques developed by its present-day practitioners, and this existence amidst old and new thinking may be contributing to some of the challenges that will be explored in this book. As Bell (2008, page 4) observes, "Forensic science is historical in practice as well as in philosophy. Many modern laboratory protocols recreate history with each rendition." Bell (2008, page 4) adds, "History and precedent lie at the heart of science, just as they do at the heart of the law. Forensic science lives where the two overlap." It is up to us to "understand where forensic science came from and how it evolved," in order to be "much better equipped to evaluate and apply it in the future" (Bell, 2008, page xiii).

It is not within the scope of this work to trace the history of forensic science when others have already done so quite admirably, such as Suzanne Bell, PhD, author *of Crime and Circumstance: Investigating the History of Forensic Science*. Bell, a forensic chemist at West Virginia University, reminds us that there was no initial nexus of information known as forensic science; the lineages of chemistry, biology, and pathology, she says, were separate from one another until early practitioners "borrowed and integrated existing science, technology and techniques" into the growing critical mass of information that could be construed collectively as forensic science (Bell, 2008, page 191). She calls forensic scientists the "archeologists of the recent past" because "We recover artifacts from a place, carefully recording their context. That place is usually a crime scene that imprisons the echoes of a moment frozen in time. The information recorded in that moment begins to decay the second it is created. We use our expertise to evaluate and interpret crime scene artifacts to recreate the likeliest scenario to explain what we found, where we found it, and in what condition. By doing so, we help sort out conflicting versions of what happened and why" (Bell, 2008, page xi).

Spitz (2006) says that the earliest association between law and medicine dates back to the Egyptian culture around 3000 BC, while more obvious medicolegal associations can be found in codes of law ranging from 1700 to 1400 BC. Ancient Greece had the work of Hippocrates, who studied medical and ethical issues and presented these opinions in court, while the ancient Roman civilizations employed amicus curiae (friends of the court) to provide expert testimony. Spitz (2006) observes, "Developments involving medico-legal investigations continued throughout the middle ages with greater reliance on medical testimony in cases of physical injury, infanticide, rape and bestiality." Medicolegal autopsies were performed as early as 1300 on victims of homicides and suicides and those individuals executed for their crimes. Spitz (2006) reports, "One of the first documents pertaining to post-mortem examinations was a Chinese handbook titled *His Yuan Lu*. It contained simple autopsy techniques, proposed general post-mortem guidelines, and discussed injuries caused by blunt and sharp instruments. It also offered comments on the determination of whether an individual in water had drowned or died prior to submersion and whether a burned victim was alive or dead at the onset of the fire."

Fast-forward several hundred years. The sixteenth century ushered in scholarly writings that further developed the concept of forensic science. Paulo Zacchias (1584–1659) came to be called the father of legal medicine for his comprehensive work on the characteristics of wounds and questionable deaths. By the mid-seventeenth century, formal lectures in forensic medicine were being held in Western Europe; as Spitz (2006) explains, "During this period, Germany had the most advanced court system in Europe and it was routine for physicians to render opinions in criminal proceedings regarding injuries and cause of death. Judicial authorities all over Europe were now using forensically knowledgeable physicians in criminal and civil trials. At this time, physicians had a limited role in regard to crime scene investigation which was typically carried out by the police; however, in complicated cases police investigators occasionally consulted a physician to discuss crime scene evidence."

The concept of medicolegal institutes through which medicolegal principles could be practiced began to spread throughout much of Europe in the 18th and 19th centuries. Spitz (2006) observes, "Continued research in forensic medicine and toxicology laid the foundation for the future of forensic pathology in Europe and the United States." The rise of the ancient coroner system in England in the twelfth century set the stage for the modern coroner and medical examiner office, and further set the wheels in motion for a more sophisticated approach to medicolegal death investigation and the practice of forensic science and criminalistics.

As Saferstein (2001) observes, "Forensic science owes its origins first to those individuals who developed the principles and techniques needed to identify or compare physical evidence, and second to those who recognized the necessity of merging these principles into a coherent discipline that could be practically applied to a criminal justice system." A number of individuals made significant contributions to the body of knowledge that was shaping up to be the field of forensic science. Mathieu Orfila (1787–1853) published one of the first treatises on the detection of poisons, and many consider him to be the one who established forensic toxicology as a scientific endeavor, according to Saferstein (2001). Alphonse Bertillon (1853–1914) created the study of anthropometry, a system of taking body measurements to distinguish one individual from another. Saferstein (2001) notes, "For nearly two decades, this system was considered the most accurate method of personal identification. Although anthropometry was eventually replaced by fingerprinting in the early 1900s, Bertillon's early efforts have earned him the distinction of being known as the father of criminal identification."

Fisher and Fisher (2007) say that despite this measurement called Bertillonage, real strides in fingerprinting came at the hands of Francis Galton, Henry Faulds, and Edward

Henry in the late nineteenth and early twentieth centuries. Edward Henry, head of Scotland Yard in the early 1900s, devised a system that became known as the Henry Classification System. It was eventually replaced by the computerized database known as the Automated Fingerprint Identification System (AFIS). Francis Galton (1822–1911) was the first to undertake a comprehensive study of fingerprints and established an early classification of prints to be used as proof of personal identification.

From a forensic serology point of view, a milestone was reached in 1901 when Karl Landsteiner discovered that human blood can be typed; however, in 1915, Leone Lattes (1887–1954) created a procedure for determining the classification of blood from a dried bloodstain, with important implications for the field of criminalistics. Alexander Wiener discovered the Rhesus factor in 1940 for various other blood subgroups. Albert Osborn in 1910 recognized the value of individualization of handwriting and other techniques, which eventually led to the discipline of questioned documents and evolved to include more modern techniques using paper, ink, and printing equipment.

In 1953, James Watson and Francis Crick used x-ray crystallography techniques developed by Rosalind Franklin to find the structure and function of deoxyribonucleic acid (DNA). There was limited use of DNA in the 1970s and 1980s, but its value was recognized. One of the first true DNA tests was created in the 1980s by Sir Alec Jeffreys, known as *genetic fingerprinting*, where DNA was digested with enzymes that caused it to break down into specific fragments that are unique to each person—these fragments were separated based on their size using electrophoresis, to create this "fingerprint" of the DNA in the electrophoresis gel image. This technique was used most famously in the Colin Pitchfork case to find the murderer of two young girls in England in 1983. Around the same time, scientist Kerry Mullis realized that DNA could be copied millions of times by mimicking natural processes occurring inside living cells—this came to be known as the polymerase chain reaction (PCR). It could be done in a lab to produce high levels of testable DNA from exceedingly small biological samples, and the tests could be run in such a way that accuracy was assured, lending further reliability and credence to the method.

Today's generation of forensic scientists owe a debt of gratitude to the individuals preceding them who pioneered the methods and mastered the critical thinking skills necessary in a profession so critical that it can convict the guilty and exonerate the innocent.

As we have seen, the nineteenth century helped forge the precursors to modern forensic science techniques, and its practitioners paved the way for the advances that were to come from successors. Building upon each decade that came before it, forensic scientists have crafted their field from the rigors of chemistry, biology, and medicine. This book recognizes that the work of a handful of notable individuals is constructed upon the study and discipline of countless men and women who helped advance the science to what it is today. As Bell (2008, page 191) reminds us, "The forensic profession crystallized around strong personalities such as Orfila, Spilsbury, Norris, McCrone, Bertillon, Galton, Kind, Helpern and others. Many stumbled into the spotlight; others chased it. Where crime, blood and murder are the subjects, there is no lack of audience." These individuals left a legacy that continues today, and as we will see in Chapter 6, the decades have not diminished the demand for their work as much as their fascinating personas. As Bell (2008, page 191) observes, "Many of today's forensic scientists can trace their professional lineage to one or more of these men, and many of them have become famous in their own right."

As Hebrard and Daoust (2013, page 274) explain, "During the second half of the 19th century, under the influence of a group of forensic pathologists and scientists, a new set of ideas and common views about forensic science and the law were introduced.

Young industrial societies were not satisfied with confession anymore; sciences had to break into the investigation process and the criminal trial in order to reinforce the judicial system. These pioneers spread forensic sciences thanks to a criminological approach and the issue of crime repetition (recidivism)."

Let's take a brief look at a few more individuals whose contributions helped shape modern forensic science. Austrian Hans Gross, who practiced a unique comparative analytical science through the late 1800s and into the turn of the century, is considered by some to be the more historic father of criminalistics, recognized for his worldview that practitioners from various disciplines could help form expert opinion and contribute to the analysis of physical evidence for the purpose of solving crimes. Gross wrote what is considered to be the first forensic science textbook, called *Criminal Investigation*, and launched a professional journal titled *Kriminologie*.

One of Gross's contemporaries was Frenchman Edmond Locard, an expert in medicine as well as in law who created the first forensic laboratory in 1910. The tenet known as Locard's exchange principle was named for him and is an offshoot of his studies and writings. Every contact leaves a trace, Locard taught, and an exchange of materials between individuals and locations can help inform the investigational process. Locard (1930, pages 279–298) once noted that "the microscopic debris that covers our clothes and bodies are the mute witnesses, sure and faithful, of all our movements and all our encounters." He also observed, "It is impossible for a criminal to act, especially considering the intensity of a crime, without leaving traces of this presence" (Houck, 2001, page xix).

Even as criminalistics was finding its own way, physicians working in clinical forensic medicine had been serving the justice system in the United Kingdom for at least a century, according to Payne-James (2016, pages 539–567), who observes, "What is remarkable is that the nature of the cases [of the late 1800s and early 1900s] is not far removed from those seen today." Bell (2008) alludes to a distinct dichotomy of the evolution of forensic science in the United States, with forensic pathology making strides in the East while criminalistics gains advances in the West.

The advent of modern policing did provide an opportunity for forensic science methods from the masters to gain recognition for their ability to help advance criminal investigations. August Vollmer, chief of police around the turn of the century in Berkeley, California, recruited faculty members from the University of California at Berkeley (UC Berkeley) to assist with casework, using the knowledge of academic experts in biology and chemistry in a newly founded school of criminology that addressed police procedures and physical evidence. In 1937, Vollmer's program became a part of UC Berkeley's academic programs, and a young upstart by the name of Paul L. Kirk, PhD, assumed the position of advisor to the criminology program. Vollmer and Kirk emphasized the importance of standardization and the adaptation of new technology for criminal investigation and evidence processing in a laboratory setting in 1916, and this was directed by Albert Schneider. While Locard is credited with establishing the first forensic laboratory, experts everywhere were beginning to create facilities that were building upon the earliest precepts from Locard.

Hebrard and Daoust (2013, page 3) note, "Since the 1990s, confession is no longer the greatest kind of criminal evidence. Forensic sciences have become the scientific benchmark that legal systems cannot do without and that stands next to, if not ahead of, other kinds of criminal evidence in priority. At the end of the 20th and beginning of the 21st centuries, information technologies joined the area of forensic sciences. Criminalistics already included fingerprints, ballistics, toxicology, arson and explosives investigations, documents and handwriting analyses, microanalysis, traffic accidentology, anthropology, entomology, and so on. The field continued to expand as new forensic fields of identification, such as DNA technology, new tools that managed evidence, such as Automated Fingerprint Identification System (AFIS), and new means of criminality, such as cybercrime, became available."

Internationally recognized forensic scientist Henry Lee, PhD, recalls the evolution of forensic science. "It was more sophisticated in the U.S. but in the 1970s, England was way ahead of the U.S.," Lee says. "The Scotland Yard laboratory had many good scientists and I got to know them and they invited me to England quite a few times. We did some joint projects. The U.S. in the 1970s there were maybe 100 laboratories, now there are probably 420 labs. The first lab was established in 1949 in the U.S.—the Chicago Police Department and the Berkley Police Department set up a lab, so over the years it has grown; the first major growth was in the 1970s because of the significant drug problem so they need drug testing labs—so most labs were busy with drug analysis. Then by the 1980s, with new protein markers, the advent of serology, so that was the second growth phase, because of a lot of rape cases and sexual assault cases where you have to do the typing. Then in the late 1980s when DNA came along, this is a major event in the forensic field—so traditional forensic evidence, such as fingerprints, document analysis, firearms, they all, in recent years, have new advances. For example, in firearms they have an automated system such as AFIS and NIBIN so in the early days you line up the bullets side by side and you look at the comparison scope and the examiner makes a very subjective call. Now, it is all computerized. In the early days of fingerprints the technician would have to do a manual search one by one. DNA, retina, fingerprints, combined, for human biometric identification. Image enhancement in recent years there has been tremendous change—everything is computerized and Internet based. And white collar crime committed by computers—computer crime units will be the next major growth."

As we have seen, while he is not a forensic scientist, the work of Sir Alec Jeffreys in the area of DNA profiling and fingerprinting paved the way for much of the analysis that is used today in modern forensic investigation. A geneticist, Jeffreys was working as a professor at the University of Leicester in Britain when he first realized the potential of DNA to identify individuals. Jeffreys had been studying x-ray images of a DNA experiment he was running in his lab when the epiphany struck, and now his techniques are a backbone of modern forensic identification methods. As Hebrard and Daoust (2013, page 3) observe, "Evolving from classical serology, DNA profiling could be considered the modern-day technique revolutionizing personal identification in forensic science. In the mid-1980s, Jeffreys developed the techniques allowing the profile analysis of DNA."

Zagorski (2006, pages 8918–8920) describes Jeffreys' recollection of his big discovery on September 10, 1984: "…'we got our first truly awful DNA fingerprint purely by chance,' Jeffreys says. Yet as soon as he took a look at what he remembers being 'a horrible, smudgy, blurry mess,' he could tell what was going on: he could spot the family group present in that blot and distinguish all three members by what appeared to be a simple pattern of inheritance. 'We suddenly realized that we'd essentially stumbled upon a DNA-based method for biological identification. My life completely changed at that point,' he says." Zagorski (2006, pages 8918–8920) adds, "After the discovery of the first DNA fingerprint, Jeffreys rushed out of the X-ray developing room and proclaimed to his group, 'I think we're onto something really exciting here.' Within a half-hour, he and his laboratory had written down a slew of potential applications, including forensics, paternity or twin testing, and conservation biology. 'We were then faced with two challenges, really. The first was to improve the technology from that blurry mess to something that would actually be reliable enough for real casework.'"

After publishing his achievements in the journal *Nature* in 1985, Jeffreys was called upon to apply his techniques to solve the first crime in 1986. Zagorski (2006, pages 8918–8920) explains: "In 1986, Jeffreys was contacted by local police regarding a murder case where two schoolgirls had been raped and murdered three years apart in an apparent copycat killing. The police had a suspect in custody, but although he confessed to the second murder, he denied the first. Jeffreys was asked to use DNA profiling to tie the suspect to both cases. The results were completely unexpected: both semen samples belonged to the same man but were not from the suspect. Jeffreys initially thought something was flawed with the DNA profile, because the police were sure they had their culprit, but repeated tests confirmed the discrepancy, and the suspect was eventually set free. 'And that's something a lot of people forget,' Jeffreys says. 'They tend to see DNA as a powerful tool for the prosecution, but don't realize it's just as powerful for the defense.'" Zagorski (2006, pages 8918–8920) quotes Jeffreys as explaining, "Then the police did something that I thought was fantastically brave. Rather than disbelieve DNA, they totally believed it and launched what proved to be the world's first DNA-based manhunt, asking for blood samples from men from the entire local community."

Zagorski (2006, pages 8918–8920) notes further, "In a Hollywood-like twist though, the perpetrator devised an elaborate deception wherein he forged his passport and had a friend stand in for him as a proxy. Fortunately, the friend confessed to the ruse while at a pub one night, which allowed for the apprehension of the real murderer, who was positively profiled via DNA testing. 'So that was the birth of forensic DNA in real casework,' says Jeffreys, 'and this was DNA potentially saving the life of future victims, which was quite sobering stuff.'"

After the British Home Office Forensic Science Service had used Jeffreys' DNA profiling techniques to identify Colin Pitchfork as the murderer of Dawn Ashworth and Lynda Mann in Leicestershire, England, Hebrard and Daoust (2013, page 3) point to an immediate commercialization of the science: "Cetus Corporation furthered the developments of DNA profiling and molecular biology techniques in personal identification during the rest of the 1980s with the development of the PCR. With PCR technology applied to short tandem repeats (STRs), it became possible to generate DNA profiles from tiny stains, minute amount of DNA, or fragmented DNA where longer variable number tandem repeats (VNTRs) failed to give any informative data." They add, "Although STR analysis together with PCR amplification enabled forensic laboratories to increase sensitivity of the method and, therefore, to obtain complete DNA profiles from low DNA templates, the problem of DNA degradation of numerous crime scene samples, leading to inconclusive results, had to be solved. During 1996, the FBI DNA Analysis Unit began using mitochondrial DNA. In 2003, STR primers were redesigned to generate shorter amplicons. This approach, named 'mini-STR,' significantly improved the success rate for poor-quality samples. Nowadays 9-plex mini-STR amplification kits are on the market, and mini-STRs are implemented in various standard 15-plex STR amplification kits. These types of analyses can be applied to compromised biological samples and samples with low quantity of nuclear DNA such as hair, old bones, or teeth, allowing the examination of evidence that may not have been suitable for comparison before the development of these techniques" (page 3).

PAYING HOMAGE TO THE MASTERS

It would be difficult *not* to be inspired by scientists such as Locard, Kirk, and Jeffreys. Much like today, forensic practitioners salute the individuals that most shaped their medicolegal perspectives and engage in a little hero worship from time to time. As Shaler (2009, page 2) explains, "Who influenced Locard the most? He attributes his revelation with respect to trace evidence's importance in criminal investigation to two seemingly divergent historical figures." Those individuals were Gross and Sir Arthur Conan Doyle, who in turn had been influenced by his mentor, Dr. Joseph Bell. As Shaler (2009, page 64) notes, "Hans Gross was a forensic giant at that time, so it is little surprise that Locard studied Gross's 1893 *Manual for Examining Magistrates*. From Locard's perspective, this arguably formed the basis of modern criminalistics, if he thought of it as that, because this was the first publication describing the marriage among science, the crime scene investigation and the law; Locard's passions. Gross combined, for the first time, fields of knowledge that had not previously been integrated. As Locard wrote in 1930, 'It would a mistake to believe that the idea of studying dust for the purpose of discovering criminological evidence is of modern origin. By seeking diligently, we may trace it to the old masters of legal medicine. However, the first author who clearly described cases where this research has been made is Hans Gross.' Continuing, he wrote, 'In his 'Manual for Examining Magistrates' Gross grouped together everything in these various teachings that would contribute to the building up of a good criminal investigation.'"

Paul L. Kirk is considered to be the American father of criminalistics, following the work of Gross and adding to the critical mass of knowledge of the field as he built the criminalistics program at UC Berkeley beginning in the late 1930s. Kirk was active in the study of and research in numerous areas of trace evidence, and authored the pivotal textbook *Crime Investigation* in 1953. Celebrity touched Kirk's life when he analyzed crime scene evidence in the Sam Sheppard case, in which the physician was accused of murdering his wife—this case was the basis of a television show in the 1960s and the 1994 movie both titled *The Fugitive*. Kirk concluded that Sheppard had not committed the crime, and blood typing and blood spatter figured prominently in court testimony.

Kirk (1953) summarizes the principle that drives criminalistics: "Wherever he steps, whatever he touches, whatever he leaves, even unconsciously, will serve as silent evidence against him. Not only his fingerprints or his footprints, but his hair, the fibers from his clothes, the glass he breaks, the tool mark he leaves, the paint he scratches, the blood or semen that he deposits or collects—all these and more bear mute witness against him. This is evidence that does not forget. It is not confused by the excitement of the moment. It is not absent because human witnesses are. It is factual evidence. Physical evidence cannot be wrong; it cannot perjure itself; it cannot be wholly absent. Only its interpretation can err. Only human failure to find it, study and understand it, can diminish its value."

According to the American Board of Criminalistics, criminalistics is defined as "the profession and scientific discipline directed to the recognition, identification, individualization and evaluation of physical evidence by application of the physical and natural sciences to law." As Bell (2008, page 195) explains, "Kirk was a forensic science generalist in the sense that he believed forensic scientists should have a broad scientific education and knowledge of many aspects of physical evidence. He considered individualization the primary skill and distinction of forensic science. Criminalists, in Kirk's view, were tasked with finding common sources and linking evidence to its source. Locard had voiced the same philosophy. In this view, identification of evidence is secondary to individualization."

Bell (2008, page 2) asserts that Kirk and Locard "considered forensic science to be the science of comparison. If a red spot is tested and if it is determined to be blood, then it can be compared to a blood sample from the victim. The science used to perform the comparison, Kirk and Locard would argue, is not forensic science. Rather it is the comparison itself and the interpretation of the results that defines the science used as forensic science." Bell (2008, page 3) adds, "In forensic comparison and classification, smaller groups are better; groups with one member are best. The goal is always to analyze and successively categorize evidence until it belongs to a group consisting of one. With proper caveats, fingerprints and DNA evidence can fall within this ideal; for any fingerprint, there is one and only one possible source. Most forensic comparisons are less definitive."

Kirk himself noted in 1963, "Criminalistics is an occupation that is poorly understood by the great majority of people, including the scientific public. It is generally assessed in terms of high-grade detective work rather than in terms of a serious and very demanding type of applied science." He added, "As a science, criminalistics is new, even though many of its techniques are not" (page 236). Kirk (1963, page 238) also asserted, "Criminalistics is an occupation that has all of the responsibility of medicine, the intricacy of the law, and the universality of science. Inasmuch as it carries higher penalties for error than other professions, it is not a matter to take lightly, not to trust to luck."

CARRYING ON THE KIRK LEGACY

Even though the School of Criminology at UC Berkeley was disestablished in 1975, a generation of practitioners had studied under Kirk and were ready to carry on his legacy. One of the practitioners following in the footsteps of Kirk is George F. Sensabaugh Jr., professor of biomedical and forensic sciences in the School of Public Health at UC Berkeley. He is also a faculty affiliate in the graduate group in forensic science at the University of California, Davis. The criminalistics program was saved and transferred into the School of Public Health, and Sensabaugh observes, "Kirk died in 1970 so he was spared the turmoil associated with the closing of the School and the move to Public Health."

Sensabaugh says that above all, a lasting legacy for the field is Kirk's staunch belief that forensic science should be a science. "It was a continuing theme throughout all that Kirk wrote and lectured about," he says. "Kirk believed that forensic science should address particular problems, as science is an exercise in problem-solving. He believed there should be certain standards for making decisions about what is established and what is in question—this concept permeated all that he did, and it is a notion to which I adhere as well."

Sensabaugh adds, "Kirk was not overly fond of the term 'forensic science' but he did like the word 'criminalistics,' a term he derived from the title of Hans Gross's *Handbuch für Untersuchungsrichter als System der Kriminalistik (Handbook for Examining Magistrates as a System of Criminalistics)*. The idea of applying the scientific approach to the investigation of crime, which was part of Gross's legacy, appealed to Kirk. He brought criminalistics into the domain of science."

With typical laser focus, Kirk (1963, page 235) identified shortcomings in forensic science: "With all of the progress that has been made in this field, and on a wide front, careful examination shows that for the most part, progress has been technical rather than fundamental, practical rather than theoretical, transient rather than permanent. … In short, there exists in the field of criminalistics a serious deficiency in basic theory and principles, as contrasted with the large assortment of technical procedures."

Sensabaugh says that Kirk was troubled by the field's struggle with that deficit in scientific principles, decades before legal scholars began documenting the trend and culminating in a number of scathing reports from government and scientific agencies.

"The concept for which he is most commonly known—individualization—requires an understanding of probability and statistics and is essential for people who are going to enter the field; but it is debated and contested even to this day," Sensabaugh says. "Several of Kirk's graduate students—Charles Kingston in particular, who is now retired but was on the faculty of John Jay College of Criminal Justice in New York—tried to develop statistical models for fingerprint evidence, for example. Kirk had the general notion that if you wanted to put some weight on some evidentiary analysis, that you needed to have some understanding of a statistical foundation for it. There are certain principles that are involved in individualization, of which probability and statistics play a part. This was a defining characteristic of criminalistics."

Sensabaugh notes the inherent contradictions involved. "In some respects, the concept of individualization is contrary to the use of probability and statistics because using DNA as an example, we can state that a particular DNA profile would be expected in a random sampling of a population of unrelated individuals to occur within one in some very large number (one in a billion, for example), but individualization is being able to say that this DNA belongs to John Doe and no one else. So the two notions—individualization, and putting statistical weight on the value of an evidentiary analysis—are not completely compatible with each other. So I think trying to figure out approaches to the analysis of evidence so that we can discriminate between samples of evidence that have different origins is something of a holy grail; it is nevertheless not something that can be stated assertively. In the various reports that have been critical of forensic science, that point was made very clearly."

In Chapter 2, we will examine in more detail the forensic disciplines and concepts that have come under fire; as we acknowledge the contributions of the earliest forensic scientists, we must accept that some of these concepts—and the forensic disciplines that employ them—are at the heart of the biggest debates.

As Page (2014, pages 26–27) notes, "Many of the traditional and formerly unquestioned areas of forensic science, such as fingerprints, have come under criticism for their lack of scientific underpinning. One of the main issues with these areas of forensic science is that their theories were developed by relying on inductive reasoning, rather than the now more favorable scientific epoch of deduction and the hypothetico-deductive model."

Regarding Locard's/Kirk's individuality principle, Crispino and Houck (2015, pages 9–10) observe, "In its strongest form, it posits that each object in the universe can be placed demonstratively into a set with one and only one member: itself. It therefore asserts the universal statement. 'Every object in our universe is unique.' ... There is little question that all things are unique—two identical things can still be numerically differentiated—the core question is, can they be distinguished at the resolution of detection applied? ... Uniqueness is necessary to claim individualization, but not sufficient. Thus, it is the degree of association that matters, how similar, how different these two things being compared are."

In addition to individualization, probability is another concept under scrutiny. In any forensic science investigation, examiners must deal with uncertainty, such as how likely it is that the recovered trace came from the suggested source. Probability is a way of assessing the likelihood of a specific event, with statistics referring to the examination of uncertainty. According to the National Institutes of Justice (NIJ), the two types of probability are aleatory (the deduction from the observation of a system), which is ideal, and epistemic (induction from the observation of a system), which is realistic. Deduction is a conclusion from a stated premise, moving from the general to the specific, while induction refers to deriving general principles from facts or instances, moving from the specific to the general. Issues and limitations associated with probability in forensic science include ensuring consistency and reproducibility.

What must be considered are two competing propositions for a particular event and the probability of the observations in each case, followed by the calculation of a likelihood ratio (LR). The greater the LR, the greater the support for the prosecution proposition. As Biedermann and Curran (2014, page 38) observe, "Statistics ... provides us with the full package that we need to address the real problems in forensic science on an operational level. On the one hand, we have probability theory that allows us to reason coherently in situations characterized by uncertainty. On the other hand, we have decision theory, which instructs us how to use coherently informed beliefs in action. We can state this more explicitly as follows: probability theory allows us to revise our belief about propositions of interest (e.g., propositions of common source), based on results of comparative examinations, which results in an indication as to whether (and if so, to what extent) or not our uncertainty about those propositions ought to be reduced; decision theory instructs us in how to make a decision based on those coherently informed beliefs, that is a decision about whether or not we ought to conclude that two compared items come from a common source."

Interpreting and communicating statistics is a key task for bench scientists, although Aitken et al. (2010) observe, "Well-informed observers have for many decades been arguing the case for making basic training in probability and statistics an integral component of legal education. But little tangible progress has been made. It is sometimes claimed that lawyers and the public at large fear anything connected with probability, statistics or mathematics in general, but irrational fears are plainly no excuse for ignorance in matters of such great practical importance. More likely, busy practitioners lack the time and opportunities to fill in persistent gaps in their professional training. Others may be unaware of their lack of knowledge, or believe that they understand but do so only imperfectly." They propose that "the objective should be to equip forensic practitioners to become responsible producers and discerning consumers of statistics and confident exponents of elementary probabilistic reasoning. It is a question of each participant in criminal proceedings being able to grasp at least enough to perform their respective allotted roles effectively in the interests of justice" (page 4). A handy reference is the Federal Judicial Center's *Reference Manual on Scientific Evidence*, which provides a valuable and instructive template. Written with the needs of a legal (primarily, judicial) audience in mind, it covers a range of related topics, including data collection, data presentation, base rates, comparisons, inference, association and causation, multiple regression, survey research, epidemiology, and DNA evidence. As we will see in an upcoming section on evidence, the underpinnings of forensic science are constantly being called into question.

The concepts of individualization and identification also continue to be debated by legal scholars. Koehler and Saks (2008) argue that no scientific basis exists for the proposition that forensic scientists can "individualize" an unknown marking such as a fingerprint or tire track to a particular person or object to the exclusion of all others in the world. However, to Kirk, individualization was everything, and as he explained, "The criminalist does not attempt identification except as a prelude to his real function—that of individualizing. The real aim of all forensic science is to establish individuality, or to approach it as closely as the present state of the science allows. Criminalistics is the science of individualization. It is concerned only incidentally with identification in its ordinary sense. This unfortunate failure of nomenclature derives from the development of methods for identifying an individual by his fingerprints or otherwise, which gave rise to the 'identification bureaus' in most police departments. What was actually done was not the identification of the fingerprint, but rather the individualization of a person as the one who left the fingerprint. Thus, the entire subject of criminalistics started with a nomenclature that was inconsistent with science at large, and the terminology has never been brought into line by making the critical distinction of the field as a separate science of individuality" (Kirk, 1963, page 236).

Like Koehler and Saks, Kaye (2010) does not believe that uniqueness has been established in any of the traditional forensic sciences such as handwriting, toolmark identification, shoe prints, or fingerprints, and he also does not believe that mere matching—without a showing of uniqueness—can establish individualization in the typical case. Many legal scholars emphasize that "court testimony by experts asserting that an object has been linked to its source to the exclusion of all others in the world is not a scientifically reliable statement in any traditional forensic science discipline given the current state of knowledge" (Koehler and Saks, 2010, pages 1163–1185).

However, Kaye (2010, pages 1163–1185) is dubious that "science cannot establish the uniqueness of objects" and suggests that "there are circumstances in which an analyst reasonably can testify to having determined the source of an object" (page 1166). He adds that "individualization—the conclusion that 'this trace came from this individual or this object'—is not the same as, and need not depend on, the belief in universal uniqueness. Consequently, there are circumstances in which an analyst reasonably can testify to having determined the source of an object, whether or not uniqueness is demonstrable" (pages 1163–1185). General uniqueness refers to all the profiles in the population, and as Kaye (2010, pages 1163–1185) asserts, "For Saks and Koehler, however, no probability of duplication is small enough to warrant an opinion that DNA or anything else is unique." Kaye (2010, pages 1163–1185) adds, "The threshold issue for the law, therefore, is not the impossibility of falsifying universal propositions. It is whether criminalists are warranted in believing, as a practical matter, that certain universals (everyone has different fingerprints, everyone other than identical twins have different genomes, every face is unique, and so on) are true. If these beliefs are warranted, and if criminalists can measure the features that give rise to these differences with sufficient accuracy, then their claims to be able to individualize are sound. If these beliefs outstrip available theory and knowledge, as Saks and Koehler claim and as the NAS committee agrees (except, it seems, for DNA evidence), then the beliefs are either premature or false" (page 1172).

Legal scholars have gone so far as to coin the concept of "the individualization fallacy," which Koehler and Saks (2010) define as "the belief that a particular known person or object must be the source of questioned markings whenever (a) the examiner judges that a sufficient number of characteristics are observable in both the questioned markings and the known, and (b) the examiner cannot otherwise distinguish the questioned markings from the known. In other words, the fallacy arises when the forensic scientist rules out all other possible sources for the unknown marking, including the multitude he has not examined, once he has found a single object or person that matches the features of the unknown marking. The fallacy is deeply entrenched in forensic science practice, where most examiners say that their knowledge, training and experience enable them to make the inferential leap from observed consistencies between markings and their putative source to a conclusion that no other object in the world could have produced those markings" (pages 1163–1185).

The issue revolves around being scientific in the application of forensic science techniques. As Evett (1993, page 73) notes, "Being an expert in any area of forensic science demands a range of qualities, some innate, some acquired through education, training and expertise." Evett (1993, page 73) alludes to three aspects of expertise for forensic scientists: pattern identification, probabilistic judgment, and reasoning, and adds, "Throughout the world, forensic scientists face growing fundamental challenges: the implementation of new and increasingly powerful techniques; increased demand from growing crime levels; and the increased pressure of budgetary restraint. In such environments it is tempting to concentrate on the purely technical and organizational aspects of our work. Techniques can be refined, organizations can be made slicker and more efficient, but the quality of the product which we deliver is determined by how good we are at handling observations and turning them into high quality information. This, I believe, is where the science of our craft lies. We are supposed to be the experts and we also claim to be scientific in the application of our expertise."

Bell (2008, page 2) says, "The best forensic scientists must have a breadth of knowledge across the sciences coupled with the ability to use that knowledge to make meaningful comparisons and draw defensible conclusions."

Instead of statements from examiners that reflect mystique ("When you've been doing the job as long as I have..."), intuition ("I rely on my gut feeling..."), complacency ("I've done thousands of cases and I've never been shown to be wrong..."), and entrenchment ("It's stood the test of time..."), Evett (1993) proposed a new ethos of scientific expertise that embraced study and debate ("What are our fundamental principles?"), continuous improvement ("Why do I do it this way? Is there a better way?"), self-analysis ("Why do I think this?"), and calibration ("Am I as good as I think I am?").

It's debatable whether or not progress has been made since Kirk observed in 1963, "With all the progress that has been made ... careful examination shows that for the most part, progress has been technical rather than fundamental, practical rather than theoretical, transient rather than permanent. In short, there exists in the field of criminalistics a serious deficiency in basic theory and principles, as contrasted with the large assortment of effective technical procedures" (Inman and Rudin, 2001, page 76).

Sensabaugh acknowledges the potential for examiner error and says its practitioners must remain vigilant. "Unfortunately, human error is always a possibility," he says. "There are a number of points in the forensic process when human error can enter, from mixing up samples in the lab, to contamination, to errors in analysis and interpretation. Some legal commentators have pointed to a case in San Jose, California where someone's DNA profile is picked up at the scene of a homicide and yet that person happened to be in jail at the time the homicide occurred. It was later discovered that the person whose DNA was found had been in contact with the EMT and when the EMT was at the scene of the homicide, apparently there was a secondary transfer of DNA to the scene. There are always going to be problems of that kind and while that case is an extreme example, it certainly makes a point that even DNA evidence is not infallible. Although, that said, the DNA did correctly identify a particular individual. The question, however, was whether that individual was involved with the homicide. And the answer to that question was, no, the individual couldn't have been involved in the homicide. And so we have to be careful when we make statements that we are presenting a proposition that a certain item of evidence originated from some particular source—whether from a person or a tool of some kind. There's the additional question of whether that particular person or tool is associated with the incident that is under investigation. It's all too easy to leap from saying we have a DNA identification, so he must be the guilty party; or a DNA identification to this particular tool means he must be guilty since it was found at the scene of the crime."

The question of DNA as a gold standard in forensic work will be discussed further in Chapter 2. Sensabaugh addresses the broader question of the capacity to put statistical weight or probabilistic weight on DNA evidence. "That issue arises because of the nature of DNA, and what it can accomplish in its biological function," he says. "For example, we know—and have known for a very long time—the fundamentals of genetics and population genetics, so we can use the population genetics models that have been developed quite independently of forensic science as the foundation for assigning a weight on the value of a particular DNA profile. We also know there are certain caveats—the standard weight is going to be based on an unrelated individual but if we are dealing with a potentially related individual, then the statistics will change and we know how to make those changes—could it have been a brother? And so the stats will change and we know how to accommodate that change in statistical weight. DNA provides a gold standard, not simply because we can put a probabilistic weight on any particular DNA profile that we obtain, but we have a very solid foundation in biology which provides the basis for making those probabilistic statements."

The challenge is transferring the gold standard of DNA to pattern evidence such as fingerprints, firearms, and bite marks. As we will see in Chapter 2, the reliability of these forms of evidence has come under continued question.

"Pattern recognition and pattern analysis have become problematic in the eyes of some people," Sensabaugh confirms, adding that the discipline has its ongoing, persistent challenges as its scientific value continues to be debated, and the aforementioned individualization fallacy continues to be asserted by critics.

"When it comes to fingerprints, we can accept as a given that every individual has a unique set of fingerprints and we can ascertain that—if not in the same kind of fundamental way we can with DNA profiles, for example—we can do it in an empirical way," Sensabaugh says. "We can look at efforts to seek matches through very large databases and determine how often we find two fingerprints that are indistinguishable from each other. To date, that has not happened. With computer-based technology we can look at millions of fingerprints and compare them to other millions of fingerprints and do comparisons. The practical issue is that fingerprints encountered as evidence are somewhat malleable, meaning that if pressure is put on a finger in a particular way, some of the fine detail of the print may be obscured or may appear to be oriented somewhat differently than it would be in an exemplar print from the same individual. A lot of that can be taken into account using mathematical construction; one can use imaging technology to consider degrees of variation that a particular mark might make or a particular mark might be missing because the print is a partial print. One can also take into account—based upon extensive database searches—how often a particular print shows some number of points of comparison. We look at how often that same sort of pattern can be found in an extensive database, and there are statistical likelihood approaches that have been developed for that."

Sensabaugh adds that the utilization of that approach—putting some probabilistic weight on a limited match of a latent print found at the scene of the crime and an exemplar print from a particular individual—has not gained much traction, particularly in the United States. "The standard practice has been to state that the print originates from a particular individual or that it did not come from that particular individual, or there is not enough information contained in the latent print to make any decision at all," Sensabaugh says. He notes that this absolutist approach has been superseded in light of the recent criticism; emerging practice is to be categorical about exclusions but to qualify identifications as very high probability but without quantifying the probability. "That kind of absolute assessment was decried by critical government and scientific reports, so the bottom line in regard to fingerprints is we have some empirical approaches that enable us to put some kind of statistical weight on the value of fingerprints but they don't track back to fundamental biology because we don't know enough about the biological formation of fingerprints. We know a fair amount but we don't know the kind of information we need to know as to why the minutia appear in particular places on a fingerprint pattern. That's an example of the fundamental background that we do have in basic genetics, and we have empirical approaches that can provide us with reasonably good answers. We can have people arguing whether the weight is greater or lesser but generally the empirical approach puts a bracket on the extent to which those arguments can be presented."

A second type of pattern evidence that critics subject to the individualization fallacy is firearms. "The consecutive striations concept that says when you have bullets fired from the same gun and you look at the striations on the bullets—bullets that are fired from the same gun will have three or four consecutive striations and the striation pattern will be the same," Sensabaugh says. "Whereas one can, with bullets fired from different guns, occasionally get some number of consecutive striations but the number of these striations has a different statistical distribution than the number of consecutive striations if they are fired from the same gun. So that provides some empirical base. Again, we have a fundamental knowledge of how marks on bullets are made, and how firing pin impressions are made on bullet casings, because we know how those are made, but being able to put them in some sort of context that enables us to put a weight on a particular impression in the absence of any other information still eludes us. I guess this is where DNA profiles stand out; we have databases that come nowhere near including the number of all of the people who exist or who have ever existed in time, but based on what we know about genetics, we can predict from any DNA profile what the frequency of occurrence that would be in a general population. We cannot do that with fingerprints or other forms of impression evidence. In order to make assessments, one has to do comparative analyses of the evidence item to exemplars and you can compare them to a large set of samples that are known to have originated from different sources."

A third type of pattern evidence that critics subject to the individualization fallacy is bite marks. "There has been somewhat of a legal withdrawal of bite mark evidence based on the fact that a lot of it has been proven to be unreliable," Sensabaugh says. To date, 24 people arrested or convicted on bite mark evidence have been exonerated by DNA, according to the Innocence Project. [A paper on bite mark evidence was just published: "Forensic Bitemark Identification: Weak Foundations, Exaggerated Claims"; it looks at the issue through a legal lens—has bite mark analysis been established as sufficiently valid and reliable to be accepted in court?]

"It's worth noting that the effort to individualize, as in the case with DNA, bite marks, firearms or fingerprints, is only one part of forensic science; it is part of a larger endeavor which is to apply science to develop a clearer picture of how a particular event happened—the event being the criminal activity in question," Sensabaugh emphasizes. "So there are many other kinds of analyses that don't fall under the rubric of individualization—forensic pathology is one example. This is a branch of medicine for which there is an existing body of knowledge but it is also clear that forensic pathologists sometimes testify to quite different interpretations of their findings. There ought to be some mechanism for assessing when the interpretation has moved from something based upon fact to something based upon speculation. Sometimes the speculation comes from limited experience. There's the proposition that all swans are white and if you see a bird that looks like a swan but is not white, you would question whether it is a swan. Well, if your experience is only seeing white swans, then you might question whether there can be a black swan; if someone else has seen black swans, he can recognize it as a swan independent of color. This is not intentional bias but that one's body of experience limits the range of information available upon which to base interpretations."

Kirk (1963, pages 237–238) has been quoted as remarking that criminalistics "is concerned with the unlikely and the unusual. Other sciences are concerned primarily with the likely and the usual. The derivation of equations, formulas and generalizations summarizing the normal behavior of any system in the universe is a major goal of the established sciences. It is not normal to be murdered, and most persons never experience this unlikely event. Yet, when a murder occurs, some combination of circumstances suddenly alters the situation from likely to certain."

Kirk (1963, pages 237–238) asserted, "According to most definitions, a science consists of an orderly and consistent body of knowledge, based on fundamental principles that can be clearly stated. Such a body of knowledge allows prediction as well as interpretation. Recognized sciences are characterized by research effort that produces constantly increasing theoretical and technical knowledge. Does criminalistics qualify?" Kirk answers that it is but cautions that "it lacks at this time the full development that will allow general recognition ... it should be developed so as to achieve full recognition as a separate scientific discipline."

Decades after Kirk's death in 1970, criminalistics remains a backbone of forensic science, but its detractors continue to allege serious flaws in the methods that Kirk and others pioneered and championed.

Sensabaugh says he thinks Kirk would be fascinated by the twists and turns that forensic science has endured in the field, in the judicial courts, and in the court of public opinion. "While I can't reflect on anyone's afterlife thoughts, I know Kirk would be pleased with some of the advances that have been made in the field," Sensabaugh says. "He operated in the realm of biology, after all, and was looking to biological approaches of individualization as one of the great areas for development. However, I think he would be disconcerted with the way work is conducted in forensic laboratories these days. What I learned from him is that each case poses a distinctive scientific problem and that one should approach each case in that manner. To that end, one could draw an analogy from medicine in that each patient presents a particular diagnostic challenge. By looking at each forensic case as a distinctive challenge, we determine if there are aspects of the case where science could provide an approach that might not be thought of otherwise; whereas if one looks upon everything as routine, one may tend not to think of alternative approaches. I think Kirk would be dismayed that we are now more removed from that sort of process. I have long harbored a notion that one of the reasons why he gravitated at mid-career toward criminalistics and away from the biological research he was doing at the time was that the biological research was becoming too routine and the challenges weren't there. With criminalistics, there was still room for an independent person to take a look at unique problems and take approaches to address them. He'd be disappointed that forensic science has moved away from that ideal."

Sensabaugh followed in Kirk's shoes by dedicating his life to teaching. Armed with a doctorate degree from the UC Berkeley School of Criminology with an emphasis in criminalistics and biochemistry, Sensabaugh began instructing undergraduate and graduate students in forensic science and biomedical sciences at his alma mater in 1972 and continues as a professor in the School of Public Health to this day. Of the numerous awards he has received, Sensabaugh says the Paul L. Kirk Award from the American Academy of Forensic Sciences (AAFS) in 1987 is a source of personal and professional pride. When it comes to contemplating his own legacy, Sensabaugh downplays his contributions.

"I'm not sure how much my research productivity will amount to a legacy primarily because forensic biology has changed so much over the last 40 years," Sensabaugh says. "Some of the things that were done some time ago are now not even on people's radar because they have been substantially displaced by other advancements. Instead, I would like to think that my legacy is a cohort of people who have gone out into the profession and done well. I represent two academic trees; Kirk's tree is one and there is a cohort of all the students that he trained and their students. I am also on an academic tree of Allan Wilson who was an evolutionary biologist and was one of the principal people at the beginning of molecular evolution. Allan's legacy continues on through his students and their students and I am just a little twig on that tree; others have made many more lasting and important contributions. But when you are in any academic areas you are either recognized because you have done something that is so noteworthy that it stands the test of time and/or that you have established a cohort of students who carry forward your values. I suspect that my research contributions are ephemeral but I would like to think that my contributions to my students are more meaningful."

Another recipient of the AAFS's Paul L. Kirk Award is Richard Saferstein, PhD, a nationally recognized forensic scientist and author. "I've always been a fan of Kirk's work," Saferstein says, adding that Kirk is one of the most-quoted thought leaders in criminalistics. "He was an awesome individual who was far ahead of his time in terms of integrating criminalistics and forensic science at UC Berkeley in the field's early years. I can't imagine what he would think of more modern advances such as DNA."

Kirk came of age professionally in a time when forensic science's association with law enforcement was not questioned. As we will see in Chapter 2, the charges directed at forensic science include its allegiance to law enforcement and to the prosecution. It's a curious position for the field to be in, considering that, as Bell (2008, page xiii) points out, "Forensic science was likely born the day after the first crime was committed." Bell (2008, pages 3–4) adds that police science morphed into the more acceptable forensic science but that "Among the modern sciences, forensic science is the screaming newborn of medicine, chemistry and biology." Criminalistics used microscopy, chemistry, botany, physics, and traditional science intermixed with serology, ballistics, and toxicology to begin establishing the framework for what Fisher and Fisher (2007, page 9) call "the long journey of bridging the philosophy of forensic principles with science."

Despite its roots in other scientific and medical disciplines, a criticism offered by Balko (2015) indicates the persistence of the notion that "most forensic disciplines weren't invented in labs, then subjected to peer review in scientific journals. Instead, most were invented by people in law enforcement, not in the quest for knowledge, but as an aide to help them solve crimes. Scientists within the same field have strong incentives to poke holes in others' theories, to find flaws in a peer's experiments. This isn't the case in forensics. A fingerprint analyst testifying for the defense might disagree with a fingerprint analyst for the prosecution, but he isn't going to call into question the premises on which the entire field of fingerprint analysis is based. He'd be undermining his own legitimacy. It was only after the onset of DNA testing, which did come from the world of science, that we began to understand just how profound these divergent incentives really are."

Granted, forensic scientists pursue knowledge within the context of a practical application, but should this knowledge be discounted solely because it is a means to an end? Forensic science draws from the scientific disciplines of chemistry, biology, genetics, and medicine, but its use is for the adjudication of crimes; it should not be vilified for its purpose, nor should its scientists apologize for their contributions to the overall justice system.

It should be understood that much of the debate lies in the argument of how forensic science is perceived by practitioners, members of the justice system, academics, legal scholars, and other stakeholders. We know that the word *forensic* is defined as "Of, relating to, or used in legal proceedings or argumentation," according to *Webster's Dictionary*. *Science* is defined by *Webster's* as "The observation, identification, description, experimental investigations and theoretical explanation of natural phenomena." On these definitions, most can agree. Where the fracas ensues is placing forensic science as a collective noun into the categories of either of the following: (1) Basic research—a systematic study directed toward a greater knowledge or understanding of the fundamental aspects of phenomena and of observable facts without specific applications toward any processes or products in mind. Basic research, however, may include activities with broad applications in mind. (2) Applied research—a systematic study to gain knowledge or understanding necessary to determine the means by which a recognized and specific need may be met (U.S. Department of Justice).

The charge that forensic science is rooted solely in law enforcement is a conflagration designed to fuel the flames of debate that still rage. While there are strong ties to policing, forensic science is moving toward independence and endeavoring to be recognized as a science in its own right, and not a factory production line to generate convictions. Hebrard and Daoust (2013, page 3) note, "After the explosion of ideas by the great forerunners at the end of the 19th century and at the beginning of the 20th century, their heirs and students ... gathered, coordinated, completed and developed their masters' fields of research and initiatives in forensic sciences. Through systematization of scientific methods and through academic teaching, they made forensic sciences a part of criminal proceedings for good."

Seeing that evidence is the driver of forensic science work at the scene and in the laboratory, it is the first place that legal scholars and other detractors of forensic science begin when attacking the field. The work of Locard, and by extension, of Kirk, comes under scrutiny. Crime scene investigators are taught to observe Locard's exchange principle, which, as we have already seen, states that whenever two objects come into contact, a transfer of material will occur; trace evidence that is transferred can be used to associate objects, individuals, or locations (Locard, 1930). The integrity and significance of trace material as associative evidence relies on proper detection, collection, and preservation, and an understanding of the transfer and persistence of trace evidence will assist the examiner in interpreting the significance of the analytical results. Because trace evidence is a building block of a criminal case, proper collection and preservation of this evidence will ensure its integrity when it arrives at the forensic laboratory for analysis. To provide proper protocol, the U.S. Department of Justice (DOJ, 1999) created its Trace Evidence Recovery Guidelines, which describe procedures and techniques for the documentation, detection, collection, and preservation of trace evidence from crime scenes, individuals, and items submitted to the laboratory for examination.

Evidence dynamics is a complex mechanism and can be an entry point for mistakes and mishandling, leading to analysis issues that have significant ramifications in the adjudication process. The downstream impact begins with evidence, and as Chisum and Turvey (2000) and Shaler (2009) have pointed out, uncertainty intercedes. As Shaler (2009) explains, "The process of crime reconstruction is often built on the assumption that evidence left behind at a crime scene, which has been recognized, documented, collected, identified, compared, individuated and reconstructed is pristine. This assumption involves the belief that the process of taping off an area, limiting access, and setting about the task of taking pictures and making measurements ensures the integrity of the evidence found within. Subsequently, any conclusions reached through forensic examinations and reconstructions of that evidence are assumed to be a reliable lens through which to view the crime. This assumption is not always accurate."

Shaler (2009) notes further that evidence dynamics refers to any influence that "changes, relocates, obscures or obliterates physical evidence, regardless of the intent. Generally, the process involved in evidence dynamics begins at the instant that a force interacts with evidence to cause a transfer until it reaches the courtroom. The thought that the process ends there is not necessarily true, either, as evidence used or not used in a legal proceeding may be required for subsequent hearings or trials. Each time the evidence is used, the potential exists for it to change or be obliterated, a process can continue until it is finally destroyed under some authority."

Giafamas (2000, page 472) sums up the challenge of criminalistics: "The premise for our work in criminalistics is based on Locard's exchange principle. It states whenever two objects come into contact with one another, there is always a transfer of material across the contact boundaries. In the 1950s, Paul Kirk added that no criminal can perpetrate a crime without leaving evidence behind or taking evidence away. Science and technology, therefore, are the limiting factors in the detection of transfers of evidence. The role of the criminalist is to recognize and collect these evidence exchanges at the scene of the crime and, through the rigorous examination of physical evidence in the laboratory, help make the facts of the case clear for an investigator, judge or jury."

No one is more familiar with Locard's exchange principle than Connecticut's famous forensic scientist, Henry C. Lee, PhD. One might think that the "C" in Lee's name might stand for "Criminalistics," since this forensic scientist has worked with 800-plus law enforcement agencies around the globe to solve more than 8000 cases, many of them some of the most challenging and famous. Lee's testimony figured prominently in the 1995 O.J. Simpson trial, and he assisted local and state police in their investigations of other high-profile crimes, such as the 1963 assassination of President John F. Kennedy; the 1996 murder of Jon Benet Ramsey; the 1993 death of White House counsel Vincent Foster; the 2001 murder of former Washington, DC, intern Chandra Levy; the 2002 kidnapping of Salt Lake City teenager Elizabeth Smart; and the reinvestigation of the Kennedy assassination.

Lee is also responsible for a number of firsts in his state, with his pioneering work establishing a path forward for his peers and subsequent generations of forensic practitioners. Lee and his protégés have made seminal contributions to the advancement of forensic science such as the enhancement of bloody fingerprints, creation of new methods for extracting DNA from samples, and estimation of blood volume at a crime scene. He has made significant contributions to the disciplines of criminal investigations, biochemistry, material science, fire and arson investigation, and law enforcement.

When asked what he believes is his greatest accomplishment, Lee points to the collaboration and teamwork that he fostered when he was the first in Connecticut in the 1970s to introduce a major-crimes squad concept. "I was lucky to have a good team, because this concept was revolutionary at that time and required working together well," Lee says. "We set up a team comprised of detectives and forensic scientists, and along with a police officer, they responded to crimes together. It was a way to address a lot of issues and solve a lot of problems that crime scenes can present. Instead of collecting hundreds of pieces of evidence where 90 percent of it is useless, we conduct the scene assessment and evaluation while we are there and collect what's key to the case. So bringing the investigator and the scientist together is what many people recognize as one of my most significant contributions to criminalistics and forensic science."

Lee adds, "Of course, you have to pay for that kind of concept. Every night I would go to three or four different crime scenes and the next morning the detective could go home to sleep but I had to analyze the evidence that we collected. I would put in so many hours in those days that my salary, divided by my hours, came out to be so little. The governor once joked that I had become the most valuable $1 man because every jump in my salary was just $1 because I worked so many hours, weekends and holidays," Lee says with a chuckle.

"We were also probably the first state to have a standardized rape kit in the early 1970s," Lee recalls. "We have 174 police departments in Connecticut and everyone was using a different label, a different kind of collection kit; some were homemade kits, using components that were purchased and assembled, while others were pre-assembled, commercial kits. So I went to the Legislation and introduced a bill for a standardized rape kit to be used by all rape centers, hospitals and police departments. We standardized the collection procedure and by doing so we were able to eliminate a number of problems related to variability."

Lee also is responsible for being a driving force in establishing a modern state police communication system as well as a sex offender and DNA data bank in Connecticut.

Lee was born in China in 1938 and grew up in Taiwan. He first worked for the Taipei Police Department, attaining the rank of captain, but he says he didn't always aspire to work in law enforcement as his first choice. "I was young and interested in police work, but when I was in high school I wanted to play basketball and hopefully become a basketball star," Lee recalls. "But then I realized I am only 5-foot-8 and regretfully I didn't have Michael Jordan's or Larry Bird's height. So I decided when I graduated high school I would enter the Central Police University in Taiwan. Taiwan has a different system than the U.S. If you want to be a police officer, you attend two years of college, and when you graduate you become a patrolman. The highest rank you can achieve is a staff sergeant; if you want to become an officer, you go to a police university. These institutions are very selective and they only accept a few students. When you graduate, they give you a lieutenant bar, and very quickly I was promoted to captain. So during that period of time we solved cases mainly by interviewing—often interrogating—the perpetrator, so interrogation became the main technique with which to solve cases. Sometimes those interrogations became so inhumane, I felt I did not really want to be a part of them. So I thought to myself, 'There must be a better way than to torture people.' Let's try to use the scientific way instead, and that's when I became interested in forensic science and criminalistics. In the early days in Taiwan, the forensic methods were primitive, with some use of ballistics, some fingerprints and document examination, so in 1965 I decided to come to the U.S. to study."

With his wife, Margaret, Lee came to the United States that year and immediately launched his quest for higher education. He earned his bachelor of science degree in forensic science from John Jay College in 1972 and then continued his studies in biochemistry at New York University (NYU), where he earned a master's degree in 1974 and his PhD in 1975. He has also received special training from the FBI Academy and the Bureau of Alcohol, Tobacco, Firearms and Explosives (ATF).

He is currently the director of the Forensic Research and Training Center and a distinguished professor in forensic science at the University of New Haven. He was the chief emeritus for the Connecticut State Police from 2000 to 2010, served as the commissioner of public safety for the state of Connecticut from 1998 to 2000, and served as the state's chief criminalist from 1978 to 2000.

In 1975, Lee joined the University of New Haven, where he created the school's forensic sciences program and later had the Henry C. Lee Forensic Institute named after him.

He has also taught as a professor at more than 40 universities, law schools, and medical schools, and lectures throughout the country and world to police, universities, and civic organizations. Lee has been married to his wife Margaret for more than 54 years, and they have two grown children, a daughter, Sherry, and a son, Stanley.

"I was very lucky to be selected by the John Jay forensic science program," Lee says. "When I graduated from John Jay I was working as a technician in the biochemistry department at NYU Medical Center. I was lucky that I got to meet Nobel Prize–wining molecular biologist Dr. Severo Ochoa because I was his technician. After I graduated from John Jay, I realized there wasn't a PhD program in forensic science, so I entered NYU, got my master's degree in biochemistry and finished my PhD in molecular biology. In 1975 after I got my doctorate degree I joined the University of New Haven as an assistant professor and started a forensic science program there. The university gave me a chance to grow, to share my experience in police work and molecular biology, so I was able to combine both skills and develop the program along the blending of those disciplines. We were fortunate in that we received quite a few grants in order to conduct research, and so many of my students—they are all retired now—became lab directors, judges, lawyers, physicians and scientists. That was 40 years ago. It's hard to believe that I have been teaching at the University of New Haven for 40 years."

While his education has been complete for some time, Lee is a recipient of more than 20 honorary degrees, including doctorate degrees of science from the University of New Haven and the University of Connecticut; honorary doctorate of law degrees from Roger Williams Law School, Mitchell College, American International University, Taiwan Scientific Technology University, and China University of Political Science and Law; as well as honorary doctorate degrees in humanities from the University of Bridgeport, St. Joseph College, and Armstrong University, in recognition of his contributions to law and science.

He has been the recipient of numerous medals and awards, including the 1996 Medal of Justice from the Justice Foundation and the 1998 Lifetime Achievement Award from the Science and Engineer Association. He has also been the recipient of the Distinguished Criminalist Award from the AAFS and the J. Donero Award from the International Association of Identification, and in 1992, was elected a distinguished fellow of the AAFS. He has also received the Lifetime Achievement Award from the American College of Forensic Examiners (ACFE) in 2000; Medal of Honor by the Ellis Island Foundation in 2004; Congressional Recognition for Outstanding Services by the US Congress in 2004; Presidential Medal of Honor by the President of Croatia in 2005; Medal of Service from the Ministry of Interior, Taiwan, ROC, in 2006; Gusi Peace Award from the Philippines in 2008; and Medal of Friendship from China.

Lee is a prolific author, having penned hundreds of articles in professional journals and coauthoring more than 40 books addressing such diverse topics as crime scene investigation and reconstruction, DNA analysis, fingerprint analysis, and trace evidence analysis. His fame as a forensic scientist, expert witness, and author has been boosted by numerous appearances on television and in movies, including a television series, *Trace Evidence—The Dr. Henry Lee Files.*

His seminal book, *Blood Evidence: How DNA Is Revolutionizing the Way We Solve Crimes*, which he wrote with Frank Tirnady, was published in 2003. Other titles that helped the world better understand forensic science include *The Real World of a Forensic Scientist: Renowned Experts Reveal What It Takes to Solve Crimes*, published in 2009 with Elaine M. Pagliaro, and *Physical Evidence in Forensic Science*, published in 2011 with Howard A. Harris. Some of his more popular books have focused on his casework, including Michael Skakel/Martha Moxley and Jonbenet Ramsay (*Cracking More Cases: The Forensic Science of Solving Crimes*, which he published in 2004 with Thomas W. O'Neil); Scott Peterson and Elizabeth Smart (*Dr. Henry Lee's Forensic Files: Five Famous Cases*, which he published in 2006 with Jerry Labriola, MD); and Phil Spector (*Shocking Cases from Dr. Henry Lee's Forensic Files*, which he published in 2010 with Labriola).

Lee shares his thoughts on how he approaches analysis of a crime scene and its resulting investigation. "One of the contributions I have made is introducing scientific logic at the crime scene," Lee says. "In the early days, we tended to use hunches, or a sort of sixth sense. You go to a scene, look around, and say, 'This guy must be guilty.' It's inductive logic like was used in the O.J. Simpson case when they jumped the gun and were too quick to say that only one man did it. Later when the whole thing was put together, they saw it could have been two people. On the first day of trial we said it could be two people; O.J. Simpson could be one suspect but there could be another person. Now everyone agrees."

Lee continues, "It's all about proper reconstruction of the crime. I am the one who first introduced that term—crime scene reconstruction—because it uses scientific principles along with deductive logic. We are also combining deductive logic with inductive logic; this third way of thinking is called abductive logic, and must use all three types of logic to solve crimes—deductive logic alone doesn't always work. Say you are at a crime scene and you find a black person's hair; you say to yourself, 'OK, it must be an African-American who committed this crime.' Maybe, but you cannot say that definitively because it can be a secondary transfer or maybe the wind blew the hair there—you have to consider everything."

Lee is also known for using crime scene profiling as one of his techniques. "In the early days I taught my students about the importance of scene profiling. Say I am investigating a case. I look at the point of entry, a window, and it's pretty high from the floor, so I know the individual has to be a certain height. In the Elizabeth Smart case, after 14 months it remained unsolved and they asked me to look at it. I returned to the scene and looked around. In profiling the scene, I said that the suspect is taller than me at 5-foot-8 and shorter than 6-foot-2 and would need to be skinny in order to fit through the small window that was positioned at a certain height. I also said the suspect had to have known or worked for the family before because they knew the right portal of entry, the window. Sure enough, we solved the case due to scene profiling and looking at the physical evidence."

Lee continues, "At the scene of a triple homicide I found a huge bloody handprint but there were no ridges. My fingerprint examiner said to me, 'Dr. Lee, there is no value here.' I said, 'There is tremendous value because that person's hand is seven and three-quarters inches in size and the suspect must be a sizable person who might also play a sport such as basketball or football. This is a logical deduction that will help us reconstruct the case to lead us in the right direction. Let's say I find a sneaker imprint and I know the size; even though I don't have the individual detail it still has tremendous value—that's called investigational value. The National Science Foundation has essentially said that if you cannot make an identification, don't use it; now, I cannot make an actual identification, but I have an investigative value. Let's say I have a hit-and-run case and I find a red smear of paint. I know I am looking for a red-colored vehicle. Of course I cannot say conclusively that this smear of paint was made by a red Honda with a specific license plate, but on the other hand, this identification of a red vehicle alone has tremendous value for the investigation."

Lee provides another example. "Say I find a 9 mm bullet at a crime scene. I know I am looking for an individual who committed a crime with a 9 mm firearm. So I was able to put together the scientific evidence coupled with the investigative technique of scene profiling. I also run some DNA and it gives me a mixture of two. I am afraid that the 2009 NAS report recommendations for the future will turn us all into laboratory technicians. In other words, don't worry about the scene, just conduct the laboratory analysis. My fear is nobody will make an interpretation of the DNA analysis. That's why over the years you can see the clearance rate in this country getting becoming so poor; I think the homicide case clearance rate is about 73 percent, 50 percent for sexual assault and 20 percent for burglary. The clearance rate is getting lower and lower because no one is thinking anymore, they just look at a chart."

Lee emphasizes that automation of analysis can't replace the human investigator who uses his or her best weapon—his or her critical thinking skills and logic. He points to a case that he says is one of his favorite cases of all time because it illustrates the concepts of logic and scene profiling.

"It was Thanksgiving night, when a neighbor made a pie for a 72-year-old woman who lived alone. When the neighbor rang the doorbell, no one answered. When the neighbor pushed on the door, it opened and they found her body in the kitchen, and they called the police. The local police called the state police major crimes sergeant, who called me. I came to the scene and looked around. Outside it was snowing and the weather was pretty bad. But the kitchen floor was clean. The woman had 11 stab wounds so logic tells me there should be a lot of blood on the floor. There were two possibilities—they are postmortem wounds and there was no bleeding; or someone cleaned up the scene. We found signs of mopping; mopping the kitchen floor can take some time, so we were certain that this individual, by induction, had to know this woman and her activities and know that there would be no visitors that night. Why mop the floor? Most likely the suspect left a bloody shoe print. This individual is probably smart enough to know that crime scene investigators use chemical formulas to raise the bloody shoeprint, and so the suspect tried to clean up. So I used TMB on the floor, and sure enough, I raised a partial footprint. So with that I know this person wears a certain brand of shoes."

Lee explains that at the time of this case, he was commissioner, running the state police. "As a forensic scientist you really don't have that much power because the investigation is run by the investigator, and then the prosecutor decides what evidence to use; however, because I was the state commissioner, I ordered the mobilization of 200 officers," Lee recalls. "I remember my chief of staff said I was going to create a lot of overtime, but I said that if the case is unsolved you will still use detectives and overtime. During the first 24 hours you have the best chance of finding the perpetrator, so I thought it was best to use our resources immediately, even if it meant overtime."

Lee says he made it a priority to check the garbage cans, with other investigators asking him why. "I told them that tomorrow morning, the garbage will be collected and then end up in the dump, and then you would have to search the garbage dump. The level of contamination would be so great that any evidence found would be unusable. The right decision-making at the very onset of an investigation is important. So the officers searched and about 30 minutes later they found a pair of sneakers that had blood on it. I looked at it and I said, 'Hairs on that bloody sneaker tell me it is Caucasian hair, so your suspect group is already getting smaller.' So usually when a person dumps a sneaker, it probably means they bought other shoes. I asked, 'Is this garbage can near a shopping center?' And the police officers said yes. I asked, 'Does the mall have a shoe store?' They said yes. I told them to wake up the manager of the shoe store. I still remember the manager when he got to the store; he was mad when he arrived but when he saw me he said, 'Oh, Dr. Lee, you are my hero, I want to take a picture with you.' I said can you first do us a favor and open up the store because we want to see who bought shoes around the 4 p.m. to 7 p.m. timeframe. It turned out that someone had indeed purchased shoes and even used a credit card for the transaction. That detail broke the case—it was the woman's nephew who committed the crime. He was addicted to drugs and asked her for money that day. When she refused, he hit her so hard the woman collapsed. He got nervous that when she becomes conscious again, she will go to the police, so he killed her."

Lee says he is bothered by seeing the worst of humanity but says, "We are lucky that we can speak for the people who cannot speak for themselves." He emphasizes, "This case is an example of that. It was daybreak the next morning when I drove home. No one thanked me, as the woman's daughter didn't have contact with her mother. The newspaper doesn't care because the woman was a nobody to them. But we solved the case, and brought the perpetrator to justice. I'm sure most investigators feel the same way about the importance of speaking for people who cannot speak for themselves."

Hebrard and Daoust (2015, page 276) acknowledge that since the dawn of forensic science through to the more modern era, practitioners wrestle with the field's challenges: "From 1963, Paul L. Kirk has pointed out the weaknesses of evidence resulting from clues and has suggested solutions to assess the validity of evidence using the implementation of strong statistical bases to assess the evidence reliability ... The current priorities for forensic science are the application of quality assurance standards in the chain of custody, from sampling procedures to examinations; the need to supervise laboratories; and an understanding of how hypotheses should be formulated from the facts of the case."

Hebrard and Daoust (2015, page 276) add, "Forensic science developed from a very pragmatic point of view. First, there was a need to identify persistent offenders. Second, there was a need to apply technical procedures to criminal investigations and implement the lessons learned. Third, protocols and scientific methods were applied to the chain of custody. Presently, a control phase has been implemented to ensure that results are accurate. By measuring uncertainty and using a fundamental scientific review approach, to give maturity to forensic science turn out to be the next perspective that could also participate to a better understanding of the science on its own."

In Chapter 2, we explore the many ways in which forensic science is called into question and how this scrutiny has set into motion a call for reform that not even Paul Kirk could have imagined.

REFERENCES

Aitken C, Roberts P and Jackson G. Fundamentals of Probability and Statistical Evidence in Criminal Proceedings Guidance for Judges, Lawyers, Forensic Scientists and Expert Witnesses. 2010. Accessible at http://www.rss.org.uk/Images/PDF/influencing-change/rss-fundamentals-probability-statistical-evidence.pdf

Balko R. A brief history of forensics. *The Washington Post.* April 21, 2015. Accessible at https://www.washingtonpost.com/news/the-watch/wp/2015/04/21/a-brief-history-of-forensics/

Bell S. *Crime and Circumstance: Investigating the History of Forensic Science.* Westport, Conn., Praeger Publishers. 2008.

Biedermann A and Curran J. Letter to the editor. Drawbacks in the scientification of forensic science. *Forensic Science International.* Vol. 245. Pages e38–e4. December 2014.

Chisum JW and Turvey BE. Evidence dynamics: Locard's exchange principle & crime reconstruction. *Journal of Behavioral Profiling.* Vol 1, No. 1. January 2000.

Crispino F and Houck MM. Principles of forensic science. In: *Professional Issues in Forensic Science*. Elsevier Academic Press. Pages 9–10. 2015.

Department of Justice (DOJ). *Trace Evidence Recovery Guidelines*. 1999. Accessible at https://www.nist.gov/sites/default/files/documents/2016/09/22/trace_evidence_recovery_guidelines.pdf

Evett IW. Criminalistics: The future of expertise. *JFSS*. Vol. 33, No. 3, 1. Pages 73–178. 1993.

Fisher B and Fisher D. *Forensics Demystified*. McGraw Hill Professional, New York. 2007.

Giafamas DM. *Criminalistics*. Academic Press. Page 472. 2000.

Gross H. *Handbuch für Untersuchungsrichter als System der Kriminalistik (Handbook for Examining Magistrates as a System of Criminology)*. 2 volumes. 1893.

Hebrard J and Daoust F. History of forensic sciences. *Encyclopedia of Forensic Sciences*. Elsevier. Pages 273–277. 2013.

Hebrard J and Daoust F. History of forensic sciences. In: *Professional Issues in Forensic Science*. Houck MM, Ed. Elsevier Academic Press. 2015.

Houck MM. Introduction. In: *Mute Witnesses*. Elsevier Academic Press, San Diego. Page xix. 2001.

Inman K and Rudin N. *Principles and Practice of Criminalistics: The Profession of Forensic Science*. CRC Press, Boca Raton, FL. Page 76. 2001.

Kaye DH. Probability, individualization, and uniqueness in forensic science evidence: Listening to the academies. *Brooklyn Law Review*. Vol. 75, No. 4. Pages 1163–1185. Summer 2010.

Kirk PL. *Crime Investigation: Physical Evidence and the Police Laboratory*. John Wiley & Sons, New York. 1953.

Kirk PL. The ontogeny of criminalistics. *Journal Criminal Law, Criminology and Police Science* Vol. 54. Pages 235–238. 1963.

Kirk PL. Criminalistics. *Science*. Vol. 140. Page 368. 1963.

Koehler JJ and Saks MJ. Individualization Claims in Forensic Science: Still Unwarranted. Northwestern University School of Law Faculty Working Papers. Paper 27. Accessible at http://scholarlycommons.law.northwestern.edu/facultyworkingpapers/272010

Koehler JJ and Saks MJ. The individualization fallacy in forensic science evidence. *Vanderbilt Law Review*. Vol. 61, No. 1. Pages 199–219. 2008.

Locard E. The analysis of dust traces. *American Journal of Police Science*. Vol. 1, No. 3. Pages 279–298. 1930.

Page M. Science and Forensic Science. In: *Forensic Testimony: Science, Law and Expert Evidence*. Elsevier, San Diego. Pages 26–27. 2014.

Payne-James JJ. History of forensic medicine. *Encyclopedia of Forensic and Legal Medicine* (2nd ed.). Elsevier, San Diego. Pages 539–567. 2016.

Saferstein R. *Criminalistics: An Introduction to Forensic Science*. Prentice Hall, New York. 2001.

Shaler RC. The Origin of Evidence, Chapter 4. 2009. Accessible at https://online.science.psu.edu/sites/default/files/frnsc200/chapter_4_-_origin_of_evidence_feb_10.pdf

Spitz DJ. History and development of forensic medicine and pathology. In: *Medico-Legal Investigation of Death: Guidelines for the Application of Pathology to Crime Investigation* (4th ed.), WU Spitz, Ed. Charles C. Thomas Publisher, Springfield, Ill. 2006.

Zagorski N. Profile of Alec J. Jeffreys. *Proceedings of the National Academy of Sciences USA*. Vol. 103, No. 24. Pages 8918–8920. June 13, 2006. Accessible at http://www.ncbi.nlm.nih.gov/pmc/articles/PMC1482540/

CHAPTER 2

Flaws and Fraud: The Accusations against Forensic Science

In the aftermath of a near-decade of accusations, forensic science is still struggling to digest recommendations, synthesize and integrate new research, implement remediation measures, and generally course-correct in the dozens of manners expected by its critics and detractors. It has been eight years since the National Academy of Sciences (NAS) issued a report that confirmed what supporters and detractors of forensic science have been debating for years—the contributions and the conflicts that characterize the justice system must be deconstructed, sorted out, examined, and reassembled into an improved enterprise. With the report's enumeration of its sins before it, the forensic science field can now set a course for addressing the allegations and emerging from this dialogue better equipped to serve the public and the U.S. justice system.

The criticisms levied against forensic science as a profession are numerous, and while some hit the bull's-eye, others are off target and reflect the machinations of the faction that predicts the field's ultimate failure. Mnookin et al. (2011, page 729) point to a combination of events—legal challenges, laboratory scandals, widely publicized errors, skeptical scholarship, and a highly critical national report that has focused attention on the forensic science and say that "these developments offer the opportunity for reflection and improvement." And as Kaye (2010, page 8) observed, "A series of highly publicized scandals at forensic laboratories and a number of successful or partially successful defense challenges to fingerprint, toolmark and other individualization evidence fueled efforts to convince the Congress to act. In addition to requiring accreditation for laboratories receiving federal funds, the Congress voted in 2005 to appropriate $1.5 million to fund an NRC study on forensic science."

As Risinger (2010, page 1) observes, "American forensic science as an organized field is less than a hundred years old. On balance, this relatively young field has almost certainly had a positive impact on the accurate determination of factual guilt and factual innocence in the criminal justice system. However, in the flush of youth, it is not uncommon for claims to outrun capabilities. For several decades now, many from the academy and some from forensic science itself have pointed to weaknesses both in various forensic fields and in the structure of forensic science practice itself—weaknesses that raised the specter of a forensic science that sometimes made unwarranted claims and that could, in practice, sometimes aid in the conviction of the innocent. These criticisms were generally dismissed without much examination by the bulk of the forensic science establishment, and the proponents of those claims were dismissed as well."

Risinger (2010, page 6) adds, "Much of the NAS report concentrates on what might be described as the problem children of forensic science. These are, in general, forensic techniques that were developed more or less at the dawn of forensic science, such as fingerprint identification, handwriting identification, firearms and toolmark identification, etc. They mostly deal with 'source attributions,' that is, determining the source item that left a trace in some relevant place, such as a crime scene. The principles relied upon by such techniques are not the products of science, as that term is currently understood, but rather the product of a kind of commonsense generalization derived from experience with the subject matter under examination. Neither the generalizations so derived nor the accuracy of the results arrived at by practitioners of these disciplines have ever been subject to the kind of systematic testing that has come to be expected as a part of anything calling itself 'science.' This does not mean that the results arrived at are necessarily always in error, but simply that we have no very good evidence about when they are likely to be in error and when they are likely to be accurate. In this way, these disciplines are probably best understood as being like folk medicine—they may be efficacious sometimes, maybe even most times, but we don't really know for sure. This is not to say that the Committee did not recognize the scientific credentials and reliability of many techniques, methods, and processes commonly used in forensic science laboratories. Indeed, it held up one such process, DNA profiling for purposes of source attribution, as (perhaps a little too uncritically) a kind of platinum standard for forensic science processes generally."

THE REPORT HEARD 'ROUND THE WORLD

In February 2009, the NAS released its report on forensic science that created seismic waves within the profession, instigated relentless commentary in legal journals, and prompted sensationalistic headlines in the mainstream media. The report, "Strengthening Forensic Science in the United States: A Path Forward," was a clarion call for reform, but to insiders and practitioners, it represented a swan song for business as usual. In a positive light, the report was able to create new awareness of the challenges that the field faces in terms of budgets and resources. But the negative fallout that ensued no doubt made the practice of forensic science all the more difficult due to unrelenting scrutiny in the press, discussion in the legal community, and debate among practitioners. As the report declared, "It is clear that change and advancements, both systemic and scientific, are needed in a number of forensic science disciplines—to ensure the reliability of the disciplines, establish enforceable standards, and promote best practices and their consistent application" (NAS, 2009).

According to Risinger (2010, page 8), "...the NAS report may be taken to identify two broad types of problems in American forensic science practice: problems in regard to our knowledge concerning the accuracy of various techniques even under ideal conditions, and problems related to the less-than-ideal conditions in which forensic science is practiced, which can potentially affect the accuracy of processes that are well researched and whose accuracy and error rates under proper conditions are well established. We may refer to the first as basic validity problems, and the second as environmental problems that undermine ideal performance."

A scathing report is nothing new to the forensic science field. As Kaye (2010) reminds us, remediation-minded studies, with varying degrees of success, reach back to the late 1920s. However, it was two DNA reports, one in 1992 and another in 1996, that "marked a turning point in the legal reception of NRC reports on forensic science," Kaye (2010, page 8) says, adding, "However, the recommendations in the two DNA reports for a government agency outside of law enforcement to promulgate standards and review scientific progress were rejected. The established powers rarely yield their authority to would-be reformers."

This call for rehabilitation encompassed several broader themes of structural and institutional reform and oversight, as well as enforceable standards by accreditation and certification mechanisms, plus education and training as a "pivotal step to promote the development of forensic science into a mature field of multidisciplinary research and practice, founded on the systematic collection and analysis or relevant data" (Kaye, 2010).

The 2009 NAS report acknowledged the contributions of the field and made it clear that it did not reach its conclusions lightly: "In adopting this report, the aim of our committee is to chart an agenda for progress in the forensic science community and its scientific disciplines. Because the work of forensic science practitioners is so obviously wide-reaching and important—affecting criminal investigation and prosecution, civil litigation, legal reform, the investigation of insurance claims, national disaster planning and preparedness, homeland security, and the advancement of technology—the committee worked with a sense of great commitment and spent countless hours deliberating over the recommendations that are included in the report. These recommendations, which are inexorably interconnected, reflect the committee's strong views on policy initiatives that must be adopted in any plan to improve the forensic science disciplines and to allow the forensic science community to serve society more effectively. The task Congress assigned our committee was daunting and required serious thought and the consideration of an extremely complex and decentralized system, with various players, jurisdictions, demands, and limitations" (NAS, 2009).

The committee that produced the report acknowledged a chorus of voices all saying the same thing: "In considering the testimony and evidence that was presented to the committee, what surprised us the most was the consistency of the message that we heard: The forensic science system, encompassing both research and practice, has serious problems that can only be addressed by a national commitment to overhaul the current structure that supports the forensic science community in this country. This can only be done with effective leadership at the highest levels of both federal and state governments, pursuant to national standards, and with a significant infusion of federal funds" (NAS, 2009).

The report did throw the forensic community a bone when it admitted, "For decades, the forensic science disciplines have produced valuable evidence that has contributed to the successful prosecution and conviction of criminals as well as to the exoneration of innocent people. Over the last two decades, advances in some forensic science disciplines, especially the use of DNA technology, have demonstrated that some areas of forensic science have great additional potential to help law enforcement identify criminals" (NAS, 2009).

While detractors of forensic science cheered the report's findings, not everyone felt the report was justified. "With regard to the legal critics who are able to find fault with so much of forensic science, it's all about finding the little chinks in the armor that can be exploited," says forensic science educator George Sensabaugh, PhD, whom we first met in Chapter 1. "Articles in law reviews regularly point fingers at forensic science but I am not sure how much impact those papers have in the real world of forensic practice. I think that courts pretty much accept evidence as it is if the evidence can be established that it is reliable; arguably not all evidence has been established as reliable to the extent that it is sometimes presented and that is quite a legitimate flaw within our field. I am not sure they are really driving the agenda in forensic science, and certainly not the research agenda."

The forensic science and medicolegal death investigation community was expecting and bracing itself for the report, as the journey to get to this point was a long and storied one. Under the Science, State, Justice, Commerce, and Related Agencies Appropriations Act of 2006, Congress authorized the NAS to conduct a study on forensic science, particularly the disciplines that exist outside of DNA. The attorney general was asked to provide funding to the NAS to create an independent Forensic Science Committee, comprised of members of the forensic science community including representatives from crime laboratories, medical examiners, and coroners; legal experts; and other scientists as determined appropriate.

The Forensic Science Committee was instructed to accomplish eight tasks:

1. Assess the present and future resource needs of the forensic science community, to include state and local crime labs, medical examiners, and coroners
2. Make recommendations for maximizing the use of forensic technologies and techniques to solve crimes, investigate deaths, and protect the public
3. Identify potential scientific advances that may assist law enforcement in using forensic technologies and techniques to protect the public
4. Make recommendations for programs that will increase the number of qualified forensic scientists and medical examiners available to work in public crime laboratories
5. Disseminate best practices and guidelines concerning the collection and analysis of forensic evidence to help ensure quality and consistency in the use of forensic technologies and techniques to solve crimes, investigate deaths, and protect the public
6. Examine the role of the forensic community in the homeland security mission
7. Examine interoperability of Automated Fingerprint Information Systems (AFIS)
8. Examine additional issues pertaining to forensic science as determined by the committee

In the fall of 2006, the NAS established a committee with the working title of "Identifying the Needs of the Forensic Science Community." The committee met on eight occasions spanning January 2007 through November 2008, where it heard expert testimony and deliberated over the information it received. Between meetings, committee members reviewed numerous published materials, studies, and reports related to the forensic science disciplines, engaged in independent research on the subject, and worked on drafts of the final report. Experts who provided testimony included federal agency officials; academics and research scholars; private consultants; federal, state, and local law enforcement officials; scientists; medical examiners; a coroner; crime laboratory officials from the public and private sectors; independent investigators; defense attorneys; forensic science practitioners; and leadership of professional and standard-setting organizations.

The issues covered during the committee's hearings and deliberations included the fundamentals of the scientific method as applied to forensic practice (hypothesis generation and testing, falsifiability and replication, and peer review of scientific publications); the assessment of forensic methods and technologies (the collection and analysis of forensic data); accuracy and error rates of forensic analyses; sources of potential bias and human error in interpretation by forensic experts; proficiency testing of forensic experts; infrastructure and needs for basic research and technology assessment in forensic science; current training and education in forensic science; the structure and operation of forensic science laboratories; the structure and operation of the coroner and medical examiner systems; budget, future needs, and priorities of the forensic science community and the coroner and medical examiner systems; the accreditation, certification, and licensing of forensic science operations, medical death investigation systems, and scientists; scientific working groups (SWGs) and their practices; forensic science practices in pattern/experience evidence; the use of forensic evidence in criminal and civil litigation;

forensic practice and projects at various federal agencies, including National Institute of Standards and Technology (NIST), Federal Bureau of Investigation (FBI), Department of Homeland Security (DHS), U.S. Secret Service, National Institute of Justice (NIJ), Drug Enforcement Administration (DEA), and Department of Defense (DOD); forensic practice in state and local agencies; nontraditional forensic service providers; and the forensic science community in the United Kingdom.

The testimonial and documentary evidence considered by the committee was detailed, complex, and sometimes controversial. Given this reality, the committee could not possibly answer every question that it confronted, nor could it devise specific solutions for every problem that it identified. Rather, it reached a consensus on the most important issues now facing the forensic science community and medical examiner system and agreed on 13 specific recommendations to address these issues.

The report's recommendations were wide ranging, and as Giannelli (2012, page 379) summarizes, "Some recommendations were structural—e.g., the creation of an independent federal entity (the National Institute of Forensic Sciences, or NIFS) to oversee the field, the removal of crime laboratories from the administrative control of law enforcement agencies, and the replacement of coroner offices with medical examiner systems. Other recommendations concerned accreditation of crime labs, certification of examiners, and standardization of procedures. Perhaps the most important recommendation was directed at research—in particular, the need for validation studies on such common techniques as fingerprint examinations, firearms (ballistics) and toolmark identifications, questioned document comparisons, hair analysis, and bite mark examinations."

The report focused on the disciplines that the committee feared had provided "substantive information and testimony based on faulty forensic science analyses" that may have contributed to wrongful convictions of innocent people. As the report states, "This fact has demonstrated the potential danger of giving undue weight to evidence and testimony derived from imperfect testing and analysis. Moreover, imprecise or exaggerated expert testimony has sometimes contributed to the admission of erroneous or misleading evidence" (NAS, 2009).

Mnookin et al. (2011, page 727) note that despite the fact that comparison and identification methods such as the pattern and impression evidence analysis seen in fingerprint examination, handwriting analysis, and firearms and toolmark comparison have served as mainstays of criminal prosecution for at least 100 years, "these methods and techniques now face more criticism and scrutiny than ever before. Latent fingerprint identification, questioned document examination, and firearms comparison have been the targets of numerous admissibility challenges."

The NAS report outlined what it considered to be forensic science's most pressing issues: the present and future resource needs of the forensic science community; maximizing the use of forensic technologies and techniques; developing programs that will increase the number of qualified forensic scientists and medical examiners; and disseminating best practices and guidelines concerning the collection and analysis of forensic evidence to help ensure quality and consistency in the use of forensic technologies and techniques.

To its credit, the 2009 NAS report acknowledged the unaddressed disparities with which practitioners had been wresting for years, including fractured processes and lack of standardization, funding, access to analytical instrumentation, the availability of skilled and well-trained personnel, and certification and accreditation. As the report stated, "...any approach to overhauling the existing system needs to address and help minimize the community's current fragmentation and inconsistent practices. Although the vast majority of criminal law enforcement is handled by state and local jurisdictions, these entities often are sorely lacking in the resources (money, staff, training and equipment) necessary to promote and maintain strong forensic science laboratory systems. By comparison, federal programs are often much better funded and staffed. It is also noteworthy that the resources, the extent of services, and the amount of expertise that medical examiners and forensic pathologists can provide vary widely in different jurisdictions. As a result, the depth, reliability and overall quality of substantive information arising from the forensic examination of evidence available to the legal system vary substantially across the country" (NAS, 2009).

The committee that produced the report scrutinized and addressed a wide range of practices within forensic science, from the fundamentals of the scientific method as applied to forensic practice such as falsifiability and replication, to the assessment of forensic methods and technologies, including the collection and analysis of forensic data, accuracy and error rates of forensic analyses, sources of potential bias, and human error in interpretation by forensic experts. Let's examine some of the key issues identified in the 2009 NAS report more closely.

PURPORTED ERRORS AND FRAUD COMMITTED BY FORENSIC EXAMINERS

A number of forensic scientists have been disgraced over unethical behavior, and entire crime labs have suffered from individual practitioners' missteps. Gabel (2014, pages 304–305) surmises, "What makes forensic error into a full-blown crime lab scandal? As with any scandal that brings down an organization, it usually includes repetitive misconduct, a failure to respond, and a culture of tolerance of such activity. The situations that push an incident from the 'problem' column to the 'scandal' column are varied and diverse. Examiners may lie about test results, produce misleading data regarding the reliability of their methods, or conceal exculpatory evidence. Other cases may involve 'dry-labbing,' where analysts record data for tests that they never conducted. Protocols may be ignored, forensic scientists may exaggerate their credentials or expertise, or tests may be tampered with. Whatever the particular problem, it cannot be denied that between 2005 and 2011, authorities identified 50 significant failures at American crime labs. These types of problems have led to scandals across the nation, resulting in full or partial closures, reorganizations, investigations, or firings at city or county crime labs."

As Upshaw-Downs (2012, page 399) states, "No one would really want to believe that a conscientious entity, public or private, least of all one charged with scientific fact-finding, would deliberately commit willful transgressions to the extent that scientific purity is compromised—or that even worse transgressions were afoot. In all likelihood, excepting actual operating criminal enterprises, no venture starts out as evil or desires to attain that status through the course of business." However, as Bell (2008, page 206) notes, "Like any discipline, forensic science has dark corners and scandals."

Upshaw-Downs (2012, page 421) notes that "...transgressions are uncommon and best avoided by proactively addressing concerns, as is mandated by accreditation and certification processes currently in operation, for none know better the dangers to the justice system of the lone rogue than the overwhelming majority whose reputation and honor are called into question by the acts of an evil few. But as history shows, it only takes a few fraudulent scientists to taint dozens of cases with devastating results. Sometimes, negligence—rather than fraud—jeopardizes the integrity of forensic analysis and can lead to wrongful convictions. This happens when training of lab employees is insufficient or when proper safeguards are not in place to prevent contamination or double-check analysts' work. In all of these instances, the government has an obligation to investigate the source and determine the extent of the problem in order to prevent it from recurring in the future." Upshaw-Downs (2012) adds, "The well-intentioned effort to legislate morality misses the point that one cannot create an ethical being simply by legislating the malfeasant away. In order to enhance the integrity of the overall system, one must start with those recruited into the field and train the next generation of practitioners in the ways of propriety and conscience."

The 2009 NAS report acknowledges, "In day-to-day forensic science work, the process of formulating and testing hypotheses is replaced with the careful preparation and analysis of samples and the interpretation of results. But that applied work, if done well, still exhibits the same hallmarks of basic science: the use of validated methods and care in following their protocols; the development of careful and adequate documentation; the avoidance of biases; and interpretation conducted within the constraints of what the science will allow" (NAS, 2009, page 113).

Science requires validation of new methods to determine their reliability under different conditions and their limitations, and to confirm the validity of a method or process such as for a forensic investigation, validation studies must be performed. ISO 17025 dictates that certain techniques be employed, such as calibration using reference standards or reference materials; comparison of results achieved with other methods; interlaboratory comparisons; systematic assessment of the factors influencing the result; and assessment of the uncertainty of the results based on scientific understanding of the theoretical principles of the method and practical experience. As the 2009 NAS report notes, "The validation of results over time increases confidence" (NAS, 2009, page 114). Forensic science has seen the greatest amount of validation with DNA analysis, as the NAS report observes, "In the case of DNA analysis, studies have evaluated the precision, reliability, and uncertainties of the methods. This knowledge has been used to define standard procedures that, when followed, lead to reliable evidence."

Bell (2008, page 208) notes, "The criticisms and challenges to pattern evidence owe their short history to the evolution of DNA evidence and the *Daubert* trilogy of court decisions. DNA evidence is presented to a jury in probabilistic terms based on genetic frequencies in the population. Not everyone on the planet has been or ever will be typed for the 13 DNA loci in use, just as not everyone will ever be typed for their ABO blood group. The frequency of types across a population can be extrapolated from a smaller subset using mathematical relationships as long as the loci are not linked to each other. The type of statistics used and how they are presented are direct results of the DNA controversies of the late 1990s; now the courts and defense lawyers are asking the same be applied to fingerprints. The contrast between DNA evidence, what lies behind it, and how the courts vet it via *Daubert* and similar standards stands in stark contrast to fingerprint evidence."

The challenge is that scientific data and processes are subject to a variety of sources of error. As the 2009 NAS report notes, "For example, laboratory results and data from questionnaires are subject to measurement error, and interpretations of evidence by human observers are subject to potential biases. A key task for the scientific investigator designing and conducting a scientific study, as well as for the analyst applying a scientific method to conduct a particular analysis, is to identify as many sources of error as possible, to control or to eliminate as many as possible, and to estimate the magnitude of remaining errors so that the conclusions drawn from the study are valid" (NAS, 2009, page 116).

As Bell (2008, page 209) observes, "Data will have to be quantitative and probabilistic with supporting evidence, peer review, standards, error measurement, and testing behind it. Every forensic practice, no matter how well entrenched, will face the same scrutiny. The history of forensic science in the 21st century will undoubtedly be intimately related to how science and the law deal with it."

As the 2009 NAS report states, "Analyses in the forensic science disciplines are conducted to provide information for a variety of purposes in the criminal justice process. However, most of these analyses aim to address two broad types of questions: Can a particular piece of evidence be associated with a particular class of sources? And can a particular piece of evidence be associated with one particular source? The first type of question leads to 'classification' conclusions" (NAS, 2009, page 117). The report defines error rates as "proportions of cases in which the analysis led to a false conclusion" (NAS, 2009, page 122). The report states further, "The existence of several types of potential error rates makes it absolutely critical for all involved in the analysis to be explicit and precise in the particular rate or rates referenced in a specific setting. The estimation of such error rates requires rigorously developed and conducted scientific studies. Additional factors may play a role in analyses involving human interpretation, such as the experience, training, and inherent ability of the interpreter, the protocol for conducting the interpretation, and biases from a variety of sources, as discussed in the next section. The assessment of the accuracy of the conclusions from forensic analyses and the estimation of relevant error rates are key components of the mission of forensic science."

The Innocence Project has documented instances of intentional and unintentional laboratory errors that have led to wrongful convictions, including contamination and mislabeling of evidence; falsified results (including the aforementioned "dry-labbing," or providing conclusions from tests that were never conducted), and misinterpretation of evidence. In the courtroom, these errors include suppression of exculpatory evidence; providing a statistical exaggeration of the results of a test conducted on evidence; and providing false testimony about test results.

The forensic science community is not the only profession seeking to gain a better understanding of misconduct among its practitioners. According to Fanelli (2009), approximately 2 percent of scientists who participated in surveys admitted to having fabricated, falsified or modified data or results at least once, and as many as one-third confessed a number of other questionable research practices including dropping data points based on intuition, and modifying the design, methodology, or results of a study in response to pressures from a funding source.

Social scientists are beginning to wonder if misbehaving scientists are becoming more the norm instead of the exception. As Fanelli (2009) notes, "A popular view propagated by the media and by many scientists sees fraudsters as just a 'few bad apples.' This pristine image of science is based on the theory that the scientific community is guided by norms including disinterestedness and organized skepticism, which are incompatible with misconduct. Increasing evidence, however, suggests that known frauds are just the 'tip of the iceberg,' and that many cases are never discovered. The debate, therefore, has moved on to defining the forms, causes and frequency of scientific misconduct."

Scientific misconduct has been defined as encompassing fabrication (invention of data or cases), falsification (willful distortion of data or results), and plagiarism (copying of ideas, data, or words without attribution). These behaviors are being driven by a publish-or-perish mentality fueled by increasing competition for funding. As Fanelli (2009) observes, "Depending on factors specific to each case, these misbehaviors lie somewhere on a continuum between scientific fraud, bias, and simple carelessness, so their direct inclusion in the 'falsification' category is debatable, although their negative impact on research can be dramatic. Ultimately, it is impossible to draw clear boundaries for scientific misconduct, just as it is impossible to give a universal definition of professional malpractice. However, the intention to deceive is a key element. Unwilling errors or honest differences in designing or interpreting a research are currently not considered scientific misconduct."

While the 2009 NAS report—as well as scores of papers written by legal commentators—alluded to bias and misconduct by forensic examiners, some critics have gone so far as to use the term *intentional fraud* in their judgments of examiners' work. Turvey (2013, pages 115–116) states, "Forensic fraud has an undeniably devastating impact: it destroys the reputations of the forensic examiners involved, if not their careers; it erodes public confidence in the institutions where they are employed; it can result in overturned convictions, individual and institutional liability, and costly civil judgments; and it is corrosive to the collective faith in the justice system as a whole. However, as mentioned in previous chapters, there is a perception that problems related to fraud and error in the forensic sciences are primarily the result of a 'few rogue practitioners' or 'bad apples'—primarily owing to the public assurances of crime lab managers and supervisors. Despite the fact that 'bad apple theory' is contradicted by established criminological theories relating to fraud and corruption, criminal justice professionals and the public they serve tend to accept this explanation insomuch as they offer little in the way of resistance to it. Consequently, and despite the broad spectrum of harm that can result, forensic fraud is given relatively narrow recognition or attention in the published forensic literature."

PURPORTED BIAS ON THE PART OF FORENSIC PRACTITIONERS

The 2009 NAS report's call for independence of crime labs and medicolegal death investigation offices is designed to eliminate examiners' and other stakeholders' preferences regarding the outcome of forensic examinations. Noting that scientists who are positioned administratively in law enforcement agencies or prosecutors' offices, or who are hired by those entities, are subject to a general risk of bias, the report recommends "removing all public forensic laboratories and facilities from the administrative control of law-enforcement agencies or prosecutors' offices" (NAS, 2009). Koppl and Krane (2016, page 157) explain, "Proposals for 'blinding' or 'masking' are meant to reduce or eliminate the knowledge required to act on one's preferences. These measures prevent examiners from learning domain-irrelevant information such as the salacious details of a crime and the criminal history of suspects." Further, Krane et al. (2008, page 1006) says that a case manager is needed to implement masking for examiners: "In many cases, an examiner must make a sequence of interlinked scientific decisions, and some of the later decisions require the knowledge of information that could bias earlier decisions. In such instances the case manager should effect a 'sequential unmasking' in which the information necessary to make later scientific decisions is revealed only when such decisions need to be made and masked while earlier decisions are being made."

Koppl and Krane (2016, page 160) argue, "When the knowledge elite of a hierarchy requires measures such as sequential unmasking, oversight becomes a blinding measure as well. Random, independent, multiple examinations of evidence is a distributed measure meant to minimize bias. Because examiners will not know whether other labs have examined the same evidence and, if so, what the results of such examinations were, it is a blinding measure as well."

While some practitioners bristle at the suggestion that blinding is necessary, commentators such as Kassin et al. (2013, page 43) assert, "Forensic science judgments are often derived from inadequate testing and analysis, if not outright fabrication; and experts often give imprecise or exaggerated testimony, drawing conclusions not supported by the data—in some cases drawing charges of misconduct. Indeed, some form of invalid or improper forensic science was a contributing factor in the original convictions of more than half of all DNA exonerees. In cases that are not subject to bias, certain forensic sciences—such as latent fingerprint identifications—offer a potentially powerful tool in administering justice. In most domains, however, there are no quantitatively precise objective measures and no instruments of measurement—just partial samples from a crime scene to be compared against a particular suspect. No two patterns are identical, so an examiner invariably must determine whether they are 'sufficiently similar' (a term that has yet to be defined or quantified) to conclude that they originate from the same source. The absence of objective standards is reflected in the lack of consistency not only between examiners but within examiners over time. Hence, not only do inter-variations exist, but intra-variations show that the same examiner inspecting the same data on multiple occasions may reach different conclusions. The lack of reliability indicates that the identification process can be subjective and that judgments are susceptible to bias from other sources."

Some commentators suggest that a monopoly on the evidence that exists in crime labs currently serves to obfuscate bias. Generally, just one laboratory examines and interprets the evidence, constituting the monopoly that Koppl and Krane (2016, page 156) say is part of the "centralization" of forensic science: "Recall that a function is 'centralized' in our sense if one entity picks the state of the system for that function. If we define the examination and interpretation of evidence in a given criminal case as a 'function' of the system, then the twofold epistemic monopoly of forensic science makes such functions highly centralized and hierarchical. The centralization is further compounded in that the system is also a monopsony. Not only do police and prosecutors typically solicit opinions from just one laboratory that serves their jurisdiction, but also that lab typically serves only one jurisdiction. The crime lab easily comes to see the monopsonistic law-enforcement agency as its 'customer' or 'client,' which becomes a source of pro-police bias."

Koppl and Krane (2016) blame the accreditation body, the American Society of Crime Laboratory Directors/Laboratory Accreditation Board (ASCLD/LAB), for the tendency to view law enforcement as the crime lab's "customer." Budowle et al. (2009, page 801) say that ISO/IEC 17025 lab standards promulgated by the International Organization for Standardization (ISO) emphasize customer service. Koppl and Krane (2016, page 157) note further, "As far as we know, the emphasis on customer service has not been criticized in the literatures on forensic science and forensic science management. But a scientific process should not be governed by a criterion of commercial success. The monopoly–monopsony relationship and the perception of law enforcement as the 'customer' create a risk of (conscious or unconscious) bias in the analyses of public crime labs."

Nearly 40 years ago, Tversky and Kahneman (1974) reasoned that confirmation bias effects could extend to the legal system insofar as "beliefs concerning the likelihood of ... the guilt of a defendant" could impact judicial decision making (page 1124). Commentators point to the concept of "forensic confirmation bias" to summarize the class of effects through which an individual's preexisting beliefs, expectations, motives and situational context influence the collection, perception, and interpretation of evidence during the course of a criminal case. As Findley and Scott (2006) have noted, the result produces a form of "tunnel vision"—a rigid focus on one suspect that leads investigators to seek out and favor inculpatory evidence, while overlooking or discounting any exculpatory evidence that might exist.

Kassin et al. (2013) refer to what they call the "elasticity of forensic evidence," in which examiners are more likely to exhibit bias when evaluating evidence that is ambiguous, consistent with the assertion that some types of evidence are more "elastic," or more vulnerable to extraneous influence than others.

While the so-called pattern evidence disciplines have received the harshest criticism, even DNA typing and testing, commonly considered to be the gold standard of forensic evidence, the interpretation of certain complex DNA mixtures requires interpretation that can be subject to bias.

Kassin et al. (2013, page 47) point out, "Although confirmation bias typically operates outside of conscious awareness, forensic examiners may have some insight into the cognitive, motivational, and emotional factors that guide their job performance." For example, interviews of experienced fingerprint examiners revealed a number of recurrent themes in their experiences, including examiners expressing a personal interest in catching criminals and solving crimes, which some reported as more pronounced in serious and high-profile cases. As Charlton et al. (2010) report, "They also expressed a strong need for closure, indicating a desire to provide definitive conclusions as a result of their work, and the feeling of joy that accompanies the discovery of a fingerprint match. At the same time, these experts consistently expressed a fear of making erroneous judgments, and in particular, a fear of committing a false-positive error that would implicate an innocent person. Thus, perhaps some experts deliberately endeavor to be conservative in their judgments to avoid such errors." Additionally, Peterson et al. (1984) studied four crime laboratories and found that very few reports excluded the known suspect from the crime scene or from a connection to the victim. It is not clear whether this result indicates that police manage to identify actual perpetrators for suspicion at high levels of accuracy or that forensic examiners have strong and biasing base-rate expectations that lab results will prove incriminating.

To address the problem of flawed evidence and erroneous reports, Kassin et al. (2013, page 49) suggest, "Examiners should work 'linear' rather than 'circular,' thus initially examining the evidence from the crime scene and documenting their findings before making comparisons against a target. This will eliminate the potential influence of the target on how information is processed and the weight assigned to it." They also suggest that potential influences stemming from examiners reassessing the evidence to fit the target are eliminated if the initial assessment is done in isolation of the target. In fact, the Office of the Inspector General (OIG) recently revised its standard operating procedures (SOPs) to include some steps to avoid bias: "examiners must complete and document analysis of the latent fingerprint before looking at any known fingerprint," and "instruct examiners conducting analysis of a latent fingerprint to analyze it for evidence of distortion, determine whether it is 'of value,' and document the data used during analysis" (OIG, 2011, page 27).

Kassin et al. (2013, page 49) emphasize that the easiest way to protect against the biasing effects of contextual variables is to conduct blind testing: "Too often, examiners are exposed to extraneous information from various sources that may taint their conclusions. It is important to shield them from this information. There is no reason why examiners should receive information that is not relevant to their work and that they do not need. Thus, we recommend, as much as possible, that forensic examiners be isolated from undue influences such as direct contact with the investigating officer, the victims and their families, and other irrelevant information—such as whether the suspect had confessed. Blind testing can shield the forensic examiner from a confession, eyewitness identification, and other information about an investigation that is irrelevant to their forensic work. But it does not protect against the simple base-rate assumption that any individual identified as a suspect is the likely perpetrator. In current forensic practice, examiners often compare a sample of material to that of a target, presumably belonging to the suspect, in an effort to determine if the two samples derive from the same individual."

Koppl et al. (2008, pages 141–159) say, "The verification of forensic decisions should be a more controlled process in which blind and double-blind procedures are used whenever possible. Such procedures would require that the verifier is not informed of the initial conclusion; if possible, that the verifier does not know who the examiner was; and that the examiner does not select the verifier (a common practice in many laboratories). Cross-laboratory verifications are also advisable to provide an independent means of checking on the propriety of the initial forensic work."

Commentators have long pointed to bias among forensic practitioners. Cooley and Turvey (2011, pages 52–53) summarize the issue by observing, "As cognitive psychologists have repeatedly documented, tested, and proven, the scientific observer is an imperfectly calibrated instrument. Their imperfections stem from the fact that subtle forms of bias, whether conscious or unconscious, can easily contaminate their seemingly objective undertakings. Observer effects are present when the results of a forensic examination are distorted by the context and mental state of the forensic examiner, to include the examiner's subconscious expectations and desires. Identifying and curtailing this kind of bias is a considerable task when one takes into account the forensic community's affiliation with both law enforcement and the prosecution. Specifically, this association has fashioned an atmosphere in which an unsettling number of forensic professionals have all but abandoned objectivity and have become completely partial to the prosecution's objectives, goals, and philosophies. They may even go so far as to regard this association as virtuous and heroic, and believe any alternative philosophy to be a manifestation of something that is morally bankrupt. So strong is the influence of this association between forensic science and law enforcement that some forensic examiners have even deliberately fabricated evidence, or testified falsely, so that the prosecution might prove its case; however, this is the extreme end of the spectrum."

Most commentators acknowledge the desire on the part of the vast majority of forensic scientists to address the issue when it arises. As Cooley and Turvey (2011, pages 52–53) state, "It is fair to say that the majority of practitioners in the forensic science community routinely acknowledge the existence of overt forms of conscious bias. That is, they generally recognize and condemn forensic ignorance, forensic fraud, and evidence fabricators when they are dragged into the light and exposed for all to see. Moreover, the forensic community seems to realize that in order to effectively serve the criminal justice system, they must immediately eliminate individuals, procedures, or circumstances that call into question examiner objectivity and neutrality (although this may be called into question in some specific cases, when forensic science organizations essentially fail in their duty to regulate membership and essentially protect inept and unethical examiners). Although the forensic community is attenuated to the potential for extreme forms of outright fraud and overt bias, it tends to be wholly unaware when it comes to understanding and accepting that well-documented forms of covert bias can taint even the most impartial scientific examinations. This is disheartening for the simple reason that covert and subconscious biases represent a far greater threat to the forensic community than do the small percentage of overtly biased, dishonest or fraudulent forensic examiners."

To impugn the integrity of the entire forensic community is folly, and at some point, the realities of humanity come into play. As Houck and Siegel (2015, page 665) emphasize, "Ethics and professional responsibilities are central to the success of and respect for a profession. Everyone is subject to bias in virtually all of their activities and interactions with others. All scientists face biasing issues by nature of their involvement in scientific activities. Forensic scientists face all of these bias issues and, in addition, they face biasing situations by virtue of their interactions with the justice system. Awareness of sources of bias is a necessary step in becoming a good professional but it is not sufficient. Forensic scientists must practice ethical behavior daily and act as role models for their peers and colleagues so that their scientific expertise aids the criminal justice system and does not damage it."

Houck and Siegel (2015, page 655) explain that bias is a preference for or against a person, thing, group, idea, or behavior: "Being biased means being one-sided and being less willing to consider alternatives ... Although most people like to think of themselves as being unbiased, fair and impartial, it is nearly impossible to be able to take a completely neutral position. All of our opinions and feelings are based upon our own experiences and ... being biased is, in a way, hard-wired into human beings but that does not mean biases cannot be overcome or controlled for. In many cases, people do not even have a conscious realization that they are being biased. Bias is not something that can be turned on or off like a switch and cannot be wished away." They add, "Forensic science is not immune to bias. In fact, forensic science has more opportunities for potential bias because of the close relationship it has with professions that are required to have a particular viewpoint, like police officers, prosecutors and defense attorneys. Remember that most public laboratories are administered and funded by a unit of government, which has the responsibility to prosecute people for committing crimes. The fact that a forensic scientist is employed by a public laboratory may imply that he or she is biased toward the prosecution and is a 'member' of the prosecution 'team.'"

Two types of bias have particular implications for forensic science. Contextual bias exists when a person is influenced by clues surrounding the topic but not the content itself. Confirmation bias is the tendency to search for and use only information that supports a belief or hypothesis; any information that conflicts with the belief or hypothesis is discounted or ignored (Houck and Siegel, 2015, page 657).

Fraud notwithstanding, it is the expressed desire of so many in the legal and forensic communities to address any appearance of or actual presence of bias. As the NAS report noted, "Human judgment is subject to many different types of bias, because we unconsciously pick up cues from our environment and factor them in an unstated way into our mental analyses. Those mental analyses might also be affected by unwarranted assumptions and a degree of overconfidence that we do not even recognize in ourselves. Such cognitive biases are not the result of character flaws; instead, they are common features of decision-making, and they cannot be willed away" (NAS, 2009).

A paper by Saks and Risinger et al. (2003, pages 77–90) is one of the more definitive attempts to characterize context effects in science. They explain that context information, including expectations about what one is supposed to see or conclude, has been found to have a "small but relentless impact on human perception, judgment and decision-making." Their work considers the vulnerability of forensic science practice to context effects, and concludes by suggesting that forensic science adopt practices familiar in other fields of scientific work, in particular blind or double-blind testing and also the use of evidence lineups.

As the 2009 NAS report emphasizes, "The goal is to make scientific investigations as objective as possible so the results do not depend on the investigator" (NAS, 2009).

It's a goal echoed by numerous legal scholars who are pushing hard for better measures of the accuracy of inferences made by forensic scientists. As the 2009 NAS report observes, "All results for every forensic science method should indicate the uncertainty in the measurements that are made, and studies must be conducted that enable the estimation of those values. For the identification sciences (e.g., friction ridge analysis, toolmark analysis, handwriting analysis), such studies would accumulate data about the intra-individual variability (e.g., how much one finger's impressions vary from impression to impression, or how much one toolmark or signature varies from instance to instance) and the inter-individual variability (e.g., how much the impressions of many fingerprints vary across a population and in what ways). With that information, one could begin to attach confidence limits to individualization determinations and also begin to develop an understanding of how much similarity is needed in order to attain a given level of confidence that a match exists. Note that this necessary step would change the way the word 'individualization' is commonly used" (NAS, 2009, page 184).

Identification and individualization are the two issues that must be resolved by the forensic scientist. In forensic science, Fisher et al. (2007, page 6) say identification is simply answering the question, "What is it?" Individualization can be thought of as the uniqueness of an object to the exclusion of all other objects like itself.

Evidence usually takes the form of an unknown in the lab. According to Fisher et al. (2007, page 8), "It is the forensic scientist's responsibility to test this unknown and determine what it is (identification) and what sets it apart from other evidence (individualization). To do this, forensics utilizes exemplars, or knowns. Exemplars are objects that are commonly encountered in investigations or the possible real object that created the evidence." They add that every facet of forensic science relies on knowns or unknowns for the process of forensic testing.

Fisher et al. (2007, page 8) add, "When the evidence in a case is linked to an exemplar or known, it is called an inclusion. Inclusions typically occur when the evidence is individualized to a known, apart from all other knowns in the case. However, if the evidence does not match the exemplar in a case, then there is an exclusion, and that exemplar is ruled out from having produced the evidence. Inclusions not only aid in matching people to people and people to places in the course of the investigation, but also by establishing these links, open more avenues or clues for the investigation. Likewise, exclusions are important because they help eliminate the suspects, places or possible events that surround a crime and can aid in narrowing down the focus of the investigation."

As we have seen from the early days of criminalistics, the concept of individualization is that an object found at a crime scene can be uniquely associated with one particular source. As the 2009 NAS report notes, "By acknowledging that there can be uncertainties in this process, the concept of 'uniquely associated with' must be replaced with a probabilistic association, and other sources of the crime scene evidence cannot be completely discounted. The courts already have proven their ability to deal with some degree of uncertainty in individualizations, as demonstrated by the successful use of DNA analysis (with its small, but nonzero, error rate)" (NAS, 2009, page 184).

Risinger et al. (2002) offer an overview of the effect of bias in the forensic science disciplines, noting that decisions regarding what analyses need to be performed and in what order also can be influenced by bias and ultimately have the potential to skew results. As the 2009 NAS report expounds, "Forensic scientists who sit administratively in law enforcement agencies or prosecutors' offices, or who are hired by those units, are subject to a general risk of bias. Bias also is introduced through decisions made about evidence collection, which controls who is listed as a suspect. Evidence collection and crime scene investigation can require scientific knowledge and judgment, and these functions are normally outside the control of forensic scientists" (NAS, 2009, page 185).

Operating under potential bias and in danger of committing unwitting errors, it would seem that every forensic scientist is looking for an opportunity to engage in malfeasance. Instead of coming to work looking to commit error or fraud, it's more than likely the practitioner is merely coping with a set of circumstances not necessarily unique to his or her professional station in life, and attempting to rise above the challenges. It may very well be that forensic science's required mix of skills is creating an environment that makes its practitioners a product of their surroundings.

As Siegel (2011, page 2) explains, "Analysis of scientific evidence is the bread and butter of forensic science. In most cases, forensic science laboratories analyze evidence brought to them by crime scene investigators or police investigators. This raises the interesting issue of, when they perform their analysis, how much a scientist should know about the circumstances surrounding the evidence. There are two schools of thought: the first, and prevailing school, says that the examiner should have as much information as possible about the crime or incident from which the evidence came. One should never analyze evidence in a vacuum. The other school is the purely scientific one that the evidence should be analyzed completely, objectively and nothing should be divulged about the evidence that would bias the examiner in any way."

Siegel (2011, page 10) insists further, "Forensic scientists do not operate in a vacuum. The culture and environment of the crime laboratory can have a profound effect on how the work gets done. The pressures on scientists from police investigators, prosecutors and defense attorneys, as well as from the adversarial system under which they must function, can cause covert—or even overt—bias to creep in and the science to become compromised." Siegel (2011, page 11) adds, "The vast majority of forensic scientists claim to be able to function effectively, maintaining a degree of objectivity and helping the evidence tell its story without regard to which side gets the benefit. It is only a few who allow bias to creep in and allow themselves to become advocates instead of disinterested scientists. In spite of all these issues and problems, the vast majority of forensic scientists love their work. Interviews with forensic scientists have shown high levels of job satisfaction because they have a chance to use their interest and background in science to help tackle serious crime, because they love to solve problems, and because of the public nature of their jobs in a courtroom."

Perhaps underlying professional misconduct are varying levels of skills and aptitudes, a reality the 2009 NAS report said needed to be addressed through professional development. "Some activities require the skills and analytical expertise of individuals trained as scientists (e.g., chemists or biologists); other activities are conducted by scientists as well as by individuals trained in law enforcement (e.g., crime scene investigators, blood spatter analysts, crime reconstruction specialists), medicine (e.g., forensic pathologists), or laboratory methods (e.g., technologists). Many of the processes used in the forensic science disciplines are largely empirical applications of science—that is, they are not based on a body of knowledge that recognizes the underlying limitations of the scientific principles and methodologies used for problem solving and discovery. It is therefore important to focus on ways to improve, systematize and monitor the activities and practices in the forensic science disciplines and related areas of inquiry" (NAS, 2009, page 38).

The observation that forensic science is in a state of flux and seeking resoluteness hasn't changed much since 2003, when James and Nordby said that the presentation of evidence and expert opinions should be made with a sense of "contrite fallibilism." As James and Nordby (2003, page 13) explain, "By this is meant an awareness of how much we do not know, and the humility to acknowledge the possibility of making mistakes. ... Forensic scientists must develop an intellect not too sure of what must remain uncertain, not too uncertain about what must remain sure. In the spirit of intellectual honesty and judicial prudence, the best advice for the forensic scientist to carry from the scene to the lab and into court throughout a long career comes from a 20th century Viennese philosopher, Ludwig Wittgenstein: 'Whereof one cannot speak, thereof one must remain silent.'"

Forensic scientists are expected to demonstrate logical acumen in applying the scientific method, and they are expected to explain their application of science to the problem at hand clearly, accurately, and responsibly. In essence, Nordby (2003) admonishes the forensic scientist to own his or her conclusions: "Once you, as a forensic scientist, write something in a report, or say something under oath, you own that forever, good, bad or indifferent." With this comes two scenarios; Nordby explains that forensic scientists' statements may either appear to be "overly definitive or precise" or appear "overly inconclusive or imprecise." Nordby adds, "When a degree of precision expressed by a conclusion fails to mirror the available precision among the data, red flags ought to fly." Going back to the issue of semantics within the context of expressions of certainty, forensic scientists face danger in using pejorative language when using words such as *likely* or *indicates*—the implication is that there is some degree of probability or even certainty to these claims. Nordby admonishes, "When couching claims with these words, the forensic scientist must be prepared to supply a foundation for the probabilistic nature of the attendant opinion." The absence of this foundation will, of course, open the scientist up to attack by the defense and cause counsel to probe for underlying scientific weaknesses, whether real or imagined.

Kiely (2003) describes the antagonism between forensic scientists and the courts that can be captured in in two questions: How far can forensic scientists go in making definitive statements about crime scenes and/or linking a suspect to them because they have a microscope? How far do we let them go because we have a constitution? As Kiely (2003) explains, "The importance of these questions lies in the recognition of how far and on what empirical basis such statements can be made at all, and the impact they may have on a jury in causing such match testimony, albeit given in a qualified manner, to be taken as true by a jury. The concern has always been that a scientist's testimony that a hair or fiber obtained from a suspect was consistent in all respects or not dissimilar will be internalized by jurors as statement of a definitive match. It is important to realize that ... the opinions of most forensic experts are routinely couched in such qualified terms."

The presentation of expert testimony is one of the primary ways in which forensic science and the law clash and forensic scientists are put in a position to render opinions and interpretations. Starrs (2003) notes, "Even though forensic scientists may be respectful of the limits of their own scientific inquiries, they may nevertheless chomp at the legal bit which curbs them in the legal forum. The law proceeds at a pace moved by restraint and conservatism. Indeed, the law's detractors in the scientific community often perceive the snail's pace of the law's acceptance of science to be a bone of much contention. Science, on its part, can and does make gigantic strides with new insights and almost magisterial new-found instrumentation."

Many critics regard forensic science as an applied science at best, as the various disciplines lack scientific rigor and empirical data. The forensic science community counters with the argument that forensic science is not a pristine discipline, and is required to engage in the kind of scientific inquiry that cannot be modeled after the traditional natural sciences. As James and Nordby (2003) observe, "Currently, legal challenges to many established forensic science techniques, such as fingerprint and hair comparison, are being made. The law is questioning whether such evidence is truly scientific. The natural sciences from this adversarial position remain theoretical, while the forensic sciences remain pejoratively practical. The forensic scientist must work to counteract this misguided view without appearing defensive." For example, James and Nordby (2003) point out that while the natural sciences are said to be, among other things, theoretical, orderly, controlled, pristine, and certain, and consist of pure knowledge, the forensic sciences are said to be practical and applied, disorderly, contaminated, chaotic, uncertain, and comprised of conjectures on the part of its practitioners.

Bell (2008, page 4) observes, "Science and the law are not the compatible bedfellows people often assume they are. Both seek to investigate events based on available evidence, articulate presumptions based on probability, and use those presumptions to arrive at the most likely interpretation of events. The more probable a presumption becomes, the closer it approaches fact. The law and science differ dramatically in their goals and methods. The goal of science is to describe the workings of the natural world, while the goal of the law is to settle disputes. Science relies on the scientific method of hypothesis, experiment and observation, and refinement to validate ideas and presumptions. The law relies on the adversarial system and argument to determine how best to resolve conflict. Theoretically and in simplistic terms, whoever makes the better argument wins in an adversarial system."

Bell (2008, page xii) adds, "Good forensic science can implicate the guilty, but also and just as importantly, it can exonerate the innocent. It has taken many years to get to this point. False prophets, fools and self-proclaimed experts marred early forensic science, often dazzling courts with salesmanship over expertise. Pseudoscience still knocks on courtroom doors and sometimes manages to slip in. In the worst case, scientific evidence can become so complex that juries simply ignore it. Scientific analysis appears so convoluted and technical that a clever attorney can easily raise a reasonable doubt to prevent a conviction. If this trend continues, courts will fumble complex cases, and public trust, the blood currency of the justice system, will be lost."

James and Nordby (2003) add, "Unlike the carefully controlled experiment set up in a laboratory, consider the slightly smudged half fingerprint on a glass. If forensic science is conjectural, operating in chaotic situations where data are likely to become contaminated, can we trust the fingerprint as evidence? The so-called covering law model of natural science accounts for expectations of scientific certainty which no forensic science allegedly approximates: epistemically certain laws of nature cover and, thereby, through deduction, explain cases."

James and Nordby (2003) emphasize that "almost all cases requiring explanation in the forensic setting involve many combinations of so-called causes all mixed together in the world existing outside of the laboratory. ... The search for some single covering law becomes sheer myth. Until we discover some such law, it is up to science to supply acceptable explanations in the absence of any so-called certain knowledge. In practice, the forensic sciences have an important element in common with the natural sciences. While their scientific goals obviously differ, their scientific common ground rests within an identical method of inquiry."

As Nordby (2003) states, "Scientifically reliable methods help forensic scientists develop reasoned opinions, views that may not be proved conclusively true, but views toward which the explanatory patterns emerging from the evidence, together with the evidence itself, most unambiguously point. Reasoned opinions developed from scientifically acceptable methods avoid subjective, unsupported, and untested hunches and guesses. While the observation may be correct, its truth is merely coincidental. Since truth often hides among the debris of coincidence, a method, one that reveals the truth more often than not, earns the mantle of reliability." Regarding these uncertainties, Starrs (2003) asserts that "guesstimates" abound in forensic science. For example, time-dating, which he calls a "perturbing complexity," is a challenge in the forensic discipline of fingerprinting and ballistics. Starrs also points to forensic pathologists who are "constantly besieged to provide more exact statements on the time of a person's death" or asked to determine the precise sequence of the creation of stab wounds or bullet holes. As Starrs notes, "The interest of the public, fed by the media, in forensic science and concomitantly, the belief that forensic science has all the answers, has risen in a geometric progression, but forensic science moves more lumberingly in its research and development according to an arithmetic formulation. Soon, if we are not exceedingly careful to rein in the public portrayals of the forensic sciences to a more realistic scientific level, the forensic sciences will be found to be wanting in credibility by juries failing to measure up to public image. Worse yet, forensic scientists, to keep pace with this public misperception of forensic science, will render opinions as experts in the courts by expressing more scientific assurance that they should or can."

James and Nordby (2003) emphasize, "How one's opinion is constructed determines its certainty. The certainty of forensic explanations is measured by assessing their explanatory justifications. This, in turn, involves showing first that the explanation is justified, and second, that the explanation is better justified than any available alternative explanation. In this forensic setting, certainty assessments address the scientific explanation's rational justification, leaving the question of the explanation's truth and role in legal deliberations of the court. This allows for a clearer understanding of requests for certainty assessments when scientists are asked by attorneys to attach some degree of certainty to their work product."

Nordby (2003) recognizes the challenges inherent in the criminal justice system when cases come down to mere semantics: "Scientific opinions involve interpretations of and inferences from data which can be subject to challenge on scientific grounds. The argument must be developed in the spirit of rational disagreement in either science or the law." Nordby sees scientific disagreements as scientific process, but these arguments and opinions must have purpose: "Forensic scientists have a scientific obligation to present their reasoning as clearly as possible, showing how their conclusions follow from the scientific work applied to a given case." Nordby adds, "Good science, and good forensic science, produces reasoned opinions." He also states that when the court asks for a statement of certainty, "it must remain solidly within the methodological realm of forensic science." He adds, "...scientists shouldn't navigate scientific waters with an eye fixed solely on conclusions. Instead we must navigate with a critical eye focused firmly on the methods dictated by logic."

With outcomes resting on the evidence, it's imperative that standardized terminology and reporting be established. As the 2009 NAS report notes, "There is a critical need in most fields of forensic science to raise the standards for reporting and testifying about the results of investigations" (NAS, 2009, page 185). The NAS report adds, "For example, many terms are used by forensic examiners in reports and in court testimony to describe findings, conclusions, and the degrees of association between evidentiary material (e.g., hairs, fingerprints, fibers) and particular people or objects. Such terms include but are not limited to 'match,' 'consistent with,' 'identical,' 'similar in all respects tested,' and 'cannot be excluded as the source of.' The use of such terms can have a profound effect on how the trier of fact in a criminal or civil matter perceives and evaluates evidence.

Yet the forensic science disciplines have not reached agreement or consensus on the precise meaning of any of these terms. Although some disciplines have developed vocabulary and scales to be used in reporting results, they have not become standard practice. This imprecision in vocabulary stems in part from the paucity of research in forensic science and the corresponding limitations in interpreting the results of forensic analyses."

To this end, on January 16, 2016, the National Commission on Forensic Science (NCFS) adopted the document, "Recommendations to the Attorney General Regarding Use of the Term 'Reasonable Scientific Certainty.'" As the NCFS explained, "Forensic discipline conclusions are often testified to as being held 'to a reasonable degree of scientific certainty' or 'to a reasonable degree of [discipline] certainty.' These terms have no scientific meaning and may mislead factfinders about the level of objectivity involved in the analysis, its scientific reliability and limitations, and the ability of the analysis to reach an individualized conclusion. Forensic scientists, medical professionals and other scientists do not routinely express opinions or conclusions 'to a reasonable scientific certainty' outside of the courts. Neither the Daubert nor Frye test of scientific admissibility requires its use, and consideration of caselaw from around the country confirms that use of the phrase is not required by law and is primarily a relic of custom and practice."

The NCFS noted additional problems with this phrase, including the fact that there is no common definition within science disciplines as to what threshold establishes "reasonable" certainty. Therefore, whether couched as "scientific certainty" or "[discipline] certainty," the term is idiosyncratic to the witness. As the NCFS remarked, "The term invites confusion when presented with testimony expressed in probabilistic terms. How is a lay person, without either scientific or legal training, to understand an expert's 'reasonable scientific certainty' that evidence is 'probably' or possibly linked to a particular source?"

The NCFS recommends that the attorney general direct all attorneys appearing on behalf of the Department of Justice to forego use of these phrases when presenting forensic discipline testimony unless directly required by judicial authority as a condition of admissibility for the witness' opinion or conclusion, and to assert the legal position that such terminology is not required and is indeed misleading. As the NCFS explains, "Because the government is the primary proponent of forensic discipline testimony in criminal prosecutions and because of its duty to seek justice, government attorneys should eschew usage of this phrasing and appropriately challenge any suggestion to a trial court that such language be used when forensic discipline testimony is presented. Science should be used in the courtroom to clarify and elucidate rather than obscure."

Legal scholars and other experts emphasize that forensic science reports, and any courtroom testimony stemming from them, must include clear characterizations of the limitations of the analyses, including associated probabilities where possible. The NAS report notes that the use of such terms by forensic scientists in scientific reports and in court testimony that describe findings, conclusions, and degrees of association between evidentiary material (e.g., hairs, fingerprints, fibers) and particular people or objects "can and does have a profound effect on how the trier of fact in a criminal or civil matter perceives and evaluates scientific evidence. Although some forensic science disciplines have proposed reporting vocabulary and scales, the use of the recommended language is not standard practice among forensic science practitioners" (NAS, 2009, page 185).

Many clinical and testing disciplines outside the forensic science disciplines have standards and protocols for data reporting, such as the ISO/IEC 17025 standard, which is an international standard published by the ISO that specifies the general requirements for the competence to carry out tests and/or calibrations. These requirements have been used by accrediting agencies to determine what a laboratory must do to secure accreditation.

As the NAS report pointed out, although appropriate standards exist, they are not always followed: "Forensic reports, and any courtroom testimony stemming from them, must include clear characterizations of the limitations of the analyses, including measures of uncertainty in reported results and associated estimated probabilities where possible" (NAS, 2009, page 186).

To that end, in its Recommendation 2, the 2009 NAS report noted, "The National Institute of Forensic Science (NIFS), after reviewing established standards such as ISO 17025, and in consultation with its advisory board, should establish standard terminology to be used in reporting on and testifying about the results of forensic science investigations. Similarly, it should establish model laboratory reports for different forensic science disciplines and specify the minimum information that should be included. As part of the accreditation and certification processes, laboratories and forensic scientists should be required to utilize model laboratory reports when summarizing the results of their analyses" (NAS, 2009, page 189).

In a document created by the Subcommittee on Reporting and Testimony, the NCFS outlined the issue at the heart of the matter: "Forensics experts are often required to testify that the opinions or facts stated are offered 'to a reasonable scientific certainty' or to a 'reasonable degree of [discipline] certainty.' Outside of the courts, this phrasing is not routinely used in scientific disciplines. Moreover, the terminology, in its varying forms, is not defined in standard medical or scientific reference materials. With respect to its use in the courts, this phrase is almost always interjected as a matter of custom, but in some jurisdictions, results from an appellate court ruling or trial judges' or lawyers' belief that it is a necessary precondition for admissibility. In the courtroom setting, the phrase risks misleading or confusing the factfinder."

The NCFS (2016) notes further, "...the scientific community should not promote the use of this terminology. Additionally, the legal community should recognize that medical professionals and other scientists do not routinely use 'to a reasonable scientific certainty' when expressing conclusions outside of the courts since there is no foundational scientific basis for its use. Therefore, legal professionals should not require that forensic discipline testimony be admitted conditioned upon the expert witness testifying that a conclusion is held to a 'reasonable scientific certainty,' a 'reasonable degree of scientific certainty,' or a 'reasonable degree of [discipline] certainty,' as such terms have no scientific meaning and may mislead jurors or judges when deciding whether guilt has been proved beyond a reasonable doubt. The Commission recognizes the right of each court to determine admissibility standards but expresses this view as part of its mandate to 'develop proposed guidance concerning the intersection of forensic science and the courtroom.'"

Historically, the NCFS explained, "The requirement of an expert testifying that a conclusion is held to a 'degree of certainty' emerged in the context of medical testimony, when witnesses in civil cases were asked about the potential future consequences of an injury or illness. In predicting future events, courts wanted to avoid speculation. As a result, they required that the testifying doctor make a prediction with some degree of certitude" (NCFS, 2016). In federal courts, neither the Daubert trilogy of cases (Daubert, Joyner, or Kumho Tire) nor the Federal Rules of Evidence 702–705 require such language. As the NCFS points out, "Both the Daubert and Frye tests, when properly implemented, serve to screen out speculative testimony and thus further demonstrate the lack of need for the 'reasonable degree of certainty' language."

Legal scholars have questioned the use of the term, notably Giannelli (2010, page 3), who states, "The term 'reasonable medical certainty' has no scientific meaning. Its legal meaning is at best ambiguous, at worst misleading." In addition, Kaye (2010) observes, "The reasonable-degree-of-scientific-certainty language almost certainly was drafted by the lawyers. Scientists have no use for this phrase (outside the courtroom). Indeed, 'a reasonable degree of scientific certainty' is not a defined concept in scientific disciplines or even in law… It is legal mumbo jumbo derived from archaic cases in which lawyers discovered that if a medical doctor did not utter the incantation 'to a reasonable degree of medical certainty,' his testimony might be excluded because doctors were not supposed to talk about mere probabilities."

As the NCFS notes, "The Commission recognizes that recommending the abandonment of a long-used phrase is only a first step. An expert's certainty in a conclusion may be an appropriate concern in a particular case, and that certainty is actually a statement of confidence distinct from the likelihood of the conclusion itself. For example, an expert may be very certain that 'X' is the most likely cause of condition 'Y.' As well, depending on the nature of the case, a court may determine that for the testimony about the existence of a fact to be sufficiently helpful, the witness must indicate that, in the expert's judgment, the fact is at least more probable than not (or meets some other threshold level of certainty). Nonetheless, the terminology at issue—reasonable degree of scientific certainty—in no way serves such a function. Work will be needed to identify the full range of appropriate language for expressing an expert's opinion. That work, particularly for forensic science, may best be undertaken through the OSAC structure or this Commission. As a first step, however, the term 'reasonable degree of scientific [or discipline] certainty' has no place in the judicial process" (NCFS, 2016).

ADDRESSING PSEUDOSCIENCE

As we have seen, there are ongoing efforts to address the terminology used by forensic scientists in their reports and in their court testimony. But the larger issue that continues to be debated before and after the 2009 NAS report by commentators is the lack of science, or the presence of *pseudoscience* in forensic science disciplines.

Cole (2010, page 444) says we err when we equate "science" with what he calls "discovery science," defined as the scientific activity designed to create new, generalizable knowledge about the natural world: "There are a wide variety of activities that we conventionally consider 'science' that would not be described as 'discovery science.' These activities would include: routine laboratory work, such as work that may be part of larger projects that may themselves be 'discovery science;' industrial science; engineering; much of medicine; descriptive science; and so on. There are armies of workers engaged in what sociologists call 'techno-scientific work' in the enterprise of modern science, who are performing work that could not, in itself, be characterized as discovery."

Therefore, Cole (2010, page 445) says, laypeople, such as judges and lawyers, tend to be familiar only with accounts of discovery science and thus seek to apply those accounts to all scientific activities: "This results in a mismatch, which can produce a variety of misunderstandings. Mundane scientific activity can be characterized according to explanations that were constructed for discovery science and can be found wanting because it does not meet expectations that were devised for discovery science." Cole (2010, page 445) adds that concepts such as *science*, *scientific method*, and *scientific culture* cannot be applied to forensic science "without thinking seriously about what sort of scientific activity forensic science purports to be."

The 2009 NAS report said that forensic science lacks adequate validation, certification, accreditation, oversight, and basic research, but it never said that forensic science was unscientific, Cole (2010, page 446) points out, adding that "...there is little use in debating whether or not forensic science is 'science' [because] it is legally irrelevant." In *Kumho Tire v. Carmichael*, the United States Supreme Court relieved courts of the responsibility to decide whether various forms of expert evidence should constitute "science" or "non-science." The court ruled that the same criteria enumerated in its *Daubert v. Merrell Dow Pharmaceuticals, Inc.* decision applied equally to all forms of expert evidence. However, Cole (2010, page 447) notes, "In turning to philosophy of science in an attempt to articulate a definition of reliable science, the Daubert Court necessarily turned to a literature that is concerned with what we might call 'discovery science.' ... For example, laboratory technicians performing routine assays ... might defensibly be called 'science,' and yet are probably not best described as efforts to discover generalizable truths about the natural world. The Daubert decision is generally believed to have been occasioned, in part, by a perception that that the courts were facing an increasing number of highly technical scientific issues. Daubert, in this formulation, was an effort by the Court to assist the lower courts by providing guidance in dealing with such issues. But most legal issues involving science do not seem to involve discovery science. Instead, most legal issues would seem to pertain to precisely those ... more mundane kinds of science: laboratory tests, medical diagnoses, epidemiology, and industrial science, among others. The paradox is that, in seeking to assist lower courts in dealing with a perceived flood of scientific issues involving what we might call 'mundane science,' the Court drew on a literature constructed exclusively around the philosophical problems raised by discovery science. This mismatch has not been sufficiently recognized, either by the courts themselves or in the scholarly literature, but it surely is behind much of the sense of dissatisfaction that continues to surround the Daubert regime."

Uniqueness has been debated for years among commentators and practitioners. What Saks and Koehler (2005) object to is the examiner's insistence that two indistinguishable marks must have been produced by a single object, to the exclusion of all others in the world, thus relying on the assumption of discernible uniqueness. As Saks and Koehler observe, "According to this assumption, markings produced by different people or objects are observably different. Thus, when a pair of markings is not observably different, criminalists conclude that the marks were made by the same person or object. Although lacking theoretical or empirical foundations, the assumption of discernible uniqueness offers important practical benefits to the traditional forensic sciences. It enables forensic scientists to draw bold, definitive conclusions that can make or break cases. It excuses the forensic sciences from developing measures of object attributes, collecting population data on the frequencies of variations in those attributes, testing attribute independence, or calculating and explaining the probability that different objects share a common set of observable attributes."

As we have seen, practitioners and legal scholars are grasping for the holy grail of certainty with which to shore up concepts of individualization. For years, practitioners and the courts believed it was DNA. After all, DNA was thought to be able to cast out the last vestiges of what critics refer to as the scourge of pseudoscience allegations that forensic science can't seem to shake. Saks and Koehler (2005), like many commentators on forensic science, laud DNA typing as the one aspect of forensic science actually steeped in traditional science and biochemistry. They say DNA typing serves as a model for the traditional forensic sciences in three important respects: DNA typing technology was an application of knowledge derived from core scientific disciplines. This provided a stable structure for future empirical work on the technology; the courts and scientists scrutinized applications of the technology in individual cases. As a result, early, unscientific practices were rooted out. Additionally, DNA typing offered data-based, probabilistic assessments of the meaning of evidentiary *matches*. This practice represented an advance over potentially misleading match/no-match claims associated with other forensic identification sciences.

According to Saks and Koehler (2005), the strength of DNA testing is that it is steeped in population genetics theory and empirical testing, a foundation they say should be emulated by traditional forensic sciences. They explain: "Each subfield must construct databases of sample characteristics and use these databases to support a probabilistic approach to identification. Fingerprinting could be one of the first areas to make the transition to this approach because large fingerprint databases already exist. The greatest challenge in this effort would be to develop measures of the complex images presented by fingerprints, tool marks, bite marks, handwriting, etc. Forensic scientists will need to work with experts in differential geometry, topology, or other fields to develop workable measures."

Saks and Koehler (2005) assert that one of the easiest ways to take a corrective course of action is to study the model provided by DNA typing and use it to inject science back into forensic identification science. They state, "This effort should begin with adoption of the basic-research model. Just as DNA scientists tested the genetic assumptions that undergirded DNA typing theory, traditional forensic scientists should design experiments that test the core assumptions of their fields. As basic research knowledge grows, experts will be able to inform courts about the relative strengths and weaknesses of their theories and methods, and suggest how that knowledge applies to individual cases."

Whether or not there is a true paradigm shift taking place at the intersection where forensic science and the law meet, Saks and Koehler (2005) have, at the very least, established a vision in which "untested assumptions and semi-informed guesswork are replaced by a sound scientific foundation and justifiable protocols." They add, "Although obstacles exist both inside and outside forensic science, the time is ripe for the traditional forensic sciences to replace antiquated assumptions of uniqueness and perfection with a more defensible empirical and probabilistic foundation."

Rudin and Inman (2005) have suggested that, for the purpose of clarity, *identification* should be used to describe the categorization of items, while *individualization* should be reserved for the process that attempts to determine if two items share a unique common source. They explain that determination of source (whether described by identification or individualization) is only one element of a complete forensic analysis. They say that forensic scientists are being limited to addressing only the question of source, "excluding us from commenting on the very relevant forensic questions of contact and event ordering. ... Whether intentional or not, this artificial constraint on the role of forensic science and forensic scientists allows others, most often attorneys, to control discussions regarding the significance of physical evidence in the context of the case. While this may provide an attorney the chance to arrange the facts to suit a particular theory in some instant case, it does not serve justice well in the long run. This is exemplified no more clearly than their circumscription of forensic science as a single-use tool, to answer only questions of source, limits their thinking about the issues they present and leads them to overly simplistic and poorly conceived solutions."

Rudin and Inman (2005) bristle at Saks and Koehler's suggestion that, "Although lacking theoretical or empirical foundations, the assumption of discernible uniqueness offers important practical benefits to the traditional forensic sciences. It enables forensic scientists to draw bold, definitive conclusions that can make or break cases. It excuses the forensic sciences from developing measures of object attributes, collecting population data on the frequencies of variations in those attributes, testing attribute independence, or calculating and explaining the probability that different objects share a common set of observable attributes. Without the discernible uniqueness assumption, far more scientific work would be needed and criminalists would need to offer more tempered opinions in court." Where Rudin and Inman agree with Saks and Koehler, however, is that forensic science would benefit greatly from partnering with researchers rooted in academia who could help define the controversial limitations involved in comparing physical objects and the patterns made by them.

Critics have long asserted the existence of pseudoscience among forensic science disciplines. Because the field was borne out of scientific, legal, and humanities communities, forensic science inherits characteristics that serve it well but also create opportunities for purists to question its heritage and its lineage. Forensic science is grounded in the traditional sciences of biology, chemistry, physics, and, more recently, genetics, thanks to DNA typing. But some commentators argue over whether forensic science is a pure, more traditional science or an applied, inherently less prestigious science. According to Inman and Rudin (2001, page 7), "Like medicine or engineering, the forensic analysis of physical evidence is an applied science, resting firmly on a foundation of the basic scientific principles of physics, chemistry, and biology."

Perhaps the problem is that forensic science has always been equal parts art and science, as Inman and Rudin (2001 , page 7) explain, "Scientific breakthroughs stand on the bedrock of many small, insignificant advances; but the final solution is often rooted in an intuition that is not fully understandable based simply on previous data. We do not mean to imply that a forensic analysis is an act of genius, only that the boundaries between art and science are perhaps less distinct than is commonly understood. The nature of forensic science lends itself to an artistic and intuitive approach. Facts are often in short supply, analytical results are rarely textbook, and human nature prompts us to fill in the gaps. The very recognition of this proclivity, however, and the institution of rigorous review procedures, serves as an effective counter to our natural tendencies."

Regarding the subjectivity of an applied science, Inman and Rudin (2001 , page 12) note, "At the same time that we strive to maintain scientific objectivity, however, we must realize that the comparison between evidence and reference, regardless of whether the items of interest are two fingerprints or two spectra, is not free of human subjectivity. Nor should it be. ... The question before the forensic scientist is not, as the uninitiated might assume, are these two items the same, but rather, can we exclude the possibility that they originate from the same source? Even the most sophisticated instrumentation cannot overcome imperfections in the samples themselves; analysts must rely on their education, training, and experience to determine whether small differences observed between evidence and reference samples qualify as significant or explainable." They add that even though there is a set of ground rules, or protocol, "No matter how clear and well-reasoned the guidelines, and no matter how conscientiously applied, two competent scientists may still ultimately disagree about the interpretation of a result. This is simply the nature of science. One could program a computer with all the interpretation guidelines in the world, but a human being still must designate and input the guidelines."

As an applied science, forensic science must be prepared for challenges under the ever-evolving standard of admissibility of evidence, as well as closer scrutiny of all forensic disciplines, as we have seen with the 2009 NAS report. As far back as 2001, Inman and Rudin observed, "Some criminalists debate whether any useful purpose would be served by demanding a more scientific treatment of disciplines that have traditionally relied on the experience and expertise of each examiner" (Inman and Rudin, 2001, page 2).

Thornton (1997) notes, "To master statistical models to explain much of our evidence may be a slow, reluctant march through enemy territory, but we must begin to plan for that campaign." To this, Inman and Rudin (2001, page 14) add, "We agree that, at least for physical evidence, providing a statistical justification for the analyst's opinion should be a goal. ... The discussion within the forensic community remains heated and current."

Koppl and Kobilinsky (2005) say that the differences between *pure* science and forensic science can be most readily demonstrated within the context of an institutional structure: "Forensic science is sometimes unreliable because the larger environment of knowledge seeking is not appropriately structured. Most forensic scientists are skillful and diligent practitioners of their trade. They find themselves in an environment, however, that does not encourage the sort of institutional self-criticism characterizing pure science. They are in an environment that can induce unconscious bias and even give the unscrupulous an incentive to lie. If competitive self-regulation has value, it is because it provides a better institutional structure for truth seeking and knowledge production."

The more things change, the more they stay the same. In 2001, Inman and Rudin (page 4) noted, "It appears that the science part of forensic science is what instigates so much consternation. Why should this be? Perhaps a partial answer may be found in modern society's perception of science. Science is believed by the average person to offer hard facts, definite conclusions, and uncompromised objectivity. Therefore, any discipline called a science gains a certain legitimacy and credibility in society's (the judge's? the jury's) view. ... Science is an oft-misused term, frequently employed to lend credibility to an idea or statement as if the aura of science automatically confers trustworthiness. Just as often, it is used to discredit a concept, as if ideas outside the realm of science have no merit. The reality lies in understanding that science is a process not a truth."

Inman and Rudin (2001, page 7) observed further that forensic science is damaged by the presumption that science embraces immutable truths: "In fact, nothing could be further from reality. At any point in time, science provides us with our best estimate of how the universe works. But soon enough, an idea or discovery comes along either to refine or refute what we once 'knew to be true.' This is simply the nature of scientific discovery; our understanding changes with new information. This revelation can be somewhat disconcerting to the layperson who perceives that science can provide hard and fast, black and white, irrefutable answers to questions about the physical realm. All science can provide is the best answer based on all the information available at that point in time."

LACK OF RESEARCH IN FORENSIC SCIENCE

One of the only ways to finally eradicate the pseudoscience allegations is to shore up the academic underpinnings of forensic science and boost its research agenda. Not only must new research be conducted, but existing research must be revisited, according to some commentators. For example, Saks and Risinger (2003, page 24) have asserted that there are numerous problems with the research that has already been undertaken by forensic practitioners, including "placing propositions beyond empirical reach by relying on subjective means of measurement; using research designs that cannot generate clear data on individual practitioner competence; manufacturing favorable test results by giving poor practitioner performances additional help or resources to reconsider their judgments; refusing to share data with researchers who wish to reanalyze or further analyze results; encouraging over-stated interpretations of data; burying unfavorable results in reports where they are least likely to be noticed; and generating disclaimers that the data cannot be used to infer the false positive error rate it reveals."

As well, Faigman (2007) has characterized the pattern evidence disciplines of fingerprints, firearms, toolmarks, and bite marks as "anecdotal" sciences with little or no research basis and depending largely on the subjective judgment of practitioners. According to Page (2014, page 24), "Faigman has stated that these sciences contain a substantive degree of subjective judgment in their application, do not test their hypotheses in any serious manner, and only look for confirmation of their practice while rationalizing or ignoring contradictory evidence."

An ambitious research agenda could overcome the lingering debate about forensic science's scientific rigors as well as the long shadow of the law, concerns voiced by other commentators such as Simoncelli (2017), who asserts that many of the "systemic, pervasive problems" stem in part from "the forensic science community's thin ties to an academic research base." As Simoncelli (2017, page 130) adds, "Rather than emerging out of academic research science, a number of forensic techniques had emerged directly out of law enforcement practice. As a result, they emerged with limited foundational research establishing their basic validity and with little if any research dedicated to understanding the effects of cognitive bias on forensic procedures."

As Page (2014, page 26) observes, "Many of the traditional and formerly unquestioned areas of forensic science, such as fingerprints, have come under criticism for their lack of scientific underpinning. One of the main issues with these areas of forensic science is that their theories were developed by relying on inductive reasoning, rather than the now more favorable scientific epoch of deduction and the hypothetico-deductive model."

In inductive reasoning, according to Page (2014, page 27), thought processes move from specific observations to more general ones, applying the theories suggested by observation of specific circumstances to broader situations: "A key feature of induction is that generally it relies on accumulation of positive instances in order to verify a theory as correct. Deductive reasoning, in contrast to inductive reasoning, works the other way: by moving from more generalized observations to developing theories about very specific things. Consequently, deductive arguments tend to be much narrower in form, and are therefore more easily substantiated."

An ambitious research agenda could also address lingering questions pertaining to validity and reliability. As Page (2014, page 29) explains, "Science and scientific hypothesis testing is only meaningful if it is conducted in a valid and reliable way." The concept of reliability reached public consciousness when the Supreme Court used it in the 1993 *Daubert* decision to distinguish science based on supporting facts, data, and reasoning from junk science or pseudoscience. Page (2014) explains that scientific validity is further divided into internal and external realms; internal validity refers to how well experiments or theories are constructed and assesses whether they were subject to bias, whether the results were accurately measured, and whether other potentially confounding variables were taken into consideration. External validity focuses on how applicable the theory or experiment is to the real-world situation.

Page (2014, page 30) asserts further, "Despite the fact that the terms reliability and validity are technically distinct from one another, one must be mindful of that much of the critical literature in forensic science uses the term 'reliability' to simultaneously encompass the meaning of validity. Similarly, most interpretations of the term 'reliable' when used in legal discussions of forensic science testimony are including both concepts of reliability and validity … What the courts ultimately want is some form of evidence that the experts can do what they say they can do, but the forensic expert should be mindful that this concept consists of both validity and reliability, and that the two are distinct, non-substitutable terms when it comes to discussing the scientific underpinning of forensic techniques."

Getting back to the high bar that DNA has set, Page (2014, page 31) insists, "The problem with much of forensic science theory is that it is largely inductive, and has never been subject to rigorous tests that specifically attempt to falsify it. It has been said that forensic scientists in general have failed to consistently appreciate the implications of the scientific method. The progression through the stages of research, formulation of a hypothesis, testing, analyzing results, and then modifying the hypothesis where necessary has the advantages of built-in evaluators, such as the calculation of error rates, as part of the process, in addition to other benefits, including its impartiality. Indeed, the Daubert indicia, while not necessarily being representative of what reliability is to all things and all disciplines, arise as being the natural products of good research. Testing allows the generation of error rates and approximations, and good quality research is generally published, thereby being subject to peer review. Standardization of techniques and theories becomes necessary so as to ensure their validity and applicability in the hands of different researchers, scientists and practitioners. Eventually, when a theory gains overwhelming support, it may even enter the realm of 'general acceptance'; however, this by itself is no substitute for these first stages of scientific endeavor."

Page (2014, page 36) asserts that practitioners need to take responsibility to ensure that the scientific basis of their own disciplines can withstand criticism and that one of the key barriers to improving the scientific standing of much of forensic science is the lack of acknowledgement that any such improvement is necessary: "Reliance on a technique simply because it has been used for many years runs the dangerous risk that the underlying theories are not as robust as once thought; comparative bullet lead analysis is a perfect example of this." Page softens the criticism by acknowledging, "That is not to say that all, or even most, forensic science is 'junk science' and of no value to the criminal justice system. The problem is that many forensic science practices lack robust support for their theoretical and scientific underpinnings, which has led to various claims based on nothing more than collective opinion. These claims have been perpetuated over the years with little challenge, to the point where some claims now verge on the ridiculous, such as the ability to 'identify to the exclusion of all others,' or claim an error rate of 'zero.' Judges can attempt to limit or even exclude evidence in certain cases, but this has a very limited effect on the overall practice of the discipline due to the inherent case-, circumstance-, and jurisdiction-specific nature of judicial precedent. The only way to reign in these patently spurious claims is to actually ascertain the boundaries of what the forensic sciences can and cannot do. Fortunately, there is already a tried and tested framework available to forensic scientists on which to base this attempt: it's called science."

Legal scholars and practitioners alike have been quick to embrace the 2009 NAS report's call for increased scientific rigor and a creation of a "culture of science," even though many may be uncertain about what that entails. As Cole (2010) ruminates, "'Scientific culture' is a rather vague and contested term that is used to mean a variety of different things. If no one agrees upon what we mean by 'scientific culture,' then the NAS Report's call to adopt it becomes an empty rhetorical gesture, easily answered by any interest group that simply chooses its preferred definition of 'scientific culture' and declares that forensic science has or has not adopted it." Cole says the NAS report's characterization of scientific culture is "based on popular accounts of science and 'the scientific method.' I suggest that these accounts are incomplete, generally considered obsolete and not particularly helpful in pointing a way toward reform of forensic science."

Cole (2010) conceives of science as work rather than method and provides a framework for how forensic science might be understood as work by dividing forensic labor into a set of general tasks. Cole divides forensic science work into the five categories of basic research, evidence collection, technical management, analysis, and interpretation, and then specifies the qualifications for each category.

In formulating his schematic, Cole (2010, page 454) points out the many ways that the NAS committee "invoked obsolete models of science," and ponders whether the NAS report's model of science impedes the achievement of its purported goal: the "adoption," by forensic science, of a vaguely articulated "scientific culture." Cole adds, "The NAS Committee had a broad ambit, and it did a fantastic job with many important matters. As a sociologist of science myself, I do not believe that the Committee's limited time would have been well spent parsing the intricacies of the sociology of scientific and technical work. I do believe, however, that the NAS report's rather cursory engagement with the nature of forensic scientific work demands that others ... think more carefully about what 'adopting scientific culture' might mean, given the nature of forensic scientific work. I also believe that, if such careful thinking is not done, the NAS report's call to adopt scientific culture risks becoming an empty gesture."

Seeking to fill the void left by the NAS Committee by not defining a standard set of principles and methods for the tasks involved in scientific work, Cole outlined his take on his aforementioned five tasks. Regarding basic research, Cole (2010, page 457) notes that forensic basic researchers should "innovate and subject their innovations to rigorous scrutiny. We want the individuals who do this work to be trained scientists, much as they are in other areas of science. We want a culture that is as much like a university—or at least like an industrial research laboratory—as possible." For evidence collection, Cole (2010, page 457) eschews "a culture centered around hypothesis testing, falsificationism or organized skepticism" and instead embraces "care, accountability, meticulous documentation and ethics," adding, "By far the greatest concern expressed in the forensic literature about evidence collection concerns the potential for contaminating the crime scene. It seems that the main concern is that we want people who are careful, meticulous, and honest. They need not know philosophy of science or be competent to practice science. Primarily, they need to be aware of the current capabilities and limitations of forensic science, so as to know what to collect and what not to collect, and what sorts of actions might lead to contamination." Regarding technical management, Cole (2010, page 457) expects individuals to "think scientifically about a case as a whole" as part of "rigorous open-mindedness and critical thinking with an emphasis on avoiding traps in reasoning, such as circularity and the transposed conditional." For analysis, Cole (2010, page 458) notes, "We do not want, or need, these analysts to think about the validity of the assays they perform. What we want is for analysts to do well at performing assays that someone else has validated. We want them to be careful, meticulous and honest in their application of these assays. We want them to document their work, and to adhere to protocols." And finally, for interpretation, Cole (2010, page 458) says "logical reasoning of the highest order" is needed, noting, "The primary values might be a determination to report the evidence as accurately and precisely as possible, as well as a sense of self-restraint that would allow the Interpreter to resist the temptation to make more inferences than are warranted by the analytic results."

Cole (2010, page 470) is cognizant of the process he calls the "de-skilling" of forensic science: "We are proposing to break the task of the forensic scientist, as classically understood, into segments that would be assigned to different individuals with different skill sets, educational backgrounds, expectations and roles. We are proposing that some of the individuals, particularly the technicians, simply will not need to know, or even think much about certain things, and this may be construed as countenancing ignorance."

This runs counter to what Cole (2010, page 470) identifies as the model of elevating the profession, as proposed by Inman, Rudin, and DeForest, and to some extent, the late Paul Kirk—a view that Cole dubs the "California School," which argues that instead of de-skilling and segmenting the profession, we should be uplifting it: "While they might agree that it was a mistake to expect technicians without significant scientific training to defend, or even talk or think coherently about the validation of techniques like latent print or firearms and toolmark identification, they might argue that the answer is not to keep those non-scientifically trained individuals in the technician role. Rather, they might argue that the goal should be to turn all persons occupying the role of 'forensic scientist' into true scientists with a scientific approach to empirical questions—in short, a 'scientific culture.' ... I think that having every individual working in forensic science trained to the level of Inman, Rudin, and DeForest would, by itself, solve most of the 'the problems that plague the forensic science community. I think that, to pose a historical counterfactual, had the profession developed so that everyone in it had the scientific training of Inman, Rudin, and DeForest, no one would ever have claimed that the error rate of latent print identification was 'zero,' and we would not have an NAS report today" (NAS, 2009, page 470).

The debate over scientific rigor and the training of forensic scientists is triggered by the interpretation of evidence and the admission of forensic science evidence in litigation. Giannelli (2011, page 58) says the advent of DNA profiling in the late 1980s, followed by the U.S. Supreme Court's decision in *Daubert v. Merrell Dow Pharmaceuticals, Inc.* in 1993, drastically altered the legal landscape for scientific evidence, a "paradigm shift" first noted by Saks and Koehler (2005). As Giannelli (2011, page 58) explains, "DNA evidence became the 'gold standard' in forensic science, and Daubert revolutionized how courts scrutinized expert testimony."

Giannelli (2011) points to work by Saks and Koehler (1991, page 59) stating that "forensic scientists, like scientists in all other fields, should subject their claims to methodologically rigorous empirical tests. The results of these tests should be published and debated. Until such steps are taken, the strong claims of forensic scientists must be regarded with far more caution than they traditionally have been."

Giannelli (2011, page 60) points to two consequences of DNA evidence in addition to establishing the gold standard—it focused attention on the lack of regulation of crime laboratories, and the use of DNA profiling to exonerate innocent convicts led to a reexamination of the types of evidence admitted to secure their convictions. "The impact of DNA profiling was reinforced by the *Daubert* decision, which enunciated a new reliability test for expert testimony. *Daubert* listed several factors that trial judges should consider in assessing reliability. The first and foremost *Daubert* factor is testability. Citing scientific authorities, the Supreme Court noted that a hallmark of science is empirical testing. The other factors listed by the Court are generally supplementary. For example, the second factor, peer review and publication, is a means to verify the results of the testing mentioned in the first factor, and in turn, verification can lead to general acceptance of the technique within the scientific community. Similarly, another factor, an error rate, is derived from testing."

As we have seen, almost 25 years ago, the U.S. Supreme Court forever changed the legal landscape when it issued a landmark ruling on scientific and expert evidence that eradicated the 70-year-old Frye test and created a new framework. Gabel (2010, page 19) explains that the decision in *Daubert v. Merrill Dow Pharm., Inc.* established "an intricate, non-exhaustive criteria aimed at assessing the validity, reliability and relevance of scientific evidence" and rejected Frye's focus on whether the expert's methodology was generally accepted in the relevant scientific community. Gabel (2010, page 20) adds that Daubert can be "as ambiguous and generous as Frye" and that "the notable difference between the two was not the elaborate inquiry established by Daubert, but rather Daubert's crowning of the trial judge as the 'gatekeeper' of scientific evidence."

Essentially, the Supreme Court ruled that, under Rule 702 of the *Federal Rules of Evidence*, a "trial judge must ensure that any and all scientific testimony or evidence admitted is not only relevant, but reliable." The court indicated that the subject of an expert's testimony should be scientific knowledge, so that "evidentiary reliability will be based upon scientific validity." The court also emphasized that, in considering the admissibility of evidence, a trial judge should focus "solely" on the expert's "principles and methodology," and "not on the conclusions that they generate."

Daubert's requirement that an expert's testimony pertain to *scientific knowledge* established a standard of *evidentiary reliability*. In explaining this evidentiary standard, the *Daubert* court pointed to several factors that might be considered by a trial judge: whether a theory or technique can be (and has been) tested; whether the theory or technique has been subjected to peer review and publication; the known or potential rate of error of a particular scientific technique; the existence and maintenance of standards controlling the technique's operation; and a scientific technique's degree of acceptance within a relevant scientific community. The court emphasized that the inquiry under Rule 702 is "a flexible one," and it expressed confidence in the adversarial system, noting that "vigorous cross-examination, presentation of contrary evidence, and careful instruction on the burden of proof are the traditional and appropriate means of attacking shaky but admissible evidence."

As the 2009 NAS report notes, "The law's greatest dilemma in its heavy reliance on forensic evidence, however, concerns the question of whether—and to what extent—there is science in any given forensic science discipline. Two very important questions should underlie the law's admission of and reliance upon forensic evidence in criminal trials: The extent to which a particular forensic discipline is founded on a reliable scientific methodology that gives it the capacity to accurately analyze evidence and report findings, and the extent to which practitioners in a particular forensic discipline rely on human interpretation that could be tainted by error, the threat of bias, or the absence of sound operational procedures and robust performance standards. These questions are significant" (NAS, 2009, page 9).

The 2009 NAS report expressed that it "matters a great deal whether an expert is qualified to testify about forensic evidence and whether the evidence is sufficiently reliable to merit a fact finder's reliance on the truth that it purports to support" (NAS, 2009, page 9). Unfortunately, these important questions do not always produce satisfactory answers in judicial decisions pertaining to the admissibility of forensic science evidence proffered in criminal trials.

As the 2009 NAS report notes, "*Daubert* and its progeny have engendered confusion and controversy. In particular, judicial dispositions of *Daubert*-type questions in criminal cases have been criticized by some lawyers and scholars who thought that the Supreme Court's decision would be applied more rigorously. If one focuses solely on reported federal appellate decisions, the picture is not appealing to those who have preferred a more rigorous application of *Daubert*. Federal appellate courts have not with any consistency or clarity imposed standards ensuring the application of scientifically valid reasoning and reliable methodology in criminal cases involving *Daubert* questions. This is not really surprising, however. The Supreme Court itself described the *Daubert* standard as 'flexible.'

This means that, beyond questions of relevance, *Daubert* offers appellate courts no clear substantive standard by which to review decisions by trial courts. As a result, trial judges exercise great discretion in deciding whether to admit or exclude expert testimony, and their judgments are subject only to a highly deferential 'abuse of discretion' standard of review. Although it is difficult to get a clear picture of how trial courts handle *Daubert* challenges, because many evidentiary rulings are issued without a published opinion and without an appeal, the vast majority of the reported opinions in criminal cases indicate that trial judges rarely exclude or restrict expert testimony offered by prosecutors; most reported opinions also indicate that appellate courts routinely deny appeals contesting trial court decisions admitting forensic evidence against criminal defendants. But the reported opinions do not offer in any way a complete sample of federal trial court dispositions of *Daubert*-type questions in criminal cases. The situation appears to be very different in civil cases. Plaintiffs and defendants, equally, are more likely to have access to expert witnesses in civil cases, while prosecutors usually have an advantage over most defendants in offering expert testimony in criminal cases. And, ironically, the appellate courts appear to be more willing to second-guess trial court judgments on the admissibility of purported scientific evidence in civil cases than in criminal cases" (NAS, 2009, page 11).

The 2009 NAS report adds, "Prophetically, the *Daubert* decision observed that 'there are important differences between the quest for truth in the courtroom and the quest for truth in the laboratory. Scientific conclusions are subject to perpetual revision. Law, on the other hand, must resolve disputes finally and quickly.' But because accused parties in criminal cases are convicted on the basis of testimony from forensic science experts, much depends upon whether the evidence offered is reliable. Furthermore, in addition to protecting innocent persons from being convicted of crimes that they did not commit, we are also seeking to protect society from persons who have committed criminal acts. Law enforcement officials and the members of society they serve need to be assured that forensic techniques are reliable. Therefore, we must limit the risk of having the reliability of certain forensic science methodologies judicially certified before the techniques have been properly studied and their accuracy verified by the forensic science community. 'There is no evident reason why ['rigorous, systematic'] research would be infeasible.' However, some courts appear to be loath to insist on such research as a condition of admitting forensic science evidence in criminal cases, perhaps because to do so would likely 'demand more by way of validation than the disciplines can presently offer.' The adversarial process relating to the admission and exclusion of scientific evidence is not suited to the task of finding 'scientific truth.' The judicial system is encumbered by, among other things, judges and lawyers who generally lack the scientific expertise necessary to comprehend and evaluate forensic evidence in an informed manner, trial judges (sitting alone) who must decide evidentiary issues without the benefit of judicial colleagues and often with little time for extensive research and reflection, and the highly deferential nature of the appellate review afforded trial courts' *Daubert* rulings. Given these realities, there is a tremendous need for the forensic science community to improve. Judicial review, by itself, will not cure the infirmities of the forensic science community. The development of scientific research, training, technology, and databases associated with DNA analysis have resulted from substantial and steady federal support for both academic research and programs employing techniques for DNA analysis. Similar support must be given to all credible forensic science disciplines if they are to achieve the degrees of reliability needed to serve the goals of justice. With more and better educational programs, accredited laboratories, certified forensic practitioners, sound operational principles and procedures, and serious research to establish the limits and measures of performance in each discipline, forensic science experts will be better able to analyze evidence and coherently report their findings in the courts. The current situation, however, is seriously wanting, both because of the limitations of the judicial system and because of the many problems faced by the forensic science community" (NAS, 2009, page 12).

DNA may not have been criticized by the 2009 NAS report the way the pattern evidence disciplines were, but newer technology is a reminder that admissibility-related issues will continue long after *Daubert*. As Gabel (2010, page 21) observes, "The sheer availability of scientific evidence in cases is indisputable. New technologies and advancements in older ones are indicators of the sharp rise. Nonetheless, availability should not necessarily correlate to admissibility. It is hotly debated whether *Daubert* has opened or closed doors to scientific evidence. I submit that *Daubert* has created significant hurdles for plaintiffs in civil cases trying to demonstrate causation through the use of expert testimony. In contrast, I am of the view that *Daubert* and its statutory contemporaries have opened the door and offered coffee and biscotti to similar evidence in criminal cases."

Gabel (2010, page 53) summarizes DNA's ironclad reputation in the courts by observing, "... the NAS report held forensic DNA testing in high regard as the standard-bearer of what forensic science should be. DNA evidence has long been held out as 'the gold standard' of forensic science. There is the belief that DNA is an absolute and infallible proof of identify. In other words, DNA means 'Do Not Acquit.'" Thus, Gabel (2010) challenges the legal and scientific communities to examine the statistics surrounding DNA, even if it is the forensic discipline with the strongest scientific grounding: "The statistics routinely deployed as evidence of the discriminating power of DNA may not be as credible as they are held out to be. Simply put, DNA does not deserve a 'free pass' on the question of admissibility." Gabel (2010) emphasizes that DNA has played a significant role in exonerations, but it is not absolute.

Legal scholars point to dangers in assuming that the examination of 13 loci on different chromosomes that comprises DNA profiling and analysis is discriminating enough to suggest a perfect match between two individuals, with the exception of identical twins. As Gabel (2010, page 53) points out, "Different people's forensic profiles may be similar to those of other individuals, especially siblings. Even unrelated persons can share similarities between their profiles." Gabel (2010) says that the population statistics associated with DNA "have been taken at face value" and that "without access to additional data these statistics are difficult, if not impossible, to challenge, and lawyers are certainly reluctant to do so. Whether DNA evidence is trustworthy is a question that must be examined carefully in each case. And that challenging task falls ultimately on the shoulders of lawyers who represent clients incriminated by DNA tests."

Even if the population statistics were infallible, critics say that human error by the analyst can erode DNA's reliability. Podlas (2006, page 124) reminds us, "Typically, testing is not in a research lab at a major institution resembling the pristine set of *CSI*. Poor testing conditions reduce the reliability of results. Unbeknownst to the average citizen, different technicians often have varying interpretations of DNA. Sometimes, forensic technicians are sloppy, use unproven methods, manufacture data points, or ignore inconsistent results. For example, experts from one well-known laboratory, Lifecodes, confessed that when faced with DNA bandshifts that did not quite match, they used a previously not-yet-validated methodology to reconcile the difference and declare a match. There is also a surprising amount of cross-contamination, mislabeling and mixing-up of DNA samples, switching the DNA amongst cases. One lab matched a slug with the wrong test gun, and another confused the DNA reference sample of a rape victim with that of the accused. In a particularly shocking known instance, the prosecution's forensic evidence 'proved' that the probability of a coincidental match was 1 in 694,000 African-American males. In fact, subsequent testing by an independent private laboratory showed that the probability of a match exceeded 1 in 8. Even further, the crime Lab failed to present DNA evidence which should have excluded [the defendant] as one of the rapists. Yet, DNA's cloak of science can mislead jurors into either ignoring contradictory evidence or foreclosing consideration of corroborating evidence. Once the laboratory inputs a conclusion into the criminal justice system, it has effectively terminated whatever processes it has in place to detect errors. Accordingly, notwithstanding reasonable doubt, a jury may be more inclined to convict."

Poor-quality evidence can be problematic. As the 2009 NAS report observes, "In order for qualified forensic science experts to testify competently about forensic evidence, they must first find the evidence in a usable state and properly preserve it. A latent fingerprint that is badly smudged when found cannot be usefully saved, analyzed, or explained. An inadequate drug sample may be insufficient to allow for proper analysis. And, DNA tests performed on a contaminated or otherwise compromised sample cannot be used reliably to identify or eliminate an individual as the perpetrator of a crime. These are important matters involving the proper processing of forensic evidence" (NAS, 2009, page 86).

Individualization used to support prosecutors' conclusions in court continues to be a significant issue cited by the 2009 NAS report. Critics charge that individualization, which is sometimes referred to as "matching" a specimen to a particular individual or other source, is problematic and must be addressed in order to staunch the flow of wrongful convictions. As the NAS report states, "With the exception of nuclear DNA analysis, no forensic method has been rigorously shown to have the capacity to consistently, and with a high degree of certainty, demonstrate a connection between evidence and a specific individual or source. In terms of scientific basis, the analytically based disciplines generally hold a notable edge over disciplines based on expert interpretation" (NAS, 2009, page 87).

On the topic of individualization, the 2009 NAS report states, "Some forensic science methods have as their goal the 'individualization' of specific types of evidence (typically shoe and tire impressions, dermal ridge prints, toolmarks and firearms, and handwriting). Analysts using such methods believe that unique markings are acquired by a source item in random fashion and that such uniqueness is faithfully transmitted from the source item to the evidence item being examined (or in the case of handwriting, that individuals acquire habits that result in unique handwriting). When the evidence and putative source items are compared, a conclusion of individualization implies that the evidence originated from that source, to the exclusion of all other possible sources. The determination of uniqueness requires measurements of object attributes, data collected on the population frequency of variation in these attributes, testing of attribute independence, and calculations of the probability that different objects share a common set of observable attributes" (NAS, 2009, page 43).

The report did recognize a hierarchy of sorts among the pattern evidence disciplines, noting, "There are more established protocols and available research for fingerprint analysis than for the analysis of bite marks. There also are significant variations within each discipline. For example, not all fingerprint evidence is equally good, because the true value of the evidence is determined by the quality of the latent fingerprint image. These disparities between and within the forensic science disciplines highlight a major problem in the forensic science community: The simple reality is that the interpretation of forensic evidence is not always based on scientific studies to determine its validity. This is a serious problem. Although research has been done in some disciplines, there is a notable dearth of peer-reviewed, published studies establishing the scientific bases and validity of many forensic methods" (NAS, 2009, page 87).

THE DNA STANDARD

The faith placed in DNA persists, but it has become more qualified over time, as Gabel (2014, page 287) states, "With the exception of DNA, no single forensic technique yet has the ability to definitively link an evidence sample to its source. Ability is very different from invariable actuality, however; even DNA evidence has its limitations and stress points. Deficiencies in forensic science have harrowing implications, and the number of exonerations in recent years has underscored the very real threat that innocent people can be convicted. The reality of wrongful convictions has risen to the forefront of public awareness through the work of the Innocence Project and other organizations. Of course, there are numerous factors that relate to wrongful convictions outside of faulty forensic evidence—witness misidentification, false confessions, jailhouse snitches—but in some ways, the public conception of erroneous convictions, and that DNA will cure them all, represents a somewhat myopic view."

Gabel (2014, page 291) adds, "DNA results culminate in the all-important statistical representation of the likelihood of a random match based on population genetics, i.e., the pervasive '1 in n billion' number. The lab-based forensic disciplines are deemed to be more analytical and thus more reliable than the more subjective 'pattern identification' disciplines, which produce qualitative results ... DNA analysis is subject to human error based on the interpretation (read: subjective analysis) of results that include, among other things, mixture samples, Low Copy Number DNA, and degraded evidence."

Lynch (2013, page 60) acknowledges, "Strong justifications currently are given for the overriding weight assigned to DNA evidence: many of the constituent techniques derive from molecular biology and are widely established in numerous fields of research and diagnostic practice; early problems with forensic uses of the techniques were aired in admissibility hearings, debated in the scientific literature, and subjected to numerous inquiries and audits; and refinements in technique and improvements in methods of probabilistic estimation have remedied the early problems. It is often said that DNA profiling has 'passed the test' both in science and in law, unlike many other forms of ordinary and technical evidence. It is now common to ... treat DNA as both the source and object of an extraordinary, and even absolute, degree of certainty in criminal law."

Lynch (2013, page 60) suggests that DNA evidence remains bound within the context of ordinary organizational and practical routines, and is not a transcendent source of "truth" in the criminal justice system: "DNA profiling is the ascendant 'gold standard' in criminal forensics, though not very long ago fingerprint identification held the title. The convictions (in both the epistemological and legal senses of the word) associated with confessions, eyewitness testimony, and many other forms of evidence are now held to be fallible and 'subjective' in comparison with DNA evidence. When compared with what Simon Cole in his article in this special section calls 'research science', forensic science is often granted separate and unequal status as a knowledge-producing culture. However, DNA profiling is often treated as an exceptional technique that has navigated the imaginary gulf between forensic and scientific culture, and has become so reliable that it can be used as a benchmark for evaluating all other forensic technologies. Like Paul Roberts in his contribution to this section, I argue that such comparisons misleadingly associate 'science' with certainty and 'forensics' with practical contingency. DNA profiling remains an integral part of criminal investigations, and whether or not one is inclined to accredit it with 'scientific' status, the evidence adduced through the practice is no less bound up in forensic culture than any other form of criminal evidence."

Lynch (2013, page 63) refers to the undeniable lure of "DNA exceptionalism" and notes, "Courts in the U.S. have placed DNA in an exceptional epistemic space, if one is to believe the chorus of testimonials in recent years voiced by prosecutors, defense attorneys, judges, legal scholars and persons who have been exonerated with DNA evidence." The extensive debates in admissibility hearings and appeal cases about practical, analytical, and interpretative procedures with DNA evidence now were viewed as evidence that DNA could now be held reliable in terms of the new standards for the admissibility of expert scientific evidence articulated by the U.S. Supreme Court in its 1993 ruling in *Daubert v. Merrell Dow Pharmaceuticals, Inc.* As Lynch (2013, page 63) explains, "The statistical procedures and correction factors, which had seemed so obscure when compared with the tidy declarations of fingerprint examiners, now stood as emblems of transparency, only now transparency did not mean intuitively apparent; instead, it referred to calculations of probative value that were logically traceable through formulae accepted by experts. By comparison, the fingerprint examiner began to be stereotyped as a quaint figure: a 'distinguished, greying individual on the stand saying, 'my opinion is based on my many years of experience in this field.' So, what accounts for this reversal of forensic fortune, or, as we have elsewhere called it, this 'inversion of credibility'?"

Lynch (2013, page 63) adds, "Criticisms of DNA profiling results were largely confined to charges of incompetence or bias levelled at particular police forces or forensic laboratories. The techniques themselves had become relatively immune to criticism. No single technical solution, legal decision, or other event was responsible for ending controversy in the courts and science press about forensic DNA profiling. Instead, a confluence of technical, legal and administrative 'fixes' worked to close debate about the reliability of the technique."

These "fixes" included the introduction of the short tandem repeat (STR) system and automated scanning of samples that replaced visual examination of profile results. The STR system enabled analysts to develop precise profile results from miniscule amounts of bodily material, and the number of DNA loci that were included in a given profile increased from four to six, and then to eight and more. As Lynch (2013, page 65) explains, "With each increase in the number of loci, the estimated probability of coincidence matches decreased accordingly, to the point that some forensic analysts argued that they should be permitted in most cases to declare that the chance of a coincidence match (for example, a match between a profile developed from a crime scene, and a DNA profile developed from a sample taken from a person unrelated to the 'donor' of the crime scene evidence) was, effectively, zero."

Lynch (2013, page 67) claims that the exceptional status granted to DNA evidence implicated other forms of evidence: "Analysts of forensic science who had once been critical of DNA profiling, began to use DNA as a baseline measure of the fallibility of other forms of evidence." He adds, "The promotion of DNA evidence as 'a scientific arbiter of truth' that exposes the fallibility of all other forms of criminal evidence suggests an epistemic status that is an exception to the 'human fallibility' that justifies administrative closure and moral certainty ... Currently, DNA evidence is treated as exceptional, but it also is upheld as a model for other forms of forensic evidence to emulate. Given the current state of forensic science, there is reason to welcome an expansion of precision estimation (expressed through probability figures), upgraded procedural standards and practitioner credentials, and protections against error. However, there also is a reason to be concerned about the possible institutionalization of a threshold of certainty ascribed to those technologies that pass the test ... [DNA's] probative value as testimony is bound up in competing and all-too-human narratives: stories about how DNA and other forms of evidence implicate 'what happened' at the scene of an alleged crime. As such, it should not be exempt from moral certainty 'within the limits of human fallibility.'"

REACTION TO THE 2009 NAS REPORT

The 2009 NAS report blamed forensic practitioners for insisting that their disciplines employed methodologies that have perfect accuracy and produce no errors and added that this has impeded efforts to evaluate the usefulness of the forensic science disciplines. No one was safe from the criticism, and as a passage in the NAS report reads, "The bottom line is simple: In a number of forensic science disciplines, forensic science professionals have yet to establish either the validity of their approach or the accuracy of their conclusions, and the courts have been utterly ineffective in addressing this problem" (NAS, 2009, page 53).

Some practitioners fired back, first admitting, "...the report did indeed examine issues in the profession and asked uncomfortable questions that needed to be addressed" (Miranda, 2015, page 147). But at the same time, this commentator noted, "I also join with many in our profession in not considering the report as the last word or authority on the matter, although it has been made so from an administrative perspective" (Miranda, 2015, page 147).

At a Senate hearing on September 9, 2009, Barry D. Matson, deputy director of the Alabama District Attorneys Association, rebuked the NAS for an "agenda-driven attack upon well-founded investigative techniques." As Giannelli (2012, page 381) confirms, "Questions were raised about the thoroughness of the Committee's research, the practicality of its recommendations, and its failure to accomplish parts of what Congress chartered the NAS to do." Giannelli (2012, page 384) adds, "While parts of the forensic science community embraced the NAS report, others dissented. Indeed, the NAS Committee proposed a new agency, NIFS, precisely because of the expected opposition to change. The report found that some federal entities were 'too wedded' to the status quo and 'have failed to pursue a rigorous research agenda to confirm the evidentiary reliability of methodologies used in a number of forensic science disciplines.'" As a result, these "agencies are not good candidates to oversee the overhaul of the forensic science community."

While some insiders found nothing new in the NAS report, those outside the forensic science community said the report triggered an epiphany. Some supporters of forensic science took umbrage; as Giannelli (2012, page 384) notes, "Sen. Jeff Sessions, a former prosecutor, remarked at a congressional hearing, 'I don't accept the idea that they seem to suggest that fingerprints are not proven technology,' and added, 'I don't think we should suggest that those proven scientific principles that we've been using for decades are somehow uncertain.'"

Pyrek (2007) documented forensic practitioners' thoughts on criticisms of their profession, quoting Henry Lee, PhD, as saying in a 2006 interview, "I have been in the field almost 40-some years now and forensic scientists are under the most pressure I have ever seen. ... Just like in any other field, we may have a few bad apples who are not genuine, and who provide interpretations beyond scientific principles. They are not forensic scientists, but they claim they are, and the public doesn't know the difference." Lee said he is bothered by critics who assert that forensic science is broken because it is not akin to the sterile confines of a clinical laboratory and thus is somehow less rigorous.

"Forensic science is not a pure or pristine scientific discipline," Lee said. "We have no control over the samples that come into the forensic laboratory. It's a different ball game than clinical laboratories where you can go to the stockroom and get a fresh, clean sample of unlimited quantity, to test or analyze. When we go to a crime scene, we find the victim lying in questionable surroundings, the body decomposing. There is no such thing as a clean sample at a crime scene. For example, you have the dirty, blood-stained clothes of a suspect retrieved from a garbage dump. That's all you have to work with, so it's unfair of anyone to say you did not meet scientific principles because this sample tested is contaminated; of course it is contaminated. But what can the forensic scientist do about it? Nothing. Some scientists don't understand that; they say every experiment demands controls. ... There is no way to replicate a sample. Critics they say we lack scientific principles and controls, but they don't understand the nature of forensic science. The beauty of forensic science is that it uses scientific principles as well as things like logic, intuition, and the ability to put the pieces of the puzzle together to solve the case. I have been involved in six or seven thousand major cases, and no two cases are alike. That's why when forensic science is criticized, it is by the people who really don't understand it. They think everything should be black and white, but unfortunately, in our profession, many times it is gray" (Pyrek, 2007).

Speaking in an interview in 2016, Lee said the 2009 NAS report sparked "a lot of controversy" and that he agreed with "about 80 percent" of the report's findings. "This report was produced by the third committee; I was on the first committee, when DNA was just introduced," Lee said. "The National Science Foundation set up the first committee and over the years we have been arguing about the same things. So, to us, that report is nothing new. A long time ago we said we should standardize our procedures. One day I was cleaning up my office and I found the first lab manual from 1976; in that document we had already started to standardize various procedures. I still remember that time when we wanted to write a standardized laboratory manual; some colleagues even ganged up against me, wanting to know why I wanted to put things to paper because now the defense attorneys can discover our secrets. I said, 'What secrets?' Whatever procedures we use, they should be guided by standard procedures and a manual. Since then we have realized the importance of education and standardization. You can't just set a standard, you have to have the education and training to along with it for guidance; otherwise it's just a standard on paper, not reality."

Lee continued, "The [2009 NAS] report is excellent, because it reminds us that we must be totally objective, and I agree wholeheartedly. But the training as well as the ethics, are up to the individual. You can't just say we'll have a standard and expect everyone to follow it without repercussions if they don't. There must be consequences for those who violate the ethics. In the early days, I was among the first group of ASCLD inspectors who were examining the crime laboratories, and we found individuals not in compliance. The lab director's responsibility is to monitor those individuals, as history has taught us that if those people violate this trust in forensic science, we all lose. There are always a few bad apples in every barrel, unfortunately. I still remember a case in North Carolina in which I was the defense expert; I said the lab analyst's interpretation of the evidence was wrong. The prosecutor said I was wrong, but several years later the analyst's misinterpretations were finally revealed. It is difficult to tell someone that they are wrong, but we must be honest with ourselves when we detect errors. So in that aspect, the NAS made excellent recommendations to help improve forensic science."

Retired forensic pathologist Marcella F. Fierro, MD, who served on the panel, says the report simply "identified areas that needed more basic research," and adds, "Funding for forensic pathology research and most of the others was essentially non-existent. Federal programs funded service i.e., more police on the beat, staff to perform backlogs of DNA tests, etc. People providing public service rarely have time or funding for the fundamental research that underpins forensic sciences—The forensic sciences grew out of need rather than scientific curiosity. Many do not lend themselves to the statistical accuracy of DNA (1 in 7 billion statistically) or toxicology (basically chemistry and measurement). Some require judgement and experience as well as science. Many of the questions, now, I think will be answered by basic research and the more experiential sciences will be validated. The social sciences often defy certainty but theories can be validated if data bases are large enough. Medicine, as another example, is an art and a science—the former based on continuing education and experience and the latter by research. I am optimistic. The 2009 NAS committee report was not as negative as it has been reported. Let's see if the recommendations for staff, research and funding are fulfilled."

Fierro says she thinks not enough attention was paid to medicolegal death investigation, especially "not when many states still have small city and county systems where elected officials whose qualifications may consist of being 21 and free of a felony are certifying a legal document stating the disease or injury someone died of and whether that death was natural, accidental or suicidal," she says. "If someone is dead it must be a pretty serious disease or injury that killed them and permitting someone who has no significant training in medicine making diagnoses just doesn't make any sense. Signing out people over 50 as dying from heart disease when death is unwitnessed or unattended is the setting for error. To make it worse, mistakes in diagnosis, or failure to recognize subtle signs of unnatural death, are then cremated or buried. The cost for a competent death investigation system is too much for some small counties and cities. They need to combine their resources and regionalize services and share the cost. There are several statewide models that accomplish death investigation in such a way that the smallest villages and towns and big cities receive the same excellence in death investigation."

Forensic pathologist Michael Baden, MD, says he read the 2009 NAS report and thinks the committee had "a legitimate concern." Baden says, "What I see is the bias of forensic science toward the prosecution. I remember going through that in my own career when Dr. Milton Helpern was chief ME and Frank Hogan was the chief DA. I was just starting out, the first day on the job when Jim Luke, who was later the ME in Washington, D.C., started with me and we were brought into Helpern's office to meet with Hogan's people to tell us, from Hogan's point of view, that justice is like a three-legged stool which requires the police, the DA and the ME to work together as a team. We thought, wow, we are just starting out and we're nobodies and yet we are already part of a team—Halpern, Hogan and police commissioner Kennedy. It made me feel very good at the time but it took me a while to realize that as MEs, we are not part of the team, we are separate. I think the NAS report touched on that concept of believing that MEs and law enforcement and prosecutors are team members; it sounds great—we are a team for the good guys—but sometimes the good guys make mistakes. That's a danger and one of the hardest things for us as medical examiners to do is be independent and not to bend science one way or the other but just to say, here are the autopsy findings and we can't be concerned about whom it helps and whom it hurts."

"After the 2009 NAS report came out I figured things would start popping," says retired crime lab director Barry A. J. Fisher. "Things would happen and for quite some time nothing happened, it was like a non-event. It only started to become something of importance when the lawyers, the defense bar and law school professors began to look at it and scratch their heads about what was happening in forensic science. If you look back at the O.J. Simpson case, DNA really was the star of that case. It had been in use but up until that time there was no real public fascination. Between the Simpson case, the *CSI* series and the *Forensic Files* show, people were becoming fascinated and fell in love with forensic science. But high-profile DNA analysis brought up the use of statistics. The community had done work in developing statistics, but you come up with these exquisitely small numbers that are questioned. The lawyers started to think about types of evidence other than DNA and tried to come up with a way of addressing the deficiencies they perceived. So the NAS report called out these various pattern evidence disciplines that didn't have the types of stats that DNA had. Analysts were relying on their academic training and experience, but there were no readily available statistics on fingerprints, shoe prints, tire impressions, firearms, toolmarks and hair examination. These are real problems and so now you have a situation where it has blossomed and people asking about these things, and the NAS study said the whole thing is just off. They based their opinions in part on some research by Max Houck showing a 20 percent error rate where people looking at hair without DNA had the wrong results. With that mindset, it became a witch hunt."

Fisher says the report took aim at analysts testifying to a scientific certainty. "Medical doctors have been doing it for years, but the terminology is usually used in a civil case where the burden of preponderance of the evidence, not to certainty beyond reasonable doubt," Fisher says. "Analysts are faced with trying to explain certainty to a layman in court, and so they think to themselves, 'How do I convey this opinion, this certainty I have, in a different way. Can I say it's my opinion? That sounds flippant.' You must have a way of conveying the level of certainty on evidence analysis. Go back to the 50s when Paul Kirk, the American father of criminalistics, came up with notion that some types of evidence could be individualized and other types identified. Picture this—your car is sideswiped and there is paint transfer; the cops remove it and send to the lab and perhaps find a car with the damage in the right area and want to compare paints. Analysts look at the two paints and conduct chemical tests using the same chemistry for both and what can they say? They can't say it came from this one particular vehicle because car makers paint their cars with same formulation within a model. But you can say it came from this car or a similarly manufactured car. You can show that the paint is the same but you can't get to the point where you can say it's unique to this sample."

Fisher continues, "Now other types of evidence are coming under scrutiny. Examiners have been looking at bullets and shell casings for years and they have conducted studies. If you go to a weapons manufacturer and watch the barrel being manufactured, it's a solid steel bar with a drilled-out center. Firearms examiners will cut through a sample piece to examine the individual barrel and the twisting marks made when the bullet is fired. Examiners also test-fire each gun, collect the bullets and examine them under a microscope. They can tell which gun the bullets are fired from due to the slight imperfections, the striations, made on the bullet casings. They are convinced this identification is unique. They didn't use stats to prove this, they just did the analysis based on their experience examining a large number of guns and casings and bullets."

Fisher adds, "Many of the things we do in crime labs that don't have an academic underpinning is kind of like that. If you are looking at tires or footwear, you are looking at imperfections in the prints left at the scene and determining what are the odds of all these nicks and cuts being in the same places, and what is not showing up in the shoe and what was left behind. So, you form the opinion that the likelihood is really small, and for all intents and purposes, it could be impossible. You go to court and testify to a scientific certainty this shoe left this mark, or this gun fired this bullet. The defense asks, 'How sure are you? What are the test results and studies you can provide to demonstrate this opinion you are providing to the jury?' They don't exist, in many cases. The NIJ is funding research in this area, but it's still not to the level it needs to be. The problem here is no one recognizes that this is the way it works, that we don't have the research that we need. This level of research would make everyone's life a lot easier, but the money to do the research is not there; the federal funding lobby has not been investing research dollars in the area like they need to be. In the interim, we have to find a way to express to a judge and jury what our conclusions actually mean and that's where we are right now. NIST and the National Forensic Science Commission are starting to look at these issues and are coming to grips with the challenges. We have no standard procedures for a forensic practitioner to be able to express certainty, and until you get some court cases that tell practitioners how to testify, it's going to be a chronic problem."

An expert who served on the committee producing that 2009 NAS report recalls the journey. "We had no idea when we started that report process that it would have the kind of impact it had and continues to have on FS," says retired forensic science educator Jay Siegel, PhD. "Over the years there have been a number of committees and commissions that have looked at forensic science and have discussed the problems, but this was the first time that the National Academy looked at forensic science as a whole so I was quite excited to get involved. I had never been on a National Academy committee before. It was an interesting experience because there wasn't that much forensic science experience in the room; there were three or four of us who could be called forensic scientists out of the 17 participants. The rest were in criminal justice or law enforcement, but we also had a chemistry professor, an engineering dean, a statistician, a government person—so there was a lot of education that needed to be done during the deliberations of the meetings. The people who were not forensic scientists were quite surprised by all of the issues that forensic scientists must confront, whereas those of us who were forensic scientists have heard all of this before. So there was a significant knowledge gap we had to overcome, and it was quite a hurdle to get everyone interested and involved at the same level so we could make intelligent decisions."

Siegel continues, "The other interesting thing was how our sessions operated; our meetings were quarterly and we spent half the time in open session getting testimony from people who were called to talk to us about the various problems and the other half in executive session hashing all of this out and working on the report. We had a tremendous amount of help from the National Academy staff—there was no way we could have pulled this off without AnnMarie Mazza and her staff and a professional writer to write the report. Once it came out we had no idea it was going to have the impact that it had. That was very gratifying and of course it spawned a lot of discussion and activity and led to the creation of the National Commission on Forensic Science which is now meeting. The commission is a creation of the Department of Justice and the National Institutes of Standards and Technology in the Department of Commerce, and it picked up where the committee left off. They are trying to implement a lot of the recommendations that we made in the report."

"Probably the most disappointing part of serving on that committee was that there was an awful lot of talk—a lot of smoke but no fire," Siegel recalls. "And we have done little but continue to talk about it since then, and that's disappointing. All of us still keep in touch through AnnMarie and we have universal disappointment that more hasn't been accomplished. I think the dialogue is very important, and we are hoping that this national commission will operationalize a lot of the issues that we raised."

Regarding urgent aspects of the report, Siegel says the standout issue is the push for federal oversight. "Despite the recommendation for an overarching entity, which the committee called the National Institute for Forensic Science, it was readily apparent that no such entity was going to be formed. I think some sort of federal oversight is critical—that's first and foremost in many people's view. Beyond that, we need to develop a national code of ethics with teeth in it. We need to get rid of some of these miscreants in the crime labs that have given forensic science a bad name and a black eye. In order to do that, there must be some sort of licensure that you can lift like there is in other professions, where if you have people who are bad actors, they get their license lifted and they can't practice anymore. We don't have that in forensic science. We don't have an agreed upon, consensus-driven code of ethics that carries with it some kind of licensure. Right now, if people violate the code of the AAFS, they can kick you out but that doesn't stop you from practicing forensic science. Along with that is mandatory certification of forensic scientists. There must be a certification process that everyone must pass; right now there are a number of voluntary ones in criminalistics and crime lab science—some are voluntary and a couple are required but it's a patchwork right now and we need standardization. In order to assure the public they are getting quality services we need some sort of mandatory certification and along with that, we need mandatory accreditation of crime labs. Now the ASCLAD Laboratory Accreditation Board is the main one and there are a couple of other accreditation agencies, they have accredited more than 90 percent of the public crime labs in the United States. That's at least 10 percent not accredited that need to be. Those issues that are interconnected are the most important ones if we are going to instill in the American public trust and faith in forensic science."

"The NAS report had different levels of impact," says John Butler, special assistant to the director for forensic science in the Special Programs Office at the NIST. "Some expected it and some didn't, and some didn't feel like it mattered that much, so you had everything along the continuum. From the forensic DNA world where I come from, we got a pass because it said nuclear DNA is fine but the other disciplines need some work. DNA is in a different ballpark; DNA still has issues; there are plenty of challenges doing DNA well but I think other disciplines may have taken a personal offense to the report's findings. Their review of the issues also missed some things, as some people have pointed out. Others have said the report is spot-on, and we need to embrace change and move forward. It has been seven years since that report came out; people constantly cite it and say these are the things that we need to do better and some are moving forward in that direction while some have to be convinced a bit more."

Regarding the claim that the report skewed according to the legal bar's perspective, Butler says, "Part of the challenge is discussing the forensic piece in the context of the adversarial environment of the courtroom. So you are going to get different perspectives, especially in the legal arena because of the prosecution and the defense both jockeying for position. Being on the Commission and seeing for myself how prosecutors and defense attorneys actually are coming to agreement on important issues and trying to move things forward, that has been very gratifying for me. Because of my position at NIST, I am not in a case-working lab so I don't see the same challenges that exist in that laboratory environment, so in some ways I am an outsider observing what is happening, and in other ways I am directly involved with the research with the Commission and OSAC and other things that are part of our responsibilities at NIST. So I am seeing lots of different perspectives, and to me, the way we move forward is getting people to realize there are true issues and getting them to realize that we can work together to improve them and that's what we are trying to do."

Butler continues, "From a scientist's perspective, which I have, there are key issues to be addressed and the only way to do that is changing the culture of labs and medico-legal offices so that they are receptive to improvement efforts. We also need to address issues scientifically and that's why I enjoy being part of this endeavor; I see the value of scientists contributing to improvement efforts, shoring up measurements and providing statistical values. Through my work in DNA I hope to share the insights I have developed over the last two decades. I hope I can influence other disciplines, to help with measurements and statistics for fingerprints or ballistics. That is why I am enjoying helping a broader community than just the DNA folks."

At the time of writing in late 2016, Butler points to NIST's goal for conducting greater levels of research within forensic science and says that the NCFS is in the process of determining priorities for the future. "There are so many issues and the question is, how do you prioritize them," Butler says. "Different groups are tackling stuff, and sometimes they are not as prioritized as we'd like them to be. We are spending some significant time talking about how we prioritize the main concerns. The Commission itself is a two-year, renewable federal advisory committee, and the current term expires in April 2017. We have about a year and so in upcoming meetings we want to see how much we can get done before then. We don't know if the Department of Justice will renew the Commission, and if they do, that's great, we will continue our work. We will be voting on seven documents that are in draft form and out for public comment right now and they deal with a range of issues including how you report testimony, what's included in a report, how you validate something and make sure it works properly, and a national call center for medico-legal death investigation, so many topics spanning across all efforts being made by the Commission. There are also 25 subcommittees of OSAC working on a variety of documents and trying to improve the practice of each aspect of issues in their purview."

The current political landscape notwithstanding, the commission members are racing the clock and feeling the pressure. "You have to have a long-term view of things because a quality system cannot be built overnight," Butler says. "We're taking the time to do that and of course we have had hiccups along the way; we have seen challenges with the processes and how they work in the Commission and in OSAC, and things are in refinement and that's what science does—it tries to evolve and improve with time. The federal government operates in election cycles and you have to keep that in mind, but you have to move forward over the long term, regardless."

Butler continues, "Bi-partisan support is what we need to secure funding and appropriations. You do the best you can to work within the budget you have available. Certainly the more money you have, the more you can do. The reality is, federal funding is needed, but 95 percent of forensic science is done on a state and local level. Nationalization and standardization at federal and state levels is a challenge, but you try to move forward the best you can despite those challenges. The 10th Amendment allows states to maintain sovereignty and that's part of our national psyche and how we look at things."

A great number of opinions have been expressed and explored in this chapter, and perhaps Kaye (2010, page 11) sums it up best by observing, "Even if the full promise of the report is not realized, its publication ultimately should strengthen the good in a system of law and science that has its fair share of the good, the bad, and the ugly."

REFERENCES

Charlton D, Fraser-Mackenzie PAF, and Dror IE. Emotional experiences and motivating factors associated with fingerprint analysis. *Journal of Forensic Sciences*. Vol. 55. Pages 385–393. 2010.

Chisum WJ and Turvey BE. *Crime Reconstruction*. Elsevier Academic Press, Burlington, MA. 2007. Page 52.

Cole SA. Acculturating Forensic Science: What Is Scientific Culture and How Can Forensic Science Adopt It? *38 Fordham Urb. L.J. 435* (2010). Accessible at http://ir.lawnet.fordham.edu/ulj/vol38/iss2/1

Cooley CM and Turvey BE. Observer effects and examiner bias: Psychological influences on the forensic examiner. In: *Crime Reconstruction* (2nd ed.). Cambridge, MA 2011.

Fanelli D. How many scientists fabricate and falsify research? A systematic review and meta-analysis of survey data. *PLOS One*. May 2009. Accessible at http://dx.doi.org/10.1371/journal.pone.0005738

Faigman DL. Anecdotal forensics, phrenology and other abject lessons from the history of science. *Hastings Law Journal*. 59 pp. 979–1000. 2007.

Fisher B, Fisher D, and Kolowski J. *Forensics Demystified*. McGraw-Hill Companies, New York. 2007.

Gabel JD. Forensiphilia: Is the Public Fascination with Forensic Science a Love Affair or a Fatal Attraction? April 2010. Accessible at https://papers.ssrn.com/sol3/papers.cfm?abstract_id=1578974

Gabel JD. Realizing reliability in forensic science from the ground up. *Journal of Criminal Law and Criminology*. Vol. 104, No. 2. 2014. Accessible at http://scholarlycommons.law.northwestern.edu/jclc/vol104/iss2/

Giannelli PC. The 2009 NAS Forensic Science Report: A literature review. *Criminal Law Bulletin*. Vol. 48. Page 378. 2012.

Giannelli P. Scientific evidence, reasonable scientific certainty: A phrase in search of a meaning. *Criminal Justice*. Spring 2010.

Giannelli PC. Daubert and forensic science: The pitfalls of law enforcement control of scientific research. *University of Illinois Law Review*. Page 53. 2011.

James SH and Nordby JJ. *Forensic Science: An Introduction to Scientific and Investigative Techniques*. CRC Press, Boca Raton, Fla. 2003.

Kassin SM, Drorb IE, and Kukuckaa J. The forensic confirmation bias: Problems, perspectives, and proposed solutions. *Journal of Applied Research in Memory and Cognition*. Vol. 2, No. 1. Pages 42–52. March 2013.

Kaye DH. *The Double Helix and the Law of Evidence*. Page 82. Harvard University Press, Cambridge, MA. 2010.

Kaye DH. The good, the bad, and the ugly: The NRC Report on strengthening forensic science in America. *Science and Justice*. Vol. 50. Page 8. 2010.

Kiely T. Forensic science and the law. In: *Forensic Science: An Introduction to Scientific and Investigative Techniques*, James SH and Nordby JJ, Eds. CRC Press, Boca Raton, Fla. 2003.

Koppl R and Krane D. Blinding as a solution to bias. In: *Minimizing and Leveraging Bias in Forensic Science*. Elsevier, San Diego, CA. 2016.

Koppl R, Kurzban R, and Kobilinsky L. Epistemics for forensics. *Episteme*. Vol. 5, No. 2. Pages 141–159. 2008.

Lynch M. Science, truth, and forensic cultures: The exceptional legal status of DNA evidence. *Studies in History and Philosophy of Biological and Biomedical Sciences*. Elsevier. Vol. 44, No. 1. Pages 60–70. March 2013.

Miranda DM. *Evidence Found: An Approach to Crime Scene Investigation*. Academic Press, Cambridge, MA. 2015.

National Academy of Sciences. Strengthening Forensic Science in the United States: A Path Forward 2009. Accessible at http://www.nap.edu/catalog/12589.html

National Commission on Forensic Science. Testimony Using the Term "Reasonable Scientific Certainty." January 16, 2016. Accessible at http://www.ascld.org/wp-content/uploads/2014/08/final_draft_views_document_on_testimony_using_the_term_scientific_certainty_0.pdf

National Commission on Forensic Science. Recommendations to the Attorney General Regarding Use of the Term "Reasonable Scientific Certainty." 2016. Accessible at https://www.justice.gov/ncfs/file/816021/download

National Research Council, National Academy of Sciences, Strengthening Forensic Science in the United States: A Path Forward. 2009.

Nordby JJ. Countering chaos: Logic, ethics, and the criminal justice system. In: *Forensic Science: An Introduction to Scientific and Investigative Techniques*, James SH and Nordby JJ, Eds. CRC Press, Boca Raton, Fla. 2003.

Office of the Inspector General (OIG). A review of the FBI's progress in responding to the recommendations in the Office of the Inspector General report on the fingerprint misidentification in the Brandon Mayfield case. 2011. Accessible at http://www.justice.gov/oig/special/s1105.pdf

Page M. Science and Forensic Science. In: *Forensic Testimony: Science, Law and Expert Evidence*. Academic Press, Cambridge, MA. Pages 23–39. 2014.

Peterson JL, Mihajlovic S, and Gilliland M. *Forensic Evidence and the Police*. National Institute of Justice, Washington, DC. 1984.

Podlas K. The *CSI* effect and other forensic fictions. *Loyola of Los Angeles Entertainment Law Review*. Vol. 27. Page 87. 2006. Accessible at http://digitalcommons.lmu.edu/elr/vol27/iss2/1

Pyrek KM. *Forensic Science Under Siege: The Challenges of Forensic Laboratories and the Medico-legal Death Investigation System*. Elsevier Academic Press, San Diego, CA. 2007.

Risinger DM. The NAS/NRC Report on forensic science: A path forward fraught with pitfalls. *Utah Law Review*. 2010.

Risinger DM, Saks MJ, Thompson WC, and Rosenthal R. The Daubert/Kumho implications of observer effects in forensic science: Hidden problems of expectation and suggestion. *California Law Review*. Vol. 90. Pages 1–56. 2002.

Saks MJ and Koehler JJ. Review: The coming paradigm shift in forensic identification science. *Science*. Pages 892, 894–895. 2005.

Saks MJ, Risinger DM, Rosenthal R, and Thompson WC. Context effects in forensic science: A review and application of the science of science to crime laboratory practice in the United States. *Science and Justice*. Vol. 43, No. 2. Pages 77–90. 2003.

Simoncelli T. Rigor in forensic science. In: *Blinding as a Solution to Bias: Strengthening Biomedical Science, Forensic Science, and Law*. Academic Press, Cambridge, MA. Pages 129–131. 2017.

Turvey BE. Forensic fraud: Prior research. In: *Forensic Fraud*. Elsevier, San Diego, CA. 2013.

Tversky A and Kahneman D. Judgment under uncertainty: Heuristics and biases. *Science*. Vol. 185. Pages 1124–1131. 1974.

Upshaw-Downs JC. Whistleblowers. In: *Ethics in Forensic Science*. Elsevier San Diego, CA. 2012.

CHAPTER 3

Quality Improvement in Forensic Laboratories

Mandates for improvement have been made for both the forensic laboratory and the medicolegal death investigation offices. Let's first take a look at the condition of the crime lab. The U.S. forensic system comprises about 320 forensic laboratories, and for decades now, these facilities have been struggling with deficits in personnel, budgets, and resources with which to perform their duties as a key cog in the wheel of the justice system.

The needs of the forensic science community are old news to anyone who has spent any time perusing government documents from the last two decades. Let's conduct a quick review of the recent history of documented needs assessments. The 2004 Consolidated Appropriations Act required the National Institute of Justice (NIJ) to submit to Congress a report addressing the needs of forensic service providers beyond the Advancing Justice through DNA Technology initiative. The act directed the NIJ, in conjunction with the professional societies serving the field—the American Society of Crime Lab Directors (ASCLD), the American Academy of Forensic Sciences (AAFS), the International Association for Identification (IAI), and the National Association of Medical Examiners (NAME)—to develop a plan to address the issues deemed critical for the forensic laboratories and medical examiner community. Each organization presented its formal comments at a summit held in Washington, DC, in May 2004 (NIJ, 2004). At that time, the NIJ (2004, page 3) reports that forensic laboratories face several important challenges, the most notable being personnel needs, as well as education and training for new and veteran forensic scientists: "Although it is difficult to quantify these needs, every forensic discipline believes that it faces shortfalls of personnel qualified to replace retiring examiners or meet increasing case workloads. In addition, examiners should be required to meet minimum training and proficiency standards in all disciplines."

Interestingly, this 2004 report came out five years before the infamous 2009 National Academy of Sciences (NAS) report, and the issues sounded the same. Data reported by the Bureau of Justice Statistics (BJS) from its census of forensic laboratories showed that the training and continuing-education budgets of the largest 50 laboratories in the United States were actually less than one-half of 1 percent of their total budgets. To close this gap, according to the forensic science organizations, the federal government should provide grants for continuing education or training academies for the forensic sciences. Some options to address the training needs of forensic examiners and managers include traditional face-to-face or hands-on training, collaborations, and alternative delivery systems such as electronic media. Regional centers would be suited for expanding the scope and delivery of training programs. Also, professional models for training and establishing competency should be encouraged. According to the NIJ (2004), the forensic science community should consider methods to encourage quality graduate education in forensic science. ASCLD suggested that a program to eliminate or forgive student loans for graduates who obtain full-time employment in public forensic science laboratories be considered.

In addition, back in 2004, the forensic service organizations recognized the need to improve the understanding of the scientific foundations of specific disciplines. They remarked that DNA analysis has a fully characterized statistical and scientific basis, in that the uniqueness of one individual's DNA profile can be quantified and presented with great accuracy. They emphasized that scientific research and the publication of best practices guides can improve the practice and acceptance of the forensic disciplines. Although Congress did not specifically ask for input concerning research and development needs, each of the forensic science organizations outlined specific needs for improved scientific understanding and technology to serve the forensic community. In particular, forensic service providers reported that basic research is needed into the scientific underpinning of impression evidence, questioned documents, and firearms/toolmark examination. The forensic science organizations believe that the federal government should sponsor research to validate forensic science disciplines to address basic principles, error rates, and standards of procedure. In addition, forensic laboratories need tools to improve speed and efficiency, extend forensic analysis to more difficult samples, and support the full range of forensic techniques. Technology is needed to improve evidence collection, crime scene analysis, and field testing of drugs and other material for investigative purposes.

The NIJ (2004) stated that these issues should be addressed more fully by a forensic science commission, which was authorized by the Justice for All Act. The creation of this commission was also part of the president's DNA Initiative, and the entity is charged with the responsibilities of developing recommendations for long-term strategies to maximize the use of current forensic technologies to solve crimes and protect the public, and identifying potential scientific breakthroughs that may be used to assist law enforcement. According to the NIJ (2004), each of the forensic service organizations supports the creation of this commission to review the needs of the forensic science community in the long term at the federal, state, and local levels. The commission was viewed by the organizations as a mechanism to identify issues and needs of particular disciplines and provide national leadership to improve the practice of forensic science.

It is only very recently that attention has turned to the needs of forensic science in a more meaningful way. From time to time, the U.S. Department of Justice (DOJ) has conducted studies to assess the status and needs of forensic laboratories. One of the latest studies, "Forensic Sciences: Review of Status and Needs," issued in February 1999, was the first update in more than 20 years. The report was the work product of a two-day meeting held in March 1997, which assembled more than 40 scientists and administrators representing state, local, and federal forensic science organizations. The NIJ, the National Institute of Standards and Technology's (NIST's) Office of Law Enforcement Standards, and the ASCLD held a joint workshop, Forensic Science Summit: Road Map to the Year 2000, March 5–6, 1997, at NIST headquarters in Gaithersburg, Maryland. The purpose of the workshop was to determine the current status and needs of forensic laboratories on training; technology transfer; methods research, development, testing, and evaluation; and analytical services. The workshop also provided a forum to explore the use of national and federal laboratory resources and how best to take advantage of this external support.

The 1999 report acknowledges a few deficits in the current operations of the laboratory system. It states in the executive summary, "For technology transfer to be successful, there must be a true partnership between local or state forensic laboratories and national laboratories. Existing strengths that are fragmented and dispersed need to be consolidated. Over the years, a large amount of development work has been done at the national laboratories that some forensic laboratories may be aware of because of their geographic location, but the work may not be known to the entire forensic community. No formal process exists for technology transfer to forensic laboratories. The key is to identify technology currently in use or under development at national facilities that can be quickly transferred for use in the forensic field. Areas of technology at national laboratories that could be applied to the forensic community include robotics, remote sensors, supercomputers for computational power, and satellite communications" (NIJ, 1999).

The 1999 report adds, "In forensic science, as in other disciplines, cost-effectiveness and budgetary constraints are constant concerns. The technology must be affordable, reliable, and in some cases portable. The forensic community needs to be aggressive and creative in securing sources of funding to ensure that quality work is performed. It is important to examine not only the needs of the forensic community, but also the consequences of not meeting those needs—how does it affect the criminal justice system and the public that the forensic laboratories serve. When police are not able to work cases efficiently, when court dates are postponed, then taxpayer money is not well spent, efficiency is reduced, and justice may not be served" (NIJ, 1999, page 3).

The 1999 report also addresses what it calls the "immense" training needs of the forensic community. It states, "Training of newcomers to the field, as well as providing continuing education for seasoned professionals, are vital to ensuring that crime laboratories deliver the best possible service to the criminal justice system. Forensic scientists must stay up-to-date as new technology, equipment, methods, and techniques are developed. While training programs exist in a variety of forms, there is a need to broaden their scope and build on existing resources. Casework, the support crime laboratories provide to those in the field, is the essence of forensic laboratory work. Casework support includes routine and traditional analyses common to all forensic laboratory settings, methods development particular to the requirements of specific cases, and the identification of analytical sources to perform work that is considered non-routine" (NIJ, 1999, page 4).

A more recent attempt to enumerate and document the needs of forensic laboratories came in the summer of 2004, when a number of forensic science organizations examined their needs and contributed to the "180-Day Study Report: Status and Needs of United States Crime Laboratories for the NIJ" as part of a larger report of the status and needs of crime laboratories in the United States. While the forensic science community was glad to have yet another vehicle through which the field could be studied and its issues validated, some practitioners were concerned about the ultimate disposition of the information they shared with the NIJ.

The recommendations that ASCLD made for the NIJ's 180-day report focused on the issue that while state and local crime laboratories are an integral part of the criminal justice system, demands for facilities' services have increased, but funding has not kept pace. The 2004 report points to the already established fact that crime laboratory backlogs cause significant delays in evidence being analyzed, resulting in delays in the courts as well as in the investigation of crimes. It also alludes to the BJS survey (Hickman and Peterson, 2004) of the 50 largest laboratories in the United States, which revealed that in 2002, laboratories faced a 134 percent increase in their backlogs. Overall, for every four requests completed by a laboratory, one request remained unworked by the end of the year.

The 2004 ASCLD report covers a wide variety of laboratory infrastructure-related needs. The primary need identified by crime laboratory managers was personnel, with additional manpower needed in all sections. The need is so urgent that in order for laboratories to achieve a 30-day turnaround time for all requests, extra personnel would cost in excess of $36 million. Other needs included equipment (estimated in excess of $18 million), supplies, laboratory space, overtime, travel, and training.

The 2004 ASCLD report notes that another urgent need was in the area of training and education. Prior to conducting analyses of evidence, forensic scientists must have both basic scientific education and discipline-specific advanced and continuing training and education. Although minimum curriculum guidelines for both undergraduate and graduate forensic science programs have been established by the NIJ and an accreditation program has been established to accredit them, continued support is required to ensure that would-be and veteran scientists receive the training they need to become proficient and to remain competent in their fields of expertise.

Training needs for forensic laboratories are significant, driven by the increased demand for trained staff and succession planning. Initial training of laboratory analysts is largely done on the job and is labor intensive, and the ASCLD report (2004) called for collaborations, innovative approaches, and alternative delivery systems for forensic analyst and manager training. The report stated that maintaining and increasing professionalism within the forensic science community requires attention to a wide range of issues, many of which are related to quality and guidelines of good practice.

The 2004 report agreed that quality improvement measures such as accreditation and certification brought to bear increased expenditures for laboratories, and these costs can become problematic for some facilities. Although ASCLD acknowledges that laboratory accreditation "is not a guarantee against error," it is a program that requires a laboratory to evaluate its operations and address issues, and it requires a time commitment and substantial fees. Adding to this financial burden is an average cost per analyst for proficiency testing at approximately $500 per year, on top of the average fee per accreditation inspection at $6500, exclusive of travel costs.

The report also acknowledged the lack of active research being conducted inside forensic laboratories due to constricted resources and manpower issues. The report indicated that practitioner partnerships are needed for these research programs, but at the same time, research takes a backseat to the primary work of the laboratory. The ASCLD report (2004, page iv) stated, "In addition to research into new techniques and the implementation of these techniques in the laboratory, crime labs must also identify innovative ways to work more efficiently and rapidly to reduce case backlogs and to bring forensic science to the crime scene. Crime laboratories barely have the resources to attend to core business and must direct resources to casework. Any innovation that does take place is largely uncoordinated."

A number of surveys and studies have documented the characteristics of these facilities as well as these aforementioned deficits. In brief, the BJS has conducted several censuses of publicly funded forensic crime laboratories. The first one, administered in 2002, established baseline information on the operations and workload of these public crime laboratories, while the 2005 census documented changes in workload and backlog that have occurred since the 2002 census. A third census was conducted in 2009, and in 2016, data from the third Census of Publicly Funded Forensic Crime Laboratories was scheduled to have been released, according to Matthew Durose, statistician with the BJS.

The census provides a comprehensive look at the forensic services provided by federal, state, and local crime labs across the nation and the resources devoted to completing the work. The Census of Publicly Funded Forensic Crime Laboratories collects data on staff, budgets, and workloads within publicly operated labs. The census also provides information on lab accreditations, proficiency tests, and other quality assurance mechanisms.

The 2005 census showed that 389 publicly funded forensic crime laboratories were operating in the United States with an estimated budget of about $1 billion, nearly half of which funded state laboratories. The BJS report cited a total of nearly 2.7 million new cases that year, including many more separate requests for forensic services. The census demonstrated that funding for laboratories had not increased with increasing demands. It also showed that staffing remains a challenge, with an average staff size of a crime lab of about 16; there were more than 11,900 full-time equivalent (FTE) personnel employed overall.

This relatively small number is felt when examining the significant case-backlog problem still plaguing labs. A 2006 NIJ report cited equipment shortages as a limiting factor in processing cases. According to the 2005 BJS data, laboratories serving local jurisdictions received about 1.3 million cases in 2005, including 727,000 cases received by county laboratories and 566,000 by municipal laboratories. An estimated 359,000 cases were backlogged (not completed within 30 days) at the end of 2005, compared to 287,000 at year-end 2002. This represents a 24 percent increase in backlogged cases between 2002 and 2005. State laboratories accounted for more than half of the backlog in both years. Among the 288 laboratories that reported this information, the median number of cases received in 2005 was about 4100. Overall, laboratories ended the year with a median backlog of about 400 cases (NAS report, 2009).

While practitioners currently wait for the data from the 2014 census, the latest information from the 2009 census (coincidentally, the year of the publication of the NAS report on forensic science) continues to document the state of labs that are lacking in resources and personnel, even though utilization of these facilities' services continues to escalate. More than 4 million forensic requests were received in 2009, and these totals do not include requests outsourced to private labs. Of the 4.1 million forensic requests in 2009, 2.4 million were made of state labs; 820,000 of county labs; 650,000 of municipal labs; and 280,000 to federal labs. An estimated 3.9 million forensic requests were completed in 2009, but about 1.2 million requests were backlogged at year-end 2008 and 2009. In a 2007 communication with the NAS committee, then-director of the Los Angeles County Sheriff's Department crime laboratory Barry Fisher warned that to manage backlogs, laboratories must triage cases, where murders, rapes, aggravated assaults, and the like have priority, as do cases going to court, cases where a suspect is being held on an arrest warrant, highly publicized cases, etc. Fisher said the use of triage is laboratories' best way to manage scarce resources. Fisher adds that another case management strategy is for investigators to become persistent, calling labs regularly to check on the status of their analyses (NAS report, 2009).

Of the total number of crime lab expenditures documented by the 2009 census, personnel costs accounted for 73 percent; supplies were 13 percent; equipment was 9 percent; and other costs (such as travel, training, and construction) accounted for the remaining 5 percent.

The 2009 census found that the average staff size was 32 employees, and of the 13,100 crime lab employees in 2009, 60 percent were forensic analysts/examiners; 9 percent were technical support; 14 percent were managers; 9 percent were clerical support; 6 percent were crime scene technicians; and 3 percent worked in other positions.

When it comes to accreditation, the 2009 census showed that 83 percent of all labs were accredited by a professional forensic science organization; that's up from 71 percent in the 2002 census and 82 percent in the 2005 census.

The mandate for quality improvement has come from a number of sources; one of the most notable in recent years has been from the 2009 NAS report, which we first encountered in Chapter 2. In Recommendation 8, the committee notes, "Forensic laboratories should establish routine quality assurance and quality control procedures to ensure the accuracy of forensic analyses and the work of forensic practitioners. Quality control procedures should be designed to identify mistakes, fraud, and bias; confirm the continued validity and reliability of standard operating procedures and protocols; ensure that best practices are being followed; and correct procedures and protocols that are found to need improvement" (NAS, 2009, page 26).

Lennard (2015, page 77) emphasizes, "Given that results generated by a forensic science facility may lead to the conviction or exoneration of an individual accused of a crime, may determine a cause of death, or may identify the victim of a criminal act ... systems need to be in place to ensure reliability, accuracy and precision. It is expected that the scientific methods employed will be fit-for-purpose and will be applied in accordance with accepted international standards. Many factors impact on quality assurance in the forensic arena, from how samples are collected and transferred, how examinations and analyses are undertaken, the qualifications and training of staff, through to how results are communicated in written reports and presented in court."

Experts define quality assurance as a program for the systematic monitoring and evaluation of the various aspects of a project, service, or facility to ensure that standards of quality are being met. As Lennard (2015, page 77) notes, "It is an activity designed to provide evidence to all stakeholders that activities related to the delivery of a service or the manufacture of a product are being performed effectively and to an appropriate standard. QA assures the existence and effectiveness of procedures that attempt to make sure—in advance—that expected levels of quality will be reached."

The FORESIGHT Project is one of the more recent examples of an attempt at quality improvement and assurance for crime labs, introduced the same year as the 2009 NAS report. As Houck (2009) observes, "Managers of scientific laboratories see themselves as scientists first and managers second; consequently, they tend to devalue the managerial aspects of their jobs. Forensic laboratory managers are no different, but the stakes may be much higher given the importance of quality science to the criminal justice system. The need for training and support in forensic laboratory management has been recognized for many years, but little has been done to transition the tools of business to the forensic laboratory environment."

The FORESIGHT Project is described as a business-guided self-evaluation of forensic science laboratories across the globe, funded by the NIJ and housed at West Virginia University (WVU), where economics, accounting, finance, and forensic faculty provide assistance, guidance, and analysis to participating laboratories of local, regional, state, and national agencies. Laboratories participating in FORESIGHT have developed standardized definitions for metrics to evaluate work processes, linking financial information to work tasks, and functions. Laboratory managers can then assess resource allocations, efficiencies, and value of services. Those who run the project say the mission of FORESIGHT is to "measure, preserve what works, and change what does not."

FORESIGHT's origins stem from a study in Europe, called QUADRUPOL, which conducted an in-depth analysis of four forensic laboratories in the European Union. At the 2006 International Forensic Business and Economics Colloquium, it was decided that a similar study would benefit U.S. forensic laboratories. Participation in FORESIGHT is voluntary but requires that an interested laboratory submit a completed Laboratory Reporting and Analysis Tool (LabRAT). The LabRAT is a spreadsheet that collects and calculates business measures about caseloads, staffing, budgets, and other important factors. While the LabRAT alone is a useful tool for a laboratory manager, submitting a completed LabRAT form allows WVU to generate a benchmarking report for the laboratory. This analysis compares the participant to others with laboratories in the study.

The 2009 NAS report acknowledges that although there have been notable efforts to achieve standardization and develop best practices in some forensic science disciplines and the medical examiner system, "...most disciplines still lack best practices or any coherent structure for the enforcement of operating standards, certification and accreditation. Standards and codes of ethics exist in some fields, and there are some functioning certification and accreditation programs, but none are mandatory. In short, oversight and enforcement of operating standards, certification, accreditation, and ethics are lacking in most local and state jurisdictions" (NAS, 2009, page 23).

Someone who knows the needs of forensic laboratories intimately is New Yorker-turned-Californian Barry A. J. Fisher, MS, MBA, who has been the face of forensic laboratory advocacy for almost 20 years. Fisher, whom we first met in Chapter 2, has made a name for himself in pursuing his interest in the interrelationship between forensic science and the law along with public policy issues concerning the timely delivery of quality forensic support services to the criminal justice system. Although now retired, he remains a go-to person for those who seek answers about forensic science—both on Capitol Hill and in the lab. Case in point: his seminal book, *Techniques of Crime Scene Investigation*, is in its eighth edition and remains a cornerstone of instruction on criminalistics. He has lectured throughout the United States and the world, speaking on forensic laboratory practices, quality assurance, and related topics.

Fisher served as director of the Los Angeles County Sheriff's Department crime laboratory from 1987 until his retirement in 2009. At the lab, he oversaw a staff of more than 300 in a lab with an annual budget of more than $25 million. But his career in criminalistics with the sheriff's crime lab dates back to 1969. From that year until 1986, Fisher worked in most sections of the crime laboratory and supervised the physical evidence and forensic toxicology sections. Duties included crime scene investigation, laboratory casework, and court testimony.

Fast-forward to 2016 at the time of this writing, and Fisher occupies his time with monitoring the state of forensic science and sharing his thoughts on social media. "I'm on Twitter, and I tweet articles about forensic science," Fisher says. "I am also active on LinkedIn, and when I see interesting news articles and publications, I post them there. I have more than 1,300 followers on Twitter, and 4,200 connections on LinkedIn. People seem to be interested in what I post; these are issues that have confounded me for years, things like needs assessments for crime labs and related issues explored in that 2009 NAS report and the aftermath, and where forensic science is going in the future. I have my ear to the ground but I am not an active player these days. I have thrown my hat in the ring to get selected on national panels but I guess the feeling is that Fisher is a has-been and it is time to get new people to examine the issues. I shake my head because I see the same issues being discussed over and over again, and without institutional memory it becomes two steps forward and sometimes three steps back."

Fisher continues, "I have been retired almost seven years now, and as the calendar pages turn, some contacts begin to fade away." Fisher says, "It's certainly not at the level it was when I was actively engaged in the game." Modest assessment aside, Fisher is sought out for key opportunities, including working with the National Judicial College, which was established at the University of Nevada to train state court judges around the country. "They received a small grant and are looking to develop a curriculum for educating judges about forensic evidence," Fisher explains. "I am the token forensic guy, and the rest are all lawyers. We will kick around some ideas for a curriculum."

That "token forensic guy" has lined up some impressive accolades, including being a distinguished fellow and past president of the AAFS, past president of the International Association of Forensic Sciences, past president of the American Society of Crime Laboratory Directors (ASCLD), and a past chairman of the American Society of Crime Laboratory Directors–Laboratory Accreditation Board (ASCLD/LAB).

But what Fisher says he is known for most is championing forensic science in ways that a lesser man may not have attempted.

"When I was at the LA Sheriff's Department crime lab I was always interested in the bigger picture, so I started getting involved in various forensic science associations and organizations, such as the California Association of Criminalists," Fisher recalls. "After a while at the lab, I saw that my forte was not in the actual doing of the forensic science work, performing various tests and analyses, working in all divisions of the lab and testifying on nearly every kind of case we were seeing. I felt I was a mediocre player in that area of lab operations. Early on in my career, I had earned a master's degree in business administration in night school and armed with my MBA I had a different perspective on forensic science matters."

Fisher describes people's reactions to his unique take on the issues facing the forensic laboratory community at the time, and how they led him to start speaking out. "I had given a talk at an AAFS meeting in the 1980s and I had used the term 'customers' and 'clients' in describing the people for which we were working, and one guy came up to me and said, 'How can you use terms like that, these are not clients,' as it seemed in doing so we are the dog wagging the tail and not the other way around. He thought we are the most important player in the whole process so we're not someone who's just serving customers. That exchange kind of stuck in my head, as well as the notion that many people in our profession did not understand the reality of how all these things work, that if you are in a crime lab, working as a forensic scientist or a criminalist, you are just a very small player in the bigger scheme of things. After all, there are lawyers, cops, judges, the public, and you must have a way to connect to these folks, and in doing that, you can use them to help you get to where you need to go. I was starting to formulate some opinions about the way things were, and still are, out there."

Fisher continues, "Around the same time in these early years I got involved in sexual assault cases, dealing with nurses and doctors in hospitals and the frustrations they were experiencing with processes. I came across some kindred spirits in a couple of sexual assault detectives and some nurses in hospitals and some prosecutors keen on making improvements to the system. It occurred to me, 'Sure, I can do a lot of this stuff myself but if I had some people helping me push these boulders uphill, it would make life a lot easier.' It would also carry more weight if people were saying the same things in unison. By the time I started to recognize this concept, I had joined the AAFS. In the 1980s I was promoted at the lab and was in management, and I started to attend ASCLD meetings. I began to meet with people in the same spot I was—running labs, people who considered themselves players in the forensic science community, and I saw that one of the things they failed to see was the notion of trying to pull people together to speak with a coherent voice."

During his tenure with ASCLD, Fisher found himself in Washington, DC fairly often, with an opportunity to engage in dialogue with the NIJ. "I saw early on that the NIJ was a benefactor because they were the only identifiable group that seemed to represent something of substance for forensic science needs. The FBI had been in that role previously but gave it up; they stirred up contention with some of the biggies in the crime lab community and ASCLD, and decided to walk away. No one was on the same wavelength anymore. But the NIJ did seem to have some people on the same wavelength, and I befriended a guy by the name of Dick Rau who is long since retired now. He became someone I could talk to about our issues, and I remember around the time I was president or maybe past-president at ASCLD, he brought his boss with him, David Boyd. David was a former Army guy, retired and working for the NIJ. We chatted and I saw that he was a bright guy who understood how politics worked. He wanted to introduce me to a guy who turned out to be the head of the White House's Office of Science and Technology Policy. So I met with one of his guys, Neal Lane, whose deputy was Duncan Moore, a physicist up at Rochester Institute of Technology. Lane and Moore met with us—we were starting to become a group of people who had been in Washington who were talking to people in Congress and the various committees, trying to get some traction on the issues. At one meeting, Neil said that what we needed to do was form an official group so that we would be speaking with a single voice, because he said individually, we were too small. He said we needed to have a consortium. I thought to myself, 'Wow, what a great idea,' so around the same time Boyd introduced us to someone doing work for the NIJ, lobbyist Bob Greenberg, who had a consulting firm in D.C., involved in law enforcement and public safety issues and was well connected. Our consortium was just getting off the ground and was too small for him so he turned us over to one of his associates, Beth Lavach, who not only became our lobbyist in Washington, but also our confidante and best buddy. She was a hard charger, and met with all kinds of people on a regular basis in D.C."

Fisher says their Consortium of Forensic Science Organizations started to gain attention from key staffers on the Hill, but the journey toward unity was a challenging one. "A guy who worked for Sen. Mike DeWine was a big supporter of forensic science. His told us that a couple people from ASCLD had stopped by the office and were saying some similar things, but he advised us to get our act together and said that if we weren't speaking from the same platform with one voice, it was never going to happen for us. So we were hearing this same thing from a couple of different people, so it seemed like forming an official consortium was the right thing to do. Our first meeting was at an AAFS meeting held in Reno, California in 2000. We all sat down and hammered out an agreement. We agreed that each of the half dozen groups that were interested in the consortium would have to kick in $15,000 to pay for our lobbyist. So we started to get together regularly, then go to D.C. regularly, meeting with as many people on the Hill as we could. We had some successes but some meetings went nowhere, but overall, it seemed like we were doing well at the end of the Clinton administration. Al Gore was the techie guy, and word on the street was he was interested in forensic science. We weren't sure if it was true, but there seemed to be something going on, and Neil Lane and the White House Office of Science Technology and Policy were actually interested in this stuff."

Fisher says he was about to get a heavy dose of political reality. "At the time, Neal Lane was working with Attorney General Janet Reno on a program in science and technology relating to public safety. So they assembled a group of folks working in law enforcement, corrections and forensic science. Neil and his deputy were coming out to Los Angeles to meet people at Caltech. I got a call from Neal's office that he was in town and wanted to see the crime lab. I showed them around and they were mesmerized—they thought it was phenomenal, and it turns out that seeing our lab was their first exposure to actual forensic science. Things were looking really good and probably if Gore had been elected, our successes would have continued. I suspected that, like Raiders of the Lost Ark, the crate with Ark of the Covenant in it would never see the light of day. All of our work through the consortium with NIJ and White House put in this government warehouse, never to be seen again. When George W. Bush was elected, all the players changed and they were not interested in anything we had done or worked on up to that time. So we had to start over with another group of bureaucrats and the person they put in charge of the NIJ—Sarah Hart—was interested in only one thing, DNA. Hart was there for almost eight years and we would go there frequently. We convinced NIJ to conduct that 180-day study, so they called us in, and we had meetings in D.C. When the study came out, virtually nothing that we had put in there during in our meetings was actually in the study, and we were miffed."

Despite this setback, old—and new—allies appeared. "Years earlier, at an annual NIJ conference on science and the law, I had met Joe Cecil. He said to me, 'Have you seen this case in front of the U.S. Supreme Court about forensic evidence?' The case happened to be the pivotal *Kumho Tire v. Carmichael*, wherein during questioning of the expert, it was determined how the tire was defective. The expert ran his hand inside the tire and found defects, and said that based on his experience it was a manufacturing problem. He was asked if this opinion had been published, etc. No, so the Supreme Court said not only does the science has to meet the *Daubert* standard, but with any type of expert evidence, the expert on the stand can't pull it out of the air and say it works. I read the Court's opinion and I said to Joe, 'Wow, this is really serious stuff because there is so much in forensic science just like this.' For example, with firearms, there is nothing in the academic studies regarding firearm evidence, and there's also not a lot of academic research on fingerprints, tire or shoe impressions, and it's a serious problem. And once the lawyers get ahold of it, it's all over. We were starting to realize we were going nowhere with the NIJ and with what the judicial landscape was looking like, we needed help. So I paid a visit to AnnMarie Mazza, who worked for the National Academy of Sciences (NAS). I was accompanied by Patty McFeeley, the president-elect of AAFS at the time, because we felt the evidence issue was something that the NAS needed to examine. AnnMarie said it was a great idea but they didn't have the budget for it; the NAS would need a directive from Congress to undertake it. So it was another hurdle to negotiate. So I tucked that away in my head and I realize that we are not getting anywhere with NIJ, so I said to Beth Lavach, we need to raise this issue again with our friends in Congress but this time have the National Academies do that study. Beth and Ann Marie started talking and we ultimately got this thing passed in Congress."

Fisher says that in his long and storied career, he is most proud of launching the consortium. "It helped move a significant number of efforts forward," Fisher says. "It made us realize the importance of getting to Washington and speaking with one voice, getting legislation passed, getting the National Academies to conduct the study and to get the NIJ to pay for it. I can't say I made it happen all by myself but through the hard work of a lot of other like-minded people, we helped push this thing along to get traction to make important things happen. When push comes to shove, I always made it a point, when I met people who were in important places, to stay in touch, engage them, send them pieces of information in hopes that when the time came they could do something to help our cause. It had nothing had to do with personal gain, it was purely something needed to be done. And we were ultimately successful. That Consortium has given birth not only to the National Academy of Sciences report in 2009, but to all the things that are happening now, including the National Commission on Forensic Science, where people are actively engaged in the major issues that we still face in forensic science."

Fisher is no stranger to the political tensions that accompany making strides in advancing the forensic science agenda. From the very beginning of his time at the LA

Sheriff's Department crime laboratory, Fisher says the politics was a significant part of the territory. "Working as a civilian in a law enforcement organization is a challenge because you are part of them but not really part of them," Fisher says. "You didn't go to the police academy or work in a patrol car, so the lab is a very different environment from police work. My worst thing was doing the right thing for the right reasons and getting clobbered for it."

Fisher describes a situation that changed his outlook on his work and how he functioned in lab management. "We had an employee who was dry-labbing drug cases. The criminalist had a master's degree in chemistry and was fully able to conduct the analyses, but for whatever reason she wasn't doing the full tests. Her supervisor accidentally discovered this, running spectra and they all matched perfectly, which is an impossibility. So the supervisor went to his boss who came to me and lays it out. When something like that happened, I got a pain in my stomach, I wanted the floor to open up and swallow me. I wanted it to go away in the worst way but by the same token I really believed in the ethics of crime lab work and doing the right thing, so I did ... the first thing we did was relieved her of duty, took away her credential and sent her home. We treated this as if it was going to be a criminal matter which meant we didn't ask her questions about what happened; as her employer we could compel her to answer without giving her Miranda rights. I took this matter to our internal affairs unit; we laid it out and decided we needed to bring in the District Attorney to look at this to see if there was any criminal misconduct. We retested all of the evidence from cases that we could lay our hands on, and we asked the state lab in Riverside, California to retest—as we would be suspect if we did it ourselves. The DA's office decided they couldn't win this case, so they ended up making a deal; they told the criminalist to retire, we'll pay you off, so go away. So the No. 2 guy in the sheriff's department said to me, 'I know you are an honest guy but I wouldn't be doing my job unless I commission an investigation of the lab.' So they did. They had a captain and two lieutenants look at the lab's processes, interview every person who worked there. I learned that if you give subordinates an opportunity to dump on you, some of them will."

Fisher describes a dark day in his career. "At the conclusion of the investigation it was decided I would be the subject of an internal affairs investigation, and I could be charged because my behavior in all this was 'unconscionable.' Why? Because there were a number of things going on at the laboratory before, during and after the incident. One of the issues was that the amount of resources the lab was getting wasn't enough to do what we needed to do. I made my pitch every year and I was told I didn't do my job well enough because I couldn't get my superiors to recognize the importance of these resources—hence my performance was 'unconscionable.' Luckily I had enough people in the Sheriff's Department who thought highly enough of me, so they brought in a captain to oversee the lab and I was the lab director without any real responsibility, the token lab director, if you will. They told me that if I fought this, I would be fired. So I was mulling this over and telling myself that I'd have to hire a lawyer and if I prevailed, I'd continue at my current pay scale, continue to have company care and I'd wind up to continue doing the administrative duties I didn't like. So I said, 'OK, I'll just take the deal and make the best of it, although it bothered me greatly.'"

He continues, "This happened in 1994, and I was dragging myself along for the next five years. I kept a journal where I regurgitated and masticated the situation endlessly and considered it all, and my wife Susan says to me, 'Maybe you're not getting it—you still have your job, the rest of the world thinks you are the crime lab director, they leave you alone. Maybe explain the problem to me?'" Fisher says with a laugh at the recollection of his wife's insistence he snap out of his funk, "I told her, it's a guy thing. It's an ego thing. But I got beyond it. That incident was right around the time I was getting involved with the advocacy work, and it freed me up to do anything I wanted. A few weeks after I resigned myself to making the situation work, I get a call from a buddy in D.C. and he says, 'We need you to testify before Congress on some of these forensic science issues' and I think to myself, 'I am living in this bizarre world where back home they think I'm a disaster, but in other places they think I am hot stuff.' So I decided to suck it up and proceed with the hot-stuff approach so I could move on. It has always troubled me that this kind of situation has happened to other crime lab directors where they are a convenient political target."

Fisher was working as an instructor and guest lecturer when his participation in hearings on Capitol Hill started to heat up. For example, in September 1997, he testified before the U.S. Senate Judiciary Committee's Subcommittee on Administration Oversight and the Courts on the subject, "A Review of the Federal Bureau of Investigation Laboratory: Beyond the Inspector General Report," and the following month, he testified before the California State Senate Committee on Public Safety on forensic DNA testing, the state's DNA data bank, and Assembly Bill 1332. In 2000, he served as moderator of a U.S. congressional briefing, Innovations in Crime-Fighting Technology, sponsored by the American Chemical Society. Fisher also spoke to stakeholders of the justice system, including addressing attendees of the 2003 annual meeting of the National Association of Attorneys General, speaking on the subject of advocacy in forensic science and the need for support in federal legislation. All throughout the 2000s, Fisher continued his advocacy work. In April 2007, for example, he addressed the NAS Forensic Science Committee, speaking on the topic of physical evidence from the crime scene to the court room, as well as gave a talk at the NIJ's technology conference about the *CSI* effect and its impact on real-life crime labs.

"The LA Sheriff's Department was wonderful in terms of leaving me alone and allowing me to represent the department during my advocacy efforts," Fisher says. "I went out of my way to never to say anything bad about them, as in hindsight I saw where they were coming from; I understood the mindset. So I immersed myself in the opportunities to interact with others on behalf of forensic science. It happened a long time ago and I have made peace with it. And I came out of it relatively unscathed, and was able to accomplish many more things than if I had been chained to my desk, I never would have attempted and been effective as I was, so, end of story. So I said to hell with it, I can get my jollies elsewhere if they don't recognize what I bring to the position, I will do it for myself. I enjoy politics, I do it well and I get results."

Indeed, Fisher spent two decades as the director of the Los Angeles County Sheriff's Department crime labs and was responsible for conceptualizing, planning, and coordinating the new Los Angeles County Sheriff's Department/Los Angeles Police Department crime lab located at California State University (the Hertzberg-Davis Forensic Science Center), as well as the creation of the California Forensic Science Institute.

As we have seen, the 2009 NAS report identifies a number of issues with forensic science that are directly related to the professionalism, the education and training levels, as well as the certification of practitioners. While acknowledging these forensic scientists' dedication, the NAS report suggests that not all were practicing at a level beyond reproach: "Numerous professionals in the forensic science community and the medical examiner system have worked for years to achieve excellence in their fields, aiming to follow high ethical norms, develop sound professional standards, ensure accurate results in their practices, and improve the processes by which accuracy is determined. Although the work of these dedicated professionals has resulted in significant progress in the forensic science disciplines in recent decades, major challenges still face the forensic science community" (NAS, 2009, page 5).

The 2009 NAS report identified several key flaws related to professionalism in forensic science, including lack of mandatory standardization, certification, and accreditation, citing fragmentation of the field compounded by the fact that "operational principles and procedures for many forensic science disciplines are not standardized or embraced, either between or within jurisdictions. There is no uniformity in the certification of forensic practitioners, or in the accreditation of crime laboratories. Indeed, most jurisdictions do not require forensic practitioners to be certified, and most forensic science disciplines have no mandatory certification programs. Moreover, accreditation of crime laboratories is not required in most jurisdictions. Often there are no standard protocols governing forensic practice in a given discipline. And, even when protocols are in place (e.g., SWG standards), they often are vague and not enforced in any meaningful way. In short, the quality of forensic practice in most disciplines varies greatly because of the absence of adequate training and continuing education, rigorous mandatory certification and accreditation programs, adherence to robust performance standards, and effective oversight. These shortcomings obviously pose a continuing and serious threat to the quality and credibility of forensic science practice" (NAS, 2009).

The report outlined several recommendations addressing professional development–related issues. As we saw in Chapter 2, the 2009 NAS report outlines recommendations for improvement overall, with specific directives for the enhancement of forensic scientists' skills, the solidifying of practitioners' ethics, and the elevation of forensic laboratories.

In Recommendation 7, the 2009 NAS report advises, "Laboratory accreditation and individual certification of forensic science professionals should be mandatory, and all forensic science professionals should have access to a certification process. In determining appropriate standards for accreditation and certification, the National Institute of Forensic Science (NIFS) should take into account established and recognized international standards, such as those published by the International Organization for Standardization (ISO). No person (public or private) should be allowed to practice in a forensic science discipline or testify as a forensic science professional without certification. Certification requirements should include, at a minimum, written examinations, supervised practice, proficiency testing, continuing education, recertification procedures, adherence to a code of ethics, and effective disciplinary procedures. All laboratories and facilities (public or private) should be accredited, and all forensic science professionals should be certified, when eligible, within a time period established by NIFS" (NAS, 2009, page 25).

Let's examine the individual elements of the 2009 NAS report recommendations and improvement efforts for the crime laboratory system.

EDUCATION AND TRAINING OF FORENSIC LABORATORY PERSONNEL

The 2009 NAS report declares, "Forensic examiners must understand the principles, practices and contexts of science, including the scientific method" (NAS, 2009, page 217). It asserts that training should move away from reliance on the apprentice-like transmittal of practices to education at the college level and beyond that is based on scientifically valid principles: "For example, in addition to learning a particular methodology through a lengthy apprenticeship or workshop during which a trainee discerns and learns to copy the skills of an experienced examiner, the junior person should learn what to measure, the associated population statistics (if appropriate), biases and errors to avoid, other threats to the validity of the evidence, how to calculate the probability that a conclusion is valid, and how to document and report the analysis."

The 2009 NAS report emphasizes that forensic science education and training must provide the tools needed to understand the probabilities and the limits of decision making under conditions of uncertainty, and that better undergraduate and graduate programs, coupled with increased opportunities for continuing education, can address and correct existing deficiencies.

Initial education and training in the forensic science disciplines prepares the next generation of forensic practitioners to tackle the rigors of their field, but ongoing professional development and lifelong continuing education ensure that forensic scientists are keeping up with the evolving advances in forensic science techniques and research.

The NIJ reports that in recent years, the demand for forensic scientists has been triggered by numerous factors, including population demographics, increased awareness of forensic science by law enforcement, increased numbers of law enforcement officers, database automation in several categories of physical evidence, jury expectations, legal requirements, accreditation and certification requirements of laboratories and personnel, impending retirement of a large number of currently practicing forensic scientists, and increased public awareness of forensic science through the media. As we will see in Chapter 4, the medicolegal death investigation field is most critical in its need for additional board-certified forensic pathologists. A high-performance education and training machine is needed in the United States in subsequent decades if this demand is to be met.

The 2009 NAS report asserts that inconsistent quality and insufficient funding have impeded the improvement of forensic science education, and observes, "Because, until recently, no nationally recognized, mandated standards existed for forensic science degree programs at any level, consistent quality cannot be achieved" (NAS, 2009, page 224).

The NIJ report, "Forensic Sciences: Review of Status and Needs," called in part for an accreditation system for such programs. Following this report, in 2001, NIJ established a Technical Working Group for Education and Training in Forensic Science (TWGED), consisting of 47 experts, including educators, judges, attorneys, crime laboratory directors, and subject matter scientists, which developed recommended curricular guidelines for undergraduate and graduate forensic science programs. These were provided in a 2004 report. In 2002, the AAFS created an ad hoc committee, the Forensic Education Program Accreditation Committee, to look into issues regarding an accreditation system. The committee was made a standing committee in 2004, at which time the name was changed to the Forensic Science Education Program Accreditation Commission (FEPAC). FEPAC is comprised of five forensic science educators, five crime laboratory directors, and one public member. FEPAC created a process for accrediting undergraduate and graduate forensic science programs using the TWGED standards.

FEPAC standards are divided into three parts; there are general standards that all programs must meet and then additional standards for undergraduate and graduate programs. An important note regarding the accreditation process is that the program must award at least a bachelor's degree in either forensic science or a natural science with a concentration in forensic science at both the bachelor's and master's levels. Programs that award certificates or associate degrees are ineligible for accreditation in this system. Additionally, at this time, only U.S. programs are eligible for accreditation. To summarize the general standards, such programs shall (1) have an explicit process for evaluating and monitoring its overall efforts to fulfill its mission, goals, and objectives; for assessing its effectiveness in serving its various constituencies; for modifying the curriculum as necessary, based on the results of its evaluation activities; and for planning to achieve its mission in the future; (2) have adequate institutional support in the form of financial resources, facilities, instructional, and support services; (3) provide adequate student support services, such as mentoring, advising, and career placement; (4) have policies and procedures for student recruitment and admissions, with advisers to students regarding requirements for employment; (5) have procedures for handling student complaints; and (6) consider the use of distance learning as an instructional technique, demonstrating that all required laboratory experiences are hands-on for all students.

The NIJ (2004, page 185) has defined training as the "formal, structured process through which a forensic scientist reaches a level of scientific knowledge and expertise required to conduct specific forensic analyses." Among its numerous observations about the ways forensic science allegedly has not met expectations by stakeholders is the presumption that forensic examiners in particular have insufficient education and training in order to "understand the principles, practices and contexts of scientific methodology, as well as the distinctive features of their specialty," according to the NAS report. Moving beyond what it called "apprentice-like transmittal of practices to education based on scientifically valid principles," the 2009 NAS report advises—in addition to the practical experience and learning acquired during an internship—that "a trainee should acquire rigorous interdisciplinary education and training in the scientific areas that constitute the basis for the particular forensic discipline and instruction on how to document and report the analysis." The NAS report adds, "A trainee also should have working knowledge of basic quantitative calculations, including statistics and probability, as needed for the applicable discipline."

The committee that produced the 2009 NAS report felt it was essential to correct some of the existing deficiencies by improving undergraduate and graduate forensic science programs. It should be an achievable task, seeing that currently, there are about 40 bachelor's and master's programs in the United States and Canada (Madren, 2013). The 2009 NAS report points to the AAFS's list of 138 undergraduate, 59 graduate, and 6 doctoral forensic science degree programs in the United States and observes, "Not all are science based—many are criminal justice programs. The curricula of these degrees range from rigorous scientific coursework amounting to a degree in chemistry or biology with forensic science content, to little more than criminal justice degrees with an internship" (NAS, 2009, page 223).

As the committee emphasized, "Legitimization of practices in forensic disciplines must be based on established scientific knowledge, principles and practices, which are best learned through formal education. Apprenticeship has a secondary role, and under no circumstances can it supplant the need for the scientific basis of education in and the practice of forensic science. In addition, lawyers and judges often have insufficient training and background in scientific methodology, and they often fail to fully comprehend the approaches employed by different forensic science disciplines and the reliability of forensic science evidence that is offered in trial. Such training is essential, because any checklist for the admissibility of scientific or technical testimony is imperfect. Conformance with items on a checklist can suggest that testimony is reliable, but it does not guarantee it" (NAS, 2009, page 238).

In Recommendation 10, the 2009 NAS report suggested, "To attract students in the physical and life sciences to pursue graduate studies in multidisciplinary fields critical to forensic science practice, Congress should authorize and appropriate funds to the National Institute of Forensic Science (NIFS) to work with appropriate organizations and educational institutions to improve and develop graduate education programs designed to cut across organizational, programmatic, and disciplinary boundaries. To make these programs appealing to potential students, they must include attractive scholarship and fellowship offerings. Emphasis should be placed on developing and improving research methods and methodologies applicable to forensic science practice and on funding research programs to attract research universities and students in fields relevant to forensic science. NIFS should also support law school administrators and judicial education organizations in establishing continuing legal education programs for law students, practitioners and judges" (NAS, 2009, page 239).

The committee also felt that the education process should extend to the stakeholders of forensic science when it noted, "Better connections must be established and promoted between experts in the forensic science disciplines and law schools, legal scholars, and practitioners. The fruits of any advances in the forensic science disciplines should be transferred directly to legal scholars and practitioners (including civil litigators, prosecutors, and criminal defense counsel), federal, state, and local legislators, members of the judiciary, and law enforcement officials, so that appropriate adjustments can be made in criminal and civil laws and procedures, model jury instructions, law enforcement practices, litigation strategies, and judicial decision-making. Law schools should enhance this connection by offering courses in the forensic science disciplines, by offering credit for forensic science courses taken in other colleges, and by developing joint degree programs. And judges need to be better educated in forensic science methodologies and practices" (NAS, 2009).

A better understanding of the current state of forensic science education and training can be achieved by reviewing a brief history. As Palmbach (2013, page 171) explains, "In 1946, Michigan State University took claim to be the first U.S. university to offer a degree program in forensic science. University of Lausanne in Switzerland offered a course in legal photography at the beginning of the 20th century and as such proclaimed to be the oldest academic institution to offer coursework in forensic science. The growth and development of forensic science programs was relatively slow. Even as recent as the late 1980s, the option of forensic science as a collegiate major was relative unknown. There were approximately one dozen American universities that were offering forensic science as a major. Further, most of these programs graduated a handful of students each year from this obscure major."

Palmbach (2013, page 171) adds, "During these early years of forensic science, the expectations of the criminal justice community and scientific limitations of the field created an environment where a major emphasis on formal educational was not necessary. For starters, society simply did not have expectations or demand the interjection of science into crime solving that it has obtained in this current CSI crazed world. A majority of criminal matters were resolved with good old-fashioned police work. Key elements of those investigations included confessions, eye witness testimony, and a solid circumstantial case constructed through investigative efforts. Over the years, it has become apparent that these investigative methods while often successful could also yield false or misleading investigative information. As forensic science began to expand and become available to everyday police work, the focus began to shift toward the scientific answers."

For most of the twentieth century, the availability of forensic science to assist in solving crimes was focused primarily on disciplines outside the direct realm of natural sciences, biology, chemistry, and physics; these included fingerprints, firearms evidence, crime scene photography and evidence collection, and handwriting analysis, says Palmbach (2013). Instead of formal education courses, these pattern-based, identification disciplines were learned under the tutelage of a skilled practitioner, who most often learned in the same manner. "Under this model, it was possible for these fields to further develop and refine their methodologies by simply assessing what works and what does not," Palmbach (2013, page 171) says. "For the most part, what was lacking was an understanding of the fundamental principles upon which these disciplines were based.

Certainly, more complex mechanisms such as the statistical analysis of the data and proper expression of that data were not addressed. Further, a majority of this work was conducted by police agencies, and outside the purview of scientists and researchers."

Palmbach (2013, page 171) explains further, "As disciplines more closely associated with biology or chemistry emerged, the need for academically trained practitioners was evident. Disciplines such as Toxicology and Serology began to expand in both practical application and research. Laboratories at the city, state, and federal levels were created to house these more traditional science specialties. In some jurisdictions, there was a move to merge the traditional services, such as photography and fingerprint analysis, into the emerging laboratories dedicated to chemical and biological-based analysis of physical evidence. Other jurisdictions, some of which still exist, elected to keep the traditional police-based identification disciplines separate from the natural science-based methodologies. During these early and transitional years, the educational requirements for these different positions began to diverge. Many of the practitioners in the police-based disciplines had no more than a high school education, but did possess some professional training and often had very extensive experience within their specialty."

As education and training for forensic practitioners evolved, it was becoming readily apparent that some individuals were still unclear about a straight and direct educational path toward high-level forensic work. As Jackson (2009, page 2) observes, "The higher education system plays an important role in establishing an educated workforce that is both scientifically adept and socially responsible. Graduates entering any law enforcement agency—whether at the county, state, or national level—assume responsibility for enforcing the policies and laws set forth by the relevant governing bodies. As such, it is critical to the success of these agencies that new employees exceed some kind of minimum standard of competence. Educators in the higher education system have a moral obligation to develop this aptitude by ensuring that their graduates receive the appropriate scientific, technical, communicative, and ethical training required for their chosen specialties. Forensic science degrees are publicized by providers as being the fastest route to careers related to criminal law, despite the fact that most employers have little comprehension of what a 'forensic science' degree entails. An unfortunate result of the 'CSI effect' is that many of the high-school graduates that choose forensic science degrees are often ill-equipped to tackle the level of scientific rigor required in the higher-quality programs that seek accreditation by Forensic Science Education Programs Accreditation Commission (FEPAC). As a result, large attrition rates are common in the higher-quality programs as most students switch to non-'hard' science majors."

The common fallacy among college students is that a criminal justice degree provides entry to the forensic field, when in reality, the hard sciences are preferred by forensic laboratories and most certainly required for a career in forensic pathology. As Almirall and Furton (2003, page 1156) note, "Over the years, surveys have repeatedly indicated that lab directors have a preference for applicants with a strong chemistry background." Results of a survey published in the *Journal of Forensic Science* in 1999 (Furton et al. 1999) reinforce that the majority of crime lab directors require applicants to have BS degrees with a preference for chemistry/biochemistry, followed by biology and forensic science with a requirement for a substantial number of chemistry and other natural science courses. According to the survey, the summary of degrees required for all positions combined was 63 percent BS, 27 percent BA, 6 percent none, 3 percent MS, and 1 percent PhD. The degree specialty required was 41 percent chemistry (including biochemistry), 24 percent biology (including genetics and molecular biology), 22 percent forensic science, 7 percent medical laboratory science, and 6 percent other (including 2 percent physics and 1 percent criminal justice).

Results of a 1986 survey to the membership of the ASCLD showed that the educational background most preferred for a career in forensic science would consist of a BS degree that has a major chemistry component and an MS in forensic science. Additional comments also suggested the need for a strong background in chemistry and a general disdain for the BS in forensic science as the terminal degree unless it has a strong hard science component (Siegel, 1988).

Almirall and Furton (2003, page 1157) point to what they call a "steady requirement of a significant scientific background for applicants, with an increasingly high expectation for areas such as criminalistics." They add, "In the past, crime scene investigators and firearms examiners routinely were sworn officers with A.A. degrees; current successful applicants are now more likely to have B.S. or M.S. science degrees. While individual professional aspirations will determine the level of education a student will pursue, it is apparent that the trend in forensic science practice includes graduate studies, especially for those practitioners interested in advanced technical positions."

Retired forensic science educator Jay Siegel, PhD, whom we first met in Chapter 2, has seen the trend firsthand. "Early on at Michigan State, we got a lot of students who thought the path to forensic science was through criminal justice," he confirms. "They would go get their degree in criminal justice and then the laboratories would tell them. 'We are looking for scientists—go back and get your chemistry degree.' Thankfully that has decreased over the years because people are realizing that this is real science and the popularity of DNA typing has really helped to elevate the public consciousness that this is real science—it isn't criminology and policing. So I have witnessed a gradual increase in people's awareness of the scientific underpinnings needed for lab work. During my last few years at Indiana, we got very few students out of criminal justice who wanted to major in forensic science. We have seen growth in the number of forensic science programs at universities and that causes its own problems because many of them started out as a criminal justice program with an internship in the crime lab and they called themselves 'forensic scientists' so it really was caveat emptor—let the buyer beware when you sign up for a forensic science program. That has been radically changed over the last decade through the accreditation process by the AAFS and ASCLD's forensic science education accreditation commission which assembled forensic scientists and crime lab directors to develop a set of standards for bachelor's and master's programs and determined what kind of background a student will need to prepare themselves for a career in forensic science. These criteria are quite strict, and not everyone will be able to meet the accreditation standards; there are probably a few dozen programs that are accredited now. It's great because it has put a lot of charlatan programs out of business."

Siegel continues, "The bottom line is that we need to ensure students are receiving a solid education. I was a charter member of this education and accreditation commission and I thought it worked extremely well to help wean people off the idea that forensic science is a social science."

Variable levels of education and training were addressed in a 1999 National Institute of Justice (NIJ) report, "Forensic Sciences: Review of Status and Needs," which indicated that the training needs of the forensic community were "immense." The report also recommended the funding of "accredited academic institutions" (NIJ, 1999). As Jackson (2009, page 4) notes, "Because accreditation with standard-setting bodies did not exist in 1999, the report suggested the establishment of an accreditation body, such as a technical working group, which could help set national standards to accredit or certify academic forensic training programs. Following these recommendations, NIJ funded WVU to help establish the TWGED, which first met in the summer of 2001. With contributions from

49 forensic practitioners, educators and members of governing bodies, NIJ published guidelines on the educational and training aspects of forensic science in order to serve educational institutions, students and laboratories."

In 2002, the AAFS established FEPAC to continue the work of the TWGED by organizing an accreditation commission for academic programs in forensic science. According to Almirall and Furton (2003), FEPAC's goals included maintaining and enhancing the quality of forensic science education through a formal evaluation and recognition of college-level academic programs.

To help clear up a number of issues and to put forth a series of recommendations for institutions of higher learning and other stakeholders, in 2004, NIJ published a document, "Education and Training in Forensic Sciences; A Guide for Forensic Science Laboratories, Educational Institutions and Students." The document was produced by the NIJ's TWGED, tasked with developing consensus guidelines for academic programs in forensic science. The group, composed of approximately 45 practitioners, laboratory directors, forensic science educators, and others, intended to assist academic institutions that are planning to offer new programs of study with a description of the minimum curricula expectations determined by a consensus of experts.

Palmbach (2013, page 172) says of the 2004 NIJ report, "The primary finding was that educational programs in forensic science must have a strong background in natural sciences and include extensive laboratory coursework. Students in graduate programs can transit from theoretical concepts to discipline-specific knowledge, and should contain a substantial research component. In addition to articulating curriculum requirements, this report addressed other qualifications necessary for a career in forensic science. Future candidates were informed of the need for personal integrity and honesty, and that they would likely be required to submit to extensive background tests and perhaps drug testing. In addition, credit history, driving record, past work performance, medical exams, and polygraph examination may all play a factor in their hiring process. Finally, these recommendations articulated what a model forensic science program would look like and what were the necessary resources, for example, faculty and facilities required to accomplish this mission."

The 2004 NIJ report outlines a detailed sample curriculum for all forensic science undergraduate programs and includes a natural science core, specialized science core courses, forensic science course work, forensic science laboratory courses, and additional upper-level course work. A recommended natural science core consisted of general biology, general chemistry, organic chemistry, physics, calculus, and statistics. A specialized core could provide instruction according to focus; for example, a biology track program would offer biochemistry, genetics, instrumental analysis, and molecular biology. A chemistry track would require quantitative chemistry, inorganic chemistry, instrumental analysis, and physical chemistry. Other mandatory courses encompassed an introduction to the law and justice system; ethics; professional practice; an overview or forensic science survey course; evidence identification, collection, and processing; quality assurance; courtroom testimony; as well as technical and scientific writing. Additional credit hours were dedicated to a laboratory component, plus a relevant internship experience. Finally, students were required to take an additional 19 credit hours that would give them greater depth in their specific concentration, such as criminal justice, legal evidence, and public speaking. Biology track students would take cell biology, microbiology, population genetics, and immunology. Chemistry-based students would take advanced instrumental analysis, drugs, analytical toxicology, materials science, and pharmacology.

Graduate programs in forensic science must require a baccalaureate degree in forensic science or a natural science. Education at this level should move beyond theoretical concepts and provide students with critical thinking ability, problem-solving skills, and advanced discipline-specific knowledge. Consistent with other science-based graduate programs, these forensic science programs need to incorporate a research component. Regardless of their specific focus, a forensic science graduate program should contain curricula that address the following topics: crime scenes; physical evidence concepts; law/science interface; ethics and professional responsibility; quality assurance; as well as additional specific courses that would address analytical chemistry and instrumental analysis, drug chemistry, microscopy, forensic biology, and pattern evidence.

Not all forensic education is created equal, however. Released within a year of each other, two reports criticized UK academic institutions for an apparent exploitation of students' interest in forensic science by offering less-than-rigorous courses more befitting an extension program for the lay community. In 2004, the Science, Engineering, Manufacturing and Technology Alliance (SEMTA) report "Forensic Science: Implications for Higher Education" was published, followed by the 2005 House of Commons Select Committee on Science and Technology seventh report, "Forensic Science on Trial," which stated the following:

> A search of the Universities and Colleges Admission Service website for "forensic" undergraduate courses produces a list of 401 degree courses at 57 universities. These range from "Forensic Science" through to; Forensic Science and Human Resource Management … and "Citizenship Studies and Forensic Science" … the expansion in provision of forensic science degrees does not reflect the limited employment prospects in forensic science nor is it in response to employers in the sector; rather, the growth was a result of student interest in forensic science, which was, at least in part, stimulated by television dramas featuring forensic scientists and high profile coverage of forensic science in books and by the media. (page 43)

Daeid (2008, page 59) says the 2005 UK report noted that these courses "provided poor preparation for a career in forensic science" and were "a savage waste of young people's time and parents' money … degree courses and other higher education opportunities [were] of widely differing standards and content, often hybrid in order to attract a wide range of students, often unsuited to the needs of employers, and sometimes encouraging unrealistic employment expectations among students."

Daeid (2008, page 59) says the 2005 UK report also emphasized the fact that, while the number of forensic science and related courses were increasing, the numbers of science courses (chemistry and physics in particular) were decreasing, and observes, "Unfortunately this decline has to a certain extent continued in the three years since the select committee report was issued. Some have advocated that the continued success of 'forensic' named courses should be capitalized upon and that it should be possible to 'teach science through forensic science.' On reflection, I have a number of problems with this statement. On the one hand, forensic science is perhaps a useful media by which to encourage students' interest in the fundamental sciences, but (in my view) one cannot become a competent forensic scientist without first becoming a competent scientist in the specific field of study. In its most fundamental form, forensic science is an application of scientific knowledge, skills, practice and evaluation, not a fundamental field of study in its own right."

As we have seen, U.S. forensic organizations prefer degrees in the hard sciences; the situation is similar in the United Kingdom, as Daeid (2008, page 60) explains, "The general consensus of the 2005 Select Committee report was that both forensic science and other science employers considered a degree in chemistry or some other pure science to be preferable to a degree in forensic science. While these were general comments and there were also a number of institutions praised for the quality of their 'forensic' degree programs and the resultant employment of their graduates within the sector. Also of interest was that at around the same time [2004/2005] similar discussions were taking place with the U.S. and Australian higher education and forensic science sectors which were facing a similar, though not quite as dramatic, issue in relation to the growth of forensic science courses in their own countries."

Since that 2005 UK report, Daeid (2008, page 60) reports that the select committee identified 401 undergraduate degree courses at 57 institutions and notes, "More than 20 percent of the 320 UK higher and further education providers now offer an undergraduate course with 'forensic' in the title. So much for the 'forensic education' bubble bursting! ... Probably a more concerning development is that since 2004–05, the number of UK postgraduate courses with 'forensic' in the title has grown from around 15 to 112 available for the next academic year offered by no less than 47 higher education institutions. The cynic within me wonders whether this has occurred as a direct response to the forensic science providers' comments within the Select Committee report which made the point that the forensic science education for prospective employees should be at postgraduate level."

The United Kingdom continued to wrestle with the issue, according to Daeid (2008). In 2006, the United Kingdom Forensic Science Education Group (UKFSEG) was established to provide a link between academic institutions and forensic science providers and trainers. The Forensic Science Advisory Council (FSAC), established in 2007, highlighted the importance of interacting with the higher education sector. The 2005 select committee recommended that the Forensic Science Society establish a higher education accreditation scheme for the forensic science component of undergraduate courses; eventually, this has been expanded to cover postgraduate degree provision.

Cassella (2008), in a rebuttal to Daeid (2008), notes, "Clearly, 10 years ago now, when the public interest in forensic science directed failing science courses to adapt their content and create new courses, it was done with a degree of haste as nationally, we watched reports of student numbers falling-off from the traditional courses such as chemistry, biology and physics. However, universities are well versed in course construction and delivery and have strict guidelines for course structure and review of the quality assurance systems for provision, delivery and assessment" (page 197).

Cassella (2008, pages 197–198) adds that "the future is very positive for students and the educational provision of forensic science in the UK" and points to the role that higher education will play in addressing research needs: "Forensic Science is a maturing discipline where the research is beginning to blossom. Can the forensic science (practitioner) community claim the same rigor to its research as is undertaken and published by universities? One only has to look how many criminal cases have collapsed due to the 'unauthenticated' forensic science research? The forensic science community should be working in conjunction with HEIs to improve the quality of forensic science research instead of criticizing it and in doing so preventing further development to the benefit of everyone. If we as a joint industry cannot be positive and forward thinking, then the outdated naval-gazing attitude will be the biggest 'criminal' in forensic science provision in the UK."

The education landscape in the United Kingdom will continue to evolve now that privatization has impacted forensic science there, as we will explore further in Chapter 6.

Back in the United States, a new education paradigm has been proposed. On December 8, 2015, by more than a two-thirds majority vote, members of the National Commission on Forensic Science's (NCFS's) Training on Science and Law Subcommittee voted to adopt a recommendation, "Forensic Science Curriculum Development." In this document, the NCFS recommends that the attorney general fund the creation of a fair and balanced national curriculum on forensic science issues expected to be brought before courts, and that this curriculum should be completed within one year. The NCFS said this curriculum should be developed initially for judges and lawyers but with a design permitting future adaptability to other audiences such as forensic science service providers (FSSPs), law enforcement, and victims' advocates.

The NCFS justifies its recommendation based on two existing conditions: "First is what has been described as the law's 'heavy reliance' on forensic evidence. The second is at the heart of this proposal: the inability of the consumers of this evidence, be they judges or lawyers, to properly assess and apply this information" (NCFS, 2015). As the NCFS explains, "The judicial system is encumbered by, among other things, judges and lawyers who generally lack the scientific expertise necessary to comprehend and evaluate forensic evidence in an informed manner, trial judges (sitting alone) who must decide evidentiary issues without the benefit of judicial colleagues and often with little time for extensive research and reflection, and the highly deferential nature of the appellate review afforded trial courts' Daubert rulings."

Citing the 2009 NAS report's Recommendation 10, which urges that a national forensic institute "support law school administrators and judicial education organizations in establishing continuing legal education programs for law students, practitioners, and judges," the NCFS asserts, "Ample data and anecdotal evidence confirm that the expert witness rules are not well understood by the legal community or forensic science stakeholders" (Moreno, 2003, page 239).

There are many organizations committed to training stakeholders on issues of law and science, including the American Bar Association (ABA), the Federal Judicial College, the AAFS, many state organizations, and graduate schools as well as other institutions. However, the NCFS notes, "There is no uniform curriculum, standardized training model, or set of training material on a national level that can be easily accessed" (NCFS, 2015, page 89).

To be perceived as neutral, the NCFS says, "A national curriculum must be developed by scientific entities independent of prosecutors and defense attorneys—in particular, entities such as the National Institute of Standards and Technology (NIST) and the Organization of Scientific Area Committees (OSAC), the American Association for the Advancement of Science (AAAS), and the National Academy of Sciences (NAS)." The NCFS says the proposed curriculum should include but not be limited to the following:

- The law governing expert opinion and scientific and technical evidence
- Probabilities and statistics
- An articulation of the strengths and limitations of the analysis of forensic evidence, including forensic medicine
- Issues concerning quality assurance, and FSSP and forensic medicine service provider management, accreditation, and certification
- Issues related to human factors
- Specific forensic and social science disciplines likely to come before the courts

The NCFS indicated that this proposed national curriculum must be assessed for its effectiveness as a teaching tool once drafted and again after its implementation.

In August 2015, ASCLD provided comments on the Initial Draft Recommendation on Developing a National Forensic Science Curriculum, to help build consensus and address areas of concern. ASCLD noted that the document states that the curriculum must only be developed by research scientists and/or academics, and commented, "This would be irresponsible based on the amount of misinformation and genuine misunderstanding that exists regarding the forensic sciences" (ASCLD, 2015).

The document states, "To be perceived as neutral a national curriculum must be developed by entities independent of the Department of Justice—in particular NIST, AAAS, and NAS" (ASCLD, 2015). ASCLD comments, "The development of an effective, transparent and comprehensive national forensic science curriculum should include many stakeholders with different relevant areas of expertise. Practitioners from the major forensic science disciplines including controlled substances, trace evidence, latent prints, firearms/toolmarks, forensic biology, digital evidence and crime scene as well forensic laboratory managers should be consulted. Additionally, the NAS report specifically cites the need for forensic scientists to be involved in the development and delivery of these education programs ... A comprehensive program should also include investigators, prosecutors, defense attorneys, judges, academics and applicable researchers."

In addition, ASCLD notes, "In order to develop a comprehensive and meaningful forensic science training and education program for criminal justice practitioners, ASCLD urges the Commission to consider the value that forensic science service providers and corresponding professional organizations such as ASCLD, AAFS, IAI, etc. bring to the development of these programs. Without the involvement of relevant experts from the professions at the focus of the program, the education program will be deficient in addressing the intended need as identified in the 2009 NAS report on education in the legal system" (ASCLD, 2015).

While the proposed curriculum targeted the stakeholders in the judicial system, ASCLD pointed out, "The recommendations by the Commission do not address a similar program for law enforcement officials as they are also in need of the same level of education and training about forensic science. In particular, law enforcement officers are often the first responders and responsible for the initial identification, collection, and preservation of crime scene evidence. Without a fundamental understanding of forensic science, law enforcement officials may be under-resourced to adequately accomplish this task" (ASCLD, 2015). ASCLD also emphasized the importance of funding "at appropriate levels to be adopted not only at the federal level, but also at the state and local levels where most forensic science is practiced and admitted into trials for use by law enforcement and legal professionals. Without appropriate levels of funding, no training beyond what currently exists at the state and local levels will be effective at meeting the needs of the legal community."

With an eye toward future educational needs of forensic scientists, Palmbach (2013, page 174) observes, "Given the recommendations of the NAS report, and need for the forensic science community to further study existing methodologies as well as properly validate emerging technologies, the need for quality education will only increase. In the early years of forensic science, up until around 1980s, many practitioners had only a high school education and some on-the-job training. As forensic laboratories grew in scope and function, bench scientists commonly entered the field with a natural science or forensic science baccalaureate degrees and more commonly master of science degrees. As research increases to address these key issues, more PhDs will be necessary to conduct and mentor the appropriate level of research and scholarly inquiry. Currently, the United States educational system is not offering a doctor of philosophy degree in forensic science. Those with PhDs working in forensic science laboratories and teaching in forensic science programs generally possess earned doctorates in analytical chemistry, toxicology, molecular or cell biology, or a similar scientific discipline. There are some criminal justice or criminology programs that offer earned doctorate degrees in which the focus is a forensic science discipline. It is still too early to predict how many institutions will elect to develop a pure forensic science doctorate."

Palmbach (2013, page 174) adds, "The demand for scholarly research, need to develop and integrate new technologies, and a very competitive employment picture, all bode well for the educational community dedicated to educating current and future forensic scientists."

At some point in his or her education, an aspiring forensic scientist would most likely have read a book penned by Richard Saferstein, PhD, one of the more prolific forensic experts who have authored seminal textbooks and technical papers in the field.

In 1977, Saferstein's widely used introductory textbook, *Criminalistics: An Introduction to Forensic Science*, was published. Currently in its 12th edition, the text is considered to be one of the classics and is instrumental to establishing a forensic practitioner's mastery of key principles and concepts. His other titles include *Basic Laboratory Exercises for Forensic Science* and *Lab Manual for Criminalistics*. He has also edited the reference books *Forensic Science Handbook, Volume 1*; *Forensic Science Handbook, Volume 2*; and *Forensic Science Handbook, Volume 3*. Saferstein has also authored the book *Forensic Science: From the Crime Scene to the Crime Lab,* in which he presents forensic science in a straightforward, student-friendly format for students with limited backgrounds in the sciences. He also has authored or coauthored more than 45 technical papers covering a variety of forensic topics.

"I was an organic chemist doctoral student and was exposed to all fields of organic chemistry and whenever there was an issue of new development, there was a monograph that came off the presses quickly to deal with controversial issues in organic chemistry," Saferstein recalls. "So there was always some kind of reference material available. But when I walked into the classroom at Trent State College to teach an introductory course in forensic science, there was no textbook and a lightbulb went off in my head. I thought to myself, 'I'm going to write a basic book in forensic science' because it didn't exist at the time. I had discipline as a doctoral student and chemist, and I had always been a good communicator in the courtroom regarding my findings. I don't like to intimidate or show off, I like to bring it down to a street level, so to speak, but at the same time I want to educate—so the book was a compromise between the two. I spent many days deciding what I should write and what to leave out, what to touch on lightly or deeply; the choices are many, and I guess they were good ones because the book has held up pretty well."

"The pinnacle of my career has been writing that standard textbook in forensic science," Saferstein adds. "In my mind, it's a significant accomplishment and I am proud of it. And when it enters its 12th edition, as it is doing this year, clearly people are interested in it and feel as strongly about it as I do." Saferstein says he is approached frequently by people who have read his books and want to share their reactions to it. "One of my fondest memories is being at a forensic science meeting in an elevator when a woman joined me and recognized my name from the name tag I was wearing," he recalls. "This young lady says to me, 'Aren't you the guy who wrote that book?' And I said I was. She said to me, 'I want to tell you if it wasn't for you and your book, I wouldn't be here.' When I walked off the elevator, I thought, 'Forget about awards or anything else, as that was the supreme accolade to me.'"

Sharing his knowledge with others has come naturally to Saferstein, who, from 1972 to 1991, taught an introductory forensic science course in the criminal justice programs at the College of New Jersey and at Ocean County College. As for his educational background, Saferstein holds degrees from the City College of New York and earned his doctorate degree in chemistry in 1970 from the City University of New York.

But what he may be most known for, books aside, is his 21-year tenure as the chief forensic scientist of the New Jersey State Police laboratory, one of the largest crime laboratories in the United States. Each year, this laboratory conducts more than 35,000 case analyses using a staff of 85 scientists.

"It was an exciting time to be a forensic scientist," Saferstein says. "I always thought of myself as an organic chemist and so I was very much interested in mass spectrometry as well as other techniques that were being applied in the 1970s in crime laboratories. It was exciting to be involved in not so much developing technology but implementing it, something from which I derived the most satisfaction. I was always thinking about how could I make my laboratory the most viable, both technically and economically, because I always faced making choices and financial decisions. It was an exhilarating time and I always felt, from the very beginning of my career, that I had a knack for identifying technologies that would be useful and applicable to forensic science; I don't think a lot of people had that knack as much as I did. I enjoyed visiting other labs outside of New Jersey and asking about equipment and ascertaining if that would be useful for our work, and often it was."

Saferstein began his career at the New Jersey State Police laboratory in 1970 and retired in 1991, but that was just the beginning of a long and successful career as an expert witness for attorneys and as a consultant to the media in the area of forensic science. Saferstein has served as an expert witness more than 2000 times in nearly 150 federal and state courts involving a variety of forensic issues. His areas of expertise encompass breath and blood testing for alcohol; pharmacological effects of alcohol and drugs; detection and identification of drugs in biological fluids; arson-related analysis; and the forensic examination of blood, semen, hair, paint, fiber, and glass evidence. His expertise includes the review and evaluation of forensic DNA evidence. During the O.J. Simpson criminal trial, Saferstein provided extensive commentary on forensic aspects of the case for the *Rivera Live* show, the E! television network, ABC radio, and various radio talk shows.

His career has been high profile, but Saferstein says he chalks it up to serendipity. "When I graduated with a baccalaureate degree, I filled out an application with the U.S. Treasury, not seeking a job in forensics but getting a job, period," Saferstein says. "I wound up working for them, then went to graduate school for my PhD and then was made aware of the opening for the chief of the state police in New Jersey. Back then, not many people had a PhD in forensics and I had some background working for the Treasury, so I did testify and I was familiar with forensic concepts so I was sort of a rare bird, so to speak. They were looking for a chief and they gave me the job. It was totally unplanned."

Saferstein continues, "Despite how I landed in the field, it was never just a job for me; forensic science was a profession I loved from day one. When conducting my doctoral research, I was never into theoretical research, I did work in chromatography, and I was always thinking about applied analytical chemistry so when I walked into the forensic field it was made for me. I knew this was what I wanted for my life's work. It was such a perfect match and I felt fortunate because most people don't have that kind of experience."

Experts' reputations sometimes live and die by the cases they pursue, but Saferstein says he takes a pragmatic view of his casework. "I have a rule that whenever I am working a case, particularly if I am called to testify, I never ever call to follow up on what happened with that case. I just don't want to get into a win-or-lose mentality," he says. "Sometimes surprisingly, when we do win, the attorney will call me, but that happens very infrequently. I don't seek it out. I just move on to the next case and do the best job I can. I think the most important attribute to have as a consultant is being able to communicate to the jury effectively. I feel I am able to accomplish that when I testify. I rarely feel hostility even though in the courtroom I can get grilled aggressively. I enjoy that because when I testify I have my ducks in a row and have nothing to hide, and so I have nothing to fear and I am comfortable in my testimony."

Serendipity seemed to follow Saferstein throughout his early career. "When I was asked to teach a course as an adjunct professor, there wasn't even a text available," he says. "So I wrote the *Criminalistics* book. So from the very beginning it was a mutual admiration society between me and forensic science, and it still is. I have been retired for 25 years but I am still involved as a consultant and work with attorneys. It keeps me connected to the field I love." He adds, "I am going to be 75 soon and I'm surprised how many of my contemporaries have dropped out of the field or retired. I am still going and I enjoy it. It's the love of my life—that and my wife," he says with a laugh. "I know people retire, but why should one leave if you love it so much? It does take some effort to remain in the field, however; to stay sharp in this profession, it requires reading the scientific literature and staying up to date and apprising yourself of current technologies and techniques by reading voraciously. Maybe when I don't want to read this stuff anymore, that will be the time I know it's best to throw in the towel. But I have not gotten to that stage yet."

CERTIFICATION OF FORENSIC LABORATORY PERSONNEL

Numerous professions require that practitioners be certified, and the 2009 NAS report states, "The certification of individuals complements the accreditation of laboratories for a total quality assurance program" (NAS, 2009, page 208). Although the accreditation process primarily addresses the management system, technical methods, and quality of the work of a laboratory (which includes the education and training of staff), certification is a process specifically designed to ensure the competency of the individual examiner.

The ABA has recommended that certification standards be required of examiners, including "demanding written examinations, proficiency testing, continuing education, recertification procedures, an ethical code, and effective disciplinary procedures" (page 208).

In addition to improving quality, certification programs can enhance the credibility of certificate holders, and the concept has been generally embraced by the forensic science community. ASCLD recommends that laboratory managers support peer certification programs that promote professionalism and provide objective standards. In 2002, the Technical Working Group on Forensic Science Education recommended certification of an individual's competency by an independent peer-based organization, if available, from a certifying body with appropriate credentials.

The AAFS formed a Forensic Specialties Accreditation Board to accredit certifying organizations, and accredited boards include the American Board of Criminalistics (ABC), the American Board of Forensic Document Examiners, the American Board of Forensic Toxicology, the American Board of Medicolegal Death Investigators, the Board of Forensic Document Examiners, and the International Institute of Forensic Engineering Sciences. Each of these entities has specific educational, training, and experience requirements, including a series of competency tests—both written and practical—and participation in proficiency testing, and provides continuing education/active participation by means of publication, presentation, and membership in professional organizations.

Certification is one way that forensic scientists can prove that they are competent to perform evidence analysis within their expertise. Although this is a critical way to demonstrate to a court that they are worthy of consideration as expert witnesses, Houck and Siegel (2015, page 664) acknowledge that in the United States, "there is no universal mandatory requirement for either certification or accreditation. Although about 90 percent of the public forensic science laboratories are accredited, the process is voluntary. Likewise, no mandatory requirement exists for forensic scientists to be certified, although there are voluntary programs set up for various forensic science disciplines. The issue of mandatory certification raises many questions, such as acceptance of certifying bodies, who pays for the certifications (which travel with the employee), and what to do about disciplines with no certifications."

Let's take a look at the current system of quality control in forensic science. In terms of quality assurance, there are two main safeguards—the certification of the forensic analyst and the accreditation of the forensic laboratory. In 1989, the ABC was formed to provide analyst certification, and in 1991, ASCLD and the criminalistics section of the AAFS had joined as members. In 1993, certification went national with the first round of testing offered, giving the analyst diplomate status—to advance to fellow, a second written examination had to be passed as well as a laboratory proficiency test. In 2007, exams were attuned to individual specialties. Lab accreditation has its roots in the 1970s, when ASCLD took shape; the charter was approved in 1974, and the first accreditation standards were applied in 1982 by the Laboratory Accreditation Board, a segment of ASCLD.

The mechanisms of quality control applied to the forensic science field are embodied within several entities, most notably the International Standards Organization (ISO); the U.S. representative of the ISO is the American National Standards Institute (ANSI). Within the analytical and forensic communities, guidance for the procedures is provided by entities such as the American Society of Testing and Materials (ASTM) International, the AAFS, and the ASCLD. Playing a key role is NIST, founded in 1901 as part of the Department of Commerce. NIST promotes the standardization of weights and measures to serve science, commerce, and technology and provide reference materials.

Critics assert that measures currently in place do not ensure quality systems. As Gabel (2014, pages 303–304) observes, "As with the individual forensic disciplines, crime labs also lack any cohesive set of mandatory standards. Depending on the crime lab, this creates a quality control issue. The crime lab accreditation process—which implies reviews, testing, and audits—is, at best, voluntary and, at worst, a charitable endowment."

The 2009 NAS report notes the lack of standards for lab management and administration. Specifically, it observes, "There is no uniformity in the certification of forensic practitioners, or in the accreditation of crime laboratories. Indeed, most jurisdictions do not require forensic practitioners to be certified, and most forensic science disciplines have no mandatory certification programs. Moreover, accreditation of crime laboratories is not required in most jurisdictions. Often there are no standard protocols governing forensic practice in a given discipline. And, even when protocols are in place ... they often are vague and not enforced in any meaningful way. History demonstrates that if a lab produces errors (on any scale), it is unlikely to affect its accreditation from ASCLD/LAB" (NAS, 2009, page 6).

PROFICIENCY TESTING OF FORENSIC LABORATORY PERSONNEL

Proficiency testing with teeth to it is another quality assurance vehicle that has been proposed for crime lab personnel. As the 2009 NAS report observes, "Although many forensic science disciplines have engaged in proficiency testing for the past several decades, several courts have noted that proficiency testing in some disciplines is not sufficiently rigorous" (NAS, 2009, page 206).

There are several types of proficiency tests, with the primary distinction among them being whether the examiner is aware that he or she is being tested (an open or declared test) or does not realize that the sample presented for analysis is a test sample and not a real case (a blind test). Tests can be generated externally, by another laboratory (sometimes called an interlaboratory test), or internally. Another type of testing involves random case reanalysis, in which an examiner's completed prior casework is randomly selected for reanalysis by a supervisor or another examiner.

Interlaboratory testing can be conducted to determine the performance of individual laboratories for specific tests or measurements and to monitor laboratories' continuing performance. It can also help to identify problems in laboratories and initiate remedial actions, which may be related to personnel performance or the calibration of instrumentation. Additionally, it can determine the performance characteristics of a method, establish the effectiveness and comparability of new tests or measurement methods, or assign values to reference materials and assess their suitability for use in specific tests or measurement procedures. As the 2009 NAS report points out, blind proficiency testing is recommended, but not required, by ASCLD/LAB as a more precise test of a worker's accuracy. Initially, mandatory blind testing was proposed as part of the federal DNA Identification Act. A DOJ panel designed blind tests, evaluated them, and estimated that it would cost $500,000 to $1 million annually for one test per laboratory. In appropriate circumstances, the NAS report suggests, proficiency testing should include blind testing.

One of the means by which ASCLD/LAB monitors compliance is by reviewing proficiency testing reports submitted by approved test providers. According to the 2002 BJS census, 33,274 of the 351 publicly funded laboratories at the time were engaged in proficiency testing. Proficiency testing was slightly less common among smaller laboratories and those serving municipal jurisdictions. Among the laboratories engaged in proficiency testing, almost all use declared tests. Slightly more than half engaged in proficiency testing use random case reanalysis. Twenty-six percent of the laboratories engaged in proficiency testing use blind tests. In addition, the BJS survey reported that almost all laboratories engaged in proficiency testing used tests that were generated externally (thus allowing comparative analysis). In addition to external tests, 74 percent of laboratories engaged in proficiency testing also used internally generated tests. Data on proficiency testing were not collected for the 2005 census.

Welsh and Aitchison (2013, page 185) say, "The skills, knowledge, and understanding required to do a role are evidenced consistently over time through performance in the workplace." It stands to reason that standards of competence can be used effectively across forensic science people and processes to ensure that staff are recruited, trained, developed, promoted, and professionally recognized throughout their career. Welsh and Aitchison (2013, page 185) emphasize that "occupational competence is more than just the skills required for the job" and that there are four subcategories of skills, knowledge, and understanding: (1) technical competence, or the occupational skills and knowledge required to be effective in a specific function and/or role; (2) managing the work process, or the ability to manage overall organizational processes such as planning, monitoring quality, and solving problems; (3) working relationships, particularly managing relationships with internal and external colleagues and customers; and managing (4) the work environment, including ethics, values, behaviors, and quality.

Welsh and Aitchison (2013, page 185) add, "Staff competence can be achieved through embedding nationally agreed standards of competence across the organization's systems and people processes." They explain, "Standards of competence, in relation to personnel in an organization, are developed to define key activities that make up the functions and roles of an organization and usually wider than this, a sector. These standards define what is required in relation to the skills, knowledge, and understanding for staff to perform effectively and consistently." Additionally, "Standards of competence must describe competent performance in terms of outcomes of an individual's work and the skills, knowledge, and understanding they need to perform effectively and consistently. They allow for clear assessment of competence and should be nationally agreed, developed for a sector, through consultation with employers in that sector across a range of workplace activities, and the different circumstances these activities require for a role. In this way, defining outcomes rather than the steps taken to achieve the outcome provides the necessary flexibility to meet the needs of individuals."

Kolowski et al. (2016) analyzed data from a proficiency test provider from 2008 to 2015 to see if laboratories were increasing proficiency testing by examining enrollment numbers and the return rate of the completed proficiency tests. Noting a key difference in domestic and international laboratories, additional data from the period of 2004–2015 was analyzed to examine the return rate of proficiency tests against the percentage of reports released to accreditation bodies. All of the data were reviewed to see if the 2009 NAS report's recommendations were being enacted by looking for an increasing number of accredited laboratories enrolling in proficiency tests, returning the test results, and reporting the proficiency testing outcomes to accrediting bodies in the period following 2009–2010. Kolowski et al. (2016) report that despite the recommendations put forward by the National Academies for increased accreditation, certification, and as a result, proficiency testing, the current data from proficiency test enrollment and return rate do not show a marked increase in proficiency testing in U.S.-based forensic laboratories, but do reflect an increase in the ratio of proficiency test results submitted to support accreditation for the laboratories.

Around the same time, on December 22, 2015, the ASCLD offered its views for consideration by the Interim Solutions Subcommittee of the NCFS for the "Proficiency Testing in Forensic Science" document. While ASCLD's board said it supported the document in its entirety, it expressed concerns "with the fiscal impact to those providers who are not currently participating in a regular program of proficiency testing. To address this concern, two questions must be answered: First, how many individual forensic examiners would be subject to a mandatory requirement and second, what is the cost to provide proficiency testing to all of them?" (ASCLD, 2016).

ASCLD acknowledged several key challenges and made appropriate recommendations. A main issue ASCLD identified was a lack of consensus as to the total number of FSSPs in the United States: "A comprehensive study determining the number of FSSPs would allow for an estimation of the fiscal impact for all FSSPs to implement proficiency testing. The criminal justice community must ensure appropriate resources are available for this endeavor" (ASCLD, 2016). As a recommendation, ASCLD suggested that the NCFS recommend the attorney general place dedicated funding for implementing proficiency testing of state and local FSSPs in the DOJ budget recommendation to the president, adding, "The magnitude of the funding request should be responsive to the results of the BJS Census of Publicly Funded Crime Laboratories currently in progress. It is important to note, however, that existing grant funding for forensic laboratories such as the Paul Coverdell grant should not be supplanted by monies made available for this recommendation" (ASCLD, 2016).

On March 16, 2016, the NCFS approved the "Proficiency Testing in Forensic Science" document; it is a key development with implications for accreditation, as proficiency testing is required of all accredited FSSPs (the NCFS had previously adopted the policy recommendation on the universal accreditation of all FSSPs). Calling it a "recognized quality control tool," the NCFS says proficiency testing should also be implemented by nonaccredited FSSPs in disciplines where proficiency tests are available from external organizations.

As the NCFS emphasizes, "Proficiency testing is one mechanism through which the performance of an organization can be checked to confirm its ability to adhere to the organization's procedures ... Proficiency testing is a quality control tool that is available to FSSPs and can be utilized prior to achieving accreditation" (ASCLD, 2016).

"ISO/IEC 17043:2010 Conformity Assessment—General Requirements for Proficiency Testing" identifies proficiency testing as an evaluation of participant performance against preestablished criteria by means of interlaboratory comparisons for the determination of laboratory performance. ISO/IEC 17043 states that the purposes of proficiency testing include evaluation of the performance of laboratories for specific tests or measurements and monitoring laboratories' continuing performance; identification of problems in laboratories and initiation of actions for improvement, which, for example, may be related to inadequate test or measurement procedures, effectiveness of staff training and supervision, or calibration of equipment; establishment of the effectiveness and comparability of test or measurement methods; identification of interlaboratory differences; education of participating laboratories based on the outcomes of such comparisons; as well as the validation of uncertainty claims.

The NCFS explains that there are different types of proficiency testing programs; in the most comprehensive form, proficiency testing involves four distinct entities: the proficiency test participant (FSSP and practitioner), the proficiency test provider, bodies that accredit the FSSPs, and the bodies that accredit the proficiency test providers. Although compliance standards vary between provider and accreditation bodies, accreditation programs require that the proficiency test user's results, however obtained, are reported within the participant's quality assurance system.

Proficiency tests come in different forms: Accrediting bodies may facilitate or host a proficiency test. Users may create and administer a proficiency test to internal and external users. Users may assess proficiency through alternatives such as observation, case presentation, or peer review. Proficiency tests may be purchased and results reported externally. Proficiency tests may be created or purchased externally and results reported internally. Proficiency tests may be created and results reported internally.

The NCFS emphasizes that in forensic science, there are definable and distinct differences between competency testing and proficiency testing, and notes, "Proficiency testing is not designed as a measure of an individual forensic science practitioner (FSP)'s competence" (ASCLD, 2016). The NCFS explains further, "Proficiency testing is intended as an evaluation of participant performance against pre-established criteria by means of inter-laboratory comparisons for the determination of service provider performance. Proficiency testing is commonly used by FSSP management to evaluate staff, training, and method validation; appropriateness of test methods, traceability of measurements and calibrations to national standards; calibration and maintenance of test equipment; documentation, sampling, and handling of test items; and quality assurance of data, including reporting of results. In forensic science, proficiency testing is used not only as a measure of the FSSP's overall performance and quality system (e.g., facility, equipment, procedures, and training programs) but also as a tool for monitoring an individual FSP's continued ability to perform work in a specific discipline or tasks. The use of proficiency testing to evaluate individual examiners continuing ability to perform specific tasks should not be confused with competency testing. Competency testing is the demonstration that an FSP has acquired and demonstrated specialized knowledge, skills, and abilities in the standard practices necessary to conduct examinations in a discipline and/or category of testing prior to performing independent casework. Competency testing is an integral part of the forensic training process and is administered as part of a comprehensive assessment of technical skills and knowledge during basic training, and prior to the initiation of case work by a forensic science practitioner on a newly validated technology, technique, or method. Competency testing includes written and/or practical testing as part of a thorough evaluation of education, training, and practical experience. It also does not address the FSSP's overall quality system and performance, methods, procedures, testimony, reports, documentation, equipment, validation, measurement uncertainty, facilities, evidence handling, security, or safety procedures used by the individual practitioner. Proficiency testing and competency testing are different tools that assess and evaluate distinct aspects of FSSPs for different objectives. They are not interchangeable, but both are necessary to strengthen and improve forensic science" (ASCLD, 2016).

ACCREDITATION OF FORENSIC LABORATORIES

Accreditation assesses a forensic lab's capacity to generate and interpret results in a particular forensic discipline and helps to ensure an ongoing compliance to industry and applicable international standards. An independent accrediting body assesses and monitors the quality of the lab's management system by examining factors that include staff competence, method validation, appropriateness of test methods, calibration and maintenance of test equipment, testing environment, and quality assurance data. Accreditation is one way to increase the quality of work and reduce the likelihood of errors. The 2009 NAS report says, "Accreditation helps to ensure both ongoing compliance to industry standards and continual improvement of a FSSP's operations" (NAS, 2009, page 195).

Traditionally, quality control in the crime lab has been achieved through mechanisms such as proficiency testing of examiners, support analysts, technical managers, and technical consultants engaged in the field of trace evidence; validation of techniques and procedures in the lab, employing methodologies that the scientific community considers to be valid; and audits of the crime lab conducted by the technical manager in conjunction with the personnel responsible for the quality assurance program (U.S. Department of Justice, 2000).

Fisher (2012, pages 286–287) describes the current state of accreditation as mostly voluntary as opposed to mandated, mostly due to fiduciary reasons: "In times of budget constraint, it should be pointed out that preparation, continued compliance and the process itself might be viewed by some as 'unnecessary expenses.'"

The other challenge is putting teeth into accreditation policies related to noncompliance. ASCLD/LAB has issued a document, "ASCLD/LAB Guiding Principles of Professional Responsibility for Crime Laboratories and Forensic Scientists," which provides a framework for describing ethical and professional responsibilities in the forensic laboratory community. As the document states, "The Guiding Principles are designed to promote integrity among practitioners, and to increase public confidence in the quality of laboratory services, whether or not the laboratory is accredited by any accrediting body." As Fisher (2012, page 286) acknowledges, "Laboratories accredited by ASCLD/LAB accreditation are expected to adopt and adhere to ASCLD/LAB guidelines. If it is shown that an accredited lab willfully failed to follow these guidelines, that lab could potentially be sanctioned by ASCLD/LAB and possibly forfeit its accreditation. A shortcoming of laboratory accreditation and the accompanying codes of ethics is again that not all forensic laboratories are accredited. With the exception of a handful of states, there is no mandatory accreditation for crime laboratories. Additionally, most police departments who do not operate fully-fledged conventional crime labs, but manage some forensic programs, e.g., latent print details and crime scene units, typically are not accredited."

That lackadaisical attitude is about to change in the near future. On December 7, 2015, U.S. Deputy Attorney General Sally Quillian Yates announced that the U.S. DOJ will, within the next five years, require department-run forensic labs to obtain and maintain accreditation and require all department prosecutors to use accredited labs to process forensic evidence when practicable. Additionally, the department has decided to use its grant-funding mechanisms to encourage other labs around the country to pursue accreditation.

The new policies arose out of recommendations made by the NCFS, which, as we have seen, was established to advance the field of forensic science and make suggestions to the attorney general on how to ensure that reliable and scientifically valid evidence is used when solving crimes. "The department believes that accreditation is one of the most important tools for ensuring that forensic science is practiced in a reliable, scientifically rigorous way," said Yates in a statement. "Accreditation provides valuable oversight by ensuring that someone outside the participating laboratory has confirmed that the lab is following their required procedures. We support accreditation and we want to expand accreditation as widely as possible."

Although department forensic labs at Bureau of Alcohol, Tobacco, Firearms and Explosives (ATF), Drug Enforcement Administration (DEA), and Federal Bureau of Investigation (FBI) are already accredited, the new policy will ensure that, by 2020, those labs will have to maintain that accreditation. Also by 2020, department prosecutors will be required to use accredited forensic labs when it is practicable. The Executive Office for U.S. Attorneys (EOUSA) has been directed to develop guidance that will ensure the successful implementation of this new policy in the field. The new policy does not apply to digital forensic labs. Instead, the deputy attorney general has asked the NCFS to develop separate recommendations on accrediting of labs that conduct digital forensic work, given the difference in the practices of forensic analysis of digital evidence.

As a result of the commission's recommendations, the attorney general also has directed two changes to the department's grant funding in an effort to encourage and support state and local forensic labs in the process of becoming accredited. First, solicitations for both Edward Byrne Memorial Justice Assistance Grant funding and Paul Coverdell Forensic Science Improvement Grant funding will be redrafted to make clear that applicants can use this money to seek accreditation, because labs have not always used these funds to seek accreditation. Second, relevant discretionary grant programs at the Office of Justice Programs will be modified to give preferences to labs that will use the money to obtain accreditation. These applicants will get a "plus factor," increasing their likelihood of getting the money they need.

Those NCFS recommendations made to the attorney general arose out of April 30, 2015, action taken by the organization's Accreditation and Proficiency Testing Subcommittee, which adopted the universal accreditation recommendation with a 96 percent affirmative vote. Essentially, the recommendation was that all FSSPs become accredited.

Accreditation, as well as best practices, standardization, and improving the quality of services, is cited as a major issue in the 2009 NAS report, which observes, "Many

FSSPs currently providing services in furtherance of criminal, civil, regulatory, or administrative proceedings in the United States are not accredited to any national or international standard. To achieve universal accreditation, the Commission recommends that the Attorney General take several actions to promote and enforce universal accreditation" (NAS, 2009, page 6). Accreditation programs specifically for FSSPs have been available in the United States since approximately 1982. Accreditation has been voluntary in many jurisdictions, and universal accreditation has not been required or achieved. Several states have passed legislation mandating accreditation and other forms of oversight of FSSPs; however, legislation and oversight requirements vary greatly from state to state.

As the 2009 NAS report notes, "Accreditation is just one aspect of an organization's quality assurance program, which also should include proficiency testing where relevant, continuing education, and other programs to help the organization provide better overall services. In the case of laboratories, accreditation does not mean that accredited laboratories do not make mistakes, nor does it mean that a laboratory utilizes best practices in every case, but rather, it means that the laboratory adheres to an established set of standards of quality and relies on acceptable practices within these requirements. An accredited laboratory has in place a management system that defines the various processes by which it operates on a daily basis, monitors that activity, and responds to deviations from the acceptable practices using a routine and thoughtful method" (NAS, 2009, page 195).

In 2003, the ASCLD/LAB Delegate Assembly approved the implementation of an ISO/IEC 17025 program, and ASCLD/LAB began offering these accreditations in April 2004. For accreditation, ASCLD/LAB requires labs to demonstrate that they maintain procedures to protect evidence from loss, cross-transfer, contamination, and/or deleterious change; engage in validated and documented technical procedures; use appropriate controls and standards; provide calibration procedures; ensure complete documentation of all evidence examination; offer documented training programs that include competency testing; provide technical review of a portion of each examiner's work product as well as testimony monitoring of all who testify; and maintain a comprehensive proficiency testing program.

This process requires oversight, and as we will see in Chapter 6, the NAS report indicates, "Oversight must come from outside the participating laboratory to ensure that standards are not self-serving and superficial and to remove the option of taking shortcuts when other demands compete with quality assurance. In addition, accreditation serves as a mechanism to strengthen professional community ties, transmit best practices, and expose laboratory employees directly to the perspectives and expectations of other leaders in the profession" (page 195).

While not a perfect system of quality control, the NAS report notes, "Accreditation cannot guarantee high quality—that is, it cannot guard against those who intentionally disobey or ignore requirements. However, over time it can reduce the likelihood that violations will occur, and reports of infractions should trigger increased scrutiny by an accrediting body. And, by requiring that education be a standard that must be met as a condition of accreditation, incremental change and quality improvement can be achieved individual by individual" (page 197).

On March 22, 2016, the NCFS's Accreditation and Proficiency Testing Subcommittee adopted a viewpoint document on critical steps to accreditation, as a supporting document to its previously adopted "Recommendation on the Universal Accreditation of all Forensic Science Service Providers (FSSP)." The NCFS says that significant progress toward accreditation can be achieved by implementing the nine critical steps and formalizing these steps with written policies and procedures. As the NCFS document explains,

"A critical outcome of preparing for accreditation is the creation of a quality management system that is aligned with recognized technical and administrative requirements. To improve the quality and reliability of forensic work, a quality management system can be created as a whole or by using an incremental process. A significant challenge; however, is to engage FSSPs in embracing a culture of quality; not because it is required; but because it is best practice. Failure to recognize these challenges could negatively impact successful accreditation."

The NCFS asserts that accreditation helps to ensure both ongoing compliance to industry standards and continual improvement of an FSSP's operations, and acknowledges that the process can be daunting. That's why it recommends incremental steps toward improvements that can be systematically implemented on the pathway to accreditation. The NCFS recommends the following elements to improve the quality and reliability of forensic work:

Written procedures for evidence (security/control/handling): Procedures should be required defining how evidence is identified, collected, preserved, stored, sealed, secured, labeled, and maintained, and how it is documented. Procedures should include how the evidence is transferred from person to person or acquired from the storage area by a person and how transfers are documented to ensure accurate chain-of-custody records.

Written reports: Written reports should be required for the results of all examinations performed. Reporting procedures should specify the required elements of a report, which may include but are not limited to report format, signature authority, and content.

Technical and administrative Review of reports and supporting records: Written procedures should include the scope of what is reviewed, the frequency of reviews, the qualifications of the reviewer, and how reviews are documented. Written procedures should include case record security and retention.

Testimony monitoring: Written procedures should include a process to assess testimony given in support of examinations and how that assessment is documented.

Note-taking: Written procedures should require contemporaneous notes that provide sufficient information to demonstrate what was done, when and by whom, test results, and what conclusions were drawn, so that a competent analyst reviewing these notes should be able to reconstruct the entire testing process.

Technical procedures: Written technical procedures should specify the required elements of a procedure, which may include but are not limited to case approach, sampling, sample preparation, methodology, quality control, instrument parameters, and data interpretation. Written technical procedures should also include information regarding instrument and equipment maintenance and quality control of reagents. Written technical procedures should be based on method validation.

Training program: A written training manual should include the goals and objectives, material covered, mechanism(s) for assessment, and how the training is documented. Prior to working independently in a discipline or category of testing, a competency test should be used as a mechanism of assessment of qualification. Prior to offering testimony, legal/courtroom training and/or a moot court exercise should be completed and documented. Training topics should include professional responsibility.

Proficiency testing: Written procedures that require proficiency testing for all forensic science practitioners and set the frequency of testing.

Corrective and preventive action process: Written procedures should be in place to address nonconforming work. Written procedures should designate appropriate authorities to investigate nonconforming work and explain how the root cause(s) of the problem(s) will be determined. Written procedures should describe how the corrective action process will address nonconforming work, prevent its recurrence, and establish notification requirements and how the investigation will be documented.

Regarding an implementation strategy, the NCFS, in its recommendation, advises the attorney general to direct all DOJ FSSPs to maintain their accreditation, and those FSSPs who are not yet accredited should prepare and apply for accreditation within five years. Additionally, accreditation should be to internationally recognized standards, and the attorney general should require that DOJ grant funding provided to non-DOJ FSSPs shall be granted only to those FSSPs who are accredited or are in the process of becoming accredited. In the future, the NCFS stipulates that any DOJ funding award should include a special condition requiring that the agency's FSSPs be accredited.

The NCSF adds that in addition to these nine steps designed to build a culture of continuous quality improvement, labs should engage in internal audits and document control promulgated by international standards.

These aforementioned standards are essential to quality control. As the 2009 NAS report explains, "Standards provide the foundation against which performance, reliability and validity can be assessed. Adherence to standards reduces bias, improves consistency, and enhances the validity and reliability of results. Standards reduce variability resulting from the idiosyncratic tendencies of the individual examiner—for example, setting conditions under which one can declare a 'match' in forensic identifications. They make it possible to replicate and empirically test procedures and help disentangle method errors from practitioner errors. Importantly, standards not only guide practice but also can serve as guideposts in accreditation and certification programs" (NAS, 2009, page 201).

Several groups produce standards for use in the forensic science disciplines, including ASTM International, an international standards organization that develops and publishes voluntary technical standards for a wide range of materials, products, systems, and services. In the area of forensic science, it offers documents such as "Standard Guide for Minimum Training Requirements for Forensic Document Examiners," "Standard Guide for Forensic Paint Analysis and Comparison," "Standard Guide for Nondestructive Examination of Paper," "Standard Guide for Forensic Analysis of Fibers by Infrared Spectroscopy," and "Standard Terminology for Expressing Conclusions of Forensic Document Examiners."

At the federal level, the NIST conducts research to establish standards in a limited number of forensic areas, for example, organic gunshot residue analysis, trace explosives detectors, and improvised explosive devices. Its laboratories develop tests, test methods, produce reference data, conduct proof-of-concept implementations, and perform technical analyses. They also develop guides to help forensic organizations formulate appropriate policies and procedures, such as those concerning mobile phone forensic examinations. These guides are not all-inclusive, and they do not prescribe how law enforcement and incident response communities should handle investigations. Instead, they provide principles for establishing policies and procedures.

Continued improvement seems to be on the horizon. In a memorandum to staff dated March 17, 2016, Attorney General Loretta Lynch announced that the department would be endorsing aspects of the NCFS proposal regarding universal accreditation. Lynch said the department would be supporting the NCFS recommendations encompassing best practices in forensic laboratories and would be taking several steps, including requiring that department entities that provide nondigital forensic science services establish or maintain protocols and policies to address when a mistake or nonconforming event occurs. The memorandum stated that all department entities that provide forensic science services should review their policies in light of the NCFS's research to determine if any change to them might be appropriate to create even more robust protocols and policies.

ETHICS OF FORENSIC LABORATORY PERSONNEL

The cornerstone of any profession should be the ethics guiding practice and defining the outer edges of acceptable behavior so that there is no mistaking a breach in conduct.

As James and Nordby (2003) state, "The commitment to ethics should be stressed in the education of a forensic scientist. The values inherent in good science ... should be a part of official forensic science curricula." They add, "Without the underpinnings of high ethical standards, forensic scientists may become what is known in the profession as hired guns. The student considering this profession should resist the temptation of selling whatever opinion is needed by defense or prosecution. Not all hired guns become forensic frauds merely through nonexistent or meaningless credentials. Properly educated, experienced scientists may also act as gunslingers through ignorance or misapplication of method. This might involve purposely omitting relevant tests or suppressing relevant results. Many such experts may develop an entirely unjustified sense of their own scientific abilities and observational powers. Generally, such experts offer firm, certain and conclusive opinions designed to fit the relevant courtroom advocate's agenda. Such a forensic expert may even resort to defining scientific error as any interpretation that disagrees with his or her own."

Swienton and Upshaw (2012, page 433) address good scientists gone bad: "Every field has it rogues, those who are patently unethical for reasons incomprehensible to most. Some do it for money, some for fame or perceived prestige, some just succumb to pressure either real or imagined. There is a broad spectrum of behavior that can range from the irresponsible or that which derives from poor or inadequate training to outright purposeful falsification or deception. Forensic scientists are human and humans make mistakes. In forensic science this can be especially egregious because someone's life or liberty may depend on the accuracy of the science being proffered. When bad science is mistakenly delivered, the honesty of the mistake may be forgivable (as long as it is identified, admitted, and rectified). However, when bad or misleading science is purposefully presented, there is no penance that can atone. Certainly, there have been a few infamous forensic scientists who have gained notoriety not for their diligent and meticulous work but instead for the sheer number of cases in which they lied or falsified or fabricated data. Is this news? Arguably. Does the public have a right to know? Certainly. Do those involved in past cases in which these scientists conducted testing and offered testimony have a right to ask that those cases be re-examined? Definitely. But what is the responsibility of the media who reports these cases to the public? How much information need be revealed? How does this exposure affect the public confidence in a system in which the majority of those working in the field are, in fact, responsible, ethical, and diligent? How will the knowledge that a few bad apples exist color the perception of future juries who are asked to weigh and evaluate forensic evidence? Does this knowledge affect their perception of law enforcement and general public safety?"

The forensic science hall of shame has included infamous cases such as forensic lab technician Fred Zain, who was accused of falsifying evidence reports, and forensic chemist Joyce Gilchrist, who was accused of falsifying evidence. Other black eyes include various laboratory scandals that have encompassed errors, allegations of dry-labbing, incidences of contamination, and reports of large numbers of untested sexual assault kits, according to Swienton and Upshaw (2012).

Houck and Siegel (2015, page 652) emphasize, "No matter what the professional culture, ethics are important in the workforce. Every profession experiences unethical behaviors that arise due to human nature, self-justification, pressures, and greed or desire. While issues, responsibilities and scenarios differ, the underlying causes remain similar and any professional culture that employs people faces the possibility for misconduct. Very simply, ethical issues can be divided into 'sins of commission' (doing the wrong thing) and 'sins of omission' (not doing the right thing). Blame tends to fall on an individual rather than on a group; people tend to like simple answers to complex problems."

Sources of ethical failures can be remembered through the mnemonic of A-B-C, according to Houck and Siegel (2015, page 652):

- Bad apple (individual)
- Bad bushel (group)
- Bad crop (system)

They add that a fourth option should also be considered, that of a bad farmer, namely, a supervisor or manager who allows inappropriate behavior to continue by supporting or turning a blind eye to it.

Houck and Siegel (2015, page 653) list the guiding principles for success in the forensic field: technically competent and employ reliable (accurate and precise) and validated methods of analysis; honest about their qualifications and staying within their area(s) of expertise; intellectually honest about their data, conclusions, and opinions; and objective when reviewing evidence and testifying as an expert.

As Houck and Siegel (2015, page 653) observe, "These guiding principles are the minimum of ethics in forensic science. Although there is no single code of ethics for forensic science, many individual professional organizations, agencies, and department codes contain similar provisions. Ethical behavior helps to ensure consistency and reliability of behavior within the forensic science profession."

Some experts believe that ethics-related issues in forensic science are heightened due to the very nature of the interactions between medicolegal stakeholders. As Houck and Siegel (2015, page 654) explain, "Forensic scientists face two major types of ethical dilemmas: those that occur because they are scientists and those that occur because they interact with the justice system. Most forensic scientists see themselves as scientists first and they concentrate most heavily on scientific ethical questions and may not appreciate the complexity and seriousness of the ones that arise from justice system interactions. One way that forensic science is unique, especially in relation to ethics, is the close professional relationship the field has with some other professional cultures. Forensic scientists, law enforcement officers, lawyers, judges, and other scientists work very closely together, but may have very different objectives, rules, and philosophies. Despite the differences, forensic scientists must find a way to get along to support the justice system without succumbing to being unduly influenced or biased by differing ethical behaviors."

Houck and Siegel (2015, page 654) advise practitioners to recognize that differences do exist, understand the governing rules of law enforcement and court personnel, and establish open and regular dialogue as all parties in the justice system work through issues early before they become unmanageable. Note Houck and Siegel (2015, page 654), "Awareness of where the pitfalls and problems may be is key to avoiding them. Examining and exploring common pressures between professions enables individuals to realize common red flags to potential ethical misconduct. Looking at the outcome of case studies or examples, and especially events and circumstances leading up to those events, is an invaluable teaching tool for students and professionals. Some ethical issues arise in the forensic science field more than others, including those that involve the use of best practices, validated methods of analysis, instances of bias, seeking notoriety of a personal nature, and becoming advocates for one side or the other."

There are other potential ethical dilemmas that forensic scientists face, including demonstrating professional credentials or qualifications when being qualified as an expert witness in court. Misrepresentations of credentials include educational degrees; professional licensures or certifications; employment history; and data about previous testimonies such as number of testimonies, locations, and areas in which the expert was qualified. Forensic scientists must also stay current in their discipline(s), being aware of the latest techniques and methods, research on limitations and errors in areas of their expertise, new instruments, and other current issues. As Houck and Siegel (2015, page 663) explain, "The hallmark of science is that it is always changing. What was true 10 years ago may not be true today; new methods and instrumentation appear constantly. It is incumbent upon laboratory forensic scientists to keep up with changes in their field of expertise and to make sure that the methods they use for the analysis of evidence represent best practices. Using outmoded practices runs the risks of results that can be refuted or proven to be the detriment of the justice system. In drug analysis, for example, there is a continuous stream of new illicit drugs showing up such as synthetic cannabinoids and steroids. In DNA typing, new methods for determination of mixtures, next-generation sequencing, familial relations, and myriad other new practices are altering the landscape of identification."

Ethics-related issues also extend to analytical procedures performed in the forensic laboratory. As Houck and Siegel (2015, page 659) explain, "Most forensic science laboratories commit their analytical procedures to writing (standard operating procedures, or SOPs), validate all methods, and develop schemes for the analysis of various types of scientific evidence. All laboratories should have rigorous protocols for administrative and technical reviews of their analyses and reports, but there are no consensus standards or uniformity across agencies for when and how to accomplish this. Potential ethical violations can occur when forensic scientists do not follow established procedures for the analysis of evidence or use invalidated methods."

Potentially unethical behavior can include a wide range of actions including falsifying laboratory examinations, ignoring evidence at a crime scene that might exonerate a suspect or be a mitigating factor, fabricating scientific opinions based on invalid interpretations of tests or evidence, examining physical evidence when not qualified to do so, extending expertise beyond one's knowledge, using unproved methodologies, and overstating an expert opinion.

According to Houck and Siegel (2015, page 660), "Perhaps the most extreme form of unethical practice in a forensic science laboratory is the practice of 'dry-labbing.' This occurs when an analyst reports results without performing the analysis; that is, he or she makes up the answers ... This practice can never be accidental except in the instance of a gross mix-up of cases and is never a training issue; the analyst simply does not do some or all of the work ... Regardless of the how or why, dry-labbing is always a serious ethical violation and it is inconceivable to construct a valid defense for willfully saying a test was performed that was never done."

As we have seen, in Recommendation 9 in the 2009 NAS report, the committee recommended a national code of ethics for all forensic science disciplines and encouraged professional forensic science societies to incorporate the national code into their own codes of professional responsibility and code of ethics. The report also recommended exploring mechanisms to enforce serious ethical violations.

Codes of ethics exist within the various professional organizations. One of the oldest regional forensic science societies in the United States, the California Association of Criminalists, has a robust code of ethics. The preamble to the document states, "It is the duty of any person practicing the profession of criminalistics to serve the interests of justice to the best of his ability at all times. In fulfilling this duty, he or she will use all of the scientific means at his or her command to ascertain all of the significant physical facts relative to the matters under investigation. Having made factual determinations, the criminalist must then interpret and evaluate their findings. In this they will be guided by experience and knowledge which, coupled with a serious consideration of the analytical findings and the application of sound judgment, may enable the criminalist to arrive at opinions and conclusions pertaining to the matters under study. These findings of fact, conclusions, and opinions should then be reported, with all the accuracy and skill of which the criminalist is capable, to the end that all may fully understand and be able to place the findings in their proper relationship to the problem at issue."

Existing codes notwithstanding, Fisher (2012, page 282) poses the hard questions about implementation: "How are these goals translated into every day practice? How should laboratory managers and practitioners meet their respective obligations? In some cases, inappropriate ethical conduct is clear, while at other times it may not be straightforward. It requires discipline and sometimes effort to 'do the right thing.' It also requires an understanding of what ethical conduct means in the context of forensic science and the criminal justice system."

Fisher (2012, page 285) adds, "Unlike other professions, such as medicine, dentistry, or law, which are regulated by state agencies, with the exception of forensic odontologists and physicians (medical examiners, psychiatrists, nurses, etc.), forensic science lacks such oversight. In addition, membership of professional associations is not a requirement for forensic science practitioners in order for them to either work in government forensic science laboratories or to testify in court. Such memberships are voluntary and are likely to give forensic scientists added credibility in the eyes of the judge or jury. As a result, codes of professional conduct or codes of ethics are not, in any strict sense, a deterrent to guard against professional misconduct. There are no real consequences—there is no hammer. One might easily voluntarily step down from membership in order to avoid sanction. In addition, there are cases where a forensic scientist had been expelled from or suspended for a period of time from a professional organization but the chastisement did not stop the offending practitioner from testifying in court."

Fisher (2012, pages 285–286) asserts that, especially in cases of gross misconduct or malfeasance, "there have been rare instances where experts have been criminally charged, however, lawsuits against experts and their agencies have been few. Plaintiffs generally wish to seek financial remuneration and that means the public agency will be sued, however, police and prosecution agencies are generally immune from such suits unless it can be shown that gross negligence was involved."

Houck and Bowen (2012, page 206) outline a set of characteristics for forensic scientists to meet the ethical obligations of the profession: They should be technically competent and employ reliable methods of analysis, while being honest with respect to their qualifications. They should be intellectually honest with respect to the scientific data upon which conclusions and opinions are based, and they must be objective in their review of evidence and delivery of expert testimony. As they note, "These guiding principles are the basics of ethics in forensic science, but to provide all forensic scientists with this understanding requires education and training. In part due to the inherent variability of the involved disciplines, there exist no universally applicable licensing or certificate requirements, no universally accepted educational or employment criteria, and no professional criteria for on-the-job training in the forensic sciences as a whole."

Houck and Bowen (2012, page 206) say that any code of ethics for the field, in order to be successful, must include an obligation to follow the scientific method in performing examinations and formulating conclusions; must require the impartial interpretation and presentation of analytical results; must mandate proper behavior concerning courtroom demeanor and delivery of expert testimony; and must insist on obligations to the profession as a whole and maintenance of one's own professional skills. They observe, "Following the guiding principles of the profession and utilizing tools such as codes of ethics should help to ensure consistency and reliability within the forensic science profession."

In 2010, the Education, Ethics and Terminology Inter-Agency Working Group (EETIWG) of the National Science and Technology Council's Subcommittee on Forensic Science developed a National Code of Ethics and Professional Responsibility for the Forensic Sciences (NCEPRFS). Further, the EETIWG recommended that all practitioners "who provide reports and expert opinion testimony with respect to forensic evidence in United States courts of law, adopt the NCEPRFS" (NCFS, 2016). According to the NCFS, this recommendation was not acted upon, and no NCEPRFS exists today.

While it noted the lack of a single code of ethics that covered all forensic disciplines, the EETIWG identified four major categories addressed by every code of ethics it reviewed: working within professional competence; providing clear and objective testimony; avoiding conflicts of interest; and avoiding bias and influence, real or perceived. According to the NCFS, "The EETIWG found that the most broadly applicable code of ethics that would best serve as the NCEPRFS was the ASCLD/LAB Guiding Principles of Professional Responsibility for Crime Laboratories and Forensic Scientists. The working group found that the principles in this document were appropriate to the work conducted in the federal forensic laboratories, and ultimately proposed that the ASCLD/LAB document be adopted as the NCEPRFS. The Interim Solutions Subcommittee of the National Commission on Forensic Sciences utilized this code as its starting point for a National Code of Professional Responsibility for all forensic science and forensic medicine service providers. The subcommittee chose professional responsibility rather than ethics as the title because ethics is a much broader term referring to many issues beyond those directly associated with forensic science and forensic medicine service providers' professional responsibilities" (NCFS, 2016).

On the federal side, there is new movement toward improved professional behavior. On March 22, 2016, the Subcommittee for Interim Solutions of the NCFS voted by more than a two-thirds majority to adopt the National Code of Professional Responsibility for Forensic Science and Forensic Medicine Service Providers. The NCFS states, "The U.S. Attorney General should require the forensic science service providers within the Department of Justice to adopt the National Code of Professional Responsibility for Forensic Science and Forensic Medicine Service Providers, that the Code be annually reviewed and signed by all forensic science service providers, and that steps be defined to address violations."

The NCFS is asking the attorney general to urge all forensic science and forensic medicine service providers, associated certification and accreditation bodies, and professional societies to adopt the National Code of Professional Responsibility for Forensic Science and Forensic Medicine Service Providers, and for their management systems to develop policies and procedures to enforce the standards embodied in this code.

As the NCFS notes, "Most practitioners in forensic science and forensic medicine are committed, hard-working, ethical professionals; however, education and guidance on professional responsibility is uneven and there is no enforceable universal code of professional responsibility. In addition, when nonconformities or breaches of law or professional standards that adversely affects a previously issued report or testimony occur, there must be a process in place for reporting and remediation ... Perhaps the key element lacking from the proposed NCEPRFS was the acknowledgement and address of serious violations of professional conduct, as recommended in the NAS Report. Oversight and enforcement are critical to compliance" (NCFS, 2016).

The National Code of Professional Responsibility for Forensic Science and Forensic Medicine Service Providers defines a framework for promoting integrity and respect for the scientific process among forensic science and forensic medicine service providers, both practitioners and agencies, including its managers. Its tenets are as follows:

1. Accurately represent relevant education, training, experience, and areas of expertise.
2. Be honest and truthful in all professional affairs including not representing the work of others as one's own.
3. Foster and pursue professional competency through such activities as training, proficiency testing, certification, and presentation and publication of research findings.
4. Commit to continuous learning in relevant forensic disciplines and stay abreast of new findings, equipment, and techniques.
5. Utilize scientifically validated methods and new technologies, while guarding against the use of unproven methods in casework and the misapplication of generally accepted standards.
6. Handle evidentiary materials to prevent tampering, adulteration, loss, or nonessential consumption of evidentiary materials.
7. Participation in any case in which there is a conflict of interest shall be avoided.
8. Conduct independent, impartial, and objective examinations that are fair, unbiased, and fit for purpose.
9. Make and retain contemporaneous, clear, complete, and accurate records of all examinations, tests, measurements, and conclusions, in sufficient detail to allow meaningful review and assessment by an independent professional proficient in the discipline.
10. Ensure interpretations, opinions, and conclusions are supported by sufficient data, and minimize influences and biases for or against any party.
11. Render interpretations, opinions, or conclusions only when within the practitioner's proficiency or expertise.
12. Prepare reports and testify using clear and straightforward terminology, clearly distinguishing data from interpretations, opinions, and conclusions, and disclosing known limitations that are necessary to understand the significance of the findings.
13. Reports and other records shall not be altered, and information shall not be withheld for strategic or tactical advantage.

14. Document and, if appropriate, inform management or quality assurance personnel of nonconformities (defined by the NCFS as any aspect of laboratory work that does not conform to its established procedures) and breaches of law or professional standards.
15. Once a report is issued and the adjudicative process has commenced, communicate fully when requested with the parties through their investigators, attorneys, and experts, except when instructed that a legal privilege, protective order, or law prevents disclosure.
16. Appropriately inform affected recipients (either directly or through proper management channels) of all nonconformities or breaches of law or professional standards that adversely affect a previously issued report or testimony, and make reasonable efforts to inform all relevant stakeholders, including affected professional and legal parties, victim(s), and defendant(s).

The NCFS is recommending that this code be reviewed annually and signed by all DOJ FSSPs. In addition, the NCFS says there must be an effective process to report and correct nonconformities or breaches of law or professional standards that adversely affect a previously issued report or testimony. The NCFS also recommends protection for whistleblowers by noting, "Policies and procedures should describe or define a system whereby individuals are protected when reporting suspicious, unscrupulous, unethical or criminal actions without punitive concerns."

Houck and Siegel (2015, page 664) note, "Forensic science has no licensure requirement and no agreed-upon code of ethics. To be sure, there are a large number of forensic science organizations that have a code of ethics, including national and regional associations, as well as discipline specific groups. Although there is obviously some overlap between these organizations with respect to the types of behaviors that constitute ethical violations, there are also significant differences. The major problem with this patchwork system is the lack of consequences for violators. The only serious consequence for violating the ethical code of the American Academy of Forensic Sciences, for example, is expulsion; this does not prevent the scientist from continuing to practice in the forensic science field, nor does it necessarily stop the unethical behavior. Unethical forensic scientists can cause significant damage to the whole justice system and there are few practical ways to stop it. The 11th recommendation of the NAS Committee report on forensic science is that there be a national code of ethics that is tied to certification. In order for this to have any real effect on the bad actors, however, there must be real consequences for serious ethical violations, up to and including loss of the right to practice forensic science, and offer expert testimony in court. Since the NAS report came out in 2009, there has been much discussion about creating a national code of ethics and a few small attempts to do so. The major problem is that there is no national organization that speaks for all forensic scientists with one voice, analogous to the American Bar Association for attorneys or the American Medical Association for doctors. The recently formed National Commission on Forensic Science will attempt to forge a consensus for a national code of ethics and hopefully the United States Congress will provide some funding and perhaps legislation to move this effort along. A national code of ethics with strong enforcement will go a long way to help reduce the number of ethical violators and advance the forensic sciences to the level of other professional fields."

Not everyone believes a code of ethics will resolve lingering issues with rogue scientists. As Kaye (2010, page 10) asserts, "Professional regulation is not especially effective in regulating the testimony of expert witnesses ... thus, the committee's proposal for 'a national code of ethics for all forensic science disciplines' such that 'those forensic scientists who commit serious ethical violations' could be sanctioned 'through a certification process for forensic scientists' could not be implemented in full without legislation. State and federal governments could require certification for employment in public laboratories, and this could go a long way toward removing 'bad apples' from the system. However, under the American doctrine of separation of governmental powers, whether legislatures have the power to prescribe the qualifications of the expert witnesses who the parties are entitled to produce in court is a significant legal question."

Fisher (2012, pages 288–289) alludes to the problems associated with a universal code of ethics: "It is evident that an enforceable code of ethics should certainly help to provide examples of appropriate behavior. At present, there are no universal forensic science ethics codes. While various codes contain similar elements, these are not identical and have dramatically different enforcement mechanisms. Furthermore, membership of professional organizations is not mandatory, thus enforcement of standards is problematic if possible at all, given the present operational structure. The issue is that there are no real sanctions for unethical conduct. Even an individual dismissed from a professional society for ethics violations, may still practice and continue their career. The absence of federal or state law saying that practitioners and forensic science institutions are required to follow a code of ethics means that enforcement of any code of conduct is problematic. Only when there is consensus among policy-makers to mandate a code of conduct and set up an enforcement mechanism will ethics have significant meaning."

Fisher (2012, pages 288–289) asserts that mechanisms of enforcement should exist for those forensic scientists who commit serious ethical violations: "Such a code could be enforced through a certification process for forensic scientists. Unfortunately, having an ideal is far from having a plan to follow to get there."

As the field awaits attempts at a mandated, universal code of professional conduct as advocated by the NAS report, Fisher (2012, pages 288–289) says the profession can adapt strategies for improvement as well as cultivate a greater self-awareness of breaches in conduct: "One could easily argue that forensic science practitioners should and do know the difference between right and wrong behavior. This is true most of the time, however, examples of ethical failing make the issue important. The question becomes one of taking action: what can or should an individual do when an examiner becomes aware of an ethics concern? What should supervisors and forensic science laboratory managers do? And what of institutional improvements? When an individual forensic examiner is found on the horns of an ethical dilemma, what might be done? Often, when faced with such situations, wishing a problem would just go away or choosing to do nothing is an easy but fruitless dichotomy. Either path is often a bad idea. One suggestion might be to speak to a trusted colleague or superior. At some later point, should a person be called to explain actions and their significance, a written account might become important and even helpful. But of course, deciding when to take such action is not always clear."

AN IDENTITY CRISIS?

Perhaps exacerbating the issue of ethics is how the forensic science community perceives and defines itself. The NAS report acknowledges that the term *forensic science* encompasses a broad range of forensic disciplines, each with its own set of technologies and practices, and therefore, there is wide variability across forensic science disciplines with regard to techniques, methodologies, reliability, types and numbers of potential errors, research, general acceptability, and published material. As the NAS report notes, "Some of the forensic science disciplines are laboratory based (e.g., nuclear and mitochondrial DNA analysis, toxicology and drug analysis); others are based on expert interpretation of observed patterns (e.g., fingerprints, writing samples, toolmarks, bite marks, and specimens such as hair). The 'forensic science community,' in turn, consists of a host of practitioners, including scientists (some with advanced degrees) in the fields of chemistry, biochemistry, biology, and medicine; laboratory technicians; crime scene investigators; and law enforcement officers. There are very important differences, however, between forensic laboratory work and crime scene investigations. There are also sharp distinctions between forensic practitioners who have been trained in chemistry, biochemistry, biology, and medicine (and who bring these disciplines to bear in their work) and technicians who lend support to forensic science enterprises" (page 7).

It takes a variety of practitioners working together to provide the services required by the justice system, but lines are being drawn by some commentators who insist that some forensic scientists are more legitimate than others. As Turvey (2013, page 36) states, "The majority of full-time forensic science practitioners in the United States work for law enforcement agencies or in publicly funded government crime labs, providing their services exclusively to law enforcement and the prosecution. However, because of the current fractured state and the past 'rebranding' of the forensic sciences, there is much confusion over who precisely the 'real' forensic scientists are—and who they are not (Inman and Rudin, 1999). This confusion exists within the forensic science community, and among those operating in the criminal justice system, which has misinformed the media and the general public."

Turvey (2013, page 38) adds, "The NAS report ultimately concludes that the forensic science community is poorly focused and badly fragmented, with no clear practice standards, consistent terminology, or standardized means of practitioner certification. That is to say, forensic science is not always practiced in a laboratory; forensic science is not always practiced by someone working for law enforcement; and forensic science is not always practiced by scientists. At this point, it is also necessary to recognize the distinction that must be made between scientists and technician practitioners of forensic science."

According to the 2009 NAS report, "There are also sharp distinctions between forensic practitioners who have been trained in chemistry, biochemistry, biology, and medicine (and who bring these disciplines to bear in their work) and technicians who lend support to forensic science enterprises" (NAS, 2009, page 7). In addition, the report notes, "The greatest distinction between the forensic scientist and the forensic technician is that of testing versus interpretation." The report states further, "Because of the distinctly different professional tracks within larger laboratories, for example, technicians perform tests with defined protocols, and credentialed scientists conduct specialized testing and interpretation. Unlike many other professions, the forensic science disciplines have no organized control over entry into the profession, such as by degree, boards or exams, or licensure ... Control mechanisms traditionally have been held through employment and job function."

As Bono et al. (2012, page 346) observe, "Forensic scientists are comfortable with laboratory practice, that is, after all their chosen vocation. Many are degreed scientists with years of training in process and interpretation, usually accompanied by long periods of practical apprenticeship before even beginning to perform casework on their own. Certain forensic disciplines, although well established and with extensive histories (fingerprint analysis, firearms analysis, and other pattern recognition sciences for example), have tended to be populated by those from within the law enforcement community. With little grant funding to be had in such disciplines, the only continuing sincere interest in shoring up the practice has come from those most dependent on the outcome—the end users. Regardless of the overall background (degreed versus practical knowledge), the practitioner in addition to the theoretical and practical training received, is also versed in the areas of chain of custody, legal questioning, biohazard safety, quality control/quality assurance, etc. One can play with test tubes and chemicals all day long, but the difference between research or academic scientists and forensic scientists is in the immediate and direct applicability of the science. The immediacy of casework requires forensic scientists to apply what they do to the criminal justice system in something approaching real time. The difference can be stark. The practicality of working cases to solve questions based on the imperfect world of submitted evidence arising under myriad circumstances in less than pristine condition, versus the institutional scientific hierarchy of intelligentsia in grant-funded research achieving necessary incremental growth in knowledge as a concept rather than in a specific scenario, is a stark contrast indeed. Regardless of the role, practical or theoretical, once the bench work is complete, the practicing scientist ventures out of the comfort of the laboratory. In the case of the forensic practitioner, this means entering a completely different (and occasionally surreal) world—the courtroom. The forensic part of the equation is an important delineation, for those called to testify tend to fall into one of two broad camps—those who thrive in the spectacle of the public forum (hence the ontogeny of the qualifier) and those for whom the witness box is an intimidating place. In order to cross that bridge, the fundamentals of the science must be sound."

Houck and Siegel (2015, page 662) acknowledge the ethical dilemma that mere employment status can present to practitioners in a world bent on divisiveness: "Most practicing forensic scientists in the United States work for a laboratory that is under the administrative control of a unit of government, federal, state, regional, or local. Most of these laboratories are within a law enforcement agency such as a police department, sheriff's department, or prosecutor's office. Public forensic science laboratories are supported by the taxpayers of that governmental unit and the scientists are paid a salary for their work. Forensic scientists who work in public laboratories are often viewed by workers in the justice system and in the general public as being part of the police department, for example, and they are viewed as being part of the police team even though the forensic scientists view themselves as unbiased, neutral scientists. This is a form of attribution bias, discussed earlier: The assumption is that because the scientists work for the police, they hold the same views. Other forensic scientists make their living working for nongovernmental laboratories in the private sector. A few of these private laboratories perform services for governmental agencies. Most private laboratories get most of their work from criminal defendants or in civil cases where they may work for either party. The scientists who work for these private laboratories may also receive a salary for their services. Still other forensic scientists have one-person laboratories and they receive a fee for service. They also do most of their work for criminal defense or in civil cases. They also face issues of attribution bias. It is a common tactic for a prosecutor to question a defense expert forensic scientist about the fees that they are collecting for appearing in court, implying that the expert is saying what he or she is being paid to say and is thus biased and unethical."

The association with law enforcement (and by extension, prosecutors) has led to the rise of the perception of forensic scientists as hired guns, or expert witnesses who gain a reputation for essentially offering testimony that is suited to the client for a fee. As Houck and Spiegel (2015, page 663) explain, "Hired guns are viewed to be unethical because they tailor their testimony to the needs of the client without regard to what the science says. They will do tests and select the results that fit their testimony. In addition, many expert witnesses will build their practice by working only as plaintiff's expert or defense expert. Thus, they are not only hired guns, but they will only work for the same side of a case in all cases, regardless of the merit. Sometimes charges of prosecution bias will be leveled at forensic scientists who work for a governmental agency such as a police department. The fact is that this is the nature of their employment. Most public forensic science laboratories are required by statute to accept cases only from law enforcement agencies and may not be permitted to work for a defense attorney. Calling these scientists hired guns is misleading."

An expert witness must state the truth, free from prejudice and subjectivity. The AAFS notes, "The forensic scientist must be impartial and unbiased. The forensic scientist must tell ... the whole truth, no matter what it is or whom it hurts or helps. An expert opinion can be offered only if there are scientific facts upon which to base it. In court, the work of the forensic scientist is carefully examined to find any flaws, whether in the test performed, the interpretation of the results, or the science upon which opinion is based. Whether the forensic scientist expert is hired by the prosecution or defense, the opposing attorney will try to undermine or discredit testimony which is against his client. The forensic witness must be qualified and knowledgeable of both his special area of scientific knowledge and expertise and the rules of evidence that govern the admissibility of opinions and conclusions. The forensic scientist often spends long hours testifying clearly and concisely in judicial proceedings concerning scientific information and what it means. Throughout he must maintain a posture of impartial professionalism" (page 3).

BREACHES IN ETHICS AND WRONGFUL CONVICTIONS

Breaches of ethics can lead to are wrongful convictions, the platform upon which legal commentators have built their case against forensic science. Koppl and Sacks (2012, page 3) assert, "Police, prosecutors and forensic scientists often have an incentive to convict someone, with little or no incentive to convict the right one. In other words, they often have an incentive to get a conviction without at the same time having any material incentive to distinguish between the guilty and the innocent."

Hastening to soften the blow a bit, Koppl and Sacks (2012, page 3) add, "The rate of false convictions is hard to estimate. It seems to be relatively low given the strength of the incentive to convict, however, which would seem to be a testament to human decency. Most actors in the system wish to serve justice. But with about one million felony convictions per year, even a low rate of false conviction can produce a high number of false convictions. Michael Risinger estimates that the rate of false convictions for rape–murders in the 1980s was not less than 3.3 percent. If that rate applied to all felony convictions today, the U.S. would have at least 33,000 false felony convictions per year. The number of false convictions could be reduced by structural changes that strengthen the incentive of criminal-justice professionals to discriminate between the innocent and the guilty. Incentives matter even when the actors are sincerely motivated to achieve justice. Thus, improved outcomes require structural changes rather than policies meant to 'get tough' with overt cheaters and frauds."

What Koppl and Sacks (2015, page 4) assert is evidence that "criminal-justice professionals sometimes respond to incentives," adding that evidence suggests that "people can respond to incentives without knowing it. In other words, 'bad apples' are not the only ones whose actions may be skewed by inappropriate incentives."

These incentives matter, according to Koppl and Sacks (2012, page 12), who observe, "They matter because people tend to do what is in their interest. The tendency to do what is in your interest can be stronger in some individuals, weaker in others."

Some believe that the observer effect is an incentive that can skew honest errors, according to Koppl and Sacks (2012), who explain, "We tend to see what we expect to see and what we hope to see," and, "Incentives (motivation and hope) can skew honest errors because they influence perception. When scholars speak of 'unconscious bias' they generally refer to 'observer effects.'" They continue, "People can make honest mistakes. They may unintentionally make choices that fulfill certain pre-existing biases. The literature on observer effects demonstrates that a person's opinion may unknowingly serve his interests in that sometimes what we observe is naturally skewed by what we expect … Observer effects are pervasive and enhanced by desire and motivation."

With an eye toward forensic scientists in particular, Koppl and Sacks (2012, page 16) state, "The errors of police officers, forensic scientists, and prosecutors may all be biased by incentives. The number of mechanisms linking incentives to honest errors is indefinitely large, and these mechanisms are diverse and dissimilar. At the same time, of course, there is a risk that incentives will lead to fraud, falsification, or fabrication. Finally, there is the great middle ground between perfectly honest error and willful fraud. Human cognition seems to be plastic enough to create degrees of consciousness regarding the bias in one's errors."

Koppl and Sacks (2012, page 27) assert that it is "relatively easy to observe whether a forensic scientist's work supports the police or prosecution theory in a case" and that it is "relatively difficult to observe whether a forensic scientist's work includes errors." They therefore note, "Unfortunately, forensic scientists do often have an incentive to produce results that support the police or prosecution theory. It might seem hard to act on this incentive without openly cheating by, say, falsifying scientific data. Surprisingly, perhaps, the incentives of forensic scientist can and do influence the content of their scientific analyses."

Koppl and Sacks (2012, page 27) point to several reasons that support their presumption First, they allege that "forensic science depends greatly on subjective judgment." Second, they cite the NAS report's comment that most forensic science methods, programs, and evidence are within the regulatory province of state and local law enforcement entities or are covered by statutes and rules governing state judicial proceedings. Thus, Koppl and Sacks observe, "High-powered incentives for police to the clear cases and secure convictions tend to produce in crime labs a similar incentive to find evidence inculpating police suspects. Forensic scientists who sit administratively in law enforcement agencies or prosecutors' offices, or who are hired by those units, are subject to a general risk of bias." Third, they say that forensic evidence is generally examined by one crime lab only, "creating a kind of monopoly on the examination and interpretation of such evidence."

"The subjectivism of forensic science matters in part because of the twofold monopoly in forensic science. First, evidence typically examined by one crime lab only. In this sense the crime lab receiving a bit of evidence has a monopoly on examination of that evidence. Second, that same lab will normally be the only one to offer an interpretation of the results of the examination it performs. No other experts in forensic science will be asked to judge what the evidence means. Typically, only the prosecution will have expert witnesses testifying on forensic evidence. Monopoly in examinations may allow errors and even fraud to go undetected. Monopoly in interpretation may allow false interpretations to go unchallenged and alternative hypotheses to go unexamined. Organizing crime labs under law enforcement creates such biases and incentives" (Koppl and Sacks, 2012, page 38).

Koppl and Sacks say that funding crime labs through court-assessed fees creates another channel for bias to enter crime lab analyses. In jurisdictions with this practice, the crime lab receives a sum of money for each conviction of a given type. Several state statutory schemes require crime laboratory fees upon conviction. For example, North Carolina general statutes require, "For the services of" the state or local crime lab, that judges in criminal cases assess a $600 fee to be charged "upon conviction" and remitted to the law enforcement agency containing the lab whenever that lab "performed DNA analysis of the crime, tests of bodily fluids of the defendant for the presence of alcohol or controlled substances, or analysis of any controlled substance possessed by the defendant or the defendant's agent" (Koppl and Sacks, 2012, page 31). Illinois crime labs receive fees upon convictions for sex offenses, controlled substance offenses, and those involving driving under the influence.

Other states have broadened the scope even further. Washington statutes require a $100 crime lab fee for any conviction that involves lab analysis. Kansas statutes require offenders "to pay a separate court cost of $400 for every individual offense if forensic science or laboratory services or forensic computer examination services are provided in connection with the investigation" (Koppl and Sacks, 2013). In addition, Arizona, California, Missouri, Tennessee, and Wisconsin also require crime lab fees in connection with various conviction types.

With states sending work to crime labs, there may be unconscious pressure to produce results favorable to the invested party. And there has been debate in the community about how much about a case a bench scientist should know when performing analyses.

"I was in a state police environment but I never experienced any pressure from the state to control the outcome of a case," remarks Richard Saferstein. "But I guess those pressures do exist subtly, and even today when I am hired by a public defender or defense attorney sometimes you can see the bench analysts and investigators have not really stepped back from the case; it comes out when you ask for alternative explanations for what may have occurred. It doesn't happen a lot but it does happen. I believe there is a need for a second pair of eyes on cases, and I'm not saying it always results in identification of a mistake or oversight. If a mistake exists in 1 out of 10 cases or 1 out of 20 cases, who's to say that it isn't worth doing a check because 95 percent of the cases are absolutely correct. Where do you draw the line?"

When it comes to separation of law enforcement from crime labs, Saferstein says that it's a challenging proposition and that the new generation of forensic scientists may find a better way to coexist, if complete separation isn't feasible. "My experiences in New Jersey, which are now at least 25 years old, may not relate to what's going on today," Saferstein acknowledges. "It's a balancing act. In my day, being within the state police and the state system in general, afforded personnel some level of protection—no one was going to come after us and close down our lab. The state police afforded us that kind of security so we never feared losing our jobs or benefits. But again, that comes at a price—often I was surrounded by semi-incompetent administrators who did not make my life easy. There was an inherent conflict between me as a civilian scientist and the officers, and I suspect it still exists today. It is a tradeoff. In the ideal world, we would be able to put the laboratory in a more secure environment free of politics, and free of economic sanctions and repercussions."

Saferstein blames everyone up and down the chain of command when crime lab scientists engage in unacceptable behaviors such as dry-labbing. "The consequences for the criminal justice system are enormous, and that can happen in any lab. And it's not just the bad behavior by the bench scientist but also poor oversight and supervision by crime lab managers. I remember many years ago there was a situation in our lab where there was an attempted cover-up of a mistake in the lab work conducted. When I investigated the error I found that the supervisor was not doing his job and checking the analyst's work. I suspended the supervisor, not the bench chemist, but the suspension was overturned by the union. You have to have a strong supervisory structure in place because unfortunately, errors will happen. Every crime lab must have a system of checks and balances built into the facility's processes."

Forensic pathologist Cyril Wecht, JD, MD, comments, "All along the spectrum there are opportunities to screw up. This field is susceptible to errors perhaps because of the multi-faceted nature of what analysts are doing, such as the failure to properly label evidence, and so on. There are a large number of touch points at which something can go wrong. I would disagree with the observation that forensic scientists are sloppier or more lackadaisical than any other scientists. In fact, I would argue that they less so. The NAS report addressed the problems of understaffing, underfunding, lack of certification, uniformity and lack of training. I think many changes have been made in the seven years since that the report came out and there is a lot more to be done."

As many forensic practitioners maintain, Wecht agrees that an adversarial legal system both exacerbates the issues of quality and brings problems to light.

"In the forensic science field, you will know about it if there is a problem with the evidence or how it was analyzed," Wecht says. "Those cases will go to court and they will be challenged. In every other field, such as medicine, you don't know about mistakes other than the ones that go to court. You read about it in the news like the O.J. Simpson case, and the debacle of the preliminary hearing, the technical errors, the things that come out on the stand. You have to keep in mind what is the lawyer is thinking and what he or she will be asking about. Many forensic scientists do learn their lessons by coming to grips with attorneys; they learn through confrontation provided by our adversarial system. I would argue strongly for the inclusion of basic legal principles in all forensic scientists' training and education. Take the essence of legal principles and feed them to forensic scientists within the course of their training and then they will have a better understanding of what's at stake and how things work."

Jay Siegel acknowledges the opportunities for things to go awry. "Forensic science is unique because you have practicing, trained, educated scientists who are applying their trade in a non-scientific atmosphere—the criminal and civil justice system," Siegel says. "But the justice system where you have trials where two parties are at odds with each other and you need to answer questions about the evidence and yet the scientists can only at times give you tentative answers or this is the answer now but check back with me in a couple of years and the answer might be different—for example, DNA has revolutionized personal identification in forensic science. So there is a natural tension between scientists and the criminal justice community and this is most often seen in the partisanship in the courtroom, so you have a prosecutor and a defendant and it's a battlefield; the two sides are marshalling their resources and the jury decides who wins. And of course, there is a tension between those two parties and then in walks the forensic scientists who might be a government scientists working for the prosecution or a scientist working for the defense and there is a tremendous amount of pull and pressure on those people to show bias about their testimony to show favor for those for whom they are working. So people who are doing this on their own and working on a consultant basis, there is a hired gun issue—there are people out there who will tell you what they are paid to say. And there are other people who will respect the science and who will only testify as to what the science says no matter who is paying them. And so that is the natural tension that has arisen between science and law, science and justice that puts forensic science in a unique position. Because a forensic scientist, as we train our students, you have to be a very good scientist to do your job but that's not enough. You also have to be an effective testifier, you have to be able to explain concepts in a language in which a jury will understand, you have to be unbiased in a very biased atmosphere; and able to maintain your unbiased nature of science. This is very difficult for new scientists but even for veterans to understand—if you spend 20 years getting nothing but cases from police and prosecutors, it's hard not to be prosecution-oriented, and if you see the carnage that people impose on each other, you want to do something about it. It's human nature. So the tendency is, 'Let's get this bad guy off the streets,' but he's maybe not the guy who did it. Just look at the 300-plus exonerations by the Innocence Project—we're not always getting it right due to poor forensic science, although not as much as the Innocence Project would have you believe. The 30,000-foot view is you have competing cultures in science and law and they meet in the courtroom, and that's where many of the problems arise."

Siegel acknowledges that the pattern evidence disciplines and their examiners have taken a hit in the 2009 NAS report and says the rebuttal lies in research and standards setting. "Research that answers any of the questions brought up by the report is good," Siegel says. "DNA is unusual in that there is a finite number of different kinds of DNA evidence and you can develop a taxonomy to classify them. That's what makes it so powerful. Once you determine how frequently each of these types of DNA occurs, then you can say something with a scientific basis about how likely it is that the DNA sample came from a person. With regard to hair evidence, the microscopic characteristics that are examined in hairs are a continuum, there's no taxonomy here. There's no way of classifying hairs as a particular type because of the variation; even in a head of hair it may exceed the variation in two people, so I don't believe that hair analysis, outside of mitochondrial DNA, is never going to get to that point. If we look at something like firearms, bullet comparison, toolmarks, questioned documents especially handwriting, and fingerprints, I think things are a little better. Again, if you look at fingerprints, there's no taxonomy in terms of ridge orientation; which is the main feature examiners use. There's not a finite number of types of fingerprints, it's almost infinite—so many ridges in so many places and so many different shapes, it's virtually impossible to develop a classification system so that you can say 'this fingerprint falls into that class and here's how common that class is.'"

Siegel continues, "That doesn't mean to say that nothing can be done with fingerprints and the other pattern evidence disciplines. What we need is research that will tell us if two fingerprints have similar characteristics, what's the likelihood they came from the same person. The problem here is that there are no standards; we don't have a standard number of characteristics between a fingerprint found and a crime scene, and a fingerprint taken from a suspect that must match each other in order for someone to declare that the fingerprint from the crime scene came from the finger of the accused. We don't have any way of expressing that probability because again, there's no taxonomy here, no classification system. The same is true for bullet striations that are used to compare microscopic markings in bullets. There's no classification system here for those minute markings and so even if you find under a microscope by observation that the markings from a test-fired bullet and the markings from a crime scene bullet are very similar to each other, you still can't state, in my view, to a reasonable scientific certainty that those bullets have a common source. Even though that kind of testimony has been offered for a hundred years, it has not been scientifically validated. This is the problem. And so, I think where we are headed with these kinds of pattern evidence is a situation where people are not going to be able to state unequivocally that two fingerprints match, that two bullets match, two handwritings match, because the science doesn't support it. It never did, and it still doesn't. More and better research will help us answer those questions but I have my doubts as to whether we will ever get over the hump and be able to say, there is no reasonable scientific doubt that these two fingerprints have a common source. I don't think we are going to get to that point. This is one of the major criticisms we leveled in the 2009 NAS report—that people were reaching conclusions about pattern evidence that were not scientifically justified and that's still the case. But old habits die hard and you have a hundred years' worth of evidence in some of these cases and no one wants to throw that all out. I think if we are going to be scientists, we have to behave like it."

REFERENCES

Almirall JR and Furton KG. Trends in forensic science education: Expansion and increased accountability. *Analytical and Bioanalytical Chemistry*. Vol. 376. Pages 1156–1159. 2003.

American Society of Crime Laboratory Directors. Commentary on Proficiency Testing in Forensic Science. 2016. Accessible at http://www.ascld.org/wp-content/uploads/2016/01/Views-doc-proficiency-testing-in-forensic-science.pdf

American Society of Crime Laboratory Directors. Comments on Initial Draft Recommendation on Developing a National Forensic Science Curriculum. August 31, 2015. Accessible at http://www.ascld.org/wpcontent/uploads/2015/09/initial_draft_recommendation_on_developing_a_national_forensic_science_curriculum.pdf

Bono JP, Anjali Swienton AR, and Upshaw Downs JC. Ethics in Testimony. In: *Ethics in Forensic Science*. Elsevier. 2012.

Cassella JP. Letter to the Editor: Forensic science on trial—Still! Response to "Educating the next generation" [Science and Justice, 48 (2008) 59–60]. *Science & Justice*. Vol. 48, No. 4. Pages 197–199. December 2008.

Daeid NN. Educating the next generation. *Science & Justice*. Vol. 48, No. 2. Pages 59–60. June 2008.

Fisher BAJ. Ethics in the Crime Laboratory and in Crime Scene Investigations. In: *Ethics in Forensic Science*. Elsevier. 2012.

Furton KG, Hsu YL, and Cole MD. What educational background is required by crime laboratory directors? *Journal of Forensic Science*. Vol. 44. Pages 128–132. 1999.

Houck MM. Overview. In: *Professional Issues in Forensic Science*. Elsevier Academic Press. Page xxi. 2015.

Houck MM and Bowen RT. Teaching Ethics. In: *Ethics in Forensic Science*. Elsevier, Cambridge, MA. 2012.

Houck MM and Siegel JA. Chapter 25: Ethical and professional issues. In: *Fundamentals of Forensic Science*. Elsevier Ltd. 2015.

Houck MM, Riley RA, Speaker PJ, and Witt TS. FORESIGHT: A business approach to improving forensic science services. *Forensic Science Policy & Management: An International Journal*. Vol. 1, No. 2. Pages 85–95. 2009.

House of Commons, Science and Technology Committee Forensic Science on Trial Seventh Report of Session 2004-05.

Jackson GP. The status of forensic science degree programs in the United States. *Forensic Science Policy and Management*. Vol. 1. Pages 2–9. 2009.

Kaye DH. The good, the bad, and the ugly: The NRC Report on strengthening forensic science in America. *Science and Justice*. Vol. 50. Page 8. 2010.

Kolowski J, Barden C, Brown C, Leete J, and Czyryca C. Proficiency testing trends following the 2009 National Academy of Sciences Report, "Strengthening Forensic Science in the United States: A Path Forward." *Forensic Science Policy & Management*. Vol. 7, Nos. 3–4. Pages 98–105. 2016.

Koppl R and Sacks M. The Criminal Justice System Creates Incentives for False Convictions. April 25, 2012. Accessible at http://works.bepress.com/roger_koppl/1/

Koppl R and Sacks M. The Criminal Justice System Creates Incentives for False Convictions. *Criminal Justice Ethics*. Vol. 32, No. 2. Pages 126–162. 2013.

Lennard C. Principles of quality assurance. In: *Professional Issues in Forensic Science*. Elsevier Academic Press. Page 77. 2015.

Madren C. Investigating the future of forensics. *AAAS*. February 26, 2013. Accessible at https://www.aaas.org/blog/depth/investigating-future-forensics

Moreno JA. Einstein on the bench: Exposing what judges do not know about science and using child abuse cases to improve how courts evaluate scientific evidence. *Ohio State Law Journal*. Vol. 64. Page 531. 2003.

National Academy of Sciences. Strengthening Forensic Science in the United States: A Path Forward 2009. Accessible at http://www.nap.edu/catalog/12589.html

National Commission on Forensic Science. Proficiency Testing in Forensic Science. March 16, 2016.

National Commission on Forensic Science. Forensic Science Curriculum Development. December 8, 2015. Accessible at https://www.justice.gov/ncfs/file/818206/download

National Commission of Forensic Science. National Code of Professional Responsibility for Forensic Science and Forensic Medicine Service Providers. March 2016. Accessible at https://www.justice.gov/ncfs/file/839711/download

National Institute of Justice. Forensic Sciences: Review of Status and Needs, Issues and Practices. 1999.

National Institute of Justice. Education and Training in Forensic Science: A Guide for Forensic Science Laboratories, Educational Institutions, and Students. June 2004.

National Research Council of the National Academies. *Strengthening Forensic Science in the United States: A Path Forward*. The National Academies Press, Washington, DC. 2009.

Office of the Attorney General. Recommendations of the National Commission on Forensic Science; Announcement for NCFS Meeting Nine. March 17, 2016. Accessible at https://www.justice.gov/ncfs/file/841861/download

Palmbach TM. Education and accreditation in forensic science. In: *Encyclopedia of Forensic Sciences*. Elsevier. Pages 171–174. 2013.

Siegel JA. The appropriate educational background for entry-level forensic scientists: A survey of practitioners. *Journal of Forensic Science*. Vol. 33. Pages 1065–1068. 1988.

Swienton AR and Upshaw Downs JC. Ethics in media. In: *Ethics in Forensic Science*. Elsevier. 2012.

Turvey BE. *Forensic Fraud: Evaluating Law Enforcement and Forensic Science Cultures in the Context of Examiner Misconduct*. Elsevier Academic Press, Waltham, MA. Page 38. 2013.

Welsh C and Aitchison G. Training to competence. In: *Encyclopedia of Forensic Sciences*. Elsevier. Pages 185–189. 2013.

CHAPTER 4

Quality Improvement in Forensic Medicine Facilities

The medicolegal death investigation system in the United States is expected to handle a heavy workload. According to the most recent data from 2004, about 1 percent of the U.S. population (about 2.6 million people) die each year. In 2004, medical examiner/coroner offices received nearly 1 million reports of deaths, constituting between 30 and 40 percent of all U.S. deaths, and accepted about one half of those (500,000, or 1 in 6 deaths) for further investigation and certification. Depending on the jurisdiction, about 40 to 50 percent of deaths referred to the medical examiner/coroner will, after investigation and examination, be attributed to natural causes, 27 to 40 percent to accident, 12 to 15 percent to suicide, 7 to 10 percent to homicide, and 1 percent as undetermined.

Just as we saw in Chapter 3 with crime laboratories, the medicolegal death investigation field faces its own barriers to accreditation and ongoing quality improvement. The 2009 NAS report enumerated the impediments, including the fact that most coroner systems cannot qualify for accreditation because of problems related to size, insufficient staff and equipment, and insufficiently trained personnel, which "inhibit their ability to perform a competent physical examination, make and/or exclude medical diagnoses on dead bodies, and make determinations of the cause and manner of death" (NAS, 2009, page 258). As the report adds, "The historic role of the coroner is insufficient to accurately perform the medicolegal and public health functions related to sudden, unexpected or violent deaths. Additionally, many medical examiner systems are constrained by budget, lack of staff, lack of equipment and insufficient facilities and cannot meet NAME standards. Also, the accreditation process requires considerable staff work, including written policies and procedures. The process requires renewal with accompanying administrative costs, so many offices do not see any benefit to accreditation." As the 2009 NAS report note furthers, "Federal incentives are lacking for states to perform an assessment of death investigation systems to determine status and needs, using as a benchmark and goal compliance with current professional standards, guidelines and accreditation requirements" (NAS, 2009, page 258).

To summarize, the 2009 NAS report outlines a long list of specific deficiencies of the medicolegal death investigation system, including systems functioning at varying levels of expertise; persistent lack of adequate facilities, equipment, staff, education, and training; lack of mandated national qualifications or certifications for death investigators; lack of one recognized set of performance standards or best practices; and lack of universally accepted or promulgated methods of quality control or quality assurance.

Let's explore these issues more closely; many of them are interrelated and confound each other. For example, a shortage of forensic pathologists, coupled with a mixed system of medical examiners and coroners, continues to exacerbate challenges within the medicolegal death investigation system.

The National Association of Medical Examiners (NAME) confirms acute personnel shortages in the medicolegal death investigation system, with a critical need for significantly more board-certified forensic pathologists than are currently available. Akin to what we have seen with forensic laboratories, medical examiner offices face significant resourcing needs, even while facing a growing demand for their services. As the 2009 NAS report observes, "Changes in the delivery of healthcare, increased patient caseloads, the inconvenience of attending scenes, the need for before and after-hours examination of decedents, and the level of remuneration have made it difficult for statewide systems to recruit busy physicians to serve as community or local medical examiners. If this trend continues, systems will rely more heavily on lay medical death investigators and will need to develop training programs that assure competency."

GROOMING AND GROWING PROFESSIONALS: CERTIFICATION AND ACCREDITATION OF MEDICOLEGAL DEATH INVESTIGATION OFFICES

The National Commission on Forensic Science (NCFS) has adopted a number of positions affecting the medicolegal death investigation system and its efforts toward quality improvement. Regarding certification of practitioners, in January 2015, the NCFS adopted the Directive Recommendation on Certification of Medicolegal Death Investigators, drafted by the Subcommittee on Medicolegal Death Investigation. The NCFS recommends that the U.S. Attorney General approve a recommendation that directs the Office of Justice Programs (OJP) to establish a priority to use grant funds to defray the cost of ensuring all medicolegal death investigators (MDIs) and coroners (who are involved in conducting medicolegal death investigations) in the United States obtain professional certification by 2020.

As the NCFS explains, "Certification is a basic credential for individuals practicing within a particular industry. ... Unfortunately, many government agencies that have the capability to provide financial support to medical examiner or coroner offices do not give priority to enhancing professional competency of our nation's MDIs. Federal funding to support certification of MDI practitioners is non-existent. The National Research Council (NRC) has published two reports which have components that emphasize the importance of improving our nation's MDI system, which is demonstrative of the fact that this vital community of practitioners is not properly supported to ensure competency. It is estimated that between 5,000 and 8,000 professionals would require certification under this recommendation. This number includes approximately 1,500 persons currently certified but requiring recertification during the next five years" (NCFS, 2015a).

The NCFS indicates that the OJP should collaborate with the National Institutes of Health (NIH) to use funds within an existing grant program or create a new grant program to defray the costs associated with certification of MDIs. OJP should also provide technical assistance and funding to enable certification programs to become formally recognized as conformant to ISO/IEC 17024. The NCFS adds that federal funding used to defray costs associated with certification would occur on a reimbursable basis when an individual or his or her employer provides documented proof of certification. It is estimated that approximately $11,210,000 will be required over five years to support such a program. As NCFS explains, "Certification costs will vary among jurisdictions and likewise it is recognized that a reimbursement-based program may not provide a strong incentive to achieve the objective. Of greater concern is how those in small jurisdictions, where work may be part-time only or involve only small numbers of cases, can obtain the necessary number of hours of supervised experience to qualify for certification. This is a matter for further study but should not preclude the certification reimbursement process for individuals who do not face such obstacles. For the purpose of cost estimates, we have used the upper estimate of 8,000 as the number of certified investigators required. Because 1,500 investigators are already certified, 6,500 additional certifications of investigators are needed. At the end of the five-year program period, individuals or their employers would be expected to cover certification costs incurred after year 2020" (NCFS, 2015a).

According to the NCFS, the total cost for a universal national medicolegal death investigation personnel certification program would range from $1.5 million to $4 million per year with a total cost of $11.2 million over the five-year period, resulting in 100 percent of personnel being certified by 2020. At the end of the five-year program period, individuals or their employers would be expected to cover certification costs incurred after 2020.

Certification of practitioners is just half of the battle, so the NCFS also adopted its Policy Recommendation on Accreditation of Medical Examiner and Coroner Offices in January 2015. In this recommendation, NCFS asks the U.S. Attorney General to approve a policy that recommends that all offices, facilities, or institutions performing government-funded official medicolegal death investigation activities, for medical examiner/coroner system, be accredited by 2020. As the NCFS explains, "Accreditation demonstrates compliance with industry and professional standards and performance criteria and provides an independent measure of assurance to the tax-paying citizens of the community served. Unfortunately, many government bodies which fund forensic science or health and human services programs do not give priority to death investigation systems, making it difficult for such systems to achieve accreditation" (NCFS, 2015b).

Unlike traditional publicly funded crime laboratories, most medicolegal death investigation offices, medical examiner, and coroner offices are not accredited. Of the estimated 2479 medicolegal death investigation offices in the United States, the NCFS reports that fewer than 100 are accredited by either the NAME or the International Association of Coroners and Medical Examiners (IAC&ME), the only two accrediting bodies in the United States for medicolegal death investigation institutions. However, as the NCFS points out, neither NAME nor the IAC&ME are formally recognized by an external standards organization to be in compliance with international standards such as ISO/IEC 17011. As the NCFS comments, "Both accreditation processes have standards that have been developed using rigorous processes and are accepted as national standards by the interested medico-legal professional associations. Formal recognition of NAME or IAC&ME by an existing external organization appears to require more resources than either entity can currently bear" (NCFS, 2015b).

The NCFS advises the U.S. Attorney General to direct the OJP to use funds within an existing grant program or create a new grant program to defray the costs associated with accreditation of medicolegal death investigation offices nationally. The OJP should also provide technical assistance and funding to enable NAME and IAC&ME to become formally recognized as conformant to ISO/IEC 17011. As NCFS notes, "Whether reimbursement, by itself, is an effective incentive to medicolegal offices to become accredited is unclear. The Subcommittee believes that it may be, especially for small jurisdictions with small budgets. An alternative might be to use federal funds to pay for accreditation inspection fees at the time an office applies to NAME or IAC&ME for inspection (rather than after accreditation is achieved). This approach would at least result in inspection (or review of the accreditation application that does not require on-site inspection), and if an office is denied accreditation, would provide the office with information to correct deficiencies and continue the process of working to achieve accreditation" (NCFS, 2015b).

The NCFS acknowledged that "preparation for accreditation requires that specific criteria be met in terms of physical space, facilities, equipment, staffing, and other factors: "These indirect costs can be substantial, and funding opportunities need to be identified for assisting with such indirect costs. This is a matter for further study and policy development."

Finally, the NCFS recognized the deficit of forensic pathologists, so in August 2015, it adopted its Views Document on Increasing the Supply of Forensic Pathologists. As it explains, "Having an adequate supply of forensic pathologists (FPs) is a public health and public safety imperative. NCFS believes that change will not come without intervention" (NCFS, 2015c). The NCFS notes several areas of significant impact, including better exposure to forensic pathology in medical schools and training programs; improved quality with autopsy performance by forensic pathologists; improvement of forensic pathologist compensation; and adequate facilities and technology.

As we have seen, currently there are not enough board-certified forensic pathologists in the United States to meet national needs, with some areas having limited or no access to forensic pathologists. As the NCFS states, "The forensic pathologist should be an autonomous and neutral physician independent of political influence and law enforcement officials. The work of the forensic pathologist should be performed in a modern, nationally accredited medicolegal system. These work conditions could help attract and retain forensic pathologists" (NCFS, 2015c).

Although no specific workload numbers exist, Weinberg et al. (2013) examined the characteristics of medicolegal death investigation offices accredited by NAME. The researchers found that in accredited offices, there was an average of 3.7 forensic pathologists per 1 million population conducting an average of 222 autopsies per pathologist, which is within the annual case load limits established by NAME (250 autopsies and autopsy equivalents per year per pathologist). As NCFS notes, "Utilizing these data, it can be extrapolated that between 1,100 and 1,200 board-certified forensic pathologists (BC-FPs) are required nationally to conduct forensic autopsies. This estimate would include fellows in training and would take into account FPs such as chief medical examiners and others who would perform a reduced autopsy load to accommodate activities such as administration or research. Unfortunately, there are estimated to be only 500 board-certified FPs currently practicing forensic pathology full time, with an average age of 52 years" (NCFS, 2015c).

Just 41 individuals annually were trained in forensic pathology between 2007 and 2013, for a total of 290. That's the sobering findings by Hanzlick (2014). Furthermore, Hanzlick and Haden-Pinneri (2011) conducted a study of 190 people who did a forensic pathology fellowship from 2000 to 2005; of these, approximately 67 percent practiced full-time forensic pathology; 21 percent did not practice at all; 7 percent practiced part time; 3 percent only did forensic pathology consulting; and 2.6 percent did not complete the fellowship. Just 67 percent of those who trained in forensic pathology eventually obtained board certification, and just 78 percent of those practiced forensic pathology full time.

The NCFS crunched the numbers and came up with the depressing calculation that "Considering an annual creation rate of 21 FPs per year, and given the current work force of 500 FPs, it would take approximately 25 years to create enough FPs to serve the current

U.S. population, assuming no population growth during that time. Compounding this issue, the FP workforce is annually decreasing due to attrition from retirement, death, and other factors, including job dissatisfaction because of the stressful nature of political, legal, and media encounters; poor working conditions; the nature of the work; and/or low salaries" (NCFS, 2015c).

To combat these statistics, the NCFS emphasizes that action is required at the earliest entry point: "The forensic pathologist supply problem starts earlier than forensic pathology fellowship programs and involves the discipline of pathology as well. Approximately 17,500 medical school students graduate each year. Of those, approximately 3 percent of graduates will train in pathology, with 7 percent of pathology trainees then training in forensic pathology. The College of American Pathologists posits that the current numbers of pathologists in training will not match the nation's need for hospital-based pathologists. Consequently, there is the potential for increased competition for the limited number of pathology residents between hospital-based subspecialties and forensic pathology. A coordinated effort is needed to recruit more medical students into pathology and forensic pathology" (NCFS, 2015c).

To accomplish this, the NCFS says forensic pathology should be introduced in the medical school curriculum within the first two years, "as this is a prime time to attract future FPs." The NCFS says the curriculum should dedicate a minimum of a two-hour block of time to a lecture on forensic pathology, and autopsy case material should be presented by a FP in association with trauma and natural disease clinical course material. In the third and fourth year, elective rotations in forensic pathology should be offered. Because medical schools receive extensive federal funding, a suggestion for establishing a block of time to lecture on forensic pathology as well as establishing elective rotations in forensic pathology would likely be honored if proposed in a strong manner. Students engaged in an anatomic pathology residency should be required to complete a minimum of four weeks of training in forensic pathology. Anatomic pathology residents should be required to spend at least four weeks in a medico-legal death investigation office accredited by NAME, assisting FPs in performing medicolegal autopsies. If there are no such opportunities locally, arrangements should be made with a medico-legal office to provide such a rotation. FPs not on the regular pathology department faculty should be compensated for their mentorship."

Once a new generation of forensic pathologists has been groomed and are placed out in the workforce, the NCFS emphasizes that to retain these professionals, "... salaries must be more competitive with hospital/academic pathology and other medical specialties" (NCFS, 2015c).

A 2011 survey by the College of American Pathologists revealed that the average annual compensation of full-time pathologists is approximately $335,000, when base salary, incentive pay, deferred compensation, and other income are considered. In comparison, Kemp (2014) found that the average salary of a medical examiner is just under $185,000; the salary is only slightly better for chief and deputy chief medical examiners, who have average annual incomes of approximately $220,000 and $190,000, respectively. In addition to the low salaries, the NCFS pointed out, the average forensic pathologist just entering the field carries significant debt from undergraduate and graduate medical education. Youngclaus and Fresne (2013) found that 86 percent of medical school graduates report having debt, and in 2012, the median debt of graduating physicians was $170,000.

The NCFS suggests that salaries and benefits for forensic pathologists can be improved through incentives, grant programs, or agreements with associated medical schools:

"Some areas of the United States lack access to forensic pathology services and may be considered 'unserved' populations. As with some clinical medical specialties, incentives to place FPs in such areas should be developed, such as medical school loan forgiveness programs similar to those offered to other physicians. Having greater options for work locations could also attract more people into forensic pathology. Although this might be viewed as a separate issue, the primitive working conditions of many offices may act as a disincentive to increasing the number of and retaining forensic pathologists. Recognition of the essential role that forensic pathology plays in the criminal justice continuum necessitates quality facilities in which to work, including integration of modern diagnostic technologies such as computed tomography, magnetic resonance imaging and genetic testing" (NCFS, 2015c).

One person not dissuaded from the field was forensic pathologist Michael Baden, MD, presently a consulting pathologist in private practice in New York City and a former chief medical examiner there.

"My first love was journalism, and I did apply and was accepted at Columbia University," he says. "But my mother persuaded me to go to medical school because she felt that was a much better profession and she turned out to be right; when I was editor-in-chief of the newspaper at City College in New York there were something like 15 newspapers in the five boroughs of New York City and now there are about four. Medicine as a profession has expanded greatly, while journalism did not."

Baden earned a bachelor of science degree from the City College of New York and a medical degree from New York University School of Medicine. He trained in internal medicine and pathology at Bellevue Hospital Medical Center where he was an intern, resident, and then chief resident. He has held professorial teaching appointments at Albert Einstein Medical School, Albany Medical College, New York University School of Medicine, New York Law School, and John Jay College of Criminal Justice. He has been a consultant to the Federal Bureau of Investigation, Veteran's Administration, Bureau of Alcohol, Tobacco and Firearm's, Drug Enforcement Agency, and the United States Department of Justice.

Baden recalls the defining moment in his choice of a medical career: "I started out initially wanting to be an internist, treating living patients," he says. "I attended New York University School of Medicine. I did my internship and residency in medicine in Belleview Hospital's internal medicine department, and along the way I would go down to the autopsy room where the medical examiners were also working at Belleview to see what the autopsies found on the patients that I had treated. One day I had a patient at Belleview who had come in with endocarditis, an infection of the heart caused by the use of dirty needles because he was a heroin addict. At one time, when a person developed endocarditis, almost everybody died because the antibiotics weren't as good as they are now. I treated this patient for about eight weeks with a heavy course of penicillin, which is all we had at the time. Miraculously, he had recovered. I presented the case at grand rounds because it was such an unusual recovery from such a severe disease at the time. A couple of days later I went down the medical examiners' part of the autopsy room and I was shocked to see that patient lying there dead. I realized that treating the disease that the person has when he or she comes into the hospital isn't always as important as the underlying condition that brings them to the hospital; that patient had gone right out from the hospital and started using heroin again. He hadn't realized he had lost his tolerance for heroin in the few months he was in the hospital and he died of an overdose upon his next usage of the drug. It struck me then that I can learn more from the dead than from the living."

Baden continues, "As an internist I would see one patient at a time and try to work out their condition, whereas down in the medical examiners' autopsy room, you see things that can help lots and lots of patients—for example, how do you deal with a person addicted to alcohol or drugs when you see the damage done to the body. I was amazed by how much the dead can tell us to help the living. At the time, I considered the work of the medical examiner and how the fact that he or she determined how people died to develop preventive measures might be more helpful as a physician than treating patients after they have acquired conditions that could have been prevented."

His experience with the heroin addict stayed with Baden, and since then, he has been a member of the board of directors of a number of drug abuse and alcohol abuse treatment programs, where he attempts to apply what he has learned from the dead at the autopsy table to the betterment of the living.

In the more than 45 years of medical examiner work, he has performed 20,000-plus autopsies. His list of accomplishments is long and studded with high-profile case work. He served as the chairman of the Forensic Pathology Panel of the U.S. Congress Select Committee on Assassinations that reinvestigated the deaths of President John F. Kennedy and Dr. Martin Luther King, Jr. in the 1970s. He was the forensic pathologist member of a team of U.S. forensic scientists asked by the Russian government to examine the newly found remains of Tsar Nicholas II, Alexandra, and the Romanov family in Siberia in the 1990s. He has been an expert in multiple Iraq-related court martials in the United States and Camp Liberty, Baghdad. He has also been an expert in the investigations concerning Medgar Evers, John Belushi, Yankee Manager Billy Martin, Marlon Brando's son Christian Brando, O.J. Simpson, Jayson Williams, Kobe Bryant, Robert Blake, and Las Vegas hotel owner Ted Binion. He has investigated deaths around the world for human rights groups and private attorneys. He has taught homicide courses for police, judges, attorneys, and physicians in most of the 50 states as well as internationally.

Despite so many high-profile deaths, Baden says he has not lost sight of the value of the more routine autopsy. "Every death is equally important," he says. "Every death has a history, has a family, has a lot connected to the dead body, so much so that I think it is a mistake to say an autopsy could be 'routine.'"

Baden also admits that despite seeing on his autopsy table the worst of what humanity can inflict upon each other, the dead aren't as problematic as the living. "It was a lot harder for me to deal with patients who were alive but dying when I was a resident and an internist at Belleview, rather than working with the dead," he says. "For me and for most medical examiners I know, it's easier to deal with death because there is no pain and suffering that we see. When I treated patients who were dying of cancer and couldn't do anything but provide comfort measures, that was very hard for me to take. But seeing someone who was hit by a car and who died, or were shot, is easier in a sense because that person probably died right away—that part of the empathy for the patient is much less."

Baden recalls his earliest work as a medical student, assisting Milton Helpern, MD, who was the chief ME in NYC at the time. "I was helping with autopsies and discovering the challenges associated with the work in the early days," Baden says. "At that time, for example, the skull bones had to be opened up with a hand saw because there were no electrical devices to cut through bone. When I was in my first year of medical school I came by the ME's office regularly to help with that part of the autopsy, and I was delighted to do it because I learned a great deal. As I was advancing through medical school, I always had an appreciation of the kind of work that medical examiners did but it wasn't until I had treated that heroin patient and I saw the futility of my treatment and that I really hadn't helped him much by curing him of his endocarditis—all I did was reduce his tolerance to heroin so that he died more easily when he took an injection in the street. That's what really turned me on to medical examiner work and I discovered that it was more suitable to me than becoming an internist."

Baden says forensic pathology allowed him to tap into his ability to communicate with stakeholders. "When I started working as an assistant ME, I noticed that I was growing in my ability to talk to the families of the dead because I had already had practice of communicating with living patients and their relatives at Belleview Hospital, explaining what was happening to them and if they died, discussing with family members how their loved one died. This experience was a great help to me; being able to correlate the autopsy with history, what I expected to find, and being able to explain things to the families. There were some MEs I worked with who went into forensic pathology because they didn't like to speak to families, and you only speak to other doctors and hospital pathologists often. I enjoyed the contact with the families of the living and I think that helped me a great deal with the families of the dead, explaining things to them and learning things from them about the decedent's history that helped me to understand and interpret the autopsy findings. In general, I was greatly helped by my two years of working in internal medicine, and learning from my two professors who won the Nobel Prize for the work on hearts and lungs and their ability to correlate the symptoms of the person and the functioning of the body during life. For example, it made me able to better understand how a heart functioned during life so that in death, I could understand what the body then presented during autopsy."

Although the autopsy process is standardized, the forensic pathologist often brings to the table certain skill sets that are unique to the individual. In his case, Baden says he found himself hearkening back to the basics of journalism. "When I was on my school paper, we were putting into practice the concept of reporting on the 'who, what, when, where and why' that is part of the tenets of good journalism," he says.

"As forensic pathologists, we do the same thing and try to answer those key questions. But the 'who' we are looking for is not 'whodunit,' but who the decedent is. It is our responsibility to know the proper name of the individual and we do that in various ways, mostly by direct identification—so that is the 'who.' How it happened, how the person died, is part of the autopsy process. What happened, the cause of death, where it happened, whether the person died at the scene or was moved there, are all important inquiries. In the case of a suspected homicide, is this a primary or a secondary place of death? How long has the person been dead? As for the 'why,' we sometimes can figure it out. The time of death is important, as well. We conduct the autopsy to determine cause of death but toxicology tells us why something happened, too."

Baden continues, "And through it all, we are divorced from whether they arrested the right guy or not. I hope the prosecutor has the right guy. When I do the autopsy and testify, I am not testifying that he had done it, as that depends on lots of things, but I am testifying about all of the independent scientific things that happened and that is part of our autopsy. I think once we get concerned about making sure that we support the prosecutor and his or her interpretation of the case, then we are faulty and that brings about a lot of problems. This is especially true in deaths during police encounters, which I think nowadays are the hardest of cases that medical examiners do because we get our information from the police. Law enforcement is usually pretty good at giving us information when they are not involved in an individual's death, but as soon as they are potentially involved, they become like every other citizen who is biased in one way or another about how the death occurred. We must be careful just to take the findings, the evidence as we find it, without trying to spin it in the favor of one party over the other."

Officer-involved incidents are of interest to Baden, and in August of 2014, he conducted the autopsy of Michael Brown, the unarmed black teenager shot dead by a police officer in Ferguson, Missouri. At the request of Brown's family's legal team, Baden performed the four-hour autopsy in a mortuary office turned makeshift examining room. The county of St. Louis had already conducted its own autopsy, and the Justice Department followed with an autopsy of its own in this controversial case. Baden's testimony aligned with the events as described by Brown's attorneys; Baden reported that there were no signs of a struggle, and he predicted that his report would be supported by the official ones that followed.

He also actively pursues work with inmates' rights. While he has many accomplishments, Baden says one of the biggest in his mind is championing the treatment of prisoners. "That work came about for me because in 1971, there was an uprising at Attica state prison in upstate New York in which 43 people were killed—something like 11 guards and 32 prisoners," Baden says. "At the time, I was working in the NYC medical examiner's office when I was asked by the governor's office to come up to Attica where the deaths had occurred and to autopsy all of the dead. There was a dispute as to why the deaths occurred and only one of the counties involved had a forensic pathologist. New York state is a combination of medical examiner and coroner offices; of 62 counties, about 15 have a medical examiner in charge. There are almost 50 elected coroners, very few of whom are doctors and certainly not trained as forensic pathologists. So, I went to Attica and re-autopsied about 40 of the bodies. I found that a lot of mistakes had been made in those original autopsies and discovered that some of the things said about how the deaths occurred were missed, such as most of the guards' deaths were caused by gunshot wounds from the police who were trying to help them. They were trying to shoot at the prisoners but instead shot the guards who were being held hostage. That fact had not been recognized at the time. As a result of that, and as a result of the reason for the uprising—which was that the prisoners said that the guards were mistreating them and killing them—some committed suicide and it was covered up as heart attacks, myocardial infarctions. After this incident was over, the governor appointed me, as the forensic pathologist, along with a few others, to start a medical review board to review all deaths in custody in jails and prisons in New York state and city. It was our responsibility to determine the causes of death so they could not be covered up as they had been in the past. I have been on that board since its inception, and I'm proud of how it is affected the quality of life of prisoners. If someone dies from maltreatment, we will pick up on that fact during the autopsy. We will also take steps to bring guards up on charges and have people's licenses revoked, if prisoners are not treated properly. Since Attica, even though there have been a number of prison uprisings in New York since, there hasn't been a singular death from such an uprising and that's because I think in part, they know it will come before our medical review board and we will seek the truth during our investigations."

Baden continues, "So that is kind of a living legacy and change that I think I am very much part of. I think that exposes now lots of problems in prisons currently, and I think New York has established a standard for the rest of the country. No one else had this kind of review board before then. Gov. Rockefeller made sure that the state review board was separate from the county, as deaths are usually handled by the counties—each has its own police and district attorney that handles them and there is too much pressure not to make trouble for the county. Rockefeller set up a state system less pressured to do things the wrong way. It works when people also die under police custody or are injured and then die due to encounters with the police. It's a tough thing to investigate but I'm glad we are able to do that."

It's a departure from the glamor of the spotlight that has followed Baden for much of his career. Baden has been highly visible on television due to consulting for networks such as Fox News, where he worked as the forensic science contributor, and for a number of years he served as host of the HBO series *Autopsy*, in which he demonstrated how the various forensic sciences assist in solving crimes. He also was a consultant for the *Crossing Jordan* television series that depicted the experiences of a female medical examiner.

Like some forensic pathologists, he has also penned a number of books. His two popular nonfiction books are *Unnatural Death, Confessions of a Medical Examiner* and *Dead Reckoning, The New Science of Catching Killers*. He is also the author, with his wife, attorney Linda Kenney Baden, of two forensic thrillers, *Remains Silent* and *Skeleton Justice*.

Amidst the time in front of the camera and behind a computer, Baden can look back on a career on both sides of the forensic pathology spectrum—government and private practice, as well as criminal and civil case work. "I worked for the city for 25 years and when I first started at that time, Milton Helpern, the chief ME, encouraged us to do some outside work on civil cases," he recalls. "As MEs, we got paid very little, far less than the hospital pathologists were, and so he encouraged us to do some outside work on civil cases that were not connected with the office. I had a smattering of experience during my early years, testifying in civil litigation that was not related to our work at the ME's office. Cases such as people dying in automobile accidents or people dying in fires that came to civil litigation, and that's where I became accustomed to the courtroom."

Baden says that after serving with the state police for 25 years, he continued to assist with some cases, but also was able to conduct private work. "I was able to do homicide cases that were not connected with the state police," Baden says. "I liked the experience of working on both sides and I learned a lot about the importance of the independence of the medical examiner's office. I realized that defendants weren't all bad guys necessarily, and that sometimes mistakes were made by police and we should be involved in terms of 'whodunit.' I could handle some homicide cases from other jurisdictions usually outside of New York state that were homicides, either for the prosecution as I did often, or for the defense, independent of my official job. My official job with the city and the state prevented me from getting involved on the defense side of any homicide cases because it would be a conflict of interest. At the time, I was with the state police, it gave me more opportunity to be involved for the defense. Since retirement from the state police, I have been able to spend more time in my private forensic pathology practice where I have more freedom to evaluate and select cases where I think my expertise might be important as opposed to official cases where I had to investigate fully everyone in the jurisdiction. I can pick and choose now and it is a freedom I enjoy; it has helped me to understand that there's good and bad on all sides in these cases and my job is to do the same job for all, as well as to do the best I can when I advise a prosecutor or defense attorney. No matter which one I am working for, I would tell them the same thing—the autopsy findings, the toxicology findings, the questions asked—it must be the same thing whether I am engaged by the defense or the prosecution. I do not get involved emotionally in the case. It's always my hope that when I am involved, the prosecutor has the right guy and when I am involved with the defense I hope that they have reasonable argument—it may not always come down to guilt or innocence. I am now in my stage of evolution as a forensic pathologist where I can pick and choose the cases where I think I can make a difference."

That difference often starts back at the autopsy table. "I think what has been most interesting to me is translating what we find on the autopsy table into actions that can help the living. For example, my interest in pathology started with that heroin-addicted patient. That case got me into forensic pathology as opposed to internal medicine. Since then I have worked with a number of organizations that assist individuals with their heroin addictions. One example is that I helped establish Odyssey House, which is working in New York to treat heroin addiction as a condition that is curable, if individuals realize the dangers. From my point of view, it's not a death sentence if people undergo proper treatment."

In the past, NAME has been agitating for change, especially when it comes to the need for at least 850 board-certified forensic pathologists, roughly double the current number, as many autopsies are still being performed by coroners—individuals without training in general pathology and forensic pathology. Because of the variability in the U.S. medicolegal death investigation system due to a mix of medical examiner and coroner offices, the level of quality also fluctuates. A needs-assessment report by NAME (2004) observed, "It is readily apparent that quality of service varies greatly from one area to another. Unfortunately, with any particular person's death, the quality of the medico-legal death investigation is predicated on where that death occurs. While there are many high-quality medico-legal offices, in order to ensure excellent death investigation throughout the entire nation, we must improve those offices that are lacking in funding, competent staff and facilities. Medico-legal death investigation requires a high level of competence, professionalism, and ethics. The work itself is critical and has widespread impact on not only the criminal and civil justice systems, but on the families of the deceased, the community, and issues of public health. The basis for a quality death investigation system is through the integrated practice of various highly trained and certified professionals."

Coroners are elected county officials who are responsible for medicolegal duties in the jurisdictions they serve; in some states, the coroner must be a physician; in many other coroner systems, this requirement does not exist. As NAME (2004) comments, "In many coroner systems, important decisions such as whether or not to perform an autopsy are made by persons without the appropriate medical education, training and experience." Medical examiners most commonly are licensed physicians appointed to perform official medicolegal death investigations and conduct postmortem examinations. Because most medical examiners are not pathologists and are therefore not trained to perform autopsies, they must rely on pathologists (ideally, qualified forensic pathologists) to perform autopsies. Although many pathologists are currently performing medicolegal autopsies, relatively few of them are trained and credentialed in the subspecialty of forensic pathology. Pathologist medical examiners are most often government employees but may be private practice or academic pathologists engaged to work for a particular medicolegal jurisdiction. The most highly educated and trained group in the death investigation field are the forensic pathologists. Forensic pathology is the distinct subspecialty within the medical field of pathology that deals specifically with the investigation of cause and manner of death and the performance of medicolegal autopsies and ancillary studies.

In some jurisdictions, the title of medical examiner is bestowed on nonpathologist physicians who respond to the initial notification of death and are responsible for screening and referring appropriate cases for further evaluation by a forensic pathologist. The term medicolegal death investigator or death investigator is commonly used for frontline lay investigators. An increasing number of jurisdictions opt to use nonphysician investigators to perform scene and background investigations in support of physician medical examiners and forensic pathologists. The American Board of Medico-Legal Death Investigators registers and certifies such practitioners in accordance with the National Institute of Justice's

National Guidelines for Death Investigation. This, however, is a voluntary program, and in some jurisdictions, investigators are not required to have any formal education in basic death investigation procedures. According to the NAME (2004) report, "It is perhaps axiomatic that the accuracy of the forensic pathologist's determinations is contingent upon important decisions and procedures initiated by the individual who receives the first notification of death and performs the initial investigation. Working closely with the criminal justice system and law enforcement agencies, medical examiners/coroners must remain independent and objective watchdogs for the public they serve. Lack of qualified investigators and forensic pathologists, insufficient and outdated facilities, shortfalls in equipment and supportive manpower, insufficient funding, and disparate availability of needed consultative services can result in miscarriages of justice or unacceptable risks to the public's health: Homicides may be missed, the innocent may be wrongly accused and/or incarcerated, the guilty may be wrongly exonerated, civil actions and outcomes may be flawed, or infectious disease epidemics can spread."

Wetli (2005) has observed that forensic pathology is "perhaps the smallest of medical specialties, yet it is the one that is often in the forefront of intense public interest." Unfortunately, the small number of forensic pathologists in the United States more or less guarantees that most systems lack the leadership of a forensic pathologist serving as a medical examiner who is especially prepared to conduct medicolegal death investigations. The primary responsibility of the forensic pathologist is to determine the cause and manner of death. In most jurisdictions, the manner of death is limited to one of five categories: homicide, suicide, accident, natural, and undetermined. Another equally important duty of the forensic pathologist is to ensure that the deceased is correctly identified.

The forensic pathologist is specially trained to perform autopsies to determine the presence or absence of disease, injury, or poisoning; to evaluate historical and law enforcement investigative information relating to manner of death; and to collect medical evidence in order to document injuries and to determine how a person received these injuries. A medicolegal autopsy is ordered by the coroner or medical examiner, as authorized by law, with the statutory purpose of establishing the cause of death and to answer other medicolegal questions.

Wetli (2005) acknowledges the subtleties that the forensic pathologist can detect relating to the position's expected responsibilities: "Traditionally, the forensic pathologist has been charged with determining the cause and manner of death of those decedents falling within the medical examiner's or coroner's jurisdiction. In reality, the cause and manner of death are already known in a great many, if not the majority, of cases. ... Hence, the real, but often unstated, focus of the forensic pathologist is to identify, document, and preserve everything of a potentially evidentiary nature. Indeed, the 'art of forensic pathology' is to anticipate the questions that will be asked in the future: today, tomorrow, and several years from today."

Forensic pathologists are trained in traditional medicine as well as nonmedical disciplines relating to toxicology, trace evidence, forensic serology, and DNA technology. The forensic pathologist acts as the case coordinator for the medical and forensic scientific assessment of a given death, making sure that the appropriate procedures and evidence collection techniques are applied to the body. And when forensic pathologists are employed as death investigators, they bring their expertise to bear on the interpretation of the scene of death, in the assessment of the consistency of witnesses' statements with injuries, and the interpretation of injury patterns or patterned injuries. In jurisdictions where there are medical examiner systems, forensic pathologists are usually employed to perform autopsies to determine cause of death.

What particularly empowers the forensic pathologist is a slate of advanced education and training. The future forensic pathologist earns an undergraduate degree, then another four years in medical school to earn an MD or DO degree. According to NAME, following medical school there are several routes by which one may become a forensic pathologist: One may spend four years training in anatomic and clinical pathology followed by a one-year residency or fellowship in forensic pathology; or one may train for several years in anatomic pathology and train for an additional year in forensic pathology. The residency training in forensic pathology involves practical experience supervised by a trained forensic pathologist. The forensic pathology resident performs autopsies and participates in death investigations.

Contrast this with the coroner system. The office of the coroner (or "crowner") dates back to medieval times in England when the crowner was responsible for looking into deaths to be sure death duties were paid to the king. The coroner's primary duty in contemporary times is to make inquiry into the death and complete the certificate of death. The coroner assigns a cause and manner of death and lists them on the certificate of death; the coroner also decides if a death occurred under natural circumstances or was due to accident, homicide, suicide, or undetermined means or circumstances. Although coroners are frequently called on to determine if a death was due to foul play, depending on the jurisdiction and the law defining the coroner's duties, the coroner may or may not be trained in medicine, law enforcement, or forensic science. Thus, the lay coroner may consult physicians, pathologists, or forensic pathologists to perform autopsies when there appears to be a question or manner of death that autopsy can elucidate. In some jurisdictions, the coroner is a physician, but in many more jurisdictions, the coroner is not required to be a physician nor be trained in medicine. A common criticism is that in the absence of medical expertise, the nonphysician coroner may have difficulty sorting out subtle nonviolent and violent causes of death.

The first formal acknowledgment of the need for medical training for coroners occurred in 1860, when Maryland passed legislation allowing coroners to require that a physician be present at an inquest. In 1877, Massachusetts became the first state to replace its coroners with medical examiners, who were required to be physicians. In 1918, New York City instituted a medical examiner system.

It wasn't until 1928 when National Academy of Sciences (NAS) first addressed the state of death investigation. The National Research Council (NRC)'s Committee on Medical Legal Problems released a report that was critical of the status quo, and made four recommendations: that the office of the coroner be abolished; that the medical duties of the coroner's office be vested in the office of the medical examiner; that the office of the medical examiner be headed by a scientifically trained and competent pathologist, selected and retained under civil service; and that the office of the medical examiner be provided with the services of a staff competent in toxicology, bacteriology, and other sciences necessary in the scientific investigation of causes of death, and with adequate scientific equipment. In addition, the committee recommended the development of medicolegal institutes that would affiliate medical examiners with hospitals and universities.

A follow-up report in 1932 reviewed existing medicolegal collaborations and again advised a larger role for medical doctors within forensic science and criminal proceedings. It wasn't until 1954 that the Model Post-Mortem Examinations Act was issued by the National Conference of Commissioners on Uniform State Laws; it noted the need for "a means whereby greater competence can be assured in determining causes of death where criminal liability may be involved. Experience has shown that many elected coroners are not well trained in the field of pathology, and the Act should set up in each state an Office headed by a trained pathologist, this Office to have jurisdiction over postmortem examinations for criminal purposes. The Office would supersede the authority of Coroner's Offices in this field" (NASEM, 2009).

Following the release of the Model Act, a number of states implemented the proposed guidelines. Between 1960 and 1979, 12 states converted from coroners to medical examiners. However, in the subsequent decades, updates to death investigation organizations slowed considerably. Between 1980 and 1999, only three states converted from coroner to medical examiner systems. Since then, 11 states with coroners have remained unchanged, and only a handful of individual counties have independently implemented recommendations from the Model Act. Several of the remaining coroner states have provisions in their state constitutions requiring that coroners be elected. Although these provisions may be amended or removed, to do so will require political momentum. However, these provisions do not prohibit the addition of appointed medical examiners.

According to some of the most recent data available, as of 2004, 16 states had a centralized statewide medical examiner system, 14 had a county coroner system, 7 had a county medical examiner system, and 13 had a mixed county ME/C system. Eight states had hybrid arrangements, with coroners and a state medical examiner office that performed medicolegal duties. The District of Columbia relies on a medical examiner system. In total, there were approximately 2342 separate death investigation jurisdictions. Of 1590 coroner offices in the United States, 82 serve jurisdictions with more than 250,000 people; 660 medium-sized offices serve between 25,000 and 249,999 people; and 848 offices serve small jurisdictions of fewer than 25,000 people. As the 2009 NAS report notes, "The hodgepodge and multiplicity of systems and controlling statutes makes standardization of performance difficult, if not impossible. Some observers believe that a revisiting of the model code is required, as has been proposed by numerous study groups over the years, in order to work toward the development of a modern model code for death investigation systems that utilizes new and available technologies that are responsive to the needs of the citizens" (NAS, 2009, page 246).

The 2009 NAS report, in Recommendation 11, stated that in order to improve medicolegal death investigation, "Congress should authorize and appropriate incentive funds to the National Institute of Forensic Science (NIFS) for allocation to states and jurisdictions to establish medical examiner systems, with the goal of replacing and eventually eliminating existing coroner systems" (NAS, 2009, page 24).

Many forensic pathologists have been vocal about the importance of abolishing the coroner system, including Pennsylvanian Cyril Harrison Wecht, MD, JD, who has been on both sides of the issue as a county commissioner, coroner, and later medical examiner of Allegheny County, Pennsylvania. And it's not just the letters behind his name that make Pennsylvanian Cyril Harrison Wecht, MD, JD, a pioneer that is able to stand at the intersection of medicine and law, but his 54 years of experience blending the two disciplines that have shaped a legendary forensic science career. A bulwark of steadfastness, Wecht has successfully fought charges of fraud brought against him, has consulted on a number of high-profile cases, and has advanced medicolegal thought. Not bad for a guy who originally worked as a concertmaster at the University of Pittsburgh because he wanted to be a musician (he plays the violin). Instead, Wecht earned his medical degree, then his law degree, and went on to forge a forensic pathology career that many professionals could only dream of.

Wecht says his unique medical and law background has served him well in his endeavors. "Based upon my education, training and experience, plus the way I have practiced over the last 54 years after completion of all of my training, I think all of those experiences come together to help me be the best I can be," he says. "Obviously in a case where I am conducting an autopsy, my thoughts are as a forensic pathologist, and I am doing what is necessary for a good post-mortem examination. But then my legal training can kick in and I am also thinking about whatever potential legal questions might arise relative to that death. And that is the essence of forensic pathology. It would be good, I think, if everyone practicing in forensic pathology could have some legal training. I don't believe they have to go to law school and get a law degree; that is not what I am suggesting. But if I were in charge of a forensic pathologist training program, I would make mandatory some exposure to some legal training at a nearby law school in order to get some experience in the basic subjects of law, criminal procedure, torts and civil procedure law. Because then the forensic pathologist has a better understanding of processes of the justice system. Remember, the typical physician—and I realize there are exceptions—is someone who went to college and was interested in science courses; then they go into medical school for more science and medicine, and then they have four or five years of specialized training during their various residencies. They are intelligent people but what do they know about the law? It's foreign to them. And of course, the reverse is true for the attorneys—pre-law students do not get a lot of exposure to the sciences. They go into law, but what do they know about medicine?"

Wecht continues, "That's why I believe that for a long time, I was one of the first persons with both degrees. There are several more people now who have achieved that accomplishment than there were when I first got started. Many forensic pathologists believe that kind of background is helpful. I went to law school and I worked hard and I was very lucky having people in charge who very graciously permitted me to go to law school when I was doing my residency. I am probably the only person who has ever done that. I would strongly urge the people in charge of forensic pathology training programs to add a few legal courses, even if it means adding another three months to the overall program. Just work it out, even if it is just one afternoon a week; I bet every law school in the country would be delighted to be part of such a program."

With regard to how Wecht approaches a case, he says, "When I conduct an autopsy, I am functioning as a forensic pathologist, using my medical knowledge, but I am thinking, what are the forensic implications of this case, what are they going to ask me on the stand in a courtroom, what are they going to be looking for, and what are they going to want to know: 'Dr. Wecht, did you check for this? Dr. Wecht, did you check for that?' So I employ both skills—medicine and law—as a forensic pathologist. As a medico-legal consultant, both aspects come into play and I am correlating all of these things, the interface of law and medicine, and that interface is nowhere more meaningful, more frequently occurring, more relevant, more played out in civil and criminal litigation than it is in forensic pathology."

Despite performing about 20,000 autopsies and reviewing or supervising another 40,000 autopsies, Wecht says he engaged in lifelong learning. "There's no question that no matter how extensive your training may have been, no matter how good your chief and the people ahead of you were in helping to educate you, you keep learning as you go along," he confirms. "After tens of thousands of autopsies, I still come up every now and then with a case that is challenging, that is new, that is different. It doesn't happen often, but it is the human body we're dealing with, and think of what we don't know yet about it. There are so many functions of the body we have yet to learn; so if that is true in medicine, we can only imagine what we may still have to learn in forensic pathology and forensic science. As part of our work we apply medical and pathological findings to legal problems, and the law is nowhere near as firm and fixed and definable and relatively uniform as medicine, especially where we have an adversarial legal system. So now, if you take things that have come from a field that is not absolute or rigid and you apply it to a field that is designed to challenge, to test, to disagree, then you can see how you can have new problems all of the time. So yes, you learn a great deal and I have learned a lot from the autopsy table as well as the courtroom—such as what makes people tick, and what to think of families, judges and juries. The more you are able to keep this in mind and the more aware and sensitive you are to all of this, the better your performance will be because you are broadening your vision; you are not narrow-minded or focusing only on one particular aspect. That is the beauty of forensic pathology and medico-legal investigation—and at the same time it is the challenge and the difficulty of the field."

Forensic pathology may still operate on century-old principles, but Wecht reminds us that it is not a static field, and that it has evolved with time and technology. "The basics remain the same in determining cause and manner of death and trying to determine when someone died and how they died, where they died, and causal relationship between natural disease and trauma injury and vice versa. But when you go back to some of the very old great books, to the medico-legal questions in them that physicians have posed and addressed, you can see that a lot of things remain the same. The Chinese addressed criminalistics centuries ago in some ancient books, and it's amazing to think that the basics of those instructions remain the same today. Of course, technology has changed a great deal, and that has evolved our techniques. DNA analysis is undoubtedly the most revolutionary finding in science that has been applied to forensic science. DNA plays out in fascinating ways in cases and we all know about the Innocence Project and the people who have been exonerated because of it. Radiology—CAT scans and PET scans—is being applied to forensic pathology in exciting ways, and we even have virtual autopsies. This kind of technology is still expensive and cumbersome and to what extent will be developed I don't know. The advances that have occurred in clinical medicine and what doctors are able to do these days is magnificent. But sadly, they don't have much impact on forensic pathology—you still just have a dead body to work with. For example, I just reviewed a case and will be testifying regarding the time of death as a major issue of this case. In this regard, today's forensic pathologists are really no better off than our colleagues were 100 or 200 years ago to some extent—rigor mortis, livor mortis, algor mortis, gastric contents—we are still using these concepts that have not changed in centuries. I would say the biggest changes in forensic pathology have arisen in an indirect fashion rather than by something of direct impact on the autopsy technique itself."

Wecht continues, "The biggest change is in terms of what forensic pathologists now know what to do, what to look for, what to collect, what to rely upon for their colleagues in toxicology, criminalistics, anthropology, entomology and odontology. We are much more meticulous and thorough, knowing especially that our society is litigious and the legal system is adversarial. You go to an autopsy and there's no big difference from last year or the last decade or the last century—you open up the body, weigh the organs, make your observations—there's nothing new there. We learn things, of course, but what's really new? Aside from DNA on a limited basis, and maybe some radiological finings, what's new in medicine is really what helps us indirectly. What medical doctors come up with and what lab analysts have done with evidence, those are the developments that have helped those of us in forensic pathology a great deal. As far as doing the autopsy and examination, not much has changed. A few things here and there, but there have not been the dramatic changes in forensic pathology that have occurred in other fields of medicine."

While he has witnessed a great deal, and while his career is not over by any means, what Wecht would like to be known for "is for others to evaluate," he says. "I would like to be known for doing my job honestly, thoroughly, efficiently and meaningfully. Whether people like me personally or not, or what side they are on, that does not impact my work, and that's what I am most proud of after doing this for 54 years. But sometimes when people ask you how much money you get from tailoring your opinion, it upsets me. How long would it be before word gets out that you are that kind of a person?"

As we will see in Chapter 5, celebrity and undue influences can get to forensic practitioners. However, Wecht says he sticks to the straight and narrow. "Lawyers from both sides of the courtroom consult me," he says, adding that he is known for being outspoken. "I am known as someone who has spoken up on controversial cases and not hesitated to express opinions, whether it is on John Kennedy, Robert Kennedy, JonBenet Ramsay or Vincent Foster—cases that, in my opinion, have not been fully, incontrovertibly and unequivocally resolved. Again, not because I'm saying I was right, but I spoke out for further inquiry."

Wecht's time as a coroner, and therefore an elected official, has sharpened his views on the importance of speaking up. "I am very proud of addressing issues of concern to the community, and that I conducted open public inquests in every police-related death and all of deaths of significant nature in which there was highly questionable situations or evidence," he says. "In police-related deaths it is often predictable that the district attorney would never make a move on the case, so I am very proud of what I did on those cases all during my coroner years. It bothers me that some of my colleagues have been reduced to silence. Abraham Lincoln once said that the sin of silence makes cowards of men, and I think that's applicable to our profession. As a forensic pathologist conducting a medicolegal procedure and investigation, our responsibility does not end upon completion and signing out of the autopsy. Instead, it is merely the beginning of putting it all together. The autopsy may be the end of the beginning but it is not the end of the matter. You have a significant role to play and you have knowledge that empowers you to speak out. And if you have a legal background, you're in an even better and stronger position to speak out. Some of my colleagues agree with me and some disagree, but it won't change what I do."

That forthrightness might best be illustrated by Wecht's criticism of the Warren Commission's findings concerning the assassination of John F. Kennedy. Wecht rejects the sole-assassin theory and maintains that more than one bullet fired in the assassination, and has been vocal about his position.

He points to the botched original autopsy, conducted by two pathologists who had never done a medicolegal autopsy before. At the time that these pathologists were called to testify, Wecht was a member of the House Select Committee of the Assassinations Pathology Panel, which was convened in 1977 to reinvestigate the deaths of Kennedy and Dr. Martin Luther King. Wecht says the pathologists missed a bullet hole in the neck, which was later explained away and then became the basis of the single-bullet theory that Wecht contests. He points out that Kennedy's brain was not dissected, and he also was the one who, while he was working as the first nongovernment forensic pathologist who was given access to the autopsy materials at the National Archives, discovered in 1972 that the brain had gone missing. "To this day, the brain's whereabouts have not been accounted for," Wecht says. He is working on a book that will promulgate his views on the JFK assassination.

Wecht also has been vocal about the contamination of evidence and a delay in the initial crime scene investigation in both the O.J. Simpson and JonBenet Ramsey cases.

Evidence was also misinterpreted, Wecht says, underscoring the need for forensic pathologists' expert opinions during cases.

Perhaps what has prompted more headlines concerning Wecht is an allegation against him brought forward by county district attorney, Stephen A. Zappala, Jr. Wecht says that at the time, as the coroner for Allegheny County, he was holding open inquests on all police-involved deaths, a policy that he had established as being immovable. Wecht says Zappala was not pleased with this policy and had the U.S. Attorney file charges against Wecht for conducting private consulting work at county facilities. Wecht went to trial on 41 charges (lowered from an initial 84), and the case ended with a hung jury of 9–3 for acquittal on 27 counts and 6–6 on the other 14 counts. The case went back to circuit court and another judge was assigned to it. However, before a ruling could be made, Wecht says the government withdrew 27 counts, leaving 14. According to Wecht, a newly assigned judge had asserted that his constitutional rights had been violated, and then suddenly, the government announced they had withdrawn all charges with prejudice.

Despite these legal headaches, at the age of 85, Wecht shows no signs of slowing down. Last year he conducted more than 450 autopsies and provided well over 100 consultations all over the country. He was born in the Pittsburgh suburb of Dunkard Township, Pennsylvania and is the only child of parents who were first-generation immigrants. Wecht says they desired for their baby boy to become a doctor one day, and without argument, Wecht seemed to accept his destiny, attending medical school then going on to earn a law degree from the University of Maryland School of Law. The resolute discipline that got him through medical school and then law school stayed with him as he advanced in his career and began adding accolades to his curricula vitae. Wecht has served as the president of the American Academy of Forensic Sciences (AAFS) and the American College of Legal Medicine, and has headed the board of trustees of the American Board of Legal Medicine. As we have seen, he served as the county commissioner, coroner, and later medical examiner of Allegheny County, Pennsylvania. He has parlayed his knowledge and experience into the written word, authoring a number of books, including *Into Evidence: Truth, Lies and Unresolved Mysteries in the Murder of JFK*, *Mortal Evidence: The Forensics Behind Nine Shocking Cases*, *Grave Secrets: A Leading Forensic Expert Reveals the Startling Truth about O.J. Simpson, David Koresh, Vincent Foster, and Other Sensational Cases*, and *Who Killed JonBenet Ramsey?* He also has written a new textbook, *Forensic Pathology in Criminal Cases*, published in 2016.

As we saw in Chapter 3, the NAS directed its scrutiny toward both the forensic laboratory and the medicolegal death investigation system and issued a report in 2009. Let's take a look at what the report asserted regarding forensic pathology and resulting improvement efforts for the forensic medicine facility.

STANDARDS AND ACCREDITATION IN THE MEDICOLEGAL DEATH INVESTIGATION SYSTEM

In a memorandum to staff dated March 17, 2016, then-Attorney General Loretta Lynch announced that her office would be endorsing various recommendations made by the NCFS. In the memorandum, Lynch stated, "The Department believes that communication among medical examiners and coroners is critical to advance the practice of medicolegal death investigation and will work with other federal agencies to support it."

The department has also reviewed the NCFS's views on increasing the supply of forensic pathologists, and as the memorandum states, "The Department agrees that forensic pathologists play a critical role in public health and public safety and we support the NCFS's goal to raise awareness of the growing need for better training, funding, and facilities. We look forward to working with the NCFS to advance these goals."

Other steps toward improvement are underway. Based on NCFS recommendations, then-Deputy Attorney General Sally Quillian Yates announced on December 7, 2015 that the department will help to establish an interagency working group aimed at bringing higher levels of scientific rigor and reliability to the field of medicolegal death investigation. The department has asked the White House's Office of Science and Technology Policy to help convene a working group that would focus on a broad range of MDI issues. Although the department does not conduct its own MDI—which is typically handled by state and local agencies—it said in a statement that it believes an interagency group will help accomplish the goals of the NCFS in strengthening medicolegal death investigation.

This progress, like other efforts we have seen on the crime lab side, stems in part from the 2009 NAS report that identified deficits in the medicolegal death investigation profession and suggested that quality control and quality assurance begin with the implementation of standardized policies and procedures by qualified staff.

Currently, the standard for quality in death investigation for medical examiner offices is accreditation by the NAME. NAME accreditation attests that an office has a functional governing code, adequate staff, equipment, training, and a suitable physical facility, and produces a forensically documented accurate, credible death investigation product. Additionally, NAME offers an individualized assessment program to enable jurisdictions to identify what they need to meet accreditation standards.

Most emphatic is the stagnation of movement toward a transition from coroner offices to medical examiner offices. As the 2009 NAS report states, "It is clear that the conversion of coroner systems to medical examiner systems as recommended by many studies has essentially halted and requires federal incentives to move forward" (NAS, 2009, page 265). The 2009 NAS report recommends updating the Model Post-Mortem Examination Act of 1954 to include the elements of a progressive and responsive death investigation law as well as to address standards for administration, staffing, and training. Taking it one step further, the 2009 NAS report also suggests that organizations serving the medicolegal death investigation system could collaborate to draft legislation for a modern model death investigation code that would include the elements of a competent medical death investigation system.

As a funding mechanism, the 2009 NAS report recommends that the National Forensic Sciences Improvement Act (NFSIA) be fully funded to support the core needs of medical examiner and coroner grantees for equipment and facilities, training and education, as well as infrastructure. As the report states, "Funds are needed to assess and modernize the medico-legal death investigation system, using as a benchmark the current requirements of NAME related to professional credentials, standards and accreditation... NFSIA is not funded sufficiently to provide significant improvements in [medical examiner/coroner] systems" (NAS, 2009, page 265).

In Recommendation 11 of the 2009 NAS report, to improve medicolegal death investigation, six action steps are necessary to effect change:

- Congress should authorize and appropriate incentive funds to the National Institute of Forensic Science (NIFS) for allocation to states and jurisdictions to establish medical examiner systems, with the goal of replacing and eventually eliminating existing coroner systems.

- Congress should appropriate resources to the NIH and NIFS, jointly, to support research, education, and training in forensic pathology.
- The NAME, the American Board of Medicolegal Death Investigators, and other appropriate professional organizations should establish a Scientific Working Group (SWG) for forensic pathology and medicolegal death investigation to develop and promote standards for best practices, administration, staffing, education, training, and continuing education for competent death scene investigation and postmortem examinations.
- All medical examiner offices should be accredited pursuant to NIFS-endorsed standards within a timeframe to be established by NIFS.
- All federal funding should be restricted to accredited offices that meet NIFS-endorsed standards or that demonstrate significant and measurable progress in achieving accreditation within prescribed deadlines.
- All medicolegal autopsies should be performed or supervised by a board-certified forensic pathologist.

In his memoir, *Morgue*, San Antonio, Texas–based forensic pathologist Vincent Di Maio, MD, alludes to the 2009 NAS report and the recommendation to eliminate the coroner system entirely: "To date, nothing has been done. What was good for the 10th century is apparently still good for the 21st. ... Despite the imperfection and inadequacy of the old coroner system, autopsies had solved thousands of crimes by 1959, when forensic pathology was first recognized as a distinct discipline by the American Board of Pathology."

Di Maio's father, Dominick Di Maio, MD, was among the first 18 certified forensic pathologists in the United States in the 1950s and 1960s. He served as New York City's chief medical examiner in the 1970s. "That first class of medical detectives comprised some of forensic medicine's lions."

NYC scrapped the coroner system in 1918, and Di Maio says the rest of the country should follow suit. He adds that there's no comparison between a board-certified forensic pathologist and a coroner when it comes down to skills. "My father's and my career encompass the entire modern era of forensics, from a time when fingerprints and basic blood typing were the most 'high-tech' forensic tools available, to today's DNA profiling and massive computer databases. But I believe with all my heart that if we could magically drop a 1940s medical examiner into a modern morgue with an afternoon's training on the new science, he'd function quite nicely. Why? Because a good forensic pathologist's best tools are still his eyes, his brain and his scalpel. Without those, all the science in the universe doesn't help."

Di Maio says the country has about 500 forensic pathologists currently, but says the country needs at least 1500 to keep up with the demands placed on the medicolegal death investigation system. As Di Maio writes in *Morgue*, "Why, at the height of the profession's popularity... is there a shortage of forensic pathologists? Because it ain't as glamorous as TV makes it. One in five new FPs drops right out after training, and over a 10-year period, we lose 10 percent more of these new doctor-detectives" (Di Maio and Franscell, 2016, page 53). Di Maio says it's a challenging profession that requires years of schooling and extra training, and yet forensic pathologists make far less than many of their medical doctor counterparts and have enormous student loans to pay off.

Di Maio has been a forensic pathologist for more than 45 years and says his profession is "at a crossroads" because there are not enough of his kind. "We train an average of 27 board-certified FPs every year but only 21 actually go to work as medical examiners,"

Di Maio notes in *Morgue* (Di Maio and Franscell, 2016, page 255). "We need more forensic pathologists. As our population grows and ages, as we trust technology more and more (and humans less and less), and as the number of new pathologists declines, forensic pathologists will hit a disastrous wall. Fewer autopsies mean fewer autopsies. Investigations suffer, evidence is lost or overlooked, crimes are unsolved. If that happens, we don't just lose money or time, we lose justice" (Di Maio and Franscell, 2016, pages 255–256).

"It sounds very mercenary but one of the major problems is salaries," Di Maio affirms. "Two people train in pathology; one does forensic and the other does hospital; the hospital pathologist usually makes at least twice the salary of the forensic pathologist. Nowadays, people graduate from medical school with a big financial burden. You have a somewhat decent salary but then you have to pay off your debt, and that influences your professional choices. I have a retirement, and I can tell you that my retirement is as good as some of the salaries of the medical examiners working full-time."

He continues, "Really, there are three problems, and the first is salary. The second is the lack of adequate facilities and staffing. In many ways, no one really cares. So if we need equipment and if it's a choice between our equipment and a patrol car, guess what gets purchased? The patrol car. When I first came to my job in San Antonio, my X-ray equipment was 25 years old. Besides salary, you definitely want a decent facility. I remember visiting another office one time and I thought I was in an old Frankenstein movie; the lights were dim, and half of them didn't work. I asked the tech, 'Do you have X-ray here?' and the guy said, 'Oh yeah, we have X-ray, here, I'll show you.' And he led me to a room and said, 'Here's our X-ray, but we're still waiting for parts to get it back up and running again.' I said, 'How long has it been?' and he said, 'Oh, two years.' So the big issues are salaries, facilities, and then we have the hold-out coroners' offices. The bulk of the medico-legal offices in the U.S. are coroners' offices, not medical examiners' offices. And some of them will hire anybody to conduct autopsies."

Di Maio adds, "And it's not a pleasant job; some people just can't take it. But you have to offer decent facilities, and a decent salary. And if you don't offer that, you're not going to get anyone good. The other thing is, no one encourages you to go into this specialty. The medical schools want you to go into academic pathology or do service pathology in hospitals. But no one is interested in forensic pathology. I remember when I went to medical school in Brooklyn, most of the medical examiners weren't even pathologists; there was an internist, a surgeon, and so there has always been a short supply of forensic pathologists. The quality of the people has improved over the years, compared to when I first started working in the field. I think we have made vast improvements since the 1960s and 1970s, but we can do even better. We must recruit more forensic pathologists. Then we have to get more equipment and better facilities, and a better system overall. For example, some places are doing thousands of cases and they have to make decisions about priorities. They are forced to say, 'We'll autopsy the homicides, then we'll autopsy the suicides.' What about the accidents? They say, 'Nah, we don't have to do the accidents, and certainly not the natural deaths.' That's not a real medico-legal system."

Di Maio says the system lacks clout when competing interests collide. "Medico-legal systems are not federal—there is only one federal medicolegal examiner's system and that is the military—they are state, county or city so you have to convince those entities to have forensic pathologists working as medical examiners, and it involves spending money," he says. "You have to build a facility and you are talking about tens of millions of dollars. Then you have to go out and hire people for even more millions. Most people in government don't care about medico-legal death investigation, sorry to say. We are a low priority. If you have a choice of holding a bond election to secure $25 million for a new medical examiner's office or to fix the potholes, the public is probably going to vote to fix the potholes. With all of the crime shows on TV, though, citizens might actually go for the medical examiner's office, but the politicians will stick to the potholes. The thing is, it's multifactorial. You have to get the doctors, you have to get the facility, and have to get the equipment. I'm lucky in that I have been in Texas for most of my professional life; Texas spends the money because Texas is serious about forensic science. If you need a facility, you'll eventually get it; you'll get the equipment, too. The salaries are not great, but compared to other communities, they are fine, especially taking into account the lower cost of living than compared to, say, New York City. If you want to get a department or organization to do things the way you want, there are only two ways—using the carrot or the stick. Well, there is no carrot. The feds give no money at all to medical examiners' ME offices. And if they do, the medical examiner gets $10,000 and the police department gets a new $90,000 cruiser."

Di Maio says forensic pathologists and up-to-date facilities are needed more than ever before due to the number of unnatural or suspicious deaths occurring in the United States that coroners could miss. He points to the case of Genene Jones, who worked as a nurse in a pediatric clinic in Kerrville, Texas in 1982. Just 18 months earlier, Di Maio had left Dallas to take the position of chief medical examiner of Bexar County, Texas, with headquarters in San Antonio. As the deputy chief medical examiner in Dallas, Di Maio worked under Charles Petty, MD, and as Di Maio explains, "Petty wouldn't retire and I was eager to run my own operation." In March 1981, Di Maio took over as chief in San Antonio, which just happened to be Texas's first medical examiner's office, established in 1956.

In his first year there, Di Maio grew frustrated with hospitals that refused to report all questionable deaths, especially at the Bexar County Hospital. By 1982, Di Maio couldn't keep quiet and he resigned from the faculty of the University of Texas Health Science Center in San Antonio in protest. It turns out that questionable deaths were quite a problem closer to home than anyone expected.

A colleague of Di Maio's at the time mentioned the Kerrville district attorney was looking into the unexplained death of a little girl, Chelsea McClellan, with the DA suspecting a doctor and nurse who had just recently worked at Bexar County Hospital. There were suspicious baby deaths at the Kerrville clinic as well. Di Maio suspected someone might be killing babies at the county hospital, as another nurse had come forward with her suspicions about a colleague. Inquiries were made and the common thread was Genene Jones.

According to Di Maio, Jones lost her first job at a San Antonio hospital for being too rough with patients as well as making clinical decisions above her pay grade. Another stint at a hospital was brief as well before she landed at Bexar County Hospital in 1978. According to Di Maio, during her time there, 42 babies had died; 34 of them had died while Jones was on duty. Essentially, Bexar County Hospital's infant mortality rate almost tripled during Jones's tenure. Despite concern at the hospital, the questionable deaths weren't reported to Di Maio. Jones was let go when the hospital decided to upgrade staff, and Jones was hired at the Kerrville clinic. Soon after, there were suspicious situations at the clinic, including involving use of a drug called succinylcholine, used to relax muscles during breathing tube insertion. The drug vial in question had gone missing and then was found to be opened, with several puncture marks made in it. A San Antonio grand jury examined the evidence in the form of medical records of 120-plus children, and this evidence pointed to Jones, who was suspected as a child killer who used succinylcholine as her lethal drug of choice.

Di Maio had examined the body of an exhumed index patient and found no needle-marks, but tissue samples revealed traces of the drug, and Di Maio suspected Munchausen syndrome by proxy. Jones was arrested and her trial began in January 1984. The defense refuted the DA's evidence, but the jury found Jones to be guilty, sentencing her to 99 years for the lethal injection of Chelsea McClellan, plus handing down 60 more years for another child's injury. According to Di Maio, in 2014, Jones was denied parole for the ninth time, but she is scheduled to be released on March 1, 2018 due to Texas mandatory release laws to prevent prison overcrowding. Di Maio says it is the first time in U.S. history that the country "knowingly and purposely could release a captive serial killer." Di Maio says old records have surfaced and perhaps new charges could be filed, but this might represent a slim chance of keeping Jones in prison.

"I feel strongly we should have a rock-solid system to detect not only suspicious deaths, but unreported deaths as well," Di Maio says. He points to a model system in Texas. "Our state is very interested in the criminal justice system and how it functions. We have set up a commission that screens individuals in forensic laboratories. In Texas, all crime lab personnel—and unfortunately this does not pertain to ME offices—have to be certified. We're setting up a place where we can license these crime lab personnel. Suppose someone has been convicted of a crime and there is a suspicion that the analysis conducted by the crime lab was incorrect. It can be the person convicted or a relative or anyone else with this suspicion; you can contact the Texas Forensic Science Commission and it will look at your complaint. If there is any validity to it, they will investigate. The crime labs will cooperate with the commission. If it is suspected that there is an analyst in a crime lab who isn't doing the drug analyses correctly, for example, that person is investigated by the commission. So 4,000 cases have been overturned because of this process. The commission sent letters to the DAs, the defense attorneys, and the people who had been convicted, and it also posted notices in all of the jails and prisons. The commission does everything it can to correct the situation. There has been a big problem with hair analysis in the U.S. and in Texas, we investigated cases going back as far as we can to the 1960s; we are pulling all the cases that went to trial using hair analysis and we'll get the transcripts and if the testimony was incorrect, we will notify people. And that's the way it should be done. But it's not in so many other places."

Di Maio says he sticks to the facts as they are and acknowledges the opportunities to stray from one's convictions. "No one has ever tried to apply pressure to me, but families will try to argue with your findings and try to get you to change them," he says. "In the Genene Jones case, one county commissioner asked me if it was it true, and I said yes, and he said thank you and that was it. I have been threatened by other people, but the politicians were good about it. It really does depend on the people involved in each case. Sometimes some medical examiners get too friendly, I think. People don't have to like me, but I want them to respect me. I've told people things that they didn't really want to hear, but they accepted it because they knew I was telling them the truth."

He continues, "Every field has practitioners who are either true believers and whores, often exaggerated by the news media during investigations and trials. This bothers me, but it will always be with us. The biggest trouble comes when people aren't transparent. Looks at the Genene Jones case; if the hospital had gone to the medical examiner's office and said, 'I think we have a problem with a nurse', they would have investigated and the authorities would have arrested her and it would have been over. They caught her in the end, and people remember her being caught, period, and not that it took so long. The

Genene Jones case was a very important case because it's a warning. When I was working in Dallas, we'd had a nurse like that, and as soon as suspicious situations started to occur, the other nurses caught on and came to the medical examiner's office. They said they investigated but were never able to get her but the nursing board was informed and they eventually took action on the matter. It was handled correctly, unlike the Genene Jones case. The news media comes along and says the authorities are doing a good job and that's it; the lab agrees and says 'We helped catch this person,' and instead of being pilloried, they are celebrated because everyone thinks they did a good job. But did they? Transparency is vital."

As we have seen, some forensic practitioners have faced undue pressure from authorities and other stakeholders in the justice system. Surveys of NAME members have revealed that medical examiner independence was important to most members, with more than two-thirds of survey respondents reporting that they had been subjected to pressures to influence their findings, and many had suffered negative consequences for resisting those influences.

In NAME's aforementioned 2011 survey (with 336 practitioners responding), 97 percent believed that the independence of forensic pathologists was an important issue demanding action. The survey found that more forensic pathologists working in a coroner's offices (21.1 percent) than medical examiner systems (4.5 percent) were directed to change their findings by supervisors, usually once a year. Practitioners also reported being asked to sign autopsy reports and/or death certificates that were not consistent with the findings at autopsy. Eighty-two percent of forensic pathologists surveyed had experienced family or political pressure to change the reported cause or manner of death, with almost 10 percent stating that this occurred on a monthly basis. Twenty-two percent of pathologists reported that they had experienced political pressure to change death certificates from elected and/or appointed political officials. One-quarter of those practitioners who resisted these pressures suffered consequences for their actions. Ten percent of individuals similarly reported pressure from outside sources on testimony provided in legal settings, and about half of these individuals suffered consequences for resisting any changes in their expected testimonies.

Melinek et al. (2013), in the "National Association of Medical Examiners Position Paper: Medical Examiner, Coroner, and Forensic Pathologist Independence," address the political or legal pressure by individuals or offices seeking to influence forensic pathologists' findings, as well as how this pressure can introduce error, bias, and corruption into the medicolegal investigation process. This position paper, developed by NAME's ad hoc Committee on Medical Examiner Independence, reinforced the principle that medical examiners, coroners, and forensic pathologists should be allowed to perform medicolegal investigations free of these influences.

Melinek et al. (2013) declare that "forensic pathologists working in or for medical examiner or coroner offices or as private consultants should be permitted to objectively pursue and report the facts and their opinions of those cases which they are investigating independent of political influences from other agencies within their respective jurisdictions and independent of the threat of litigation."

NAME's standards state that medicolegal death investigators "must investigate cooperatively with but be independent from law enforcement and prosecutors," explaining that "parallel investigation promotes neutral and objective medical assessment of the cause and manner of death." The standards also state that to promote competent and objective death investigations, all medicolegal death investigators should operate without any undue influence from law enforcement agencies and prosecutors. In spite of this goal,

Melinek et al. (2013) said that many MDI practitioners are exposed to significant pressure to modify their diagnoses.

In its position paper, NAME asserts that "medical examiner and coroner independence is an absolute necessity for professional death investigation."

NAME states that even though forensic pathologists need to work independently from law enforcement, that does not mean that they should be restricted from seeing police investigative reports. As Melinek et al. (2013) observed, "The ability of forensic pathologists to interpret autopsy findings depends on the context of the investigation. As such, forensic pathologists working in coroner's and medical examiner's offices need to have access to good medico-legal death investigations and should have the ability to request or direct some of the investigations, as needed, in order to get the information they will rely on to interpret the cause and manner of death correctly. Ideally, this means that the medico-legal death investigators will be under the direction of the forensic pathologist, medical examiner or coroner, and independent and separate from law enforcement. In offices that rely solely on law enforcement for their death investigation, there needs to be recognition that this may bias the perspective of the information received and does not constitute a truly independent investigation."

As we have seen previously with forensic laboratories, performance standards also play a key role in the quality of the medicolegal death investigation system's performance. Efforts by the NAME to promulgate practice standards began in the 1970s, and according to NAME, these early efforts subsequently became focused on the operational aspects of medical examiner offices, resulting in the NAME Office Accreditation Checklist. More recently, in 2005, NAME developed standards that address the professional aspects of death investigations and offer a constructive framework that defines the fundamental services provided by a professional forensic pathologist. To promote competent and objective death investigations, NAME standards mandate, in general, that medicolegal death investigation officers should operate without any undue influence from law enforcement agencies and prosecutors.

As Melinek et al. (2013) note, "For preservation of a fair and just judicial system, it is imperative that forensic pathologists. medical examiners. and coroners remain independent officials, and be available for consultation for both prosecuting and defense attorneys throughout the United States." They added that forensic pathologists, medical examiners, and coroners, in the performance of their duties, should be considered neutral experts and not as "prosecution experts" or "defense experts," except when explicitly hired by these parties. They should also be protected from political pressure from government officials and from litigation directed at intimidating pathologists in their determination of cause of death. Additionally, NAME stated that they should not be penalized for providing testimony that proves to be helpful for plaintiffs, prosecution, or defense.

It may not be possible for many offices to escape that pressure. Medical examiner and coroner offices are governed differently, with varying forms of organizational oversight. The 2009 NAS report found that 43 percent of the U.S. population are served by systems that are independent, 33 percent by offices residing administratively in public safety or law enforcement organizations, 14 percent by offices in health departments, and 10 percent by offices within a forensic laboratory. Over the years, various government reports have recommended that a medical examiner system should be an independent agency or should report to a commission so that it avoids any conflicts of interest and so that it reports directly to the jurisdictional governing body. When this is not possible, the 2009 NAS report suggests that incorporation into a health department, instead of into law enforcement agencies, seems to provide the next most compatible location.

The NAME position paper also sought protection for whistleblowers in cases requiring investigation and/or testimony where a public entity has been involved in the death of a person, such as in an officer-involved shooting or a death in jail or in a state mental institution. As Melinek et al. (2013) emphasized, "For the integrity of the public trust and quality assurance in these institutions, it is imperative that the forensic pathologists who investigate these deaths are free of pressure from the public entities involved and if they should uncover abuse or criminal activity in these settings, have full 'whistleblower' protections afforded to them under the law. Forensic pathologists working for coroners or medical examiners should enjoy civil service status, contractual agreements, or other similar types of protection, to ensure that they can only be dismissed or disciplined for appropriate cause."

Forensic practitioners and their supporters say that their performance would be enhanced if resources could be bolstered. This includes everything from well-trained full-time equivalent (FTE) employees, to adequate autopsy facilities and equipment, to sufficient budgets to meet demand for services.

Efforts are restricted by budgets, and budgets vary widely, ranging from $18,000 to $2.5 million annually for county systems, depending on the size of the population. A 2007 survey conducted for NAME by Hanzlick revealed that county systems' per capita cost ranged from $1.31 to $9.19, with an average of $2.89. State systems benefit from economies of scale and function more economically at $0.64 to $2.81, with a mean of $1.76. As the 2009 NAS report observes, "The large variation in qualifications, staffing, budgets, and the multiple skills required for competent death investigations, especially in small jurisdictions, has resulted in marked variation in the quantity and quality of death investigations in the United States. Physical facilities also vary in adequacy. Only one-third of offices have in-house facilities to perform the histology needed to make microscopic diagnoses on tissues sampled at autopsy. Only one-third have in-house toxicology capabilities to identify drugs present in the deceased that either contributed to or were the primary cause of death. One-third do not have radiology services in-house that would allow the identification of missiles, disease, bony injury or identification features in decedents. Some coroner systems do not have any physical facility at all. It is clear that death investigations in the United States rely on a patchwork of coroners and medical examiners and that these vary greatly in the budgets, staff, equipment, and training available to them, and in the quality of services they provide. No matter what the level of quality of other forensic science disciplines that are supported by a particular jurisdiction may be, if the death investigation does not include competent death investigation and forensic pathology services, both civil and criminal cases may be compromised" (Hanzlick and Haden-Pinneri, 2011).

To combat these deficiencies if no other quality improvement measures are implemented, the 2009 NAS report says that industry-standard best practices must be observed. Although there is no lack of standards—including materials from NIJ and NAME such as The NIJ document Death Investigation: A Guide for the Scene Investigator; Medicolegal Death Investigator: A Systematic Training Program for the Professional Death Investigator; the NAME Autopsy Standards and Inspection Checklist; and NAME's Forensic Pathology Autopsy Standards—there is no incentive for death investigation systems to adopt them. As the 2009 NAS report notes further, "Compliance is further limited because of heavy caseloads, deficiencies in trained staff, absence of equipment, non-availability of required day-today and consultative services, and the presence of contradictory policies and practices."

Accreditation is another mechanism for quality assurance and improvement. Currently, the standard for quality in death investigation for medical examiner offices is accreditation by NAME. Accreditation attests that an office has a functional governing code, adequate staff, equipment, training, and a suitable physical facility, and produces a forensically documented accurate, credible death investigation product. Of all ME/C systems nationally, only 54 are accredited by NAME. The NAME accreditation checklist is available online and describes the requirements for accreditation. Accreditation is for a period of five years. NAME also offers an individualized assessment program to enable jurisdictions to identify what they need to meet accreditation standards.

NAME says that its accreditation standards have been prepared and revised by NAME for the purpose of improving the quality of the medicolegal investigation of death in this country. Accreditation applies to offices and systems, not individual practitioners. The standards emphasize policies and procedures, not professional work product. The standards represent minimum standards for an adequate medicolegal system, not guidelines. NAME accreditation is an endorsement by NAME that the office or system provides an adequate environment for a medical examiner in which to practice his or her profession and provides reasonable assurances that the office or system well serves its jurisdiction. It is the objective of NAME that the application of these standards will aid materially in developing and maintaining a high caliber of medicolegal investigation of death for the communities and jurisdictions in which they operate. The NAME Accreditation Program is a peer-review system. Its goal is to improve office or system performance through objective evaluation and constructive criticism. The inspector is the medical examiner's peer and serves as a guest consultant to the office or system. The accreditation program is intended to evolve over time. Procedures ensure the review of standards and procedures, and a mechanism is established for setting standards. Accreditation is conferred for a period of five years.

The 2009 NAS report enumerates the impediments to developing systems that meet accreditation requirements. For example, most coroner systems cannot qualify for accreditation because of problems related to size, insufficient staff and equipment, and insufficiently trained personnel, which inhibit their ability to perform a competent physical examination, make and/or exclude medical diagnoses on dead bodies, and make determinations of the cause and manner of death. The historic role of the coroner is insufficient to accurately perform the medicolegal and public health functions related to sudden, unexpected, or violent death. Additionally, many medical examiner systems are constrained by budget, lack of staff, lack of equipment, and insufficient facilities, and cannot meet NAME standards. Not to mention, the accreditation process requires considerable staff work, including written policies and procedures. Finally, the accreditation process requires renewal, which incurs administrative costs; therefore, many offices do not recognize the benefits accreditation affords them.

Furthermore, the 2009 NAS report says forensic practitioners must demonstrate competency in their skills on a regular basis. For lay medical investigators, registration and certification by the American Board of Medicolegal Death Investigators requires standard performance procedures. For forensic pathologists, basic competence is initially documented by examination and certification and subsequently by recertification by the American Board of Pathology. Written office and morgue policies and procedures with scheduled reviews and updates help ensure consistent performance over time. Professional performance parameters, such as the NIJ investigation guidelines for investigators and the NAME forensic autopsy standards, are offered as national documents that all systems should be able to follow.

Critics of the medicolegal death investigation system assert that professional continuing education should be mandatory. For forensic pathologists to maintain professional standing, they must earn continuing medical education (CME) credits in accordance with the number required by their state medical licensing board. Attendance at forensic educational meetings, such as the annual meetings of NAME and the AAFS, helps keep medical staff current. Other opportunities that offer valuable CME credits are meetings that focus on pediatric forensic issues and general pathology updates. AAFS meetings are multidisciplinary and afford an opportunity for updating in forensic anthropology, forensic odontology, and other forensic disciplines.

On July 2, 2009, NAME's executive committee passed a resolution endorsing all of the recommendations of the NRC of the National Academies encompassed in the report *Strengthening Forensic Science in the United States: A Path Forward*, the 2009 NAS report to which experts have referred extensively. Regarding the recommendation is that a new and independent NIFS be established to promote the development of forensic science into a mature field of multidisciplinary research and practice founded on the systematic collection and analysis of data, NAME sees it as the foundation for the remainder of the report's recommendations. If creation of the NIFS is unattainable, NAME says the duties of this agency should be placed as a bridging step into a new Office of Forensic Services (OFS) within an existing agency fulfilling the spirit of the NRC recommendations. NAME (2009) states that "an essential function of NIFS would be to conduct periodic forensic science needs assessments at the federal, state, regional and local levels in order to ensure optimal provision of resources to service providers. Such assessments should also consider research needs. The assessment results should be presented in a report."

NAME (2009) also supports the recommendation that all public forensic science laboratories including medical examiner and coroner offices should be independent from or administratively autonomous within law enforcement agencies or prosecutor offices, and notes, "Provisions should be made to assure the technical and professional autonomy of forensic service providers at all levels. The goal is to have unbiased professional testing and reporting and the absence of real and perceived conflicts of interest. We agree, that to achieve this end will require incentive funds as indicated in the report." Additionally, NAME endorses the recommendation that research programs on human observer bias and sources of human error in forensic examinations including studies to determine contextual bias in forensic practice should be encouraged. However, NAME urges caution in the arena of contextual information and forensic pathology: "Medical examiners are physicians who operate in the medical paradigm of using a clinical history and information about the circumstances surrounding a death to generate hypotheses about potential causative diseases and injuries. The autopsy and laboratory examination allows a forensic pathologist to confirm or refute these hypotheses and reach medical conclusions. Autopsy is the practice of medicine. The history and circumstances provide the context for the autopsy and laboratory findings. In addition to determining cause of death, medical examiners are directed to determine the manner of death, which is largely based on the circumstances surrounding death" (NAME, 2009).

NAME supports the recommendation that laboratory accreditation and individual certification of forensic science professionals should be mandatory and all forensic science professionals should have access to a certification process. In the arena of medicolegal death investigation, NAME believes that all death investigators should at least be certified by the American Board of Medicolegal Death Investigators at the registry (basic) level. All pathologists performing medicolegal autopsies should be certified by the American Board of Pathology in forensic pathology. All medicolegal death investigation offices and agencies should be accredited using professional consensus practice standards such as those developed by NAME. "To achieve such ideals will require funding to improve the organization and operations of many medicolegal death investigation offices," NAME notes. "Training programs and certifying and accrediting bodies will likely also need funding to process increasing numbers of applicants" (NAME, 2009).

NAME also supports the ideal recommendation that incentive funds should be provided to states and jurisdictions with the goal of replacing coroner systems with medical examiner systems: "These funds should be used to build facilities, purchase necessary equipment, improve administration, and ensure education, training and staffing of offices. To foster this transition, NAME supports the recommendation that NIFS should work with the National Conference of Commissioners on Uniform State Laws, the American Law Institute and NAME to draft legislation for a modern model death investigation code. NAME also supports the recommendation that all medicolegal autopsies should be performed or directly supervised by a board certified (American Board of Pathology) forensic pathologist and that this standard should be phased in over a defined period of time. As a more immediate step, NAME believes it essential that all medicolegal death investigative systems incorporate the leadership of a board certified forensic pathologist. Efforts to achieve more uniformity in medicolegal death investigation can be hindered by the severe lack of resources (financial, personnel, equipment, and training) on a national level. Each of these resources should be addressed in order to improve our national medicolegal death investigation infrastructure on a jurisdictional or state level" (NAME, 2009).

The report also recommends that NIFS and the NIH promote scholarly, competitive peer-reviewed research and technical development in forensic medicine and develop a strategy to improve forensic pathology research. This recommendation includes the provision of research funding and the development of a study section to establish research goals and evaluate research proposals. NAME says it supports these recommendations and adds that "Forensic pathology supports both public health and public safety but this combined role has often remained unrecognized. Historically, minimal research funds have been provided for forensic pathology research by the Centers for Disease Control and Prevention and the National Institute of Justice" (NAME, 2009).

NAME also supports the recommendation that NIFS/NIH in conjunction with NAME and the American Board of Medicolegal Death Investigators establish an SWG for forensic pathology and medicolegal death investigation. NAME agrees that this committee should develop and promote standards for best practices, administration, staffing, education, training, and continuing education for competent death scene investigation and postmortem examinations. NAME believes that this committee should be led by and have strong representation from board-certified forensic pathologists. NAME supports the concept that all medical examiner offices should be accredited pursuant to NIFS endorsed standards and believes that professional consensus accreditation standards such as those developed by NAME should become the NIFS standard. Restricting federal funding to offices that are accredited or making measurable and significant progress toward accreditation is appropriate.

As outlined in the report, recruitment of qualified practitioners into the forensic pathology should be enhanced, NAME says, adding that funding in the form of medical student loan forgiveness and/or fellowship support should be made available to pathology residents who choose forensic pathology as their specialty. Increasing the numbers of forensic pathologists will facilitate the transition from coroner to medical examiner systems.

As a rule, research in medicolegal death investigation has not been a priority, as forensic pathologists carry heavy caseloads and often have little to no dedicated time, expertise, facilities, or funding for research. Research is further limited because many offices operate training programs independent of university medical schools. As the 2009 NAS report notes, "Occasionally, a specific case may inspire 'litigation research' directed to the elucidation of a specific problem related to a case that is being litigated actively, but this does not replace broad and systematic research of a forensic issue. Few university pathology departments promote basic pathology research in forensic problems such as time of death, injury response and timing, or tissue response to poisoning. In general, research interest often is inspired by a national goal that is funded through grants" (NAS, 2009, page 261).

As we have seen, the 2009 NAS report highlighted the need for research across all disciplines. Of the many impediments to academic research in forensic pathology in the United States, the most significant are the lack of understanding of forensic research challenges, the lack of a perceived need and national goals, the lack of grant funding of any kind to support research, the lack of forensic pathology researchers, and the lack of recognition for efforts directed to forensic pathology research within the university community. Grant funding drives research, but virtually no funding is available to encourage departments of pathology to make forensic pathology research a focus, and there is little tradition of collaboration between academic and forensic pathologists. Translational research bridges the gap between basic science discoveries and their practical applications. In the case of forensic pathology/medicine, this means taking basic science research knowledge to the autopsy table. Given the large numbers of autopsies performed in the United States in medical examiner offices, there is a great need for new knowledge that will filter down to the autopsy pathologist and for opportunities for practicing forensic pathologists to identify problems that need basic research.

This kind of research was exactly what one forensic practitioner may have had in mind, albeit decades before critics started singling out the deficits of forensic pathology and related disciplines such as forensic anthropology and forensic odontology. Not every practitioner can claim he or she started a Body Farm or cowritten a series of fiction books with an Indiana Jones–like protagonist. But William Bass can, and as a foremost expert in the field of forensic anthropology, he has pioneered in numerous aspects of scientific and literary endeavors, and was ahead of his time in terms of identifying unmet needs and the critical research that could address them.

If forensic pathologists say the body they autopsy can tell them a story, then forensic anthropologists quite possibly can claim that the human bones have a lot to say. Just ask Bass, who for four decades has been listening to tales from the crypt.

Bass says bones are reliable in how they can inform scientists about potential cause and manner of death. "If you go back in time and look at crimes in the past, the idea was that if you lost soft tissue, then there wasn't much you could tell about what happened," Bass says. "This is simply not true. You just haven't looked closely enough at what to look for in bones."

As Bass writes in one of his books, *Death's Acre*, "Flesh decays; bone endures. Flesh forgets and forgives ancient injuries; bone heals, but always remembers: a childhood fall, a barroom brawl, the smash of a pistol butt to the temple, the quick sting of a blade between the ribs. The bones capture such moments, preserve a record of them, and reveal them to anyone with eyes trained to see the rich visual record, to hear the faint whispers rising from the dead" (Bass and Jefferson, 2003).

Forensic anthropology, the application of anthropological knowledge and techniques in a legal context, involves detailed knowledge of osteology to assist in the identification and cause of death of skeletal remains, as well as the recovery of remains using archaeological techniques. A lifelong student of human osteology, Bass almost missed his calling had he chosen to pursue his intended field, psychology.

"I attended the University of Virginia as an undergraduate and majored in psychology—mainly experimental psychology and not clinical—and in my junior year I had the opportunity to take some other courses," explains Bass, a Staunton, Va. native. "I found archaeology and I took four courses my junior and senior year at the University of Virginia, one each semester. Looking back, I can see that I was hooked by the first course but it took me a while to realize that. I graduated while the Korean war was raging and so I went into the service. I spent three years in the military, being assigned to the Army medical research laboratory because of my scientific background. When my military career was over I decided I wanted to return to college and work on a master's degree. I attended the University of Kentucky with an intention to major in counseling and minor in anthropology. About midway through, in the fall of 1954, about a month into the fall semester I thought to myself, 'I don't know if I want to talk to people with problems all day.' By then I was married and so I asked my wife, a military dietician also working at the University of Kentucky, if she minded if I switched my major and minor. She didn't, and I did."

Bass graduated with a master's degree in anthropology from the University of Kentucky in 1956 and earned his doctorate degree, also in anthropology, from the University of Pennsylvania in 1961. Bass held teaching positions at the University of Pennsylvania, the University of Nebraska, and the University of Kansas, before becoming a professor and head of the Department of Anthropology at the University of Tennessee in the summer of 1971. Through the late 1950s, Bass cultivated extensive experience in field research in the Northern and Central Plains, and throughout the 1960s and 1970s, Bass was a sought-after forensic anthropology consultant to law enforcement throughout the country.

When he was a graduate student at the University of Kentucky, "Charles Snow was head of the department and I took a course on osteology from him. One day he said to me, 'I have an identification case, would you like to go?' and I said, 'Sure, I'd love to,' because I'd gotten into the study of bones and identifying skeletal remains. There had been a truck wreck in Frankfurt, Ky.; there had been a fire and when the fire was put out there were three people in the two trucks—two drivers, but they had never identified the third person. Authorities suspected the third person was probably the common-law wife of one of the truck drivers but they had not been able to identify her. A lawyer in Lexington, Ky. who knew about this case called Dr. Snow and asked if he could identify someone burned in a truck wreck. Arrangements were made to have the woman exhumed from a church cemetery in eastern Kentucky. So, I accompanied Dr. Snow, and it was the only case during which I had thrown up. She had been badly burned and had not been embalmed, and so she really smelled badly." As Bass recalls in *Death's Acre*, "The body was burned, rotted and waterlogged, quite a contrast to the immaculate bone specimens I had studied in the university's osteology lab. Traditional anthropological specimens are clean and dry; forensic cases tend to be wet and smelly. But they're intellectually irresistible too—scientific puzzles demanding to be solved, life-and-death secrets waiting to be unearthed."

Bass continues, "Dr. Snow was able to make a positive identification of the body and I thought, 'Aha, that's what I want to do!' It was one of those situations where the light came on and I knew what I wanted to do with my life." As Bass writes in *Death's Acre*, "It was fascinating to see the way burned and broken bones could identify a victim, solve a long-standing mystery, close a case."

Bass became a forensic anthropologist, best known for his research on human osteology and human decomposition as well as the assistance he has provided local, state, and federal authorities in the identification of human remains. He credits Snow and "bone detective" Wilton Krogman, whom he calls "two of probably the best forensic anthropologists in the 1950s," as setting him on the path to his life's work. Bass studied under Krogman at the University of Pennsylvania; Bass notes in *Death's Acre* that "Krogman was guiding me, case by case and bone by bone, down a marvelous path."

Perhaps an unlikely teacher has also been death itself. Bass says he lost his father to suicide as well as two wives to cancer. "I don't like death, and I don't like mourning, I don't like any of that scene at all," Bass says. "But it's interesting what your mind can do when you are determined. I never see a forensic case as a dead body; I see it as a challenge of whether I have the ability to identify that person and figure out what happened to him or her. The knowledge I have gained through education has encouraged me to look at things that most people could not look at, and determine for science and society what happened to these individuals." And as he writes in *Death's Acre*, "... I deal daily with death. I have spent decades actively seeking it out. I immerse myself in it."

Bass says forensic anthropology provided him with a sense of satisfaction that he knew his former major of psychology never could. He also sensed that academia was the place for him. "When I was taking counseling I never felt as though I had learned anything, though I received a lot of information," he says. "Anatomy and osteology courses are very concrete; in other words, in every culture no matter what race or how old you are, the femur is always the femur. I derived real pleasure out of learning something that was concrete, and knowing that what I learned yesterday was applied today and into tomorrow. So, I felt very comfortable getting out of psychology and getting into something that was more structured. I looked back and saw that I had done a much better job academically after I got out of the so-called soft sciences—once I got into something that was concrete I felt more comfortable and began to build on that foundation."

In 1971, Bass joined the faculty of the University of Tennessee in Knoxville, not knowing that his passion for forensic anthropology would lead him to create the world's most unique research facility, the Anthropological Research Facility, more commonly known as "the Body Farm." In the 1970s, very little was known about how the body actually decayed, and Bass knew there had to be a better way to study the decomposition process, specifically using unclaimed cadavers donated by mortuaries.

In *Death's Acre*, Bass describes how this unique research facility was named: "When we first began researching human decomposition back in 1980, our facility didn't even have a name. After all, it was really just a two-acre patch of ground, fenced off to keep carnivorous animals and curious humans out. The original fence was chain-link, but after a few passersby caught traumatic glimpses of the bodies inside, we added a wooden privacy fence. At some point, probably when we began writing up our research results for scientific journals, we decided we should probably call it something scientific-sounding. So, we named it the Anthropology Research Facility, or ARF. Well, it wasn't long before some wag with the local district attorney's office suggested renaming it the Bass Anthropology Research Facility, or BARF. Luckily, that name never caught on; instead, police and FBI agents gradually started referring to it as 'the Body Farm.' Before long, I started calling it that too" (page 197).

Such a complex research facility had surprisingly simplistic origins. As Bass recalls in *Death's Acre*, "People who know about the Body Farm today seem to think it sprang into existence fully formed, but that's not the way it happened at all. It came from humble beginnings and it progressed by small steps. The questions we hoped to answer were almost laughably elementary: At what point does the arm fall off? What causes that greasy black stain under decomposed bodies, and when? When do the teeth fall out of the skull? How long before a corpse becomes a skeleton? To find answers, we first had to find research subjects. We had the farm, now we needed the bodies" (page 96).

Bass sent letters to 95 medical examiners and funeral directors in Tennessee's 95 counties, soliciting cadavers; in 1981, Bass picked up the first donated research subject, a 73-year-old male, identified as 1-81. As Bass notes in *Death's Acre*, "In life he'd had a family and a name; in death he would be known simply as 1-81, the anthropology department's first donated body of 1981" (page 97).

The first research subject was laid to rest at the Body Farm on May 15, 1981, and as Bass indicates, decomposition was swift with a warming weather trend and insect-assisted activity. According to Bass, within a month, 1-81 had taken the journey from fresh corpse to bare skeleton. Before their eyes, Bass and his research students were able to witness the four broad stages of body decomposition: the fresh stage, the bloated stage, the decay stage, and the dry stage. As Bass recalls in *Death's Acre*, "The graduate students and I watched in utter fascination. As far as I knew, no scientist had ever done this before; deliberately set out a human body to decompose, then simply sat back and watched, taking systematic note of what happened and when" (page 112).

While 1-81 had died of disease, Bass wanted to create a collection of bones that reflected all manners of demise, including trauma, so that students could learn both the distinct and the subtle differences between the two causes of death. Research subject 1-81 continued to teach in his own special way; as Bass describes it in *Death's Acre*, 1-81 was a teaching tool for years to come, and that "Learning the size, shape and feel of every bone in the human body is an enormous challenge for anthropology students. The only way to do it is to study actual bones—real ones, not plastic or plaster casts of them—for countless hours."

And once his students had spent sufficient time poring over those bones, Bass subject them to his "black box test." He explains in *Death's Acre*: "I'd put several bones inside a black box that had circular openings cut into the sides; to pass the test, the student would have to reach in and tell me, just by feeling them, what bones were in the black box" (page 115). It was a test of the nuances and subtleties of bones that Bass expected his students to master. As Bass says, "Even something as subtle as weight and texture can be crucially important."

The power of astute discernment is needed to tell the difference between disease and trauma inflicted on the bones. Bass says it's critical for forensic anthropologists—and, for that matter, forensic scientists of all disciplines—to cultivate keen powers of observation. "When you are dealing with forensic anthropology cases, you need a rock-solid foundation in osteology so that you can read bones," he says. "There are many subtle things that happen to people during trauma. For example, in the case of someone who has been stabbed, it's very hard to stab somebody and not leave a mark on the bone. That is not the same as a gunshot or a big blast to the bone; it can be a very small nick and easy to miss if you don't look at it and feel the bone. I am a touchy-feely person—I look at the bone, I rub my hand up and down the bone; I run my fingernail over the bone to see if I can pick up any nick left by a blade. Those are the things that you learn from the Charlie Snows and the Wilton Krogmans of the world. You just don't look at a bone, but you pick it up, you touch it and see if there is something amiss there. Not to be critical, but I have looked at a few cases that other experts had examined and who missed stab wounds on bones. I think it's because I am looking for tiny nicks; you run your fingernail down the bone and if it stops, you look at it carefully with a magnifying glass and see if it is something that could be caused by a very sharp instrument or a blade of some kind. These are things you pick up from good professors and also things you pick up from experience."

Bass continues, "If people don't run a fingernail over a bone and they miss a nick and don't even think about it, they are losing valuable data when they do that. We tell our students they must look closely at these things because it gives them more data with which to solve a crime. I think as a whole, forensic anthropology has expanded, it has gotten more scientific, which it should. And in the last 100 years as a whole, I think forensic science has become better at knowing what to look for. And hopefully our training is better than it was 100 years ago."

For forensic anthropologists, so much of what is currently known can be traced back to the research conducted on the Body Farm, which has played a pivotal role in many professionals' careers—both scientists and novelists. In 1993, author Patricia Cornwell asked Bass to conduct an experiment whose results Cornwell could use in one of her Kay Scarpetta mystery novels. Initially hesitant, Bass relented, the curiosity getting to him over what a body would be like and what would it leave behind if a murder occurred in a basement and then the body was moved some time after. Not only was the experiment's results useful for ongoing knowledge, but the detail was exactly what Cornwell had hoped to use in her book. Cornwell decided to title the book *The Body Farm*, and it was one of her most successful titles to date.

"I really thought that no one would ever know about it," Bass says. "I thought this would be an obscure little research facility in the hills of Tennessee, but along comes Patricia Cornwell whose fifth book was called *The Body Farm*. When it was published, I no longer had an obscure little research facility; it seemed as if everyone in the world knew about it then."

It also triggered immense curiosity among the public. As Bass describes in *Death's Acre*, "It wasn't long before a parade of reporters and television crews was beating a path to Knoxville and the Body Farm. Even now... the parade hasn't stopped... Flattering as the attention was, it was also distracting. If we'd been willing to give up research, teaching and writing, we could have devoted 24 hours a day to giving tours of the facility." The high profile that the research facility had achieved through exposure in the media was a blessing, Bass says, because more attention has been given to the issue of body donation for research.

However, the Body Farm has been the target of protesters and negative coverage by some journalists. In the mid-1990s, Bass and his students had been studying adipocere, the waxy substance that often coats the bodies of floaters. By studying the degree of adipocere, forensic anthropologists could provide a better idea of how long the body had been in the water. The experiment that Bass and his students had devised had been videotaped for training purposes at the UT continuing education program called the Law Enforcement Satellite Academy of Tennessee (LESAT). A television reporter that was there to cover LESAT had viewed the adipocere videotape. That had led to a series of reports on the Body Farm that included the fact that deceased veterans' bodies had been used, and this coincided with some local protests, a perfect storm of disapproval that reached the Tennessee commissioner of veterans' affairs. The commissioner had persuaded members of the state legislature to sponsor a bill that would have eliminated the Body Farm's research using unclaimed bodies from medical examiners. As Bass writes in *Death's Acre*, "Given that those bodies accounted for a sizable percentage of our research subjects, the effect would have been crippling. I was stunned that matters had reached such a crisis. This was the only scientific facility of its kind in the world. In our first few years of research, we'd published pioneering data on the processes and timing of human decomposition. And that basic data was used all over the world. That data had helped police and prosecutors put dozens of murderers behind bars... my former graduate students had become scientists whose research at the Body Farm was beginning to establish them as leading experts in their own right. And we'd only begun to scratch the surface. There we so many more variables to study, so many more techniques to develop and refine" (pages 206–207).

Bass enlisted the help of law enforcement and prosecutors to petition to keep the Body Farm viable. The committee voted 5–4 to shelve the bill, and as Bass notes, "We'd avoided catastrophe by the narrowest possible margin."

Bass says he is still surprised by the longevity of the Body Farm and pleased with its contributions to science. He says it was an indirect result of an experience he'd had during his earlier field work on the Plains.

"I wasn't walking down the street one day and saw a bright light and said to myself, 'Let's start a Body Farm,'" Bass says. "There's a bit of history involved. I taught at the University of Kansas at Lawrence from 1960 to 1971, and during that time I identified skeletal material for law enforcement agencies in Kansas. In western Kansas in the late 1960s the Kansas Bureau of Investigation (KBI) was having trouble with cattle rustling. If you watch westerns you see the bad guys round up the cattle over the hill and they are gone. Well, the bad guys don't do that today; the bad guys either own or rent a refrigerated truck and they will go out on these large ranches in the western Plains and they will kill the cows in the field and butcher them, hang the meat up and drive off. The rancher comes along a week or several weeks later and finds all these cow carcasses lying around and the question for law enforcement is, how long have they been dead? This tells law enforcement where they need to look for the sale of the meat."

Bass continues, "We had a case like this in western Kansas, and I received a letter from the director of the cattle investigation at the KBI asking me if I could look at a cow carcass and tell how long it had been dead. I wrote back and said I can't do this, but if you could get a rancher to kill a cow, I will look at it every day to see what happens with the decomposition. In my letter's PS, I wrote that we really needed the rancher to give us four cows—one for each season of the year because the major factor in decay is temperature. Well, nothing ever happened with that."

But the need to find a better way to determine rates of decomposition stayed with Bass, especially as he began to encounter cases where bodies were decaying differently due to geography and weather.

"I came to Tennessee in 1971," Bass says. "I knew the medical examiner, a forensic pathologist named Jerry Francisco. I wrote Jerry and told him that I was coming to Tennessee, and he wrote back and asked if I would be the state forensic anthropologist for the medical examiner's office. I wrote back and said I'd be happy to. It wasn't long after I came to Tennessee that instead of skeletal remains, I started getting maggot-covered bodies. Ninety-five percent of the cases that I had in Kansas were skeletal remains, but Tennessee has a lot of maggot-covered bodies; I think the reason is that in Kansas you have twice the amount of land and half as many people as Tennessee. So, if you die in Kansas the likelihood of being found in an active decay stage is not very good; you are found a year or five or 10 years later by ranchers. In Tennessee, we have half the amount of land and twice the number of people as Kansas, so the possibility of being found in an active decay stage is very good. And active decay usually means maggots."

Bass adds, "The police ask you two questions about a body; who is it, and how long has the person been dead. Well, both of those answers are complicated; but for the latter, there was very little literature available. After I retired I started writing books with Jon Jefferson and we began to wonder, who has looked at decay and Jon Googled all this stuff and he found that there's really nothing in the literature until you reach back in history to about 1200 A.D. In other words, in 800 years I'm sure people thought about decay rates but no one had investigated and published on this topic. I'm sure people looked at these things but nobody wrote them down. I thought to myself, 'If I am going to be talking to police, I better know what I am talking about.' So, in the fall of 1971, I went to the dean of the University of Tennessee (UT) and said, 'I need some land to put some dead bodies on.' He didn't say anything; he picked up the UT phonebook and made a few calls. (UT is also the land-grant institution for the state, and it's the agricultural campus too, so we have lots of land.) He sent me over to the ag campus to see the dean who handles land; I started with a sow farm and we began putting bodies out there to see what was going on."

"Now in order to do this, you need people in the vineyard to 'pick the grapes,' so to speak," Bass says, describing his recruitment process. "When I came to UT in 1971 to start a graduate program, the anthropology department was an undergraduate program only, of course. We started a master's program in 1973 and a doctorate program in 1975. By the 1980s we were getting graduate students who were really interested in doing research, and we had enough people to work in the research facility."

But the logistics were problematic. According to Bass, "To get to the sow barn took about 45 minutes to get out there from campus and 45 minutes back, so you essentially shot a morning or an afternoon going out there. So, I went back to the university and asked for land closer to campus. The dean gave me three acres in back of the university hospital, which had been the area where the university used to burn its trash. When the EPA banned open burning, the university stopped its burning and the area had grown into woods and briars. That's when our research really took off. My graduate students and I began to scientifically look at what happens when a body decays and begin to standardize our observations and the measurements. This also ushered in the field of forensic entomology, as the first critters to be attracted to a decaying body are the blowflies. Entomologists had studied this process but never in relationship to actual humans decaying in real time."

Bass says that his graduate students began to suggest a number of great ideas for research projects. "Let's say you are a graduate student in forensic anthropology and for your thesis or dissertation you want to decide how much weight a cadaver loses per day. Well, that means you are looking at the seasons of the year, so we'll schedule you for four bodies, one for each season. So, we eventually had hundreds of bodies to study; we looked at numerous changes and factors—was the body found in the sun or the shade? Was it clothed? In cotton clothing or wool or synthetics? The number of variables related to decay rates are astounding, as it's not one size fits all—there are hundreds of factors you have to deal with when the police ask you how long a person has been dead. Although through continued research we are getting much better at answering these questions, I'm sure we will never reach the stage that *CSI* did on television where the forensic scientists can tell you the body has been dead for exactly 14 hours and 47 minutes, or something precise like that. People ask me if I watched *CSI* and no, I don't—there is just too much artistic license taken."

The original Body Farm got so much use that other sites had to be established. "I have started two other farms since the original Body Farm," Bass confirms. "The original Body Farm you hear so much about is the one on the three acres behind the university hospital. We had so many graduate students using that facility, and we have so much research going on, that there was no sterile land left at the first Body Farm. Say you want to come here to get a doctoral degree and study the effect of something but you want undisturbed or unpolluted ground, well there is none left in that three-acre facility. So, we started more farms to accommodate the demand."

Bass continues, "Since there was no more room at the Body Farm in Knoxville, there is an additional facility in Oak Ridge, Tenn. that is 17 acres, and it's in the UT arboretum which is the forestry department in the College of Agriculture. At this facility we allow bodies to decay or we scatter or bury bones and students go find them. More recently, we opened a third body farm in the Cumberland Mountain area on UT-owned land. We fenced in one acre just this past year and it is set up so that when we expand, we will have the room we need. This is only for teaching law enforcement personnel right now."

Bass continues, "Up until I retired in 1997, I used to take people out to the Body Farm. But when I retired, the UT lawyers said they didn't think letting people tour the Body Farm was such a good idea anymore. The reason being that someone may visit the facility and then contract some kind of illness or disease and this leaves the university open to legal liability. I can understand that, as the Body Farm is not Disney World. It still amazes me because I absolutely had no idea at all that this would be something that people would be interested in. But some people are fascinated with death and they are not able to satisfy their curiosity. If you are driving down the road and there has been a wreck involving fatalities, you don't usually see the bodies lying out on the road, they are usually covered with a tarp. Whoever comes to pick up a body or bodies, they take them to the morgue or to the funeral home; when you go to the funeral home, you don't go to the embalming room; if you ever see that individual again, it's probably in a casket or you probably would not see them again. They are covered up and they are buried. A lot of people wonder what goes on in that period from death until burial. There's not much in the literature dealing with this and so I can see why people are interested. This is a big grey area and that door is locked to prevent further exploration. So, people are curious."

Bass says the Body Farm has helped forensic anthropologist make significant strides in their research. "The data used all over the world to determine time since death, has come out of that research that my graduate students have done at the Body Farm, so there's some good stuff that has come out of that endeavor."

It's not just forensic scientists and medical examiners who have benefited; law enforcement personnel have as well.

"Forensic science has been studied and that 2009 National Academy of Science report questioned certain approaches in some forensic disciplines; it was advised that these disciplines should be more scientific than they have been in the past," Bass says. "This is true, we do. So, UT started the National Forensic Academy, which is a training program for law enforcement officers. Participants must be a law enforcement officer and they must have crime scene investigation experience. What we are trying to do is upgrade these officers' knowledge of science. We have more of them than what the Body Farm can accommodate, so the training of this group is conducted in Oak Ridge, Tenn. Law enforcement officers are not doing the research, but they are studying dead bodies, and they are digging up dead bodies. We are teaching them how to locate a body, and when you dig it up, we teach them you don't just dig it up and look at the body, but you must look at the entire scene, the environment. Let's say you kill someone and you have to dig a grave; you take a shovel from your garage. Perhaps that shovel blade has a nick in it from hitting a rock when you are digging that grave, and you are running the shovel blade along the side of the hole; that little nick leaves a little mark along the side of the dirt. This is all theoretic at this point; you think you know who the killer might be and when you go to that person's house, you see if you can find a shovel with a nick in the blade that will match the nick mark left on the wall of the grave. This is just one example of hundreds of things we teach the police."

Teaching is at the heart of what Bass has cherished for more than four decades. Says Bass, "The Body Farm may be what I will be remembered for most, but I would also like to be acknowledged for being a good faculty member who produced good students. I may be what people consider to be the founder of the Body Farm but I may not live on through that, it's really the people who used that facility, my students, through whom I will live on." Bass adds, "I feel as though I have two families; I have a biological family of three sons and I have an academic family of probably 50 to 70 doctoral and master's students, and they have done very well in general. If I have left a mark I really think it will be through my students."

Millions of armchair detectives who have read Bass's fiction books might disagree. Bass teamed with Tennessee-based journalist Jon Jefferson to form Jefferson Bass, the pen name under which the duo created a fictional forensic anthropologist named Bill Brockton for their *Body Farm Novels* series. "Our next book, our 12th title, is coming out on Oct. 4, 2016 and it's called *Without Mercy*," Bass says. "I don't like that title, but it deals with racial deaths. I am 88 and Jon is 61 so there is a 27-year difference in age; I am getting to the stage where I think Jon ought to start on his own. We have signed contracts with Harper Collins to do one more book next year; this has been a good partnership but I would much rather have Jon go off on his own. It has been fun but I am getting a little too old for some of this. I want to slow down and enjoy life a little more."

Fiction aside, Bass is also an accomplished author of notable nonfiction works. His seminal text, *Human Osteology: A Laboratory and Field Manual*, was first published in 1971 and discusses ways to identify human bones and how to reconstruct a skeleton, with application for both forensic anthropology and for archaeology.

"My osteology book is still used all over the world," Bass says. "It's nice to know that I did something that other people are interested in."

Bass partnered with Jefferson for the aforementioned *Death's Acre: Inside the Legendary Forensic Lab the Body Farm Where the Dead Do Tell Tales*, a 2003 book that is part memoir, part celebration of some of his most intriguing cases. In 2007, the duo followed up with *Beyond the Body Farm: A Legendary Bone Detective Explores Murders, Mysteries, and the Revolution in Forensic Science.*

During his long career, Bass counts among his many accomplishments the leadership of the anthropology department at the University of Tennessee, creation of a forensic anthropology section of the AAFS, and serving for several decades as the Tennessee State forensic anthropologist. He has cultivated innumerable relationships with police departments and district attorneys, as well as with the FBI and other law enforcement agencies. He has lectured frequently and testified in court, as well as appeared on the news or quoted in newspapers for particularly newsworthy cases. Among Bass's numerous awards are the AAFS Physical Anthropology Award in Recognition of Outstanding Contributions to the Forensic Sciences in 1985. He was honored at a joint session of the Senate and House of Representatives of the State of Tennessee for Outstanding Contribution to Higher Education in 1986. And he was given the Distinguished Fellow Award by AAFS in 1994.

For his endeavors and contributions to science and to education, it's not surprise that Bass is the third generation in his family to have an educational building named after him. The Dr. William M. Bass III Forensic Anthropology Building dedication ceremony was held September 27, 2011, near the Body Farm.

"There is an elementary school in Lynchburg, Va. named the William Marvin Bass Elementary School and it is named after my grandfather," Bass says. "There is an elementary school in Frederick County, Va. named the Bass Hoover Elementary School and that is named after my father. And there is an academic building at the University of Tennessee called the William M. Bass Forensic Anthropology Building. So, three generations—grandfather, father, son—all have academic buildings named after them. That doesn't happen very often. I think education is fun—to me, it's wonderful to learn something new. I have enjoyed my career, and I think if you enjoy what you are doing, you can do a better job. So hopefully I have done a better job at everything I have attempted in my life. I was chosen as the National Professor of the Year in 1985 and this was in all fields in the U.S. and Canada and so obviously, I must have done something to deserve this honor. I always tried to bring out the best in my students."

Bass continues, "I enjoy teaching and I enjoy research and finding out things that in some cases no one else has ever discovered before. When you are working a forensic case and you are trying to figure out what happened and all of a sudden you find the one clue and it's an aha moment—that's exciting."

As Bass notes in *Death's Acre*, "There are moments in life when, in hindsight, you realize everything has changed forever. I'm proud to say the publication of *The Body Farm* was one of those moments in my life, and in the life of the Anthropology Research Facility I created" (page 199).

At the time of this writing, Bass had just turned 88. In *Death's Acre*, Bass answers the question he frequently receives: when you die, will your body go to the Body Farm? As Bass notes, "Will I practice what I preach; see it through to its logical conclusion?" (page 280). Bass says his first wife said yes, his second wife said no, and his current wife is leaning toward a more traditional final resting place, but as Bass notes further, "I leave the final call to Carol [his current wife] and the boys [Bass has three sons]. The scientist in me wants to sign the donation papers. But the rest of me can't forget how much I hate flies. Either way, you'll still find me at the Body Farm when I die. Not anytime soon, though. I don't want to die now. I have too much to do. Books to write. Grandchildren to play with. Killers to catch."

REFERENCES

Baden M and Roach M. *The New Science of Catching Killers*. Simon & Schuster, New York. 2001.

Bass B and Jefferson J. *Death's Acre. Inside the Legendary Forensic Lab, the Body Farm, Where the Dead Do Tell Tales*. G.P. Putnam's Sons, New York. 2003.

College of American Pathologists (CAP). College of American Pathologists 2011 Practice Characteristics Survey.

Di Maio V and Franscell R. *Morgue: A Life in Death*. St. Martin's Press, New York. 2016.

Fisher BAJ. Letter to the NAS Committee. June 12, 2007.

Hanzlick R. Incoming Forensic Pathology Fellow and Fellowship Program 2014–2015. Prepared for Forensic Pathology Subcommittee of National Association of Medical Examiners. 2014.

Hanzlick R and Haden-Pinneri K. Forensic pathology fellowship training positions and subsequent forensic pathology work effort of past forensic pathology fellows. *Academic Forensic Pathology*. Vol. 1, No. 3. Pages 322–327. 9. 2011.

Kemp WL. Forensic pathologist salaries in the United States: The results of Internet data collection. *Academic Forensic Pathology*. Vol. 4, No. 4. Pages 505–513. 13. 2014.

Melinek J, Thomas LC, Oliver WR, Schmunk GA, and Weedn VW. National Association of Medical Examiners Position Paper: Medical examiner, coroner and forensic pathologist independence. *Academic Forensic Pathology*. Vol. 3, No. 1. Pages 93–98. 2013.

National Academy of Sciences. Strengthening Forensic Science in the United States: A Path Forward. 2009. Accessible at http://www.nap.edu/catalog/12589.html

The National Academies of Sciences, Engineering and Medicine (NASEM). Strengthening Forensic Science in the United States: A Path Forward. Medical Examiner and Coroner Systems. Current and Future Needs. Page 242. 2009. Accessible at https://www.nap.edu/read/12589/chapter/11

National Association of Medical Examiners (NAME). Preliminary Report on America's Medicological Offices. Atlanta, GA. Page iv. 2004.

National Association of Medical Examiners. Forensic Autopsy Performance Standards. 2005.

National Association of Medical Examiners (NAME). 180-Day Study. 2004.

National Association of Medical Examiners (NAME). Resolution National Association of Medical Examiners Executive Committee. July 2, 2009. Accessible at https://netforum.avectra.com/public/temp/ClientImages/NAME/b21b1126-3124-42f1-b73f-0a689113084f.pdf

National Commission on Forensic Science (NCFS). Directive Recommendation on Certification of Medicolegal Death Investigators. January 30, 2015a. Accessible at https://www.justice.gov/ncfs/file/788026/download

National Commission on Forensic Science (NCFS). Policy Recommendation on Accreditation of Medical Examiner and Coroner Offices. January 30, 2015b. Accessible at https://www.justice.gov/ncfs/file/787236/download

National Commission on Forensic Science (NCFS). Views Document on Increasing the Supply of Forensic Pathologists. August 10–11, 2015c. Accessible at https://www.justice.gov/ncfs/file/787356/download

National Commission on Forensic Science (NCFS). Views of the Commission Regarding Critical Steps to Accreditation. March 22, 2016.

National Institute of Justice. Status and Needs of Forensic Science Service Providers: A Report to Congress. 2006. Accessible at http://www.ojp.usdoj.gov/nij/pubs-sum/213420.htm

National Library of Medicine. Marcella Fierro. Accessible at https://www.nlm.nih.gov/changingthefaceofmedicine/physicians/biography_111.html

Office of the Attorney General. Recommendations of the National Commission on Forensic Science; Announcement for NCFS Meeting Nine. March 17, 2016. Accessible at https://www.justice.gov/ncfs/file/841861/download

U.S. Department of Justice. Trace evidence quality assurance guidelines. *Forensic Science Communications*. Vol. 2, No. 1. January 2000. Accesible at https://archives.fbi.gov/archives/about-us/lab/forensic-science-science-comunications/fsc/jan2000/swgmat.htm

Weinberg M, Weedn VW, Weinberg S, and Fowler D. Characteristics of medical examiner/coroner offices accredited by the National Association of Medical Examiners. *Journal of Forensic Sciences*. Vol. 58, No. 5. Pages 1193–1199. 2013.

Wetli CV. Foreword. In: Forensic Pathology: Principles and Practice. 1st Edition. Academic Press, Cambrigde, MA. Page xxi. 2005.

Youngclaus J and Fresne JA. Physician Education Debt and the Cost to Attend Medical School 2012 Update. Association of American Medical Colleges. 2013.

CHAPTER 5

Celebrity and the Forensic Scientist

The individuals interviewed for this book are some of the most high-profile professionals in their field, noted for their expertise in practice, their contributions to advancing the profession, and their visibility in forensic science and medicolegal issues. But which came first, the celebrity forensic scientist, or the high-profile case and subsequent trial that made them a celebrity, and the notoriety that grew with each subsequent trial? There's always a case or a crime that vaults a rising star to superstardom, or catapults a heretofore unknown scientist into the limelight and launches a high-profile career. It would be disingenuous to suggest that fame is a product of cases and trials only; the hard work and continuous study that is required of these individuals as they perfected their craft over many decades cannot be overlooked. That said, it is a curious thing to behold the sense of celebrity that follows these forensic scientists, whether it is wanted, warranted, or wasted. Society loves a celebrity, and it has crowned some members of the profession as Hollywood royalty because of high-profile cases and trials that vault them into the media spotlight by virtue of association.

As Bell (2008, page 1) observes, "The response of the forensic science community to newfound fame is a predictable mix of excitement and dismay. It is fun to be at the center of attention, but at the same time being the subject of books, movies and television shows inevitably leads to false impressions and unrealistic expectations." Bell (2008, pages xiii–xiv) adds, "Forensic science is science first; forensic is easy, science is hard. The dedicated people who make it through a demanding curriculum and a competitive job market rarely care about money, fame or the perceived glamor of the field. Rather, bench forensic scientists care about making a difference every day and live for the endless variety of cases that come through their doors. ... Unlike most fictional portrayals, forensic scientists must keep their distance to protect their objectivity. Some mistake this detachment for indifference or even callous denial, but nothing could be farther from the truth. The good forensic scientists, and there are thousands of them, care passionately or they would not be where they are."

Practitioners are generally advised to eschew celebrity; James and Nordby (2003) say that it is not part of the equation: "In the real forensic sciences, individual scientists always work as members of a larger team, perhaps with other specialized scientists, law enforcement investigators, prosecutors, defense attorneys, judges, juries, and the media, each contributing his or her efforts toward the bigger picture of a public trial, or an investigation capturing the public interest. The job of a forensic scientist is not one of glamorous celebrity."

But the cult of celebrity is difficult to avoid. Whether it is the expert witness who is larger than life in the minds of jurors, or the glamorization of forensic science as the Hollywood starlet in its own right, the perception of the public is becoming increasingly significant to the legal and forensic science communities. Forensic science is vilified through the so-called "*CSI* effect," a modern-day crucible in which the very tenets of forensic disciplines and the criminal justice system are reworked like alchemy of old. James and Nordby (2003, page 6) state, "Forensic scientists must be prepared to battle dubious cultural expectations, either inappropriately elevating or denigrating the powers of science. Such expectations are usually generated through crime novels, popular theatre, movies, and television. These inappropriate expectations, when found among jurors, lawyers and even judges, can negate conservative scientific testimony."

Gabel (2014, page 290) describes the heavy weight that rests on the shoulders of forensic scientists and expert witnesses: "Despite the authority with which television and movie crime dramas depict forensic science results, the practice sometimes falls short of that 'used and done right' standard. Popular culture, news outlets, and public perception guide the belief that forensic evidence is reliable and absolute proof of an individual's guilt. In fact, forensic evidence has the essential hallmarks of certainty that juries need and society craves. Most people agree that it would be a miscarriage of justice to imprison an innocent person. Consequently, we want to be sure that we are convicting the right person. In many cases, forensic evidence closes the confidence gap left open by these concerns and seals the defendant's fate. It has the power to move the jury from maybe to guilty, and everyone can sleep better at night because 'science' solidified the conviction. The forensic analysts, then, are the criminal justice system's rock stars, bringing their objective scientific skill and authority to an otherwise emotionally charged process."

Is this kind of celebrity rooted in a cultural mindset that embraces the scientist for his or her notoriety as much as for his or her skill sets as a forensic practitioner? And are real-life scientists merely viewed as extensions of much-beloved fictional detectives? After all, society loves a larger-than-life character that solves crimes and restores justice, and embodies all of the noble, altruistic characteristics and attributes we want for ourselves.

LIFE IMITATES ART

Everyone likes a good story, and Hollywood has noticed that forensic science has many of them to tell. As Kirby (2013, page 92) notes, "Science would seem to be at odds with the process of storytelling used in the creation of entertainment texts. Science is perceived as 'truth' while entertainment storytelling resides in the imagination. For this reason, many people believe that science and storytelling make each other uncomfortable. Julian Petley (1996) claims, 'Fact plus fiction equals friction.' Yet... science has become a common narrative element across contemporary entertainment media including television, movies and computer games." Kirby (2013, page 92) adds that, "The fact that science has successfully been employed for storytelling purposes in numerous popular texts shows how science and storytelling not only can co-exist together, they can also thrive." And in fact, Kirby (2013, page 93) claims that "... the origin of modern crime fiction is intimately connected to the growth of forensic science." Thomas (2004) argues that the nineteenth century crime novels functioned as "devices of truth," and as Kirby (2013, page 93) notes, "While the novels gained validity by including forensic science, the emerging field of criminalistics itself gained legitimacy through the fact that fictional detectives were using its methods to solve crimes. Fictional detectives never failed to discover a criminal's identity through the application of science, technology and reasoning, which enhanced public faith in science's ability to solve crimes. French scientists Edmond Locard even instructed his colleagues and students to read Sherlock Holmes stories to understand the principles of forensic science."

The line between fiction and reality can be a blurred one, to the chagrin of commentators and the bemusement of forensic practitioners. As Kirby (2013, page 96) observes, "Most forensic scientists agree that the science portrayed in these shows does not match forensic reality by being simultaneously both simplified and exaggerated. The timeframes for procedures are highly accelerated, techniques are not as precise or as specific as portrayed, forensic personnel perform the duties of more than one technician, and most real-world crime labs cannot afford the types of equipment that routinely show up in television crime dramas."

Perhaps the caricature of the detective and/or forensic scientist is more in keeping with society's expectations for the embodiment of the righters of wrongs. In *The Adventure of the Abbey Grange*, the fictional detective Sherlock Holmes says to his colleague Dr. John Watson, "Your fatal habit of looking at everything from the point of view of a story instead of as a scientific exercise has ruined what might have been an instructive and even classical series of demonstrations" (http://www.literature.com/read.php?titleid=returnofsherlockholmes&abspage=270&bookmark=1).

When he wrote that scathing assessment of Watson, Holmes's faithful narrator and scribe, creator Sir Arthur Conan Doyle probably could not have imagined the modern television crime procedurals whose sole purpose is to tell an interesting, entertaining story and taking as many technical liberties as possible. The romantic portrayal of detective work in fiction began with Holmes in the late nineteenth century and remains a favorite among consumers of this literary genre. As Thomas (1999, page 4) explains, "Detective fiction as a form is generally recognized as an invention of the 19th century, coincident with the development of the modern police force and the creation of the modern bureaucratic state."

The genre has given us some memorable and much-loved fictional archetypes including the amateur detective such as Agatha Christie's Miss Marple; the private investigator such as Holmes and Christie's Poirot; the police detective such as Kojak and Columbo; and the forensic specialist such as Kay Scarpetta, Quincy, and the CSI teams. Detective fiction raised the profile of the detective significantly, thus setting the stage for the celebration of the forensic method—long before it came into its own as a structured discipline. "At the center of virtually every detective story is a body upon which the literary detective focuses his gaze and employs his unique interpretive powers," writes Thomas (1999, page 2). "His goal is to explain an event that seems to be inexplicable to everyone else. At stake is not just the identification of a dead victim or an unknown suspect, but the demonstration of the power invested in certain forensic devices embodied in the figure of the literary detective—the fingerprint, the mugshot, or the lie detector, for example—all of which enable the detective to read the clues to a mystery that is written in the suspect body."

Bell (2008, page 13) says that Sherlock Holmes will forever serve as inspiration for Hollywood, which can't help but take it one step beyond its place in Victorian literature. "Sir Arthur Conan Doyle's Sherlock Holmes stories were the first medium to bring scientific detection to the public's attention, but it took modern American pop culture to enshrine, embellish and mythologize it."

Prescience was an early hallmark of Conan Doyle's Sherlock Holmes adventures, as the author tapped into police–science techniques that were barely formative at the time. As Thomas (1999, pages 4–5) explains, "While the narratives of writers like Poe, Dickens and Conan Doyle often reflected and popularized contemporary scientific theories of law enforcement, the detective stories they wrote also sometimes anticipated actual procedures in scientific police practice by offering fantasies of social control and knowledge before the actual knowledge to achieve either was available. At times, these texts seemed to call those technologies into being. It became commonplace for early criminologists to attribute inspiration for their theories to the methods of a Sherlock Holmes or an August Dupin. In developing what he called 'a new police science,' which focused on the examination of microscopic particles on the criminal body, for example, the pioneering French forensic scientists Edmond Locard went so far as to instruct his colleagues and students to read over such stories as *A Study in Scarlet* and *The Sign of the Four* in order to understand the basis of the principles he was recommending."

Fast-forward more than 100 years and booksellers are still reaping significant profits from the detective fiction genre, although forensic science as we know it is front and center in most of today's best sellers. Many of the most popular series have at their core a fictional character based loosely on real-life forensic scientists and forensic pathologists.

In 1991, former journalist and computer analyst-turned-writer Patricia Cornwell debuted her first novel, *Postmortem*, in which we were introduced to chief medical examiner Dr. Kay Scarpetta. Borrowing heavily from real life, Cornwell parlayed her six years of work at the Office of the Chief Medical Examiner of Virginia and for the Richmond Police Department into fictional works that captured a truer essence of a forensic pathologist than readers had seen previously. To date, Cornwell's books have sold some 100 million copies in 36 languages in over 120 countries. (Former police-beat journalist Michael Connelly achieved similar success with his series of Harry Bosch detective fiction, creating a niche where reporters could blend fact with fiction in a believable, engaging storyline that keeps readers coming back for more with each subsequent title that delivered intriguing character development along with the police work.)

Following closely on Cornwell's heels in 2001 was physician-turned-writer Tess Gerritsen, who introduced the world to her Rizzoli & Isles series with *The Surgeon*; detective Jane Rizzoli was soon partnered with medical examiner Dr. Maura Isles. The series eventually was developed for television on the TNT network and lives on in syndication. While the 1970s had *Quincy* and the 1990s had *Crossing Jordan*, perhaps the queen of books developed into a monster television hit is Kathy Reichs, creator of the Temperance Brennan series that became the show *Bones*, recounting the adventures of a veteran forensic anthropologist. Reichs has competition from the team of Jefferson Bass—composed of journalist Jon Jefferson and fellow forensic anthropologist William Bass, the founder of the Body Farm at the University of Tennessee. The Body Farm series centers around the exploits of Dr. Bill Brockton, the fictional forensic anthropologist and founder, not surprisingly, of the University of Tennessee's postmortem decay research lab. Jefferson Bass debuted their first work of fiction, *Carved in Bone*, in 2003, along with several nonfiction works, as we saw in Chapter 4.

Sometimes it's just more fun to stretch reality to its breaking point when it comes to televised detective and medicolegal programming; take *Dexter* for instance. This Showtime hit in the early 2000s featured a protagonist by the name of Dexter Morgan, a Miami Metro Police Department bloodstain pattern analyst and forensic science technician who helped solve crimes by day and by night, employed his forensic skills to deliver some vigilante justice of his own as he secretly murders criminals and covers his tracks. On the flip side, forensic experts are trying their hand at fiction. For example, forensic pathologist Michael Baden, MD, has written several works of fiction, 2005's *Remains Silent* and 2009's *Skeleton Justice*, with his coauthor and wife Linda Kenney Baden. Or as we just saw in Chapter 4, retired forensic anthropologist William Bass has parlayed his professional experiences into the *Body Farm* series.

For the forensic professional upon whom a fictional character is based, it's a mixed blessing. Just ask Virginia's former chief medical examiner Marcella F. Fierro, MD, the inspiration of Patricia Cornwell's aforementioned protagonist, Dr. Kay Scarpetta. Fierro, now 75, retired from her post in 2008 after more than 30 years on the job, handling difficult cases such as the Virginia Tech massacre and Richmond's Southside Strangler killings. In 1984, the chief medical examiner at the time assigned Fierro to sit for an interview with Cornwell that was part of the writer's research for her detective protagonist's development, and Cornwell has been quoted as saying that "I would not be where I am today in my life were it not for Dr. Fierro" (Gelineau, 2007). According to Fierro, the medical examiner in Cornwell's novel was a minor character who later morphed into the main character.

As the National Library of Medicine notes, "Dr. Fierro's skill and dedication inspired mystery writer Patricia Cornwell to write a series of crime novels in which the protagonist, Kay Scarpetta, was modeled after Dr. Fierro. Cornwell knew Dr. Fierro because she had worked as a computer analyst in Fierro's office of chief Medical Examiner. As a result of the widespread success of Cornwell's novels, the work of forensic pathologists has become familiar to the public in a way that would not have otherwise been possible" (NLM, n.d.).

Gelineau (2007) quotes Cornwell as saying about Fierro, "What she does have in common with Marcella is this amazing database between her ears, a tremendous compassion for the victims, and she will fight to the death for them. She has always been a tremendous advocate for those who can no longer speak for themselves." Gelineau (2007) adds that Fierro took her responsibility as chief medical examiner very seriously: "We are physicians. And our mission is to take care of our patient—who just happens to be dead. They have a story to tell. And they tell us their story through the physical examination and the testing that we do—just as if they were living people."

As Gelineau (2007) writes, "Aside from their jobs and penchant for Italian food, Fierro sees little resemblance between her and the fictional doctor" and quotes Fierro as saying, "Kay [Scarpetta] is blond, blue-eyed and 115 pounds. I've never been blond, I have brown eyes, and I haven't weighed 115 pounds since I was 12."

Fierro maintains she is not the sole inspiration for the Scarpetta character. "Scarpetta is an amalgamation of many forensic pathologists that Patricia Cornwell knew," she says. "Cornwell was and is a meticulous researcher. If she says it, you can take it to the bank. This was the first of the genre, clearly differentiating fiction from police procedure stories, police thrillers, etc. She was the first to write fiction about forensic pathology and the forensic sciences."

Whether or not she has had a fictional character modeled after her, as we will see in Chapter 6, Marcella Farinelli Fierro, MD, has had a forensic career worthy of writing about. She may be most known for serving as chief medical examiner for the Commonwealth of Virginia, overseeing the medical examiner investigations of all violent, suspicious, and unnatural deaths there.

What lured her to forensic pathology? "Love of medicine and curiosity," Fierro says. "It's all about solving the puzzle."

Those puzzle pieces fell together as she advanced in her education and training, first earning a bachelor's degree in biology cum laude from D'Youville College in Buffalo, New York. Upon deciding to become a physician in 1962, she pursued her medical degree from the State University of New York at Buffalo School of Medicine (now known as the University at Buffalo Jacobs School of Medicine and Biomedical Sciences), graduating in

1966. Following an internship and residency at Ottawa Civic Hospital in Ontario, Canada, she completed her residency training in pathology at the Cleveland Clinic and the Medical College of Virginia, Virginia Commonwealth University from 1973 to 1974. She was a fellow in forensic pathology and legal medicine at Virginia Commonwealth University and the Office of the Chief Medical Examiner in Richmond, Virginia. She became certified by the American Board of Pathology in anatomical, clinical, and forensic pathology.

She served as professor of forensic pathology and professor and chair of the Department of Legal Medicine at Virginia Commonwealth University from 1994 to 2008. She also codirected the Virginia Institute of Forensic Science and Medicine, offering week-long courses on topics such as advanced death investigation to medical examiners, crime scene investigators, judges, law enforcement investigators, prosecutors, forensic scientists, nurses, and others working in forensic science.

A native of Buffalo, New York, Fierro has been on the faculty of the Department of Legal Medicine and Pathology at Medical College of Virginia Campus of Virginia Commonwealth University since 1973. She was a clinical professor of forensic pathology at the University of Virginia, Charlottesville, from 1983 to 1992 and again in 1999 to 2002. Fierro served as a professor of pathology at East Carolina School of Medicine in Greenville, North Carolina from 1992 to 1994.

Fierro has been active in professional organizations as a member of the Forensic Pathology Council of the American Society of Clinical Pathologists and chair of the Forensic Pathology Committee of the College of American Pathologists. She is the past president of the National Association of Medical Examiners (NAME) and served on the board of directors and the executive committee of that organization and currently serves on several committees. Fierro is a Fellow of the American Academy of Forensic Sciences, was a member of the Forensic Science Board for the Commonwealth, and has served as a consultant to the Federal Bureau of Investigation (FBI) for the National Crime Information Center Unidentified and Missing Persons Files and on federal panels and committees that are developing best practices in mass fatality management.

She has been active in the legislative process, serving as a resource and advocate in Virginia for matters related to forensic and medical examiner issues. She was a legislative resource and testified on a bill amending homicide and malicious wounding statute to increase the penalty for the murder or malicious wounding of a pregnant woman, and initiated a bill mandating mothers receive a DNA card for infant identification in addition to the almost always useless baby footprint. Recent activities include establishing child and maternal mortality review teams that characterize deaths and develop strategies for prevention. Fierro initiated participation in the National Violent Death Reporting System and Family and Interpersonal Violence surveillance programs for Virginia.

Fierro has published in professional journals, edited a textbook, contributed chapters to several books, and presented at international meetings. Fierro served as a reviewer for the *American Journal of Forensic Medicine and Pathology*. She received Virginia's Public Health Hero Award and the NAME Service award, and she was elected to Alpha Omega Alpha as a distinguished alumna of the School of Medicine, State University of New York at Buffalo. Among her many awards is the Lifetime Achievement Award she received in 2001 from the School of Medicine and Biomedical Sciences Medical Alumni Association, State University at Buffalo.

She has appeared on the Discovery Channel's *New Detectives* series and on BBC regarding Cornwell's novel *From Potter's Field*. Fierro advised Cornwell on all her Scarpetta books, including *Postmortem*, *Body of Evidence*, *All that Remains*, *Cruel and Unusual*, *Body Farm*, and *From Potter's Field*.

In an interview with the National Library of Medicine, Fierro says her biggest obstacle was a lack of career guidance for women in the 1950s and 1960s when she was getting her education, and there were very few women physicians and medicine was vastly "unknown" to women. An early mentor was a woman physician named Ellen Eckstein Rudinger who was a refugee from the Nazis and had left Germany to attend school again in order to become an internist.

With a storied career, Fierro remains modest in what she pinpoints as her greatest accomplishments to date. "It's being able to speak for the dead—telling their story to family, friends and to the courts. I am able to perform a public health function and criminal justice service, so I can serve both the living and the dead."

Fierro considers her most professionally satisfying experiences as her alumni election to Alpha Omega Alpha national medical honor society and service as a panel member and one of the authors on the Committee on Identifying the Needs of the Forensic Sciences Community, National Research Council 2009 Report: Strengthening Forensic Science in the United States: A Path Forward.

While never an easy job, Fierro says there are aspects of forensic pathology that she both enjoys and finds challenging. "Figuring out the pale of physical findings from the autopsy and correlating them with the circumstances to tell what happened to the person is rewarding," Fierro says. "However, bodies in poor condition were sometimes difficult."

Forensic pathologists frequently state that the bodies they are autopsying can help tell them the story of their demise, or at least provide significant clues to the cause, manner, and timing of death. Regarding her method when conducting the autopsy, Fierro says, "My approach is to take the broad body of knowledge of human disease (pathology) comparing it to what the body shows and documenting that in detail. Being able to recognize the various types and mechanisms of injury and subtle markers of injury are the most exciting parts. It is never business as usual because you do not know what you will find until you look. It is very detail-oriented work."

Fierro retired in 2008 but by no means did she leave forensic pathology. As many former medical examiners do, she now serves as a consultant. "I review cases for families, lawyers, the courts and others who have an interest in what happened to a person," Fierro explains. "Sometimes I can add nothing, sometimes I can raise questions (the retrospectiscope always has questions) and sometimes there are errors. All human work, despite our best effort, is subject to error."

Throughout an immensely challenging career, including working the mass shooting deaths at Virginia Tech on April 16, 2007, Fierro says she does not feel the sense of celebrity that some forensic pathologists and other forensic practitioners have attained in their careers. "I strive for and have largely managed to keep a low profile for public service work for 34 years," she says. "I do enjoy talking about forensic pathology and have done some work with reputable TV folks. By and large the celebrity status of high-profile pathologists is positive although a few are borderline, in my opinion."

In a day when men still outnumber women as forensic pathologists, Fierro recalls how it felt to be a woman in a male-dominated field. "Early on, when there were very few, police and lawyers were not sure I could handle the unpleasant aspects of the job and whether I would hold up in court," Fierro says. "That vanished pretty quickly in Virginia. I was the ninth woman certified by the American Board of Pathology in forensic pathology so there were a few pioneers before me. Judith Lehotay of Buffalo, N.Y. was the first. She worked in my home town, and I admired her."

Thousands of cases later, Fierro says there are too many memorable cases to list, but remarks, "I can say that some cases where all the medical issues were resolved and correlated perfectly with the circumstances and were perfect for explaining in court, never saw a court. The accused would work out a plea agreement in the face of overwhelming evidence—not just because of my component but all the others too. At quiet times, some cases bubble up in my memory and I feel the same grief for decedents and their families that I felt then. People compartmentalize all the time. You have to let it go or you will go crazy. You do your best job and then recognize there is/was nothing more you could contribute to your patient. All medicine deals with life, suffering and death and it isn't pretty. However, medicine does have the advantage of actually being able to comfort, treat, discover, explain and do something for the sick, dying or dead patient. Non-medical people do not have that opportunity to directly do something helpful. That is very satisfying and allows you to put it away when you are done. If the work does not reward you then you need to leave medicine and find work that does. I used to joke to myself that I needed to practice medicine as much as medicine needed me to fill its ranks."

LIGHTS, CAMERA,... COURTROOM

When the armchair detective finishes his or her favorite novel starring a forensic practitioner, he or she can then switch over to being an armchair juror, partaking in the legal voyeurism afforded by reality television. In *As You Like It*, act II, scene VII, William Shakespeare reminds us that "All the world's a stage, and all the men and women merely players; they have their exits and their entrances, and one man in his time plays many parts..." Centuries later, Boorstin (1962) tells us that, "Television reporting allows us all to be the actors we really are" (http://www.columbia.edu/itc/journalism/j6075/edit/boor.html).

Forensic scientists have become celebrities in their own right thanks to the 24/7 cable news and the continued proliferation of commentary. Gabler (1994) notes that celebrities are "people who take the national stage, do their act and leave, invited to return only when they have something new to perform" (http://www.nytimes.com/1994/10/16/arts/the-brief-half-life-of-celebrity.html?pagewanted=all). In other words, celebrities only gain their status as granted by an adoring public; it is symbiotic relationship built on fascination, intrigue, and fascination—currency that can be devalued in an instant. For forensic scientists who have become as famous as the defendants in high-profile trials, they are consistently in the spotlight thanks to a steady supply of trials warranting coverage by the media.

The public's fascination with celebrities and reality television helped made Court TV's debut a success, satisfying people's need for drama unfolding in real time, and the taste for legal proceedings that extract intimate details of celebrities' or prominent persons' lives. The public has also developed a taste for seeing the law in action and watching how the law really operates as opposed to last week's rerun of *Law & Order*. It may also represent a chance for the armchair juror to seek justice from the small screen. As Chiasson (1997, page ix) observes, "Unlike life with all its shades of grey, a trial is black or white, someone is guilty or innocent; there is crime, there is justice, there is punishment. Perhaps it is that simplicity most of us find so compelling, and perhaps that is the reason trials so often grip our attention. We gravitate to the natural drama of a trial, and some have significance that far exceeds our understanding. The trial of a carpenter's son, for example, still holds the world's attention after 2,000 years. Perhaps the intoxicating mystery of a trial is that elusive concept called justice... It is what we blindly stumble after in life and what we hope to attain in court. It may be wishful thinking, of course, to believe that we can bottle and dispense in a courtroom what we can hardly identify in life, but God bless us, we try."

If celebrity is a byproduct of being in the public eye, forensic scientists certainly can shape the public's perception of forensic science–related issues on one of the biggest and most visible stages possible—the courtroom witness stand. Chiasson (1997, page x) observes, "The true American theater is the courtroom. How the public views that stage is often left to the media. The jury renders a judgment, but public opinion often determines the final verdict in terms of the lasting historical significance of the crime, the trial, and the accused." Chiasson (1997, page 204) continues, "[Trials] have all the elements of good fiction: conflict, suspense, rising and falling action, deception and surprise, heroes and villains." Chiasson (1997, page 203) adds, "[Trials] are real-life soap operas that allow the public to gawk at others' malfeasance and tragedy."

Gregory (2008) says, "There are many reasons for contemporary society's interest in trials. One scholar identifies the following reason for such interest: 'It is the combination of wealth, glamour and extreme notoriety that make cases such as this...so interesting to the general public.' Society enjoys the glamour, wealth, and extreme notoriety of celebrities without adding the drama of a trial. Once a celebrity is involved in a trial, the combination of all of these factors makes a celebrity trial even more appealing to the public."

The outcomes of trials constitute fodder for the media and ensure continued viewership from the armchair juror as the post-trial feeding frenzy continues. As Chiasson (1997) notes, "Judges have issued decisions that defied legal logic, attorneys have used tactics or antics that fiction writers couldn't have dreamed up, and trial participants haven't always been the quiet, respectful person they were expected to be. Juries, of course, have gone so far afield from the evidence and issued such outrageous judgments that the results actually have wound up in Hollywood."

Without the media and outlets such as Court TV, verdicts—and the reactions they provoke—might not be so incendiary. As Haggerty (2009) notes, "At their best, the media have helped advance public literacy, fostered a greater understanding of distant cultures, undermined traditional authority structures and buttressed democratic processes through the development of a public sphere (Habermas, 1989). At their worst, the mass media feed public appetites for the sensational, cynically capitalize on the horrific, and institutionalize a culture of celebrity."

What happens when forensic scientists become as celebrated as star prosecutors, defense attorneys, and the celebrity defendant? Steenberg (2013) says that, "The *CSI* Effect has made criminalists (such as Dr. Edmond Locard), forensic anthropologists (such as Kathy Reichs) and forensic pathologists (such as Dr. Michael Baden) household names." We'll explore the *CSI* effect in a subsequent section in this chapter.

Forensic experts take on a life of their own within the courtroom, a trend that some observers find disconcerting. Steenberg (2013) explains that, "The forensic celebrity expert is built through several dichotomies: insider/outsider, fact/fiction and authentic/mediated. Forensic celebrity builds an authenticity by maintaining such distinctions while simultaneously exploiting both halves of these dichotomies. Kathy Reichs is a best-selling crime fiction author, television producer and the basis of a television character, Dr. Temperance Brennan in Bones. Celebrity FBI behavioral scientists John Douglas and Robert Ressler have each published true crime books and appeared on tabloid television documentaries discussing their rise to celebrity status, framed by their most interesting—or disturbing—cases. Both men also claim to be the inspiration behind the character of Jack Crawford in The Silence of the Lambs. These forensic experts depend on their ability to navigate both fact (their education and professional forensic qualifications) and fiction (their media personas). Their celebrity expert status also depends on the maintenance of the distinction between the two. Reichs promises to reveal the truth behind Bones.

Douglas and Ressler promise to reveal what goes on behind the scenes and in 'real' life. The celebrity of the forensic expert is yet another example of the feedback loop of tabloid forensic science and its hyper-real epistemology. Celebrity forensic experts base their fictions on fact. Their facts then become the stuff of fiction and they are called upon to represent the facts behind the fiction. The circular logic of the feedback means that tabloid forensic expertise and celebrity is often lucratively self-sustaining."

Finding fulfilling work in this field that also crossed paths with the courtroom wasn't an issue for Richard Saferstein, PhD, a retired crime lab director, consultant and author based in New Jersey. "I testify a lot and I really enjoy that," he says. "I like strategizing with the attorneys. I enjoy being called by attorneys for the defense in the criminal arena and in the civil arena working cases up, and to me that's what I wake up for in the morning." Saferstein says he feels the weight of the outcome of cases but that it has never influenced his analyses. "I never felt any pressure to control the outcome of a case; I always let the cards fall as they may. I think all I can do is do the best job I can and call it as it is, even though the spotlight is on me. Celebrity is an interesting thing; when people gush it's nice to hear, as I like people gushing over me," he says with a laugh. "But I don't seek out adulation. People come up to me and say nice things to me and it reinforces the feelings of pride I have that my work and my writing have touched so many people's lives and work. I have been lucky to have that experience."

Forensic pathologist Michael Baden, MD, says that in or out of the courtroom, he doesn't succumb to pressure in the spotlight. "I don't feel pressure with high-profile, high-stakes cases," he conforms. "I feel the pressure to do the same thing whether it is a high-profile case with a famous person involved, or a low-profile case involving an indigent person found on the street. It's only when the members of the media get involved and they ask us lots of questions; it can be dangerous how we answer those questions and for good or bad reasons, the high-profile cases come under much more scrutiny than the run-of-the-mill cases. We have to make sure we do the run-of-the-mill cases as well and as competently as we do the high-profile cases, because the dead body on the autopsy table doesn't have a bank account or doesn't have a fancy dress or a suit on—all bodies look alike to us in the forensic way on the autopsy table. I think for those people who do only mediocre, routine work—which isn't right—and when a high-profile case comes along they do a lot better work, that will catch up with them. You can't do good work on high-profile cases if you don't do good work on low-profile cases all of the time. This is what I tried to tell the residents and fellows when I was chief ME; you have to do good work on all of the cases in order to do good work on the high-profile cases."

Baden insists on integrity with all cases, continuing, "The main thing is to treat everyone the same and do the best work on every death investigated. For example, poor or wealthy—we can't tell from doing the autopsy whether people care or don't care about the decedent—I think we always have to do the best job we can and if we cut corners, we make mistakes. Unless the forensic pathologist is doing the best job he or she can, with every autopsy he or she does, then mistakes will be made and that's unacceptable. One of the things that forensic pathologists have more trouble with than other physicians is when mistakes are made. All doctors make mistakes sometimes, and hopefully they are not serious. If he or she does make a mistake, often it is an issue that is only between the family, the practitioner and the insurance company. But maybe it will go to trial, and the courts will be involved. When an ME makes a mistake, because of the interest of the media and the fascination with dead bodies on the part of the general public, it usually becomes more publicized. So, the ME makes one mistake in 10 years and that might hit the front page; whereas if a family doctor makes 10 mistakes in 10 years, it's only between him and his insurance company and the family. One of the reasons people don't go into forensic pathology is because of the danger of getting into a lot of trouble in the media if you make a mistake."

And if you happen to be a celebrity ME, the stakes are even higher, Baden says. "There may be 20,000 brain surgeons in the country but there are a limited number of forensic pathologists. Brain surgeons, unless they are very prominent, don't get followed by the media, as a rule. In our business, there are maybe 400 or 500 forensic pathologists who do this work full-time and they are distributed in such a way so that there may be five or 10 states that don't even have a forensic pathologist in the whole state. And when somebody dies who is high-profile, they will die usually in Los Angeles or New York or maybe Florida, as high-profile people tend to live and die where the money is. So, with a limited number of forensic pathologists available to do these high-profile autopsies or review these cases, they tend to attract attention more so than any other type of physician. (Famed coroner) Tom Noguchi performed a lot of direct examinations of famous people who died in Los Angeles, and he was subjected to a lot of scrutiny because of it."

Baden says that celebrity can bring notoriety that is at once both good and bad. "I find that even when it is good, it is still notoriety as opposed to earned wonderment," he says. "And then when people die and families want a second opinion, of those 400 or 500 forensic pathologists, there may be only 20 or 30 who contract to do that, because many who work for the government or law enforcement agencies can't do outside work. There are a number of people around who have earned some degree of notoriety, such as Noguchi, Cyril Wecht, Bernard Spitz, and Lakshmanan Sathyavagiswaran. To me, the notoriety usually interferes with proper progression of a case until it is all over. I have learned that the hard way. I learned early on that if it is a high-profile murder case, the media are invariably involved and watching. In my youth, when I worked in the New York City Medical Examiner's Office, I made some comments to the news media about my thoughts on a case and it came back to haunt me at the time of the trial because whatever I say can be used to question me later on. So early on, I learned to keep my mouth shut. That helps dispel some of the harmful things that occur from notoriety. I have learned not to speak about any cases until the case is over, and that has served me well."

Cyril Wecht, MD, JD, the forensic pathologist in private practice in Pennsylvania, has endured celebrity due to the cases in which he has been involved, including Jo Kopechne (in which Sen. Ted Kennedy as implicated), Elvis Presley, Sunny Van Bulow, Tammy Wynette, Jean Harris, the Waco Branch Davidian fire, and Anna Nicole Smith and her son Daniel Smith.

Wecht, who was a coroner, an ME and a forensic pathologist for 20 years in Alleghany County, says he doesn't go looking for cases, but rather, they tend to find him. "As a forensic pathologist I am contacted by the coroner or the district attorney, and requested to conduct an autopsy or review case findings," he says. "I am independent, I am not their employee, and I get paid by the case. I function as an independent medical legal consultant now. Since 2006, I have worked as an independent forensic pathologist doing autopsies for several counties. Now as a medico-legal consultant I pick and choose; I have every right to reject a case, but that has been very rare. I don't advertise, so the cases come to me, and I don't limit myself to one side of the other. I am contacted by defense attorneys in criminal cases not in jurisdictions where I have done the autopsies. In criminal cases I would say that as far as testifying, I wind up testifying much more for the prosecution because I have done those coroners' cases and they go to trial as homicides; but when you set those aside, in terms of consultations in homicide cases, they are about 100 percent from the defense because the prosecution rarely reaches out for other forensic pathologists beyond their own coroner or ME; they have the autopsy on Joe Jones but their practitioner called the death a homicide and that forensic pathologist will then be called to testify. It's only in some very high-profile, controversial, highly problematic cases that the prosecution attorney will reach out to me because they need an additional forensic pathologist. It does happen; I have had a few over the years. On the civil side, I get cases from both sides. I don't keep track, and I don't keep a scorecard but I would estimate that my consultations from attorneys probably run about two-thirds from the prosecution and the rest from the defense. I do consultations all over the country, and I don't have a preference for the kinds of cases I'll take. I try not to be biased."

Wecht continues, "I'll tell you this, it's a hell of a lot easier to be testifying for the prosecution than it is for the defense. The person has been charged, the jury is supposed to be unbiased and in the meantime even the average person knows we talk about innocent until proven guilty. That's not how it plays out in people's minds. You read in the paper that Tom Brown has been arrested for murder and the first thing you think of is Tom Brown is innocent, right? Or do you think that Tom Brown is guilty, and how did he do it? When I go in as a defense expert in a criminal case, I anticipate the worst, the most egregious, the most obnoxious behavior; I anticipate aggressiveness, and if it's anything less than that, I'm surprised."

Wecht says he is put off by the behavior in some courtrooms and the seemingly worst that humanity has to offer. "As a sensitive person, I think a lot about people, their beliefs and philosophies. I am not a callous person, so I think a lot about cases in which people have been injured or murdered, and especially children and innocents—they remain with me. I don't suppress it, and I frequently discuss cases with my wife, who is an attorney. We have four children—one is a justice on the supreme court of Pennsylvania, two are doctors, one is program director of the Wecht Institute of Forensic Science and Law at Duquesne University—and I talk to them about what people can do to each other. Cases remain with me, especially the people who have been tortured; you remember those details. I also remember cases in which I feel injustices have occurred, cases that bother me greatly because of the barbaric nature of the death as well as justice not being served. People who are guilty according to the evidence who have been tried and not convicted, and on the other side, there are innocent people who have been convicted. These things bother me greatly."

Wecht continues, "The JFK assassination is of course No. 1, as there is no question in my mind that the Warren report is total nonsense. That bothers me. The JonBenet Ramsay case bothers me, too. I speak frequently on these cases and every time I talk about them it bothers me greatly—the people responsible were never charged and tried. Those things bother me because of my sense of justice, when I hearken back to my legal training and knowing how the justice system is supposed to work, and how it actually works. It is thwarted and aborted and misapplied and abused. Big cases are tried in the court of public opinion thanks to the news media; those pressures mount and sometimes reach editorial pages and public opinion can influence the medical examiner who may not have the courage to buck the system and go against public opinion. Pressure applied by elected officials who appointed you is common; those officials are going to be running for re-election and it does not help them if their appointed medical examiner comes up with something diametrically opposed and antithetical to what the public wants and expects. It's another strong reason why the ME is more qualified and more respectable, there is validity to their training. But what about the elected coroner? They have been elected by the people, so who do you answer to? When you say you are appointed and you are independent, that's an oxymoron—if you are appointed by somebody other than God, aren't you answerable to somebody? So how can you say that you are independent? So much public pressure, so much public opinion, decisions made before the determination of guilt or innocence... so here you are, the ME, and the cops have arrested someone, the DA charged him and already had the press conference, you are then doing the autopsy—how likely and how realistic is it that you, Mr. ME, are going to go against the detective and the DA? But if you are truly independent, at least if you have spunk, some sense of personal morality, and professional ethics, then at least you have the opportunity to speak out, despite the glare of the spotlight."

"The pressure of celebrity can be difficult," Wecht adds. "Sometimes you are a target because of it and attorneys try to make something of it, and I just deal with it honestly. I have had some legal problems of my own but I was totally exonerated of it legally. I just love in a deposition when an attorney wants to touch on it or challenge me; fine, let's talk about it—you discuss it candidly and repeat what you have always said and stood for. Sometimes people try to ridicule or attack you for something that has played out unbeknownst to you. I deal with it by not being afraid to talk about it, not being cowed or boastful. I try not to become offended or angry but deal with it and let it play it out."

Wecht says celebrity has also driven potential bias which in turn has marred the profession. "The unsuspected, the unappreciated, subconscious politicization of the system is there and you can't eliminate it completely because we are human beings," he says. "People have their biases, and forensic scientists are no different—they are basically a microcosm of American society in that regard and they have their own biases to deal with; you have to be careful that you don't allow personal beliefs to influence you. A good percentage of forensic pathologists, I think, if they hadn't been so damn smart and their parents hadn't pushed them into medicine, they would have been in law enforcement. They would have loved being a homicide detective—that mentality is there that you are helping the criminal process. When you have that kind of mindset, that mentality to begin with and now you are planted within the field in which people with that mentality are paid to pursue it, it can be a fine line."

Bell (2008, page 14) observes that, "Forensic science professionals respond differently to attention. Some embrace it, welcoming the scientist-as-hero portrayals. Youth growing up watching *CSI* and other media become interested in science and may decide to pursue it as a career, bringing fresh blood and new ideas into the forensic system. Less-enthused practitioners argue that unrealistic publicity bring false expectations that come to rest squarely at the laboratory doorstep. A few forensic scientists have embraced popularity by writing novels. Fewer still have exploited it for fame and financial gain."

Why are forensic experts serving as expert witnesses in trials so irresistible to watch? The likes of Henry Lee, Michael Baden, and Cyril Wecht have become household names following their exposure on television and in the print media. They are admired for their knowledge, their astute observations, and the complete authority with which they present their findings. They fascinate us because they represent a world that is exclusive and mysterious, and the media is a conduit from our dull, ordinary lives to this magical inner sanctuary where people's fates are decided.

Glynn (2000) suggest that tabloid media "can offer a space where marginalized people have access to expert knowledge and to knowledge formation." As Glynn (2000, page 72) explains, "Promises to reveal that which is known and done by the socially powerful—that which takes place behind the scenes, as it were—have potentially immense resonance with readers who are routinely denied access to information by dint of the very structure of power relations and therefore of communication flows in an unequal society. Consequently, the tabloids' reports are often framed in terms of the revelation of various forms of insider information."

Glynn (2000) continues, "The forensic expert facilitates the spectator's access to this insider information not only about the cases at hand but to the meta-narrative of tabloid forensic science itself—its legitimacy as a discipline, its ability to provide truths about the world and its ability to provide upward mobility for its practitioners. The practice of forensic science can be, and in its mediated articulation frequently is, a social leveler—demonstrating both the victimhood and especially the guilt of the socially powerful" (http://www.biblioteca.unlpam.edu.ar/pubpdf/anclajes/n06a15basabe.pdf).

Glynn (2000) adds that, "Despite their ability to provide insider information to spectators who, as Glynn argues, are barred from the channels of official information by virtue of their social status, it is important to remember that experts... like Reichs are sanctioned members of powerful institutions—law enforcement and academia. They are providing what Aaron Doyle calls inner-circle crime reporting... inner circle reporter and experts have a vested interest in seeing that the institutions they represent are protected from criticism. Their unwillingness to damage the organizations to which they belong is often one of the reasons why they are granted access to information that an unbiased reporter might be denied. While forensic story lines may revel in the humiliation of the corrupt police officer, the philandering businessman or the greedy trophy wife, celebrity forensic experts on reality programming and in the media must be careful not to disgrace the sources on which they depend for their insider information. Because of the close symbiotic relationship between the forensic expert and law enforcement, the subversive potential of the tabloid media imagined by Glynn is contained" (http://www.biblioteca.unlpam.edu.ar/pubpdf/anclajes/n06a15basabe.pdf).

At the peak of a trial that involves a celebrity, politician, or other notable individual, the mass media reaches a frenzied crescendo, and the news is blanketed with opinions and analyses. The preponderance of commentary—some insightful, some muckraking, is inescapable, with pundits pontificating for ratings, and forensic experts providing their perspectives.

For as many news outlets that exist, there are experts to provide commentary. Whether the former may have created the latter and vice versa is up for debate, but the pervasiveness of criminal trial commentary is a byproduct of the age of 24/7 television news. While not all states televise trials, there is no lack of reporting on the trials, the testimony, and the titillating details desired by a general public with a voracious appetite for the strange, the lurid, and the scintillating.

Most criminal trials satisfy this hunger, and the media is eager to provide a steady diet. Sensationalism aside, most, if not all, forensic science experts who provide commentary do it with a sense of responsibility and gravity befitting the situation. While the details that come out at some criminal trials are highly sensational, it is incumbent on the forensic expert to stick to the science on TV, as they are expected to do during trial.

We need these experts because in the 1990s, criminal trial became a self-guided tour of sorts. You can't have talking heads without an audience, and much of modern reporting on trials was shaped in 1991 by the debut of Court TV (which eventually became TruTV in 2008). Creator Steven Brill, an attorney and founder of *American Lawyer* magazine in 1978, told *The New York Observer* that the network was successful because "People are always interested [in true crime]. It's why Court TV worked. It's natural drama, there's a beginning, middle and end, and people want to know what happens."

One of the earliest high-profile trials covered by the fledgling network was that of three of the defendants in the Central Park jogger rape case. The shows were essentially live trial broadcasts—delayed by 10 seconds to preserve confidential information about jurors, witnesses, and attorney–client privilege. Gerard (1990) reports Brill as saying, "By covering trials like the jogger case, we have the opportunity to take what the public may think is an open-and-shut case and explain that if they get off it's not because the system is stupid, but there are substantive reasons" (http://www.nytimes.com/1990/05/24/arts/new-cable-network-plans-to-cover-jogger-trial-live.html).

In an *Entertainment Weekly* article, Svetkey (1991) describes the trial-turned-entertainment genre: "Part C-SPAN, part Monday Night Football, Court TV hit the airwaves July 1, offering its 4.5 million subscribers gavel-to-gavel coverage of three or four different trials every day."

The *Entertainment Weekly* article notes further, "There's been criticism from inside the courthouse. Predictably, many defense attorneys and some prosecutors are uncomfortable with televised trials. 'It's a bad idea,' says Roy Black, William Kennedy Smith's lawyer. 'Cameras in the courtroom add pressure to the proceedings and skew the court's ability to judge fairly. Members of the jury are supposed to be concentrating on the evidence, not worrying about how they look on TV. If I had my way, I'd prefer that cameras not be there'" (Svetkey, 1991).

The *Entertainment Weekly* article quotes Brill as remarking, "Study after study proves that videotaping trials has no adverse effect on the outcome. All it does is educate the public about how the court system works. If ever there was a trial that a defense attorney should want on TV, it's the Kennedy case. After all, we'll be showing the whole thing—not just sensational little snippets on the evening news" (Svetkey, 1991).

Right or wrong, Court TV changed the way Americans viewed the justice system and paved the way for a new brand of voyeurism that became further entrenched with each new—and bigger—trial. As Eddy (2015) observes, "The first Menendez brothers trial, in 1993, ended with a deadlocked jury. Their subsequent retrial did not allow cameras in the courtroom; due to both that fact and because viewers were likely a bit 'Menendez-ed' out, the do-over received far less media attention. (As it happens, they were both eventually convicted of first-degree murder and received life sentences.) Probably the most important Court TV case came a year later, when O.J. Simpson went on trial for murder. But by then, televising trials was big business. The Simpson case wasn't just huge for Court TV; it was breathlessly covered by every major network. In a 2014 opinion piece looking back at the case with a 20-year perspective, *Variety* TV critic Brian Lowry discussed 'TV's corrosive influence' on the legal system: 'In cable circles, CNN, HLN, and Court TV pretty much dominated the Simpson coverage, with the case having preceded the 1996 birth of Fox News Channel and MSNBC. Even those networks, however, have ceded immediacy to a Web culture that frequently reports first, and sorts out details later.'"

A trial is not as common as most laypersons assume, so for any trial to reach the courtroom, let alone television, it takes a politically charged situation or famous individual. The prosecution may dismiss charges due to a lack of evidence, or prosecutors decide not to refile charges after a felony defendant prevails at the preliminary hearing. Some defendants escape conviction through pretrial motions, such as a motion to suppress evidence. However, most cases end pursuant to a plea bargain. For example, the U.S. Attorneys' Annual Statistical Report, FY 2013, reports that in U.S. District Courts, U.S. States Attorneys' offices received 172,024 criminal matters. After review, the offices declined a total of 25,629 criminal matters during the year; the reasons most commonly reported for the declination of these matters included weak or insufficient evidence, lack of criminal intent, agency request, suspect to be prosecuted by another authority or on other charges, and no federal offense committed. The United States Courts website estimates that more than 90 percent of federal cases resolve in a plea bargain, and a 2012 *New York Times* article reported that 97 percent of federal cases and 94 percent of state cases end via plea bargain.

Although trials are the exception, not the norm, in the criminal justice system, the ones that do reach the courtroom often leave an indelible mark on the US legal system. Increasingly, these kinds of trials also make their mark on forensic science as a discipline. If so few trials are decided by juries these days, it stands to reason that the trials that do go to court trigger considerable interest—particularly if they involve a high-profile defendant. The watershed case in the United States just may be the O.J. Simpson trial.

Nicknamed "trial of the century" by many pundits, the O.J. Simpson case sparked a staggering collection of legal opinions and seemed to characterize so much of what commentators have pointed to as deficits in criminal investigation, expert testimony, and courtroom theatrics. The trial was to decide if Simpson was guilty of the June 12, 1994 double homicide of Nicole Brown Simpson and Ronald Goldman.

Alan Dershowitz, a Harvard law professor and a member of the Simpson defense team, explained why the case became all-consuming, the strategies of prosecution and defense, and why the verdict so divided the country in a 2005 interview with Frontline for the Public Broadcast System (PBS): "The trial shows what the defense is capable of doing if they have the ability to use all of the constitutional protections that are given them by the Bill of Rights… what can happen if the defense has access to the best experts and lawyers. So it showed… that in fact the system will operate on the principle of better 10 guilty go free than one innocent be wrongly convicted. And you know what? The public doesn't like the system. The public much prefers the old system in which the prosecution really doesn't have to prove the case beyond a reasonable doubt" (Dershowitz, 2005).

Many say the O.J. Simpson trial was a watershed in Americans' perception of the law. On October 3, 1995, an estimated 150 million people stopped what they were doing to witness the televised verdict of the O.J. Simpson trial. "For more than a year, the O.J. saga transfixed the nation and dominated the public imagination," according to a Frontline special on the case, produced by PBS.

Dershowitz (2005) says, "It was a transforming case in American social, racial and legal history. You can't understand the legal system in America without understanding the O.J. Simpson case. You can't understand the reaction people have. It still continues to have an effect on some jurors. Jurors expect a higher level of proof today. Jurors are much more suspicious of policemen and police testimony today. I think all in all, it probably had a beneficial effect on law in America."

The Simpson case cast a bright light on quality issues relating to criminalistics, says Kiely (2003): "… The O.J. Simpson trial was a timely catalyst for the current renewed focus by trial counsel and judges on the rights and wrongs of crime scene investigation and testing, including alleged failure to conduct an adequate investigation, contamination of samples, deficient testing, and a host of other crime scene-related issues." Kiely adds that the case also prompted law schools to reemphasize the importance of forensic evidence instruction for attorneys.

Jones (2005) places the magnitude of the Simpson double-murder trial into perspective: "It went on for nine months. There were 11 lawyers representing the man in the dock and 25 working around the clock for the largest prosecutor's office in the country. It became the most publicized case in U.S. history. It was the longest trial ever held in California, costing over $20 million to fight and defend, running up 50,000 pages of trial transcript in the process. There were 150 witnesses called to give evidence before a jury that was sequestered at the Hotel Intercontinental in downtown L.A. from January until October.

"The case received more media coverage and was accompanied by more unadulterated hype than any other criminal trial since the Lindbergh kidnapping-murder case in New Jersey in the 1930s, even exceeding the notorious Manson Family trial of the early 1970s. The media influence, in fact, became so intense that one poll showed 74 percent of Americans could identify Kato Kaelin [a witness in the trial] but only 25 percent knew who the Vice President was. An incredible 91 percent of the television viewing audience watched it, and an unbelievable 142 million people listened on radio and watched television as the verdict was delivered. One study estimated that U.S. industry lost more than $25 billion as workers turned away from their jobs to follow the trial." Jones adds, "Two-thousand reporters covered the trial; 121 video feeds snaked out of the Criminal Courts building where it was held. There were over 80 miles of cable servicing 19 television stations and eight radio stations. 23 newspaper and magazines were represented throughout the trial, the *Los Angeles Times* itself publishing over 1000 articles throughout the period. Over 80 books and thousands of articles have already been published, authored seemingly by everyone with any role in the trial."

This megatrial was the ultimate example of courtroom procedure and strategy in a double-homicide case, and set the tone for many more celebrity trials to follow in the 1990s and 2000s, including those of Robert Blake and everyman-turned-celebrity Scott Peterson. The prosecution's initial goal was to attack Simpson's reputation and establish a motive for murder based on Simpson's history of domestic violence, an obvious attempt to knock Simpson off the pedestal. The tactic failed with jurors; those jurors who had been excused made it known to the press that they didn't get the connection and that the domestic violence had nothing to do with the double homicide. Dershowitz (2005) comments, "The prosecution made a terrible mistake in how it used domestic violence. What it did is make the first weeks in the trial all about domestic violence. They were trying to create the impression that if you have beaten your wife or threatened her, you necessarily must have killed her. Obviously, that doesn't follow, and the jury didn't fall for that. The better way of trying the case would have been to start with the dead bodies and work backwards, not turn it into a case about motive, but turn into a case more about the physical evidence."

As Arenella (2005) states, "I think the prosecution frankly played into the defense's hands. They went to trial before they were ready, before all the physical evidence had been collected. They went to trial, and they started the trial with not the physical evidence linking Simpson to the murders, but with a story of domestic violence going back to 1989. To start a trial on murder that shows not how Mr. Simpson did the murder but suggested why he might be motivated to do the murder, to start the trial that way is to start the trial with character assassination. Now, if it works, terrific, but the story of domestic violence didn't work. It didn't strip Mr. Simpson of his legitimacy in the eyes of the jury. It made the prosecution look bad."

The prosecution then turned to the physical evidence in the case, including the notorious bloody glove. The defense team poked holes in the prosecution's case by asserting that the glove had been obtained without a warrant and was possibly even planted by police. The defense asserted that if law enforcement crossed the line, a juror couldn't believe anything they said. Arenella (2005) observes, "The defense essentially was, 'You can't trust the messenger because the messenger has lied to you, and that means that you really can't trust the message they're presenting to you. So, if you have police officers that are lying to you, that aren't testifying to you truthfully, there's no reason for you to believe that all of the physical evidence that they've collected and presented is as reliable as they suggest. There's reason for you to fear incompetence and worse: corruption of the physical evidence. And you certainly can't trust the story they're telling about Mr. Simpson.'"

A number of legal commentators asserted that various members of the Los Angeles Police Department (LAPD) were working in concert to boost the probative value of evidence in the case. However, they also questioned—regardless of whether the evidence they had collected at the estate was thrown out because the police lacked a warrant—whether the prosecution would still have had a case against Simpson. Dershowitz (2005) comments, "There is no elected judge in the state of California who would have thrown out the bloody glove, even though the law required them to do so. There isn't an honest judge in the state of California who wants to be re-elected or promoted who would have thrown out the major piece of evidence in the O.J. Simpson case. That would have been the right thing to do, but it never would have occurred to a political judge—and judges are by their nature political—to become the worst villain in California history; namely, the man or woman responsible for freeing a guilty murderer."

Some legal experts maintain that had the bloody glove been thrown out as inadmissible evidence, the case might have taken a dramatically different turn, as the glove opened the door to a torrent of scrutiny of the forensic evidence. For this reason, the O.J. Simpson case stands out as an example of a case under which forensic science was undeniably under siege by the defense camp.

As Jones (2005) comments, "Having worked hard at destroying the credibility of the police officers involved in the investigation, the defense team then turned their considerable abrasive talents in the direction of the witnesses for the prosecution who were called to give evidence regarding the blood samples found at the crime scenes. This would prove to be the most complicated and technical part of the trial, leading many people to believe that a jury of laypeople was simply unable to grasp the complex and, at times, stupefying dense evidence."

According to Dershowitz (2005), "The prosecution's theory was very simple: mountain of evidence. How can you explain the blood on the glove, the blood on the socks, the blood on the floor, the blood on the gate? It was a circumstantial case with overwhelming evidence, and a case that the prosecution easily could have won if they hadn't made so many mistakes. No. 1, they relied on lies. They overstated their case. They planted evidence. They didn't have to, but they did. They put on a policeman who was a Nazi lover and a perjurer and an evidence planter. That made our day, as the defense. And the defense decided to do something very simple: put on only truthful expert witnesses; put on no one who was in any way really controversial. So, the defense presented a credible case, and we were able to show that the prosecution's case was full of lies. That doesn't mean that ultimate truth was on one side or the other, but the defense got the jury to focus on the lies of the prosecution rather than on the innocence or guilt of the defendant."

Regarding the success of the defense team's strategy, Dershowitz (2005) notes, "The theory of the defense was when you find a certain amount of lying and evidence planting on the other side, you can't trust any of the evidence, so the mountain wasn't enough to convict if a few of the hills and valleys were corrupted. And it was summarized by our expert witness (Dr. Henry Lee), who said, 'If you find a cockroach in a bowl of spaghetti, you don't look for another cockroach before you throw out the whole bowl of spaghetti.' And the argument was, you couldn't trust anything these policemen said or did because we proved that they lied about certain things and planted at least some evidence."

Key to the unraveling of the prosecution's case, some commentators say, is the slow and steady obliteration of the testimony of lead criminalist Dennis Fung, who spent a considerable amount of time on the witness stand being grilled by Simpson's counsel during cross-examination. Jones (2005) says that Fung, "explained to the jury about the painstaking process of collecting bloodstains and smears and other evidence and how it was catalogued and stored. The prosecution maintained that DNA evidence tied Simpson into both of the murders and it came from blood on the glove found behind the guest bungalow, in the Ford Bronco, on the pair of socks found in his bedroom at Rockingham Avenue and on the footpath at South Bundy."

Taking aim at the DNA evidence presented by the prosecution were attorneys Barry Scheck and Peter Neufeld, now most famous for their establishment of the pro-bono organization, the Innocence Project, founded at the Benjamin N. Cardozo School of Law in 1992. The organization looks into the cases of individuals who assert they have been wrongfully convicted and push for the retesting of DNA evidence. Scheck and Neufeld viewed DNA "fingerprinting" as a powerful tool to help exonerate those who had been wrongly convicted and imprisoned, as well as a major leap beyond conventional serology typing, according to Jones (2005).

According to Jones (2005), "Scheck started out on Fung wanting to know why the Ford Bronco had not been sealed off as a vital evidentiary object in the Rockingham crime scene, why he was the only criminalist employed on both sites, and what impact on evidence corruption the blanket that covered Nicole's body may have had. Scheck also zeroed in on why junior criminalist Andrea Mazzola was allowed to collect most of the blood evidence. Over the period of Scheck's cross-examination, he brought up the fact that a crime scene photograph showed an ungloved hand holding the blood-spattered envelope containing Mrs. Brown's eyeglasses. Fung also agreed that he had only collected 'representative' smears of the blood in the Ford Bronco, which was why stains were still found in the vehicle six weeks after it was impounded. He also admitted to placing blood samples into plastic bags, which he claimed was purely a temporary measure, although doing this could foster bacteria growth, which in turn could distort test results. Scheck accused Fung of destroying evidence in an effort to conceal when he received the vial of O.J. Simpson's blood. The criminalist remembered that in fact he had given the vial of blood to his assistant, Mazzola, and she had carried it out to their evidence truck in a black plastic bag. There was also a heated debate over a missing page from the crime scene checklist, which Scheck claimed was replaced as it showed that Fung could not have received the vial at the time he stated he had. The missing page however, subsequently turned up in a crime laboratory notebook, and Judge Lance Ito ruled that its misplacement was inadvertent" (https://www.scribd.com/doc/145924174/The-Murder-Trial-of-OJ-Simpsons).

Jones (2005) explains that "Neufeld tried hard to show that Mazzola did a sloppy job, using videotape as evidence of her resting a hand on a dirty footpath, wiping tweezers with a dirty hand, and dropping several blood swabs. She admitted that there were times when she had made mistakes in the collection of evidence, but denied emphatically that anyone, including herself, would have deliberately altered evidence. She was unable to confirm that she had carried out to the evidence truck the vial of Simpson's blood returned to the scene by Detective Vannatter, thus reinforcing the defense's notion that the blood was never handed over to Fung that day, and this delay gave the police ample time to plant blood evidence."

The prosecution's witnesses included a chief forensic chemist and the supervisor of the serology unit of the crime lab, who asserted that how a criminalist collected evidence at a crime scene had little impact on the quality of the evidence, and that Mazzola's actions as viewed on the videotape would not have necessarily contaminated the evidence being collected. The chemist testified that the blood drops leading away from the murder scene were consistent with Simpson's blood, pointing out that only one person in 200,000 have that blood type. Jones (2005) reports that "There had been a total of 45 blood samples taken for DNA analysis from the Ford Bronco, Rockingham Avenue and South Bundy. The defense's strategy was to imply that not only was the blood identified as their client's planted at the sites by corrupt police officers, but that the tests carried out on this and other blood samples were open to doubt."

Also serving as a witness for the prosecution was Dr. Robin Cotton, laboratory director of Cell Mark Diagnostics, which had performed the majority of the DNA typing of the blood samples taken from the crime scene. Cotton explained the nature and function of DNA and the tests used to analyze it; she asserted that the analyses indicated a match between Simpson's blood and the bloodstains found leading away from the bodies at South Bundy, as well as confirming that the blood on the socks found in the main bedroom at Rockingham had the same genetic fingerprint as Nicole Brown Simpson's. Cotton claimed that the odds that the blood found near the bodies could have come from anyone other than Simpson were about 1 in 170 million. Neufeld challenged the statistical calculations of the analyses and the random-match probabilities, and also suggested that if criminalists tainted the biological evidence through mishandling, Cellmark's analyses would have been flawed.

The prosecution continued to call a number of other expert witnesses to discuss the specifics of DNA typing while the defense argued that the results were open to interpretation. Jones (2005) explains, "The final technical expert called by the prosecution was Colin Yamauchi, another LAPD criminalist who was the first to test much of the key evidence. Scheck was back into action... needling away at numerous areas, trying to show that Yamauchi mishandled much of the evidence, failing to change gloves before handling different tests, failing to adequately document blood testing and generally not following the department's rules designed to safeguard against contaminating blood samples. Yamauchi confirmed that at one time during testing, he inadvertently transferred blood from the Simpson vial onto his plastic gloves, and Scheck tried hard to infer that this blood may in fact have then been transferred onto the leather glove found at Simpson's home. He denied that at any time he had been part of a police conspiracy to frame Simpson for the murders."

In the battle for the jurors' favor, both the prosecution and the defense presented a mountain of technical and scientific evidence. According to Jones (2005), "The jury was subjected to forensic evidence examination for almost two months. In 50,000 pages of trial transcript there are 10,000 references to DNA." Jones reports that Alan Dershowitz, a professor at Harvard Law School, was admittedly overwhelmed by certain parts of the trial. Jones reports Dershowitz as remarking, "Much of the expert testimony was incomprehensible to me—and I have been teaching law and science for a quarter of a century." Jones adds further, "If most of it was above Alan Dershowitz's head, it is hard to see just how members of the jury could have absorbed it. The linking of the blood to Simpson and the victims through the crime scenes was perhaps the most crucial part of the trial, but the prosecution obviously failed to make these connections as far as the jury was concerned. According to Armanda Cooley, the forewoman, it was 'witness after witness, day after day they lost us. (Dr. Cotton) talked down to us, and when you talk down to people, you tend to lose them. When we went on a break, everybody heaved a sigh of relief. Colin Yamauchi was too busy trying to protect his department. Fung and Mazzola, I think they just got caught up and were in a rush and just mishandled things, and then tried to cover it up with explanations that never added up. Their techniques just started getting sloppy; it's impossible to believe that this is the first case that they had 30 or 40 errors on.'" Jones comments, "So much of the 'mountain of evidence' seemed to lose its credibility, either because the prosecution did a less than stellar job in preparing and presenting it, or because Simpson's lawyers were smooth enough to re-interpret it in such a way that they kept introducing reasonable doubt into the minds of the panel of jurists."

As Arenella (2005) comments, "Jurors themselves did a terrific job trying to pay attention, but the prosecution's best evidence was the evidence that was most hard to understand and the most easily attacked by the defense. And the defense, especially Barry Scheck, did a terrific job of giving the jury little lifeboats to understand some of the evidence, metaphors like 'garbage in, garbage out.' And that allowed the jury, if it couldn't follow the technical aspects of the challenges to the evidence, to think about the problem very simplistically: If the police screwed up in gathering the evidence, if there were problems in collection, perhaps that meant that the evidentiary results were corrupted. Only a real expert in DNA evidence could discriminate between legitimate challenges to DNA evidence in that case and challenges that were based on speculation or exaggerated hypotheses. I don't think the jury could follow that, but neither could the media, so the jury focused more on the evidence they could understand: the timeline and motive evidence."

Jurors began their deliberations at approximately 9:16 a.m., and at about 2:28 p.m., jurors notified Judge Ito that a verdict had been reached. Ito announced to the court that he would disclose it the following morning at 10 a.m. Court clerk Deirdre Robertson read aloud the jurors' verdict: "Supreme Court of California, county of Los Angeles in the matter of the state of California versus Orenthal James Simpson, case number BA 097211. We the jury, in the above-entitled action, find the defendant, Orenthal James Simpson, not guilty of the crime of murder." A USA Today/CNN/Gallup Poll administered on October 3, 1995, revealed that regarding the Simpson case, 57 percent of those surveyed believed the jury reached a verdict too quickly. The same poll revealed that 56 percent of respondents disagreed with the verdict, and 72 percent of respondents stated they thought the prosecution did a good job in trying the case.

Some commentators expected a hung jury in the case, which would have triggered a second trial and provided the prosecution with a chance at redemption. Dershowitz (2005) remarks, "A second trial would have been a great victory for the prosecution. They never would have tried on the gloves. They never would have put Fuhrman on the witness stand. They would have cleaned up their act, and they very well might have gotten a conviction on a second trial."

The Simpson case was seen by some commentators as the opportunity to place DNA on trial, a trend that continues today. In an analysis for Court TV's Crime Library, Ramsland (2006) takes a look at the blood evidence and how the science played out in the courtroom: "Several droplets of blood at the scene failed to show a match with either of the victim's blood types. Then Simpson's blood was drawn for testing (after the droplets had already been collected) and comparison between Simpson's DNA and that of the blood at the scene showed strong similarities. Contrary to what Simpson's defense team was to say after his arrest, this blood could not have been planted after Simpson's blood was drawn. The tests indicated that the drops had three factors in common with Simpson's blood and only 1 person in 57 billion could produce an equivalent match. In addition, the blood was found near footprints made by a rare and expensive type of shoe—shoes that O.J. wore and that proved to be his size. Next to the bodies was a bloodstained black leather glove that bore traces of fibers from Goldman's jeans. The glove's mate, stained with Simpson's blood, was found on his property. There were also traces of the blood of both victims lifted from inside Simpson's car and house, along with blood that contained his own DNA. In fact, his blood and Goldman's were found together on the car's console" (http://roohit.com/36984).

Ramsland (2006) continues, "The reliability of this evidence came to be called the 'DNA Wars,' and three different crime labs performed the analysis. All three determined that the DNA in the drops of blood at the scene matched Simpson's. It was a 1 in 170 million match, using one type of analysis known as RFLP, and it was a 1 in 240 million match using the PCR test. Nevertheless, criminologist Dr. Henry Lee testified that there appeared to be something wrong with the way the blood was packaged, leading the defense to propose that the multiple samples had been switched. They also claimed that the blood had been severely degraded by being stored in a lab truck, but the prosecution's DNA expert, Harlan Levy, said that the degradation would not have been sufficient to prevent accurate DNA analysis. He also pointed out that control samples were used that would have shown any such contamination, but Scheck suggested that the control samples had been mishandled by the lab—all five of them" (http://roohit.com/36984).

What damaged the prosecution's case more than anything else, according to Ramsland, "were the endless explanations of the complex procedures involved in DNA analysis. The defense kept it simple and thereby befriended the jury. They then intimated that Detective Mark Fuhrman, who had been at O.J.'s home the night of the murder, was a racist and had planted evidence. They offered no proof of the latter statement, but allowed it to flow from the former, which they did manage to prove. The evidence was damning, but the defense team managed to refocus the jury's attention on the corruption in the Los Angeles Police Department. Then Simpson made a clear statement of his innocence, though he was not on the stand, and the defense attorneys disputed the good reputation of the forensics labs, proving that the evidence had been carelessly handled. Deliberating less than four hours, the jury bought all of this and freed Simpson with a not guilty verdict. They defended themselves in interviews after the fact by simply stating that the prosecution had not made its case. It may be that those attorneys made some serious errors, but the doubt by the defense about DNA was ludicrous and did some damage with the public to the credibility of this type of evidence."

In addition to its emphasis on DNA, the Simpson case also was notable for its sheer fire power on the witness stand, particularly on the defense team; the list of expert witnesses frequently read like a "Who's Who" of forensic science. While these so-called "hired guns" can get the job done, they often draw criticism for potentially eclipsing key evidence by their celebrity status.

Dershowitz (2005) explains, "This was a case with a level playing field. This was a case where the defense had not quite as many resources as the prosecution, but roughly the same resources. We had the best forensic pathologists. We had the best lawyer on DNA, Barry Scheck. We had the best trial lawyer for a Los Angeles jury, Johnnie Cochran. We had F. Lee Bailey, who had more experience than any lawyer in America. We had Jerry Uelmen and me, who could do the sophisticated legal research. We had forensic pathologist Dr. Michael Baden; we had Dr. Lee. We could stand mano-a-mano against the prosecution. And the public didn't like a level playing field, because in a level playing field, when the burden is on the prosecution to prove guilt beyond a reasonable doubt, the defense will often win."

Some questioned whether such a rigorous defense was necessary when the prosecution already faced a sizable burden of proof. Dershowitz (2005) says, "I think most defense attorneys honestly believe the principle that says, 'better 10 guilty go free than even one possibly innocent person be convicted.' We generally don't know whether our client is innocent or guilty, certainly not at the beginning. We presume them innocent. We think they may be one of those who possibly is guilty, but our job is to press the system as hard as possible to make sure that no innocent person is ever falsely convicted, and to achieve that goal we are willing to see the occasional release of the guilty person. That's part of the system."

Arenella (2005) states that the Simpson case set into motion much-needed reforms: "On the good side, we have criminalists who do their jobs better. The LAPD crime lab and labs across the country learned valuable lessons about how not to collect evidence, about how to do their jobs in a more professional and competent fashion. We have defense lawyers across the country that learned valuable lessons from Barry Scheck and the defense team in how to attack the reliability of DNA evidence so that lawyers across the country went to school based on things that they saw in the Simpson trial.... The negative legacy of the Simpson trial focuses mostly on the public's perception of our criminal justice system, the public's misunderstanding of the defense counsel's role, which I believe was a problem before the Simpson case and was only aggravated by the distrust generated by the media's framing of the defense playing the race card from the bottom of the deck. This is ironic since the defense counsel in Simpson performed admirably and showed the adversarial system as it is supposed to function in a criminal trial, and yet they were harpooned for that by the public's reaction to it."

Regarding the potential for another Simpson-like three-ring circus, some commentators say the Scott Peterson murder trial was a contender, especially from an evidence point of view. Dershowitz (2005) comments, "You don't quite ever see the O.J. Simpson case again, although you see every day some part of the O.J. Simpson case. If you look, for example, at the Scott Peterson case and compare it to the case of Robert Blake, you get an acquittal in the Blake case and a conviction in Scott Peterson, and yet the evidence in Blake seemed to be more compelling than the evidence in Peterson. Why the difference?

"In the Peterson case you had a terrific victim—two victims: a wife, a baby. In the Blake case you had a victim about whom nobody seemed to much care about, and so you get verdicts that aren't based necessarily on the evidence, but based on external factors that aren't supposed to figure into the evidence. Take Robert Blake: He was acquitted, and nobody said a word. Nobody complained that it was a miscarriage of justice. Why? Nobody cares. First of all, there were some doubts, but second of all, nobody cares about the victim."

The O.J. Simpson case and others beg the question of whether or not the jury system, as well as the selection of legal representation and judges, is triggering a backlash against the US criminal justice system and rocking the public's faith in this system to serve justice. A USA Today/CNN/Gallup Poll administered on October 3, 1995, found that 38 percent of respondents said the jury system should be substantially changed; 58 percent said it should remain mostly as it is.

Arenella (2005) observes, "I think that the media's role in how it covers the criminal justice system has taken a turn for the worse, because we've really gotten to a point in this country where we see criminal trials as forms of mass entertainment. It's as if every next high-profile trial is the next Roman circus, and let's all watch and be entertained by it. So, we've disconnected from the reality of what these criminal trials are supposed to be about, and instead we convert them into theaters of entertainment. We even now have actors repeating the trial the day after so that people can get more entertainment from it.

"Trials aren't supposed to be entertainment for the masses. They're supposed to be serious public processes in which juries are asked to do a very difficult job. And instead of respecting the job that jurors do, we discount it; we discredit it. We in the public act as the 13th juror when we're not in a position to know what the jurors know, to see what the jurors saw, and we feel entitled to express our opinions about guilt or innocence based on what we don't know, apart from media reports of what goes on."

Writing a few years after the Simpson verdict, Kurland (1997) observes, "For sheer human interest, the ability to catch public attention and cleave to it from start to finish, nothing else in real life equals a good murder trial. A prominent victim, or, even better, a prominent defendant; a bit of mystery surrounding the facts of the case; two prides of high-powered attorneys facing each other across the courtroom; a cluster of witnesses, each contributing a few tantalizing facts to a tale of human fallibility; a bevy of expert witnesses to explain the unexplainable; a man or woman's life or freedom hanging in the balance—these are the makings of high drama." Kurland also describes the components of an "ideal trial" as an independent judge, an adversary trial, an unbiased jury, established legal precedent, and a just verdict. In reality, many trials are impacted by fallible individuals in an imperfect system, as Kurland notes: "Circumstantial evidence is suspect, eyewitnesses are unreliable, forensic evidence is only as good as the laboratory that (analyzed) it. On the other hand, circumstantial evidence, if properly interpreted, can tell the story of the crime; eyewitnesses can be good observers; and a professionally run forensic laboratory can (analyze) evidence that is trustworthy" (http://jimfishertruecrime.blogspot.com/2014/06/criminal-justice-qoute-murder-trials.html). Equally so, individuals who have committed murder and have been tried, are acquitted "due to inadequate evidence, incompetent prosecution, a brilliant defense, or a jury not disposed to convict," Kurland adds.

Court TV remained on the air until 2007, with Brill departing in 1997. Other similar news shows followed, with Headline New Network's Nancy Grace and others that covered trials; series that delved into the details of crimes soon appeared, the most notable being the seminal *Forensic Files*, introduced to the world in 2000. This show reflected Court TV's desire to develop original programming. *Forensic Files* profiled actual criminal cases and the scientific sleuthing conducted by the coroners, medical examiners, and police detectives who solve them. The launch of *Forensic Files* coincided with the debut of the fictional series *CSI: Crime Scene Investigation* on the CBS network, suddenly creating a forensic juggernaut on television and fostering a rabid viewership among the American public.

As The Gale Group, Inc. (2005) observes, "The resulting public interest in all things forensic made *Forensic Files* a smash hit by cable television standards... Buoyed by its success with *Forensic Files*, Court TV expanded its original programming. Among the new shows it introduced was Dominick Dunne's *Power, Privilege and Justice*, a look at cases involving people from high society hosted by the noted author, and *From the Case Files of Dayle Hinman*, a real life criminal profiler. It also began to show original movies, based on one of the many crime documentaries Court TV produces each year. As a result of all this, five years after Brill's departure, Court TV's ratings had increased 10-fold. It had moved from being available in 30 million homes to being available in 70 million homes. And advertising revenue grew to $64 million, from $15 million in 1998."

Some forensic practitioners are anti-celebrity, even if their cases are high-profile. San Antonio, Texas-based forensic pathologist Vincent Di Maio, MD, served as a consultant to the defense for neighborhood watch volunteer George Zimmerman, who shot and killed Trayvon Martin on Feb. 26, 2012 in Florida. Zimmerman was found not guilty of second-degree murder, and the case set off a firestorm of debate over racial profiling.

An arduous discovery process characterized this contentious case, and although Zimmerman's defense didn't have much funding, it did require an expert to help examine the evidence. Zimmerman's defense attorney reached out to Di Maio in September 2012, 10 months before the trial was to start. As Di Maio recalls in his memoir, *Morgue*, "They might not be able to pay me, but it was an important case that raised important questions for America" (Di Maio and Franscell, 2016, page 18).

Six years previously, in 2006, Di Maio had retired as chief medical examiner in Bexar County, Texas where he had created a respected forensic medical facility and had conducted more than 9000 autopsies, examined more than 25,000 deaths, and continued to consult in unexplained or questionable death cases around the world. As he recalls in *Morgue*, "...George Zimmerman's defense wanted me to connect the forensic dots in the last three minutes of Trayvon Martin's life" (Di Maio and Franscell, 2016, page 19).

Di Maio says he did not to get caught up in the headlines that the case triggered, maintaining a laser-like focus on the task before him and ignoring the pressures brought to bear by observers. As Di Maio notes in *Morgue*, "Our determinations impact the living more than the dead. The dead are past caring, but the living can go to jail. ... Innocence can be determined. Questions can be answered, suspicions authenticated. So, medical examiners bear a heavy burden to reach an unbiased, fact-based, scientific conclusion, no matter what a dead person's family, friends, enemies or neighbors wish it to be. Truth is always better than what we merely wish to be true." He adds, "I don't take sides. What I know is vital; how I feel is irrelevant. The forensic pathologist's mission is the truth. I'm supposed to be impartial and tell the truth. Facts have no moral quality, only what we project upon them" (Di Maio and Franscell, 2016, page 19).

Di Maio's job was to document Martin's injuries, trace the path of the bullet and its physical damage, and examine Zimmerman's injuries to show whether they were all consistent with Zimmerman's account of the struggle. As he comments in *Morgue*, "I wasn't hired to contrive an opinion to help the defense but to offer my expert opinion about whether any of it supported the shooter's account. I wasn't a hired gun coming to town to do the defense's dirty work. I hate that medical examiners sometimes appear to say what they've been paid to say—and undoubtedly, some might—but I don't work for the defense, the prosecution, the killer, the family of the victim, or the cops. I didn't get this far by selling my opinion to the highest bidder" (page 21). He adds, "But the rest of the world had already taken sides. Without the benefit of facts, a lot of people saw this tragedy through the prism of their own biases and reached unyielding conclusions. This wasn't the first or the last time this happened in my career, but it was among the most stark." He adds, "This was a complicated case only in cultural terms. Forensically, it wasn't complicated at all. It was tragically simple" (Di Maio and Franscell, 2016, page 21).

The Zimmerman trial began on June 24, 2013, and the central question according to Di Maio was, who was the aggressor when the shot was fired? Ten days into the trial, no answer had been provided. Di Maio testified on the eleventh day of the trial, reporting that Zimmerman's injuries were consistent with his story. On the stand, Di Maio said the forensic evidence proved that Martin had been leaning forward, not lying down when he was shot, consistent with Zimmerman's account that Martin was kneeling or standing over Zimmerman, beating him, when Zimmerman fired his gun at Martin.

As Di Maio notes in *Morgue*, "None of us was there. There are no pictures or videos of the fatal moment. We cannot know what truly happened, and we certainly cannot know what was in those two men's hearts. But the scientific evidence told a story that many people didn't want to hear and refuse to believe even now. That's how it is with the truth. It isn't always welcome."

The jury deliberated for 16 hours, coming back with a verdict that Zimmerman was not guilty of any crime in the shooting of Trayvon Martin.

"Even now, it's difficult for many people to hear this, but the question of Trayvon Martin's death was not a miscarriage of justice, but rather a painfully perfect example of justice itself," Di Maio writes in *Morgue*. "Our system worked as it was intended. Questions were asked, scenarios explored, theories argued. It is simply the nature of any homicide—justifiable or not—that there will be winners and losers when the question must be settled" (Di Maio and Franscell, 2016, pages 25–26).

Di Maio adds, "While many people made George Zimmerman's case about black and white, it was anything but black and white. The real problem wasn't injustice, but an unfortunate series of ordinary human faults that led to a fatal overreaction by both men. A white guy misjudged the behavior of a black teenager, who misjudged the behavior of the white guy. They profiled each other. They saw each other as a threat. And both were wrong" (Di Maio and Franscell, 2016, pages 26–27).

While the ability to voice reasoned expert opinions came with time, the capacity to make sound decisions about his life developed at a surprisingly young age for Di Maio, who says he always knew he wanted to be a doctor since the time he was a child. "Not a single day passed when I thought I'd do anything else," Di Maio writes in *Morgue*. "I just assumed I would be a doctor. Before I even knew what a future was, I knew what I'd be doing in it." He surmises it is in his DNA, as his father and maternal grandfather were physicians, and since the 1600s, all but one of the men on his mother's side were doctors (with one stray lawyer). Both of Di Maio's parents were first-generation Americans, children of educated Italian immigrants who recognized significant opportunity in America. Di Maio says they brought with them the traditions of hard work, adaptability, and risk for reward and were "driven by a willingness to be uncomfortable." Di Maio was born in his doctor-grandfather's Brooklyn home, with his physician father and grandfather attending; Di Maio says it was a good omen and seemed to steer his life's path from day one.

Growing up, Di Maio was exposed to both medicine and to death, a foreshadowing of his career to come. Di Maio points to a childhood memory of seeing his grandmother lying dead on the dining room table during her wake. Even as a young child of 5, Di Maio says he knew she was dead although he can't fathom how he comprehended that fact. He recalls feeling an almost clinical response that was well beyond his tender years. As Di Maio grew into his life's work, he cultivated the same pragmatic approach to death: "I see humans as an ear of corn, with an outer, disposable husk and an inner core of kernels—the seeds of life itself. When I see a dead body, it is just a husk. The soul is gone. I don't autopsy people. I autopsy bodies. A person is something alive and vibrant and different. Bodies are just what they leave behind."

Di Maio's father, Dominick Di Maio, expected good grades from his children, and Di Maio says he was a good student but didn't love school. He describes himself as a reserved child, more prone to reading than sports. He says his childhood home, while austere, was filled with books. He says he was a voracious reader and frequent patron of the public library. He says as an adolescent he had an introverted nature and, with hair that started prematurely turning gray at 13, he found himself more at home with his books than with his peers. Those books unknowingly helped him develop an expertise on gunshot wounds; Di Maio explains that one day while perusing the library stacks, he discovered the section on guns and his favorite subject—history—was suddenly forgotten as he devoured every book available on firearms.

The planets began to align for the senior and the junior Di Maio when Dominick developed an interest in forensic pathology "even before it was a recognized specialty," Di Maio notes. Dominick began working part-time for the chief medical officer of New York in 1950 and was hired in 1957 as the full-time deputy medical examiner for Brooklyn. As Di Maio writes in *Morgue*, "In our house, death and life co-existed. Death was just something we lived with" (Di Maio and Franscell, 2016, page 36). Di Maio adds, "My father dragged me and my three younger sisters to hospitals and morgues at a young age. He didn't want us to be afraid of death. It was partly because he just assumed we'd all be doctors someday, but also because his own relationship with death was casual. He wanted us to respect the tragedy of dying, but be drawn to its mystery, too." Di Maio and his sisters—who also became doctors—satisfied their curiosity by stealing glances at crime scene photos in their father's files. Di Maio says he wasn't bothered by any of it, including when the entire family would accompany Dominick to the morgue on Sunday afternoons when he worked, afterwards picnicking behind the morgue, which at the time was surrounded by open fields and undeveloped land.

Di Maio began his quest for higher education as a chemistry major at St. John's College in Queens, NY. in 1958 but then switched to biology. During his junior year, he applied to medical schools; at 19 he passed his MCAT exam and sent in his application to State University of New York (SUNY)'s medical school. In 1961 Di Maio was notified that he had been accepted to medical school without yet possessing a college diploma—he was to start in the fall. Despite being so young, Di Maio says he knew failure wasn't an option and that he couldn't be anything but a doctor. He says he detested medical school, describing it as "four years of Marines-like boot camp, but not as pleasant," but stuck it out and graduated in 1965.

At the end of boot camp—i.e., medical school—he had to select a medical specialty. Di Maio says he learned in med school that he had no bedside manner, much like his father, and he'd realized, "I'd be better with patients who didn't require reassurance and operations that didn't require lifesaving knots. Pathology was perfect. Pathologists were doctors' doctors" (Di Maio and Franscell, 2016, page 47).

Di Maio conducted his one-year pathology residency at Duke University Hospital in Durham, North Carolina, where he decided to pursue forensic pathology. He did his three-year residency at Kings County Medical Center in Brooklyn and concurrently performed autopsies for the chief ME's Office in Brooklyn under his father. As Di Maio writes in *Morgue*, "By the time I finished my residency, I had already done more than 100 autopsies before I worked a single day as a certified forensic pathologist" (Di Maio and Franscell, 2016, page 47).

Dominick Di Maio had become chief medical examiner in New York City in 1974 and taught medicolegal death investigation classes at Brooklyn Law School. Di Maio says his father played a role in some of the most high-profile cases in NYC history but "didn't run to the *New York Times* with every high-profile death" (Di Maio and Franscell, 2016, page 38). For example, while his father worked in the ME's Office, the serial killer known as the Son of Sam was on the loose; Dominick also examined remains thought to be Jimmy Hoffa's but weren't; he saw cases associated with mob hits and also tended to celebrity cases.

Coincidentally, one of Dominick Di Maio's most notable cases came after his retirement in 1978. Bernhard Goetz, nicknamed the "Subway Vigilante," was accused of shooting four black teenagers on the subway in December 1984 because Goetz felt he was about to be robbed. It was the world's seminal "stand your ground" case, deciding whether Goetz had fired in self-defense or was a deliberate act of racism. Di Maio says it was an eerie precursor to the cases of Trayvon Martin in Florida and Michael Brown in Ferguson, Mo., where observers were divided along racial lines. Goetz was acquitted of murder and assault charges, but he was convicted for illegal possession of a weapon and served eight months in prison.

Not only were some of their cases similar, but senior and junior Di Maio collaborated on a textbook, *Forensic Pathology*, in 1992, which remains in print today. Di Maio says he and his father would engage in "lively professional dialogues" once Vincent started medical school and started blazing a trail of his own. "Our discussion could be epic and maybe a little loud, but I never stopped believing in my father. He set a standard I still aspire to. I still live with his expectations of me" (Di Maio and Franscell, 2016, page 43). Di Maio adds, "When I check my baggage, I find my father's energy, his sense of justice, his fascination with mystery, his tendency to work away from the limelight, his ability to corral his emotions. I also find my mother's austerity, her pragmatism, her love of books and history" (Di Maio and Franscell, 2016, page 43).

"We talked about everything, cases, work, life," Di Maio says. "There was some contention when we may have seen casework differently, but we both loved our work." Di Maio says that he believes he fulfilled his father's big expectations, and in doing so, established his own legacy. "I'd like to be remembered for my work on gunshot wounds," he adds. "All that knowledge started with my interest in books and reading about guns, and being given a gun by my father, which had been passed down through the family. And then when I went into the military I was appointed head of the firearms section. I think the specialty of firearms injuries found me that way."

Di Maio says he had a rich and interesting—yet ever pragmatic—home life from which to draw upon and that it served his life's aspirations and career choice well. When asked if there is anything in his life or career that he would have done differently, Di Maio is resolute in his answer: "No, I wouldn't do anything differently. No regrets at all."

Di Maio may have tapped into the sense of integrity he has fostered his whole life when he consulted on the trial of music mogul Phil Spector, who was accused of shooting and killing B-movie actress Lana Clarkson, who was moonlighting as a hostess at a LA nightclub. Confounding evidence at the scene, a messy case, and further mystery created by the presence of only Clarkson's DNA on the gun, and only her hands had a lot of gunshot residue. Spector's hands and clothing were clear of GSR. No fingerprints found on the gun. Evidence leaned toward homicide according to autopsy of Clarkson. Spector was arrested but out on bond. The central question was homicide or suicide—Spector was charged with murder, Spector pleaded not guilty. As Di Maio notes in *Morgue*, "In Los Angeles, celebrities seemed to have the magic Get Out of Jail Free card. The acquittals of O.J., Robert Blake, Michael Jackson and so many other stars left a bad taste. Money, influence and powerful friends had redefined justice in a city where entitlement, delusion and egomania are celebrated virtues, not ugly quirks" (page 195).

Di Maio was contacted by attorney Linda Kenney Baden (the wife of forensic pathologist Michael Baden), who was on Spector's defense team; they needed a gunshot wound expert. Di Maio agreed to look at the evidence. As Di Maio recalls in *Morgue*, "Spector had already begun building one of the most powerful teams of forensic experts ever amassed for a criminal trial: Baden, Dr. Werner Spitz, Dr. Henry Lee and others... Spector was desperate to avoid a conviction, and the prosecution was equally desperate to nail him" (page 196). Di Maio wasn't sure he wanted to be involved: "Celebrity cases are a pain. Such trials are too often about the celebrity—whether he or she is the defendant or a victim—instead of the physical evidence" (page 196). Di Maio says he found no hard evidence that absolutely proved Spector to be innocent of the crime, or guilty. But he did identify "a few cracks in an imperfect case against him," he says. Di Maio says he thinks it remains a largely circumstantial case; he had seen hundreds of people shot in the mouth in his then-38 years, and all but three were suicides. There was no physical evidence to prove Spector was holding the gun when it fired, but there was evidence that Clarkson was holding it. Baden, Spitz, and Lee reached similar conclusions when they examined the evidence. Suicide might have been a distinct possibility, some experts believed. The trial began April 25, 2007 and upon deliberation some days later, the jury was deadlocked at 10-2 in favor of conviction; the judge declared a mistrial. A year later, a new trial was launched; that jury reached a verdict of guilty of second-degree murder, Spector was sentenced to 19 years to life, eligible for parole in 2028. The conviction was appealed but upheld.

The Spector trial emphasized a public fascination with and a DA's distrust of expert witnesses. As Di Maio observes in *Morgue*, DA Alan Jackson accused Spector's experts of being "pay to say" mercenaries and quoted Jackson as saying at Spector's second trial, "If you can't change the science, you buy the scientist." As Di Maio explains, "That's what happens in a trial: One side calls experts to explain something highly technical or hard to understand, and the other side calls them liars, charlatans, idiots and hired guns. Both sides need expert witnesses, and both sides undermine them. During the Spector trial (and others) I was called innumerable names, none good, inside and outside of the courtroom. Why? Simply because my forensic opinion ran counter to the perceptions of onlookers who had already made up their minds" (page 203). Di Maio keeps it in perspective and adds, "Expert witnesses seldom ride in with all the answers that everyone else was too stupid to glean. They aren't always right. Justice doesn't teeter on their knowledge. They are experts, not the final word on everything. What an expert witness says must be evaluated by every juror for credibility and given its proper weight" (page 204).

Di Maio says there are some hired guns in forensic pathology and are usually exposed. There are also the expert Di Maio calls "true believers," who identify more with cops and prosecutors and may unconsciously find evidence suggesting guilt. Some are labeled whores for one side or the other and writes, "Some try to blunt this criticism by testifying for both sides, but that merely causes them to be labeled a whore for anybody who'll pay. It's a no-win situation." Di Maio says he has walked away from cases and has also been excused from cases if his forensic conclusions didn't align with the attorney's strategy. He adds, "As a medical examiner and a forensic consultant all of my adult life, I've testified for the prosecution and defense, for plaintiffs and defendants, in criminal trial and civil trials, in big cases and small. My conclusions aren't swayed by money" (page 205).

When it comes to the nuisance of celebrity, Di Maio shrugs it off and says, "I feel you should do the case properly, regardless of what is going on around you. And you shouldn't seek out these cases. Even in the Zimmerman case, they called me, and what I do is, I testify and I leave the courtroom. And that's it. I don't believe in publicity. It's interesting how with well-known people, it cuts both ways. If they like you, it helps, like O.J.; everyone I know says he's very likeable. And then if they don't like you, you can be innocent and they'll crucify you. What I often say is that the news media's goal is to free the guilty and imprison the innocent."

Di Maio says that cases, like celebrity and the media circus it can cause, don't stick with him. "I just do my work and that's it."

The stigma of being seen as the proverbial "hired gun" is reason enough for many scientists to want to avoid serving as an expert witness. As Hansen (2000, page 17) remarks, "Not long ago expert witnesses were considered to be friends of the court, people whose willingness to take time out of their busy professional lives and participate in the judicial process entitled them to absolute immunity from civil liability for anything they said on the witness stand. But somewhere along the way, we stopped viewing them as the courts' friends and started seeing them as hired guns, people who were willing to testify on just about anything for a buck. And short of a vigorous cross-examination, the risk of professional sanctions, and the threat of a criminal prosecution for perjury, there was virtually nothing anybody could do to hold them accountable for the consequences of their testimony."

Risinger (2000) asserts that there has been the development of an "unbridled expansion of asserted expertise in civil and criminal courtrooms, limited only by the imagination of an attorney with a point to prove and a hole in her more conventional evidence." The impetus for this groundswell, he says, includes questionable levels of sufficiency of evidence, coupled with "decidedly lax threshold standards of admissibility for expertise." Risinger comments, "...the stage was set for the acceptance of some fairly questionable practices in the utilization of expertise by litigants. Consequently, although all sides were free to play the game, the result was generally much more favorable to parties with the proof burdens (generally civil plaintiffs and the prosecution in criminal cases, though criminal defendants were substantial players in regard to various affirmative defenses)."

THE *CSI* EFFECT

Gabel (2010) alludes to the trend of "forensiphilia," which she defines as the place "where forensic science is itself a celebrity that captivates and enchants audiences." As Gabel (2010, page 237) notes further, "The forensic seduction via *CSI* has created a popular obsession with glamorized methods that are far removed from true science, the ultimate result of which is an unrealistic expectation for modern forensic techniques… It is easy to divorce television from reality when characters like McGyver save the world by manipulating a paperclip. Manipulating the intricacies of forensics, however, makes it more difficult to sort fact from fiction. One forensic scientist estimates that upwards of 40 percent of the so-called—science on *CSI* simply does not exist. For a show that publicly claims to regularly consult with forensic scientists, forty percent leaves a healthy cushion for artistic liberty. This steady stream of exaggeration and misinformation is not innocuous; public beliefs about forensic science have been influenced by fiction years before *CSI* arrived on the scene. *CSI* simply upped the ante with its alluring machinery, methods, and cast."

Forensic programming on television is blamed for skewed perceptions of the justice system and legal proceedings, collectively referred to as the "*CSI* effect," which for a number of years in the early to mid-2000s seemed to appear in the media fairly regularly—no doubt prompted by the enormous success of the titular show, *CSI*, which followed the exploits of a fictional team of crime scene investigators at the Las Vegas Police Department crime lab. *CSI* debuted on October 6, 2000, and according to Nielsen Media Research, the premiere was watched by more than 17 million people. You couldn't have had a pulse in the 2000s and not notice the spin-offs of *CSI* in rapid succession, as the franchise sought to replicate the skyrocketing viewership of the flagship series and burn itself into the collective cultural zeitgeist.

In a review of *CSI* published on December 16, 2000, *TV Guide* said about the new series, "Little did TV bosses know that the biggest new stars of 2000 would be maggots, decomposing pigs and torn fingernail fragments." While viewers were dazzled by the cinematography and the special effects used to explain the various forensic disciplines used to help solve crimes, real criminalists and forensic scientists were less pleased with the depictions of their work at the crime scene and in the crime laboratory. As Longworth (2002, page 289) notes, "John Houde, a veteran of 20 years as a forensic scientist, said *CSI* was "make-believe entertainment." Houdes charged that "The show has as much to do with criminalistics as *Baywatch* has to do with being a lifeguard."

The show's creators defend *CSI*'s technical accuracy. As Longworth (2002, page 97) points out, Liz Devine, a former CSI veteran from the Los Angeles County Sheriff's Department, was recruited by the show runners to ensure its authenticity. According to *CSI* creator and executive producer Anthony Zuiker, Devine left her day job to work on the show full time, and episode 15, "Too Tough to Die" was written by Devine and was loosely based on her experience on a case when she was in the field.

Despite the liberties taken in depicting how actual lab processes work, supporters of the show insist it has made significant contributions. Longworth (2002, page 97) once asked Zuiker, "How much of a role can your show play in terms of helping society?" Zuiker answers, "I think we send a message to America, and I think we send a message to criminals, that there are people out there who can solve almost any crime using sophisticated methods. Hopefully our show could make a criminal think twice."

Whether *CSI* is primer for criminals on how not to get caught, or a stern warning not to even attempt a crime, the bigger debate along legal scholars is how much influence the show has on the proceedings and outcomes of trials. Schweitzer and Saks (2007, page 358) summarize the issue: "In recent years, the television program *CSI* and its spin-offs have portrayed forensic science as high-tech magic, solving crimes quickly and unerringly. Of course, *CSI* is only fiction. One forensic scientist estimates that 40 percent of the 'science' on *CSI* does not exist, and most of the rest is performed in ways that crime lab personnel can only dream about."

Schweitzer and Saks (2007, page 358) note that, "The hypothesis heard most often is that *CSI* has raised the public's expectations for the kind of forensic science evidence that could and should be offered at trials to such heights that jurors are disappointed by the real evidence with which they are presented." They add, "An alternative hypothesis, which runs in the opposite direction, is that *CSI* has fooled the public into thinking that forensic science is far more effective and accurate than it actually is. If true, jurors may be likely to readily accept whatever conclusions forensic science witnesses point them to. The two hypotheses are not necessarily at war with each other. The prosecution might benefit when it presents any forensic-science evidence, and the defense might benefit when there is no forensic-science evidence. Whether the '*CSI* effect' helps the prosecution or the defense, the commentators seem to agree on one thing: that *CSI* is convincing the public that forensic science not only is science, but it is super-science. If true, this is high-tech forensic science to exist for all kinds of crime scene residuals and to be able to solve all kinds of crimes."

Schweitzer and Saks (2007, page 358) add, "Evidence actually offered at trials disappoints, because either too little (or no) forensic science is presented or what is presented is less impressive than what is seen on television. Either way, goes this theory, jurors are acquitting more defendants because in court they are not seeing enough forensic science to persuade them of guilt."

Those unfamiliar with the inner workings of medicolegal issues use *CSI* as a frame of reference and therein lies the problem; the expectations are both idealistic and unrealistic, and lead to a manufactured perception of reality as it relates to how the criminal justice system works. As Houck (2006) observes, "The gap between public perception and reality, however, is vast. And the popularity of these shows has led to complaints of a '*CSI* effect;' at least some lawyers and judges have the impression that jurors schooled on *CSI*, which has been on the air since 2000, now demand unreasonable levels of physical evidence in trials. Whether the *CSI* effect truly exists as a quantifiable influence on courtroom behavior is still a subject of debate. Of no debate, though, is the effect that the *CSI* programs have had on the activities of police, who now collect more pieces of physical evidence than ever before; in academia, where some forensics programs are growing exponentially; and in overburdened working laboratories, which are a far cry from the glitzy, blue-lit analysis palaces of TV."

Byers and Johnson (2009, page xv) say that the science trumps character development in *CSI*, and is the star of the show: "The series capitalizes on new technologies in their production and in the series narratives. The shows have extremely high production values and use special effects technologies extensively. Most significantly, these technologies allow viewers to ride bullets and blood spatter forward and backward in time; they take us into bodies and in so doing suggest a venue through which the dead can speak. At the same time, the series are hyper-oriented toward a display of forensic technologies that is clearly fetishistic."

Bethke (2006, pages 84–89) calls the portrayal of forensic science techniques in shows such as *CSI* "reality-based fiction" that is decently researched and attempting to reflect some of the realities of forensic science—but in a glossier, far more stylized fashion. Part education, part entertainment, *CSI* is among the shows that forensic scientists love to hate publicly and watch privately. The American public gobbled it up, flaws and all, leading Houck (2006) to observe, "Crime shows have opened up a public fascination and respect for science as an important profession unseen since the Apollo space program."

Houck (2006, pages 84–89) traces the origins of the so-called *CSI* effect to 2003, when the media began talking attorneys and judges about what appeared to be an evolution in the behavior of jurors: "In 2005 Oregon district attorney Josh Marquis, vice president of the National District Attorneys Association, told CBS News, 'Jurors now expect us to have a DNA test for just about every case. They expect us to have the most advanced technology possible, and they expect it to look like it does on television.' Indeed, jurors in a Los Angeles murder case complained that a bloody coat had not been tested for DNA, even though such tests were unnecessary: the defendant had already admitted to having been at the crime scene. The judge noted that TV had taught jurors about DNA tests but not about when they should be used. In a study in Delaware of how juries deal with evidence, one juror tangling with a complex DNA case complained that these kinds of problems did not happen 'on *CSI*.'"

It's a double-edged sword. Shows such as *CSI* have helped elevate awareness of forensic science, but the cost to the credibility of the science itself, and of verdicts leading to alleged wrongful convictions, has been a high price to pay. As Houck (2006, pages 84–89) notes, "Before *CSI* became popular, attorneys mostly worried about whether a jury was going to understand the complexity of DNA evidence. Now, though, many spend time clarifying the difference between television and reality—it is common for lawyers to ask prospective jurors about their exposure to forensics-themed TV programs. And some prosecutors are attempting to preempt any potential fallout from the *CSI* effect. In trials in Arizona, Illinois and California, they have put so-called negative evidence witnesses on the stand to alert jurors to the fact that real-life detectives often fail to find physical evidence, such as DNA or fingerprints, at crime scenes."

Byers and Johnson (2009, page xviii) argue that, "We see government through crime at play in the fact that commentators, particularly in the commercial media and the criminal justice system, have credited *CSI* with significantly impacting contemporary ideas and practices outside the television realm through what is ubiquitously known as the *CSI* effect. This is primarily understood to mean that watching *CSI* inspires an anti-prosecution tendency in North America and especially U.S. jurors, by raising their expectation and perception of the need for forensic evidence of guilt in all criminal investigations and trials. In other words, the CSI effect is understood as a dangerous hindrance to crime fighting on several fronts: it is framed as effectively de-legitimizing the traditional policing and prosecutorial arms of the criminal justice system by showing that crime is best fought through the allegedly impersonal techniques of science and high technology, it is envisioned to over-empower juries with unrealistic expectations for forensic evidence in trials and to over-burden criminal forensic labs with endless testing of every molecule possibly relevant to crimes, and so on."

Some experts say the evidence that the *CSI* effect is real is merely anecdotal in nature. Cole and Dioso (2005) emphasize, "That television might have an effect on courtrooms is not implausible.... But to argue that *CSI* and similar shows are actually raising the number of acquittals is a staggering claim, and the remarkable thing is that, speaking forensically, there is not a shred of evidence to back it up. There is a robust field of research on jury decision-making but no study finding any *CSI* effect. There is only anecdotal evidence."

The bottom line is that *CSI* is pure entertainment that just happens to foster interest in science. Can't we accept it for what it is? That query seems to be made by Byers and Johnson (2009, page xx) who observe, "We argue that the dominant popular criminology narratives offered by the CSI franchise, their huge (and interestingly now waning) commercial success, and the primary definition of the CSI effect in inspiring an anti-prosecution tendency in jurors, reflect a wider shift in the end-goals pf popular culture and criminal justice, but also an illustration of how fiction and fantasy can bring pleasure and catharsis through engagement with risk in a relatively formulaic manner, and a repeated resolution that it is 'impossible' in real life."

But as much as we relish the show for its ability to take us to a world where crimes are solved inside of 60 minutes, critics insist *CSI* is inflicting intractable damage. As Byers and Johnson (2009, page 5) insist, "As much as we wish that science could answer our questions unequivocally, subjective judgment and individual expertise are an irreducible part of the production and interpretation of forensic evidence. The CSI shows present forensic science in a way that denies the potential fallibility of scientific processes and hides the skill, expertise and subjective judgments involved from the time evidence is collected until it is delivered in a courtroom. Instead, small-screen forensic scientists are presented as allowing the evidence itself to reveal the identity of the perpetrator, as they manipulate that evidence with a myriad of high-tech procedures indicated by flashy visual effects and machines."

They continue, "Television's ability to collapse reality into reframed manageable segments, carefully delineated in time and space, may create a hyper-reality in which television portrayals appear to be more immediate and real than the correspondingly slower-moving pace of daily life. This immediacy draws viewers in and inspires them to create new realities that are actually media-inspired events. Research also shows that viewers often simply forget where they learned specific pieces of information with which they construct their world views" (Byers and Johnson, 2009, page 6).

Houck (2006) notes that "Fictional forensics programs also diverge from the real world in their portrayal of scientific techniques: University of Maryland forensic scientist Thomas Mauriello estimates that about 40 percent of the forensic science shown on *CSI* does not exist. Carol Henderson, director of the National Clearinghouse for Science, Technology and the Law at Stetson University College of Law, told a publication of that institution that jurors are 'sometimes disappointed if some of the new technologies that they think exist are not used.' Similarly, working investigators cannot be quite as precise as their counterparts on the screen. A TV character may analyze an unknown sample on an instrument with flashing screens and blinking lights and get the result 'Maybelline lipstick, Color 42, Batch A-439.' The same character may then interrogate a witness and declare, 'We know the victim was with you because we identified her lipstick on your collar.' In real life, answers are seldom that definite, and the forensic investigator probably would not confront a suspect directly. This mismatch between fiction and reality can have bizarre consequences: A Knoxville, Tenn., police officer reported, 'I had a victim of a car robbery, and he saw a red fiber in the back of his car. He said he wanted me to run tests to find out what it was from, what retail store that object was purchased at, and what credit card was used.'"

"I think the toothpaste is out of the tube and you can't put it back," says retired forensic science educator Jay Siegel in regard to the *CSI* craze. "The show did a couple of things—besides making forensic scientists crazy—it did raise public awareness of the value of good science and good investigations and good evidence. Any way you can engage the public in aspects of the criminal justice system is a good thing, so I think that was a very good fallout. Another good fallout is that it got a lot more students and faculty interested in looking at problems in forensic science, and those of us who were in education at the time, got a lot of free publicity and an army of students. Now, there had to be some unlearning based on *CSI* however; you don't show up to crime scenes in your Armani suits and your Maserati—they can be very nasty, uncomfortable situations. *CSI* did bring a lot of students into the forensic programs and then they get sorted out during the educational process, and I think that's a big plus from the *CSI* and *Law and Order* shows."

Siegel continues, "I think the downside has been unfulfilled expectations. All of these shows have to solve a crime in 45 minutes minus commercials, and they have to tie it up neatly and that's not the way it works in the real world, of course. I think this has set expectations of the general public—as well as judges and attorneys—too high to the point that forensic science can't meet those expectations and then people say, 'Well what's wrong with forensic science? Why can't you look under a microscope and declare that you have at least two kinds of DNA?' I saw that very thing on a show and that made me nuts. People think, 'They do it on television, why can't they do that here?' That's an educational process that I think will lessen a bit with time because the shows will be off the air and people's attention spans in this country are notoriously short. I think the longer-lasting effects will be the consciousness-raising about issues involving forensic science. For now though, these 'reality' shows are immensely popular with the public and I think that will continue to resonate; we haven't seen any drop-off in students wanting to study forensic science—it's still a very attractive career prospect. I have been retired now for a few years but the program I left at Indiana is booming and has more students than ever. Some of the effects are going to be persistent but I think the *CSI* effect itself is unreasonable expectations that hopefully will ebb a bit with time."

"Even the actors got tired of it," NIST scientist John Butler says with a laugh. "CSI lingers on, as does the unrealistic attitude that people have toward science in general, and not just forensic science. There's a sense of, 'I can't understand this, so I'll just believe whatever is there and not try to question it.' The concepts of critical thinking and digging deeper into something or accepting something for more than it is or sometimes digging too deep—all of those various aspects are part of how people perceive crime scene investigation and analysis of the evidence."

Is the lack of discernment on the part of the American viewing public the responsibility of forensic scientists? It would be ludicrous to assume so, yet some commentators have tried, despite the efforts of some academics to prove the *CSI* effect as illusionary.

As Houck (2006, pages 84–89) observes, "What appears to be the first study of the CSI effect was published in February by Kimberlianne Podlas, an attorney and assistant professor of media law and ethics at the University of North Carolina at Greensboro. Podlas concluded that the chances of, and reasoning for, acquittals were the same for frequent CSI viewers as for prospective jurors who did not watch the show—she saw no CSI effect. Several participants, however, said that a lack of forensic testing was an issue, despite the fact that physical evidence would not have resolved the hypothetical charges. Studies of real juries have been advocated, and at least five graduate students (three in the U.S. and two in England) are preparing theses examining the effect."

In remarks prepared for a lecture at the August 2010 Impression and Pattern Evidence Symposium, Podlas (2010, page 1)explains the importance of television to the law: "... the stories that television tells and the way it tells them communicate norms and ideologies, focus us on issues, influence how we think through them, and cultivates expectations and beliefs. This is particularly true with regard to the law; research reveals that most of what the public knows—or thinks it knows—about law and the legal system comes from television. For example, though few people have any personal experiences with courts, trials or lawyers, millions have seen them on TV." Podlas (2010, page 2) says, "Despite pop cultural perceptions otherwise, television generally does not affect viewers in a direct, immediate way... research, however, demonstrates that television can impact audiences in a number of long-term, subtle and attitudinal ways." To that end, Podlas (2010) says that one of these ways can be explained by the cultivation theory, which asserts that the heavy, long-term exposure to television's imagery cultivates in viewers' attitudes and perceptions of social reality that are consistent with that imagery. Meaning that "a viewer who constantly sees a representation on television will presume that that representation is common in the real world." And "Ultimately, these perceptions can mature into attitudes about legal policies" (Podlas 2010, page 3).

Another way is heuristic processing, which helps people process information quickly and draw inferences about events or behaviors, such as innocent people don't run from the police. Podlas (2010, page 4) explains that "The heuristic processing model proposes that heavy television viewing impacts cognitive processing, by broadcasting programs and plots that include many vivid examples of behavior and causation." Podlas (2010) notes, "Television's stories of law and the biases in these serve as heuristics about the legal system. They help us understand how trial evidence will unfold and become the standard against which testimony and behaviors (of witnesses, litigants, attorneys and judges) are compared."

An additional potential way TV creates impact is through framing—that the way television consistently presents a story or frames an issue can impact the way people understand it. Addressing the *CSI* effect, Podlas (2010, page 11) says, "The basic premise that a popular, long-running television show like *CSI* could somehow impact jurors is plausible. After all, case law and legislation regarding pretrial publicity rests on the notion that television can bias jurors. If, however, *CSI* has an effect, it does not appear to be one that harms the prosecution; notwithstanding the press devoted to the *CSI* effect, no empirical evidence has found any anti-prosecution CSI effect on guilty verdicts. Rather, research employing psychological, sociological and media studies approaches have all concluded that, in rendering not guilty verdicts, frequent viewers of *CSI* are no more influenced by *CSI* factors than are non-frequent viewers."

Podlas (2010, page 13) notes further, "The general message of *CSI* is that police forensics are legitimate. It portrays forensics as the ultimate crime-fighting weapon and fosters an aura of forensic infallibility. The experts are never wrong and the science is always absolute. This might encourage jurors to overvalue anything labeled 'forensic' and ignore problems in the data presented." Instead, Podlas (2006/2007, pages 105–106) observes: "Viewers are not taught that the prosecutor must present forensic evidence for the verdict to be guilty (or that when the prosecutor does not do so, the only correct verdict is not guilty). Instead, they are taught that all of the scientific investigation took place long before trial and led to the defendant's arrest... a juror may interpret *CSI's* dominant narrative (i.e., of perfect forensics identifying the guilty and being the precursor to arrest) to mean that: Arrests are based on forensics; forensic proves guilt; and therefore, anyone arrested and on trial has already been proven guilty."

Going to the heart of the debate is whether or not shows such as *CSI* instills in its viewers unreasonable expectations about the commonality of forensic evidence and teaches them that proof of guilt is just a simple forensic test away. So, when these viewers become jurors, they will expect the prosecution to present forensic evidence as a prerequisite to conviction. If a prosecutor does not supply such evidence—even if it is irrelevant or supplanted by testimonial evidence—jurors will equate its absence with reasonable doubt and they will wrongfully acquit. As Podlas (2006, page 91) says, "Furthermore, besides requiring forensic corroboration, *CSI* might cause jurors to demand that such proof exhibit a certain degree of sophistication. Where the prosecution presents forensic evidence that does not resemble *CSI's* standard, jurors might discount it. This may also make it tough for the government to prove cases. Some believe that this elevates juror expectations to beyond the already-high burden of proof,[25] thereby leading to acquittals. If jurors require forensic evidence to convict-regardless of the strength of testimonial evidence or relevance of forensics the prosecution's burden may rise from proof 'beyond a reasonable doubt' to 'beyond all doubt.'"

Following extensive research, Podlas (2006, page 92) declares, "Despite the magazine covers and newsprint pages warning of a *CSI* effect, there is 'not a shred of evidence' to back it up. Rather, it appears that the *CSI* effect better resembles an urban legend among prosecutors and police officers that has gained credence through repetition. To date, the only proof of a *CSI* effect is that some individuals believe in one." Podlas (2006, page 125) adds, "What is labeled a *CSI* effect may more accurately be described as a rationalization embraced by members of law enforcement who find themselves on the losing side of a prosecution. By attributing a loss to *CSI's* wrongful influence, a prosecutor can obtain an explanation yet maintain a belief that an acquittal was misguided. Although this cognitive rationalization is understandable, it should not be mistaken for empirical proof that the *CSI* effect operates anywhere other than in the minds of those proposing it."

Smith et al. (2011) point to the case of *State v. Cooke* in which the Superior Court of Delaware explored the relevance and impact of the *CSI* effect. "Cooke challenged the prosecution's use of 10 types of forensic evidence (including DNA, footwear impressions, toolmarks, handwriting, and fabric impressions, among others) as being either exculpatory or unreliable, and as such it should have been excluded. The State argued that it needed to produce this evidence for the jury for two reasons: to demonstrate to the jury that it has a solid case grounded in the products of a thorough investigation; and to offset the heightened expectations of the prosecution that the State believes jurors hold due to the *CSI* effect. Although the Court found that there was no scientific evidence to support the existence of the *CSI* effect, it also could not deny its own experience of juries' heightened expectations of forensically relevant evidence."

Smith et al. (2011) also conducted a content analysis of the first seasons of *CSI* and *CSI: Miami* in order to document the types of forensic procedures portrayed, the frequency of errors, and the frequency with which criminals were caught. The researchers found that in the two first seasons, more than 75 types of forensic evidence were portrayed in the series' storylines, with the two most popular forms of evidence presented were DNA (19 percent) and fingerprints (12 percent). The perpetrator was identified in 97 percent of the storylines, and technical errors and mistakes were rare and were always caught before any negative consequences could arise.

The study by Smith et al. (2011) also affirmed some of the more unrealistic aspects of crime shows, in that crime scene investigators conducted 72 percent of the scientific tests portrayed on *CSI*, whereas in actual investigations, specialized laboratory technicians conduct the majority of tests. Intrigued, the researchers then conducted a survey of 15 forensic experts employed by Canadian police agencies in a wide range of forensic analysis work to further assess these discrepancies between reality and fiction. These experts were presented with 73 forensic techniques, identified by name and a description of how the technique was portrayed on *CSI*. (Experts commented only on those forensic techniques for which they had expertise.) Overall, experts indicated that the accuracy levels of the *CSI* show to be relatively low, rating them as 2.5 on a 7-point scale. The specific techniques, however, were given relatively positive ratings. The realism of the procedures came in at 4.6 on the 7-point scale, and experts rated the scientific research supporting the use of the portrayed techniques at 5.9. The reliability/accuracy of the techniques, however, were rated at 1.9, which the researchers suggest likely reflects that *CSI* often portrays highly technical, experimental techniques.

In two subsequent studies, the researchers surveyed other professionals to assess their views on the *CSI* effect. When queried about their perceptions, 127 death investigators confirmed that crime dramas are somewhat inaccurate in their portrayals and have changed the way in which police practice, investigate, and interact with the public. The majority (94 percent) of the death investigators indicated that television crime shows had influenced the public's expectations of their profession and conduct. In a survey of police officers, the researchers found that 68 percent indicated that *CSI* had no effect on their behavior, but 92 percent indicated that the shows had some effect on public expectations. As Smith et al. (2011, page 6) comment, "Interestingly, all respondents felt that *CSI* affected people's perceived knowledge of forensic techniques, but most thought that knowledge gained from these shows was inaccurate. Police officers estimated that the shows depicted a 94 percent solution rate (very similar to our content analysis findings), yet they estimated that only 40 percent of crimes are solved in the real world."

Based on the results of the studies that they and others have conducted, Smith et al. (2011, page 7) say that "... it seems clear that some form of CSI effect does exist. In addition to bringing their life experiences and common sense to the deliberation room, jurors may also be bringing their understanding of the legal system and forensic evidence as portrayed on recent episodes of *CSI* and *Law and Order*. Shelton et al. suggest that the source of jurors' increased expectations of forensic evidence is not simply television crime dramas but the result of a more widespread cultural change linked to a technological and scientific revolution. They argue that a more accurate term for this phenomenon is the 'tech effect.' Regardless of which terminology is used, are jurors' demands for and expectations surrounding forensic evidence jeopardizing justice? To our knowledge, there is no evidence supporting this notion."

Some commentators believe that the more it is discussed, the more the *CSI* effect is ingrained in our collective cultural mindset. As Tyler (2006, page 1083) comments, "The CSI effect has become an accepted reality by virtue of its repeated invocation by the media," and while it is "consistent with empirical findings in other areas of legal psychology" and "accords with the intuitions of participants in the trial process," "no existing empirical research shows that it actually occurs." As Tyler (2006, page 1053) notes further, "While the CSI effect has been widely noted in the popular press, there is little objective evidence demonstrating that the effect exists. As often is the case with legal issues, the pace of public discussion has outstripped the ability of scholars to research the issue. Lacking any empirical data, discussions of the CSI effect have instead been based upon the personal impressions of lawyers and legal scholars. The argument that CSI has influenced jurors fits with many people's intuitions—including those of judges and prosecutors—about how jurors operate."

As Tyler (2006, page 1053) points out, "The rapid development of widely held views about the changing nature of litigation is not new. After the O.J. Simpson verdict in Los Angeles and the mistrial of the Menendez brothers, the media discussed the idea of juries becoming increasingly 'acquittal prone.' Yet when social scientists looked at acquittal rates in federal trials and across five states, they did not find statistical evidence in support of this widely assumed 'fact.' " (Vidmar et al., 1997). Tyler (2006, page 1055) argues that the existence of an effect linking *CSI* to juror judgments is initially plausible and consistent with the findings of empirical research in legal psychology. He also disputes the conventional wisdom that exposure to *CSI* raises jurors' standards for conviction. He suggests that "it is equally plausible that the *CSI* effect will be found to lower standards by creating a mystification of scientific evidence, leading jurors to ignore or minimize the limits in the data they see." Tyler (2006, page 1050) says there are alternatives to the traditional *CSI* effect hypotheses, namely, that *CSI* promotes the need for closure—seeing the guilty party identified and punished, but they lack the ability to take actions that satisfy this desire. As he explains: "We can never know for certain whether O.J. Simpson, Robert Blake and Scott Peterson killed their wives, whether Michael Jackson molested children… This uncertainty about the truth makes it more difficult to achieve justice in a psychologically satisfactory manner. Both decision-makers and the general public are left with a sense of unease and lack of completeness, as crimes are unsolved and uncertainty remains" (page 1064).

Another alternative to the *CSI* effect is overbelief in the probative value of evidence. "There is widespread evidence indicating that people already overestimate the probative value of scientific evidence. Given the general lack of connection between actual and perceived probative value, it is not difficult to imagine that perceived probative value shifts in response to jurors' psychological desires and needs. The effect may be unconscious" (page 1068). "…How does this connect to *CSI*? The general message of *CSI* is that scientific methods and evidence are legitimate and reliable." Yet another alternative is that *CSI* creates a one-sided view of the law, according to Tyler (2006, page 1073): "*CSI* also potentially assists prosecutors by showing only the investigation and leaving the impression that the trial is a mere formality.… The story ends in *CSI* when the investigator solves the mystery. The ultimate deliverance of justice is left as a foregone conclusion."

Tyler (2006) points to the potentially unsatisfactory results that a trial delivers: "In terms of resolving uncertainty, then, guilty and not-guilty verdicts are not equivalent. A guilty verdict identifies someone responsible for a crime and provides a sense of psychological completeness and closure. A not-guilty verdict prevents an injustice to a potentially innocent person but does nothing to resolve the psychological desire to see justice done, either for the victim or the population at large. Finally, irrespective of the verdict they render, jurors often remain uncertain about their decision, leaving any verdict shrouded in a mist of doubt."

The appetite for shows such as *CSI* may have been whetted by the pioneering Courtroom Television Network (Court TV), a cable network devoted to explaining law to the layperson. As The Gale Group, Inc. (2005) observes, "Founded in 1991, this novel venture in television programming was a long shot: few thought a 24-hour-a-day, seven-day-a-week diet of live trials and legal analysis would succeed. Within two years, though, the network ranked fourth in the Nielsen Company's daytime cable ratings. It built this record with gavel-to-gavel coverage of civil and criminal trials, including a string of highly publicized cases in the early 1990s, as well as with a mixture of regular programs that examine in simple language how the legal system works. This nuts-and-bolts approach coincided with—and, to an extent, helped influence—controversial changes in legal journalism. Lawyers, judges, and the media are divided over whether the public is served or misled by the Court TV approach, and this debate only intensified after comprehensive coverage of the O.J. Simpson murder trial in 1995."

The Gale Group, Inc. (2005) explains further that changes in the media and the law paved the way for Court TV: "From the 1960s to the 1980s, reporting on legal affairs was largely the business of two markets: specialized publications for lawyers and daily newspapers. The former was highly detailed; the latter took a broad, general approach. Television took the most sparing look at the law, usually in small slices of news broadcasts. But as state laws increasingly permitted television cameras in state courtrooms, the role of television increased. At the same time, another trend shook up television itself: the public's appetite for so-called reality programming, a format popularized by shows such as the National Broadcasting Company's Unsolved Mysteries and the Fox Network's Cops and America's Most Wanted. Cheaper to make than dramas and sitcoms, this programming subsequently glutted the airwaves in the form of cops-and-criminals shows, tabloid journalism, and 'infotainment' (the combination of information and entertainment)."

Johnson (2002) quotes Herbert Terry, an Indiana University telecommunications professor who studies media and the law, as remarking, "In some ways [Court TV] was early reality television. It was successful at representing the drama of real life and people in stressful situations before we invented `Survivor.' It's more real than reality TV." Johnson (2002) goes on to say, "Terry says he can't disagree with Court TV's claim to have performed a valuable civic function over the years. 'While there's clearly a tendency of the service to choose extraordinary cases if they can,' he says, 'I don't think it's entirely disingenuous for them to say, 'We've helped educate people'. The other impact has been for the most part positive on the judicial system and the opening up of courts to cameras.'"

In the years since Court TV was launched, there have been a number of high-profile criminal trials that continued to capture the imagination of the millions of "armchair attorneys" among the American public.

As Wood (2013) observes, "For 17 weeks, couch-lounging court-watchers have sat transfixed as the trial of Jodi Arias—the crazy-eyed photographer/Mormon/vixen accused of murdering her boyfriend, Travis Alexander—has unfolded. Approximately 500,000 viewers have tuned in to HLN (sister channel to TruTV, formerly known as Court TV) daily, as coverage of the often-salacious case has permeated every corner of the cable news channel's programming. Throughout the day, courtroom cameras roll nonstop, with the 'action' paused and restarted only for commercial breaks and quick commentator analysis. And just in case viewers were panicked at the thought that they may have missed one second of testimony, the channel's production team has created enormous on-screen 'Play' and 'Pause' buttons in order to allay any such fears. Regular programming has ceased to cover much but the Arias trial and they've even added a special late-night talk show, HLN After Dark: The Jodi Arias Trial, in which lawyers argue a new 'bold accusation' nightly (Did Jodi torture Travis? Is Jodi a sexual deviant?), while a group of 12 fake jurors decide on the outcome. Mock trials haven't been this fun since Arrested Development."

A precedent does exist for this trial-to-TV trend; on April 11, 1961, the trial of war criminal Adolf Eichmann was the first to be completely televised. The William Kennedy Smith trial in 1991 stands out because it was "deemed a victory for televised courtroom proceedings, as it gave everyday viewers an up-close look at how the American justice system truly operates," Wood (2015) asserts. William Kennedy Smith was the 30-year-old Kennedy clan member charged with rape following what he professed was a consensual sexual encounter in Palm Beach, Florida. The trial was broadcast by CNN, and the network hit ratings gold in terms of numbers of viewers when Smith was acquitted of all charges.

But the nontelevised cases are the ones that seemed to stick with the public. The 1970s and early 1980s gave us the likes of convicted serial killers Ted Bundy and Jeffrey Dahmer. Wood (2013) notes, "Shortly before he was executed in 1989, convicted serial killer Ted Bundy copped to murdering 30 women across the country between 1974 and 1978 (though some believe the true number to be more than that). Handsome and charismatic, Bundy's arrest and subsequent showboating made worldwide headlines (he was assigned five court-appointed attorneys, but the former law student insisted on leading his own defense, speaking in the third person and everything). More than 250 journalists from around the globe descended on Miami in the summer of 1979, when proceedings began in the case of the Chi Omega murders—where Bundy broke into a sorority house at Florida State University and attacked four women in less than 15 minutes, killing two of them. Bundy's trial was the first to be televised nationally, and it didn't end well for him; a guilty verdict brought him two death sentences, with a third following six months later after a separate trial in Orlando."

Regarding Dahmer, Wood (2013) says, "When it came time for cannibalistic serial killer Jeffrey Dahmer to stand trial for the murder of 15 boys and men, Court TV was there—but on a 10-second delay, in order to carefully edit out those exhibits and discussions that might be too disturbing to viewers. On Feb. 17, 1992, more than 60 global news organizations were on hand to broadcast the guilty verdict. Dahmer was sentenced to 15 consecutive life sentences for his crimes; on Nov. 28, 1994, he was beaten to death by a fellow prison inmate."

While more recent cases threaten to knock it out of first place, most legal scholars and commentators agree that the O.J. Simpson case, which was tried from June 1994 to October 1995 as we have seen, was the biggest, most sensationalistic, and most-watched trial of all time. As Merrefield (2011) explains this national and international obsession, "The trial that set the bar for round-the-clock media coverage, and the case that made one network—Court TV (now TruTV)—a household name. This wasn't just the O.J. show, kicked off by a low-speed police chase with the Juice lying in the back of the infamous white Ford Bronco. This case was full of characters good, evil, and devious, from Johnnie Cochran to Judge Ito, Kato Kaelin to Mark Fuhrman—even a certain black leather glove got its fifteen minutes, and then some. Today, the O.J. Simpson trial is still the standard bearer when it comes to sensational court cases. Indeed, seemingly the entire country gasped on Oct. 3, 1995, when the jury returned its verdict: not guilty. What other trial can say it sucked the air out of a nation?"

Wood (2013) asserts that interest in the O.J. Simpson trial "was certainly bolstered by the ex-NFL star and occasional-actor's celebrity status. The trial also made a household name of Johnnie Cochran, Simpson's prone-to-theatrics defense attorney, who famously declared during his closing arguments, in reference to a pair of gloves assumed to be used by the killer that did not fit The Juice's hands, 'If it doesn't fit, you must acquit.' The jury agreed, delivering a 'not guilty' verdict as more than 100 million interested parties watched from home (which is about as many people as tuned in for the 2010 Super Bowl)."

In terms of other celebrity cases, the trial of pop star Michael Jackson, which was tried from November 2003 to June 2005, kept viewers glued to their TVs for every morsel of information. He was arrested and indicted on seven counts of child molestation and other charges, but was acquitted on all charges. The televised trial kept coming, including the 2011 case of Jackson's physician, Dr. Conrad Murray. As Wood (2013) observes, "Just three months after the Casey Anthony trial concluded, HLN attempted to recapture ratings glory by presenting beginning-to-end coverage of the trial of Conrad Murray, the physician eventually found guilty of involuntary manslaughter in the death of Michael Jackson. While viewership never reached Anthony-level highs, it did boost the channel's October ratings by 98 percent over the same month the previous year, with 2.1 million people tuning in to watch the verdict read live."

The trials of actors and other high-profile and slightly off characters made for excellent ratings. Actor Robert Blake was charged with murdering his wife in 2002, and his trial ran from April of that year through March 2005. When he was acquitted, the Los Angeles District Attorney was reported as saying that the jurors were "incredibly stupid." The jurors explained to reporters after the trial that there simply wasn't enough direct evidence that Blake had committed the crime. The trial of music producer Phil Spector in 2007 for the murder of actress Lana Clarkson and his retrial in 2009 was a boon for the likes of Court TV, which documented Spector's bizarre behavior during this trial, which ended with a hung jury. Cameras were not allowed into the court for his 2009 retrial, where the jury declared Spector guilty of murder in the second degree.

Private citizens have been turned into overnight sensations because of their criminal trials. Made-for-TV drama came nicely packaged in the trial of brothers Lyle and Erik Menendez, whose first trial ran from March 1990 to January 1994. They were convicted of murdering their parents in 1989, and during trial alleged years of parental abuse as the reason. As Wood (2013) explains, "With cameras rolling and millions of viewers watching, the brothers' sordid defense for killing their wealthy parents—claiming dad was an abusive pedophile and mom was a self-absorbed drug addict—turned the proceeding into worldwide media fodder, particularly as the brothers were tried together (though a separate jury decided each one's fate). In the end both juries were deadlocked, leading to a second trial in 1995, in which no cameras were allowed. The second time around, it took only four days for the brothers to be convicted—both on two counts of first-degree murder—and sentenced to life in prison." And as Merrefield (2011) notes, "Another coup for Court TV, which covered the trial extensively, the Menendez brothers are currently serving life terms in prison." The Scott Peterson trial, which was tried from April 2003 to March 2005, had it all—the intrigue of a husband allegedly killing his pregnant wife for money and self-interests, as Merrefield (2011) points out, "The Scott Peterson trial was a case tailor-made for the likes of the Dateline NBC crowd, with a prosecution witness even engaging the services of the loquacious Gloria Allred." Peterson was found guilty of killing his wife and unborn child, and is being held on death row at San Quentin prison.

Two women, within two years of each other, would become the reigning queens of televised courtroom drama. As Wood (2013) observes, "If it weren't for polarizing personality Nancy Grace—a former prosecutor and now HLN's most popular host and legal commentator—the case of Casey Anthony, the young Florida mom charged with murdering her 2-year-old daughter Caylee Marie, might not have been such a national cultural obsession. Largely spurred by Grace's outrage over the case (in which she nicknamed the defendant 'Tot Mom'), HLN offered all-Casey coverage all the time for the entire six weeks of the trial—not to mention the hundreds of hours logged analyzing the evidence in the three years that elapsed between Casey's arrest and the final verdict. In the 15 minutes it took for the jury to announce its acquittal of the 25-year-old, 5.2 million people watched the verdict on HLN, bringing in the channel's highest-ever ratings (to this day). Grace's response to the judgment? 'The devil is dancing tonight.'"

Not long after the 2011 Casey Anthony case, armchair jurors were treated to another sensationalistic trial, that of Jodi Arias. As Wood (2013) notes, "Comparisons to Casey Anthony began almost immediately after Jodi Arias was arrested: Both defendants are attractive young women prone to lying and accused of murdering a close confidante. Even as the trial enters its 17th week, Arias remains HLN's highest priority. Day and night, all of the channel's regular programming (including 'Showbiz Tonight,' its entertainment-themed late-night show) focuses primarily on the Arias case, with a series of talking head psychologists, legal experts and regular court-watchers weighing in with their opinions and analyses. With closing arguments set for next Thursday and Friday, the live verdict audience is sure to trump the currently average daily viewership of around 435,000."

It may surprise practitioners that a few of their peers don't necessarily believe that the glamorization of trials and the forensic profession is wrong. "Anything that raises the profile of forensic disciplines is great," says Marcella Fierro. "We are so short staffed in all disciplines. Young people have so many choices of occupation and will not choose forensic science without hearing about it first. I think most folks have got over the *CSI* effect and attorneys are very good at explaining it as are the expert witnesses when they testify about their discipline."

RISE OF THE SCIENTIFIC CELEBRITY

The rise of the scientific celebrity, be it forensic science and any other scientific discipline, has not gone unnoticed by Hollywood, which has certainly done its fair share to promulgate the trend of late. Think Russell Crowe's portrayal of Dr. John Nash in the film *A Beautiful Mind*, Jodie Foster's turn as a scientist-turned time/space continuum traveler in *Contact*, and Matthew McConaughey's depiction of an astronaut in *Interstellar.* In the book *Lab Coats in Hollywood: Science, Scientists, and Cinema*, author David A. Kirby examines the intersection of science and cinema, including how science consultants make movie science plausible, how filmmakers negotiate scientific accuracy within production constraints, and how movies affect popular perceptions of science. Kirby says that cinema can influence science as well: Depictions of science in popular films can promote research agendas, stimulate technological development, and even stir citizens into political action.

Also exploring the scientist as Hollywood hero is Declan Fahy, an assistant professor of communication at American University, author of the book, *The New Celebrity Scientists: Out of the Lab and Into the Limelight.* Fahy (2014) says *Interstellar* is "emblematic of two powerful recent trends in the presentation of science in popular culture. First, the obsessive drive towards creating more accurate depictions of science on screen. And second, the increasing movement toward the portrayal of scientists as heroes."

No small thanks in part to the scientists who serve as technical consultants for film and television, who do their best to try to keep it real—*CSI* notwithstanding. Fahy (2014) notes, "As science studies scholar David Kirby noted in *Lab Coats in Hollywood*, science consultants have a role beyond helping directors incorporate realistic science into their movies. They also give the films a stamp of scientific approval. *The Guardian* picked up on this idea, writing in its 'Interstellar' review that the inclusion of [the science consultant]'s name as producer may be intended as an extra-textual guarantee of authenticity. Kirby argued that science consultants get another benefit from the cinematic collaboration. The presentation of their ideas in such a powerful medium makes often-hypothetical concepts more real and more persuasive, drawing increased scientific and public attention to their work. Science consultants' impact should not be overestimated—after all, the filmmakers have the final word – but their role has influence. Organizations such as the National Academies of Science and its Science & Entertainment Exchange program support and facilitate these relationships by hooking scientists up with TV and movie makers."

Fahy (2014) says that while science communication researchers who have studied on-screen scientists say the recent trend has been toward presenting scientists as heroes and voices of virtue, "there is only limited evidence about the effect these portrayals have on audiences. Researchers agree that an individual viewer's background is crucial to how they interpret science on screen. For example, one 2011 study found Americans without college science experience who watched a lot of television had a stronger belief in the promise of science. But Americans with college science experience who were heavy consumers of television had stronger reservations about science. What is missing from much science in entertainment is what David Kirby in a recent book chapter called the systems of science. That is, an authentic portrayal of the methods of science, how scientists interact, and the links between science, the state and wider culture and society."

In a 2015 article in the *Bulletin of the Atomic Scientists*, "Scientists as Celebrities: Bad for Science or Good for Society?" physicist Lawrence M. Krauss is another expert who addresses the role of scientist celebrities. As Krauss (2015) observes, "We should be encouraged, not discouraged, if at least some scientists successfully break out beyond the confines of science to become genuine public celebrities. Whatever their background and experience, they are a priori no less worthy than those other figures from sports, politics, or entertainment who help steer public opinion."

Krauss (2015) says that it is critical for scientists to "reach out beyond the walls of academia to the general public," and that "For scientists to have a public impact, they generally need to reach out to the public using those tools that have a public presence—from books to newspapers to radio, and particularly television and film—and not rely on their scientific accomplishments or reputation among their colleagues. Indeed, there need be little correlation at all between the two." Krauss emphasizes that "Public adulation should not be confused with scientific impact," and that scientists must recognize that this privilege "implies a responsibility to… both promote science in the public arena and to adequately and accurately represent the scientific enterprise."

Krauss points to scientists such as Albert Einstein, Carl Sagan, and Stephen Hawking as examples of scientists with high profiles and an elevated sense of awareness of their celebrity as a reason to portray mathematics and science as a mechanism for the greater good. "Those scientists who have a public audience have an opportunity, and also in some sense a responsibility, to help combat scientific nonsense, motivate young people to study science, and also to help steer public policy discussions toward decision making based on empirical evidence and sound theory," Krauss (2015) says. "Happily, many of the most recognizable names have a good track record of doing just that." Krauss says Einstein was the first modern A-list science celebrity who established a precedent for scientists to reach out to the public.

Krauss (2015) emphasizes accountability among scientists: "The scientific community has a responsibility to communicate to the public both the results of the knowledge it generates and also the possible public impact of that knowledge, not only because the public funds us, but also because an informed public is an essential part of a healthy democracy."

For every high-profile scientist, there is an equally recognizable interviewer providing a necessary platform. As Upshaw-Downs and Swienton (2012, page 425) observe, "The criminal justice professional is faced with unprecedented ethical dilemmas when it comes to media coverage of all aspects of a criminal case, from pre-arrest chatter and speculation, to social interest pieces investigating the background of suspects, to live trial coverage and the subsequent commentary from panels of pundits with a variety of expertise. Likewise, those who cover the media have an obligation to their constituents to inform, while ensuring that they balance the rights to privacy and protection of those accused but not yet convicted of crimes, and those who have fallen victim to crime."

Attorneys are often as visible as forensic scientists when it comes to celebrity status. They also face a decision themselves, as Upshaw-Downs and Swienton (2012, page 426) note, "A second career for the legal practitioner may be that of legal commentator. Many former legal practitioners have made successful careers out of dissecting the legal technicalities of high profile cases for the masses, including Geraldo Rivera, Nancy Grace and Greta Van Susteren. However, the actual amount of information being provided to the lay person versus the amount of 'performing' and emotional inciting of the masses that occurs on many of these programs calls into question whether these commentators are serving the public, or merely their own egos."

We come full circle when celebrity touches the accused as well. As Lawrence (2009, page 10) observes, "We do not afford people the same adulation and unconditional forgiveness. When O.J. Simpson was on trial for murdering his wife, the nation was divided. For all who assumed his guilt, there were as many people ready to spring to his defense. But when Scott Peterson faced charges for murdering his wife and unborn baby, everyone immediately assumed he was guilty, even before the trial began."

REFERENCES

Arenella P. "The O.J. verdict." *Frontline Special*, Public Broadcasting System. Air date: October 4, 2005. Accessible at http://www.pbs.org/wgbh/pages/frontline/oj/.

Bell S. *Crime and Circumstance: Investigating the History of Forensic Science*. Praeger Publishers, Westport, CT. Page 1. 2008.

Bethke B. Alimentary, my dear Catherine. In: *Investigating CSI*. Cortez D, Ed. BenBella Books, New York. Pages 117–130.

Boorstin DJ. *The Image: A Guide to Pseudo Events in America*. Atheneum. 1962. Accessible at http://www.columbia.edu/itc/journalism/j6075/edit/boor.html.

Byers M and Johnson VM, Eds. *The CSI Effect: Television, Crime and Governance*. Lexington Books. 2009. Accessible at https://books.google.com/books?id=qN3DB7_VkgQC&pg=PA22&dq=Law+and+the+Lab,+Wall+Street+Journal&hl=en&sa=X&ved=0ahUKEwico_q4pYDNAhXE8YMKHUzmDhEQ6AEIMTAB#v=onepage&q=Law%20and%20the%20Lab%2C%20Wall%20Street%20Journal&f=false.

Chiasson L, Jr., Ed. *The Press on Trial: Crimes and Trials as Media Events*. Greenwood Press, Westport, CT 1997.

Cole S and Dioso R. Law and the Lab: Do TV Shows Really Affect How Juries Vote? Let's Look at the Evidence. *The Wall Street Journal*. May 13, 2005.

Dershowitz A. "The O.J. verdict." *Frontline Special*, Public Broadcasting System. Air date October 4, 2005. Accessible at http://www.pbs.org/wgbh/pages/frontline/oj/.

Di Maio D and Di Maio V. *Forensic Pathology: Practical Aspects of Criminal & Forensic Investigations* (2nd ed.). CRC Press, Boca Raton, FL. 2001.

Di Maio V and Franscell R. *Morgue: A Life in Death*. St. Martin's Press, New York. 2016.

Eddy C. A Brief History of Court TV, Where Many a True-Crime Obsession Was Born. June 1, 2015. Accessible at http://gizmodo.com/a-brief-history-of-court-tv-where-many-a-true-crime-ob-1708115679.

Fahy D. Scientists as Hollywood Heroes. November 13, 2014. Accessible at http://theconversation.com/scientists-as-hollywood-heroes-33978.

Gabel JD. Forensiphilia: Is the public fascination with forensic science a love affair or a fatal attraction? *New England Journal on Crime and Civil Confinement*. 2010. Accessible at http://ssrn.com/abstract=1578974.

Gabel JD. Realizing reliability in forensic science from the ground up. *Journal of Criminal Law and Criminology*. March 22, 2014. Accessible at https://www.thefreelibrary.com/Realizing+reliability+in+forensic+science+from+the+ground+up.-a0372696653.

Gabler N. The brief half-life of celebrity. *New York Times*. October 16, 1994.
Gelineau K. Famed medical examiner retires. *USA Today*. December 31, 2007. Accessible at http://usatoday30.usatoday.com/news/nation/2007-12-31-628525464_x.htm.
Gerard J. New cable network plans to cover jogger trial live. *New York Times*. May 24, 1990.
Glynn K. *Tabloid Culture: Trash Taste, Popular Power, and the Transformation of American Television*. Duke University Press, 2000.
Gregory K. Celebrities: Who they are, how they gain popularity, and why society is so fascinated with them and their court cases. Eastern Michigan University. 2008. Accessible at http://commons.emich.edu/cgi/viewcontent.cgi?article=1149&context=honors.
Habermas J. *The Structural Transformation of the Public Sphere*. MIT Press. 1989. Accessible at http://pages.uoregon.edu/koopman/courses_readings/phil123-net/publicness/habermas_structural_trans_pub_sphere.pdf.
Haggerty KD. Modern Serial Killers. In: *Crime, Media, Culture*. Page 173. 2009. Accessible at http://www.forensicresearchdigest.com/yahoo_site_admin/assets/docs/Crime_Media_Culture-2009-Haggerty-168-87.183144436.pdf.
Hansen M. Experts are Laible, Too. ABA Journal. November 2000. Page 17.
Houck MM. CSI: The reality. *Scientific American*. July 1, 2006. Accessible at https://www.mcdb.ucla.edu/Research/Goldberg/HC70A_W10/pdf/CSIReality.pdf.
James SH and Nordby JJ, (eds.) Here We Stand: What a Forensic Scientist Does. In: *Forensic Science: An Introduction to Scientific and Investigate Techniques*. CRC Press, Boca Raton, FL. Page 4. 2003.
Jones TL. The Murder Trial of OJ Simpsons. 2005. Accessible at https:www.scribd.com/doc/145924174/The-Murder-Trial-of-OJ-Simpsons.
Johnson S. Even as it seeks terror trial, Court TV looks beyond the gavel. *The Chicago Tribune*. January 7, 2002. Accessible at http://articles.chicagotribune.com/2002-01-07/features/0201070214_1_court-tv-herbert-terry-midlevel-cable-channel.
Kiely TF. *Forensic Evidence: Science and the Criminal Law*. Boca Raton, FL. CRC Press. Pages 30–31. 2003.
Kirby DA. Forensic fictions: Science, television production and modern storytelling. *Studies in History and Philosophy of Biological and Biomedical Sciences*. Vol. 44. Pages 92–102. 2013.
Krauss LM. Scientists as celebrities: Bad for science or good for society? *Bulletin of the Atomic Scientists*. Vol. 71, No. 1. 2015. Accessible at https://gehrcke.de/2015/01/krauss-about-the-role-of-sceintist-celebrities/.
Kurland M. How to Try a Murder: The Handbook for Armchair Lawyers. Castle Books, Edison, NJ. Page 1. 1997.
Lawrence C. *The Cult of Celebrity*. The Globe Pequot Press. Page 10. 2009.
Longworth JL. *TV Creators: Conversations with America's Top Producers of Television Drama*. Vol. 2. Syracuse University Press. 2002.
Merrefield C. The Daily Beast. 20 Biggest Trials of Past 20 Years. July 8, 2011. Accessible at http://www.thedailybeast.com/articles/2011/07/08/casey-anthony-trial-o-j-simpson-scott-peterson-more-big-trials.html.
National Library of Medicine (NLM) (n.d.). Marcella Fierro. https://www.nlm.nih.gov/changingthefaceofmedicine/physicians/biography_111.html.
Petley J. Fact plus fiction equals friction. *Media, Culture and Society*. Vol. 18. Pages 11–25. 1996.
Podlas K. *The Potential Impact of Television on Jurors*. August 2010.

Podlas K. The *CSI* effect and other forensic fictions, 27 Loy. L.A. Ent. L. Rev. 87 (2006). Available at: http://digitalcommons.lmu.edu/elr/vol27/iss2/1.

Ramsland K. *DNA & O.J.* 2006. Accessible at https://www.yumpu.com/en/document/view/12057131/investigating-csi-background-material-table-of-contents-i-/63.

Risinger MD. Defining the Task at Hand: Non-Science Forensic Science After *Kumho Tire Co. v. Carmichael*. Page 767. 2000. Accessible at http://law.shu.edu/faculty/fulltime_faculty/risingmi/articles/37washleelrev767.pdf.

Schweitzer NJ and Saks MJ. The CSI effect: Popular fiction about forensic science affects the public's expectations about real forensic science. *Jurimetrics Journal*. Vol. 47. Pages 357–364. Spring 2007.

Smith SM, Stinson V and Patry MW. Fact or fiction? The myth and reality of the *CSI* effect. *Court Review: The Journal of the American Judges Association*. Paper 355. 2011. Accessible at http://digitalcommons.unl.edu/ajacourtreview/355.

Steenberg L. Forensic Science in Contemporary American Popular Culture. 2013. Accessible at https://books.google.com/books?id=38RvNefh4UgC&pg=PA113&lpg=PA113&dq=celebrity+status+of+forensic+scientists&source=bl&ots=-q6a6c3e8g&sig=5sXmm41UVRw1wB8pU7lIDQH9Gg0&hl=en&sa=X&ved=0ahUKEwi3ov_ggezMAhVM6oMKHbi2AW4Q6AEIKjAB#v=onepage&q=celebrity%20status%20of%20forensic%20scientists&f=false.

Svetkey B. Introducing Court TV—A new network offers a long, live look into cable-ready courts across the country. August 2, 1991. Accessible at http://www.ew.com/article/1991/08/02/introducing-court-tv.

Swienton AR and Upshaw-Downs JC. Ethics in Media. In: *Ethics in Forensic Science*. Elsevier. Pages 425–426. 2012.

Upshaw Downs JC and Swienton AR. Ethics in Media. In: *Ethics in Forensic Science*. Elsevier, San Diego. 2012.

The Gale Group, Inc. Courtroom Television Network. *West's Encyclopedia of American. Law*. 2005. Accessible at http://www.encyclopedia.com/doc/1G2-3437701197.html.

Thomas R. *Detective Fiction and the Rise of Forensic Science*. Cambridge University Press, Cambridge. 1999.

Thomas R. *Detective Fiction and the Rise of Forensic Science*. Cambridge University Press, Cambridge. 2004.

Tyler TR. Viewing *CSI* and the threshold of guilt: Managing truth and justice in reality and in fiction. *Yale Law Journal*. Vol. 115. Pages 1050–1085. January 1, 2006. http://www.yalelawjournal.org/review/viewing-ligcsilig-and-the-threshold-of-guilt-managing-truth-and-justice-in-reality-and-fiction.

US Attorneys Annual Report, Fiscal Year 2013. Accessible at https://www.justice.gov/sites/default/files/usao/legacy/2014/09/22/13statrpt.pdf.

Vidmar N, Beale SS, Rose MR and Donnelly LF. Should we rush to reform the criminal jury? Consider conviction rate data. *Judicature*. Vol. 80. Pages 286–289. 1997.

Wood JM. 11 of the most-watched television trials. May 2, 2013. Accessible at http://mentalfloss.com/article/50232/11-most-watched-television-trials.

CHAPTER 6

The Future of Forensic Science

The preceding chapters have endeavored to tell the story of more recent forensic science challenges and opportunities through the two primary prisms of politics and practitioners. Supporters and detractors of forensic science likely agree that the only constant for the field in the future is change, and at a breakneck speed to keep pace with evolving demands.

Tjin-A-Tsoi (2013) says growth in forensic science has been driven by three main factors: the introduction of new technological capabilities, the increased general awareness among customers regarding the value and efficiency of forensic science, and the advent of new types of customers from outside the scope of traditional forensics. Regarding new technology, most notable are high-tech biometrics (predominantly forensic DNA), forensic information technology (IT), and forensic chemistry. The challenge, however, is to balance the need for speed of adoption with the necessity of prudent maturation and validation.

As Tjin-A-Tsoi (2013, page 4) observes, "That these new technologies should lead to growth is not surprising. When any new investigative technique is introduced, the pressure to put it into practice quickly increases. Of course, in forensics—as in other fields (e.g., healthcare)—ethical and quality issues may need to be resolved before a new technique can be used. Otherwise, if it provides valuable information, there will be a strong demand for it to be used immediately and on a wide scale. Since, in this way, any new scientific insight or technology creates its own demand, forensic innovations are likely to continue to spur growth in the field." Additionally, growth is achieved through the continuous improvement of existing technologies and techniques. As tests become more sensitive, the amount of relevant information that can be retrieved from traces will increase, as will the number of traces that can be analyzed in the first place. For example, a decade or more ago, a relatively large sample was needed for reliable forensic DNA analysis. Today, forensic laboratories need just a fraction of that; traces that in the past would have yielded no relevant information can now alter the course of an investigation.

Regarding greater awareness of the value, efficiency, and potential of forensic science, Tjin-A-Tsoi (2013, page 5) notes that, "The use of forensic investigations has increased not only due to the advent of new technologies but also due to an increased awareness of what forensics has to offer. Existing and potential end-users, the press and the public are all more aware today of the extent of forensic capabilities. This, in turn, is generating an increasing demand. Forensic investigation is gradually assuming a more central and high-profile role, and is becoming an essential tool for law enforcement, homeland defense, and others entrusted with maintaining justice, social order and security. Increasingly, court cases depend on DNA evidence, security and terrorism threats are being prevented on the basis of digital traces, and a wide variety of investigators are taking an interest in what forensics has to offer them."

Finally, in terms of generating new customers, Tjin-A-Tsoi (2013, page 6) says that, "The capabilities of forensic service providers have not passed unnoticed in domains outside of criminal justice and law enforcement. In fact, a wide range of governmental organizations—involved in everything from defense and intelligence to administrative law and regulatory oversight—are using forensics in their investigations. This new demand for forensic science is a main driver of growth in the sector as a whole." As a result of these trends, a new outlook of the forensic community is emerging, says Tjin-A-Tsoi (2013, page 7) who adds, "It no longer solely provides forensic services in the fields of law enforcement and criminal justice. Forensic institutes become first and foremost high-tech knowledge hubs, filled with knowledge workers who deliver their services to the (mostly government) agencies that may require these and who enrich the hub in the process."

As we will see in this chapter, change—both as it refers to reform and to seizing new opportunities—can be achieved through several key drivers, including oversight and quality assurance, education and training, and standards development.

Houck (2015, page xxi) observes that, "The scientific discipline of forensic science may be overflowing with methods but the profession is lacking in information, knowledge and methods for operations and strategic planning to improve its products and outcomes... Attempts have been made over the years to try to understand the scale and scope of the profession and its operations but it has been difficult."

Houck (2015, page xxi) adds, "Forensic stands at a tipping point: It has all the tools and resources to become a recognized, legitimate science whose practitioners know how to manage the greatest effect of limited resources. Whether it pulls all these together to become the discipline and profession that it could be remains to be seen. The efforts of the entirety of the forensic enterprise are necessary, for this transformation to be possible; strategic leadership will be necessary to make it happen."

Despite decades of criticism levied against them, forensic scientists try to remain positive about their profession. Coming at the issue from a more cheerful perspective of the past, present, and future, Bell (2008, page 217) observes, "Paul Kirk or Edmond Locard could not have predicted the direction that forensic science has taken, but they doubtless would have been pleased. The body of scientific knowledge has ballooned such that the true forensic generalist is a profession of the past. However, the same goals can be achieved by combining forensic specialties together creatively to generate ideas such as entomotoxicology. The heart of it remains the fundamental and distinctively forensic arts of comparison, classification, observation and documentation. From that creative synthesis, born at the intersection of science and the law, circumstance was, and continues to be, revealed."

Houck (2013, page 1) observes, "With disasters galore and governmental attention, money usually flows to provide activity, if not solutions. Why, then, has forensic science had such difficulty fulfilling its role as an honorable star among scientific professions?" He explores three main obstacles: resources, the lack of independence of the forensic enterprise, and the value proposition provided by forensic scientists.

As we have seen, resources—specifically education and training, personnel, and funding—have been an ongoing challenge. In terms of education and training, Houck (2013, page 1) says the field has made significant strides with accreditation of forensic science programs, but the momentum must be sustained: "Doctorates in forensic science are needed as mainstays of research, to help fill the research gaps that exist in the literature, and to teach. Training in the profession is a hodgepodge of approaches, content, and standards. While jurisdictions influence processes and, therefore, training, the content is another matter. Sufficient resources exist... to produce training standards that are international. People, as a resource, seem plentiful; these accredited forensic programs are creating graduates yearly. A lack or a lag of staffing in several areas, firearms being the most prominent, nevertheless exists. How do we close this gap? Universities won't start Departments of Firearms any time soon but it is these disciplines that are the most scientifically vulnerable. Finally, funding is a matter of political will; make the topic important enough and the resources follow."

As we saw in Chapter 2, the lack of independence of forensic offices and facilities has hampered the profession's credibility and progress toward quality improvement and bias elimination. As Houck (2013, page 1) suggests, "Leave the public safety to the police, the science to the scientists, and let them negotiate across the boundaries. As the U.S. National Academy of Sciences 2009 report, 'Strengthening Forensic Science in the US: A Path Forward' recommended, 'Ideally, public forensic science laboratories should be independent of or autonomous within law enforcement agencies. In these contexts, the director would have an equal voice with others in the justice system on matters involving the laboratory and other agencies. The laboratory also would be able to set its own priorities with respect to cases, expenditures, and other important issues. Cultural pressures caused by the different missions of scientific laboratories vis-à-vis law enforcement agencies would be largely resolved. Finally, the forensic science laboratories would be able to set their own budget priorities and not have to compete with the parent law enforcement agencies.'"

Houck (2013, page 1) says the situation is "less a matter of ethics and politics than autonomy and budgetary control," and adds, "Independence, whether derived politically or financially, is central to forensic science moving forward. The failing of forensic science to marshal financial (meaning political) resources mentioned before comes in part from this dependence upon parent agencies. Fear of angering superiors or retribution stymies many in the forensic professions from speaking up or out. Moreover, forensic science needs to legitimize itself to other sciences. Our profession is more than a book of applied methods... and we need to start exploring the basis for what we do and why we can do it. Forensic science needs to embrace the precepts and processes of other sciences and leave behind the cherished fantasies of our profession's youth, like individualization and the heresies of our adolescence, such as zero error rate. No other science will take us seriously unless we grow up."

Finally, Houck (2013) advises that forensic scientists must strive toward the application of more accurate forensic science intelligently to policing, public safety, and the criminal justice process. If not, Houck (2013, page 1) asks, "If forensic evidence does not make a difference in the majority of cases (as several studies have indicated), then what are we doing? Why shouldn't our budgets be cut? If we cannot justify our existence, what is our purpose? Unless and until we can clearly articulate that we are a separate science, validate our methods transparently, and establish our value to the public, forensic science will never get beyond a bunch of mere technicians being told what to do and for whom. Independence and transparency go far in providing intellectual infrastructure forensic science needs but they are not enough. Transformational change in education, culture, and the services we provide is needed to move forensic science forward as an enterprise."

The 2009 NAS report addressed forensic science's political realities within the quality conundrum, and surmised that because most forensic science methods, programs, and evidence are within the regulatory province of state and local law enforcement entities or are covered by statutes and rules governing state judicial proceedings, "Congress cannot directly fix all of the deficiencies in the forensic science community." Despite a call for federal oversight, the 2009 NAS report acknowledged that under the federal system of government, "Congress does not have free reign to amend state criminal codes, rules of evidence, and statutes governing civil actions; nor may it easily and directly regulate local law enforcement practices, state and local medical examiner units, or state policies covering the accreditation of crime laboratories and the certification of forensic practitioners" (page 13).

But, a back door exists, the 2009 NAS report notes, and it is the funding and appropriations from entities such as the Department of Justice (DOJ) that are the lifeblood of the profession. As the NAS report bluntly points out, "If these programs are required to operate pursuant to the highest standards, they will provide an example for the states. More importantly, Congress can promote best practices and strong educational, certification, accreditation, ethics and oversight programs in the states by offering funds that are contingent on meeting appropriate standards of practice. There is every reason to believe that offers of federal funds with 'strings attached' can effect significant change in the forensic science community, because so many state and local programs currently are suffering for want of adequate resources" (page 13).

The committee did exercise caution before drawing conclusions and avoided being too prescriptive in its recommendations. It also recognized that, given the complexity of the issues and the political realities that may pose obstacles to change, some recommendations will have to be implemented creatively and over time in order to be effective. Most importantly, it acknowledged that insiders recognize as a fragmented system, rife with politics and variability that can impact medicolegal outcomes.

As the 2009 NAS report observes, "The forensic science disciplines currently are an assortment of methods and practices used in both the public and private arenas. Forensic science facilities exhibit wide variability in capacity, oversight, staffing, certification, and accreditation across federal and state jurisdictions. Too often they have inadequate educational programs, and they typically lack mandatory and enforceable standards, founded on rigorous research and testing, certification requirements, and accreditation programs. Additionally, forensic science and forensic pathology research, education, and training lack strong ties to our research universities and national science assets" (page 14).

In February 2014, the White House issued a progress report designed to provide an update on any and all strides made since the National Research Council issued its sweeping report, "Strengthening Forensic Science in the United States: A Path Forward," in 2009 on the state of forensic science, as we saw in Chapter 2. The progress report noted the many contributions that forensic science has made to the justice system, observing, "Science and technology are essential to the pursuit of justice and are critical to the appropriate collection, assessment, and application of evidence in the criminal justice system. To ensure that the best forensic science is brought to bear in the pursuit of justice, the Administration has from its earliest days supported a wide range of research and policy activities" (https://obamawhitehouse.archives.gov/sites/default/files/microsites/ostp/forensic_science_progress_2-14-14.pdf). It added, "Strengthening forensic science is a complicated challenge that will require considerably more work and a sustained commitment on the part of the federal government as well as the broader forensic science community" (https://obamawhitehouse.archives.gov/sites/default/files/microsites/ostp/forensic_science_progress_2-14-14.pdf). Let's take a look at the main areas of reform and progress since 2009.

CREATING FEDERAL OVERSIGHT AND QUALITY ASSURANCE

As we saw in preceding chapters, reformers sought better oversight of the profession and outlined their desires for federal oversight from a central entity in the 2009 NAS report. However, Gabel (2014, pages 315–317) characterizes the attempts to gain consensus on how to accomplish the creation and implementation of national forensic science standards promulgated by such an entity "has remained an uncatchable shadow" and adds, "Indeed, many forensic science practitioners disagreed with a federal entity running the show. Consequently, the Standards Act highlights the problem of too many ideas floating about to translate into one workable system. Even assuming a slight consensus that a federal entity should (or could) promulgate national forensic standards, two questions remain: (1) whether the federal government has the power to effectively create and enforce such standards; and (2) if so, how such a program should operate." Gabel (2014, pages 315–317) observes that "the federal government likely has the power to regulate at least parts of the forensic science community, but it would need support from state and federal courts to enforce the standards it promulgates," and adds, "...even with judicial support and the express authority to cram federal legislation down the state pipeline, resistance would be stiff, and the requisite buy-in from crime labs and forensic organizations is lacking."

In 2010, the DOJ and the National Institute of Standards and Technology (NIST) created a framework for collaboration between the two entities to make strides toward fulfilling the goal of strengthening forensic science. Two new organizations and the accompanying infrastructure were established—the National Commission on Forensic Science (NCFS) and the Organization for Scientific Area Committees (OSAC). NCFS is composed of scientists, forensic practitioners, members of the legal community, and other stakeholders who develop forensic science–related policy recommendations for the Attorney General. OSAC represents 600-plus forensic science practitioners and other experts who support the development and promulgation of forensic science standards and guidelines. According to Butler (2015), NCFS subcommittees have been formed to perform work between the full Commission meetings. This subcommittee work is then vetted and discussed in the public NCFS meetings. The seven initial subcommittees are (1) Accreditation and Proficiency Testing, (2) Human Factors and Cognitive Bias, (3) Interim Solutions, (4) Medicolegal Death Investigation, (5) Reporting and Testimony, (6) Scientific Inquiry and Research, and (7) Training on Science and Law.

As Butler (2015, page 10) explains, "As of late 2014, NIJ and the FBI stopped funding the vast majority of SWGs... it is expected that the activities and efforts of the SWGs will be transitioned into the OSAC efforts that were first described to the forensic science community in February 2014 and are in the process of being established."

OSAC is a NIST-administered effort to provide subject matter expertise to the development of forensic science documentary standards within the United States. The goal of OSAC is to populate a registry of standards and a registry of guidelines with documents that can be used to improve the practice of forensic science and adopted by accrediting bodies to evaluate the quality of work in forensic laboratories. The enforcement of OSAC standards will come through the voluntary accreditation process and the performance of laboratory audits, according to Butler (2015, page 10), who adds, "OSAC consists of 33 operating units: A forensic science standards board (FSSB), three resource committees, five scientific area committees (SACs), and 24 subcommittees that focus on specific discipline needs. OSAC is more expansive though than the SWGs with the addition of an odontology subcommittee and two DNA subcommittees where one focuses on methods and the other on data interpretation. The availability of resource committee expertise in human factors, legal issues, and quality infrastructure further strengthen the overall capabilities of OSAC."

According to Simoncelli (2017, pages 129–131), "Each of these organizations has created a committee dedicated to 'human factors,' namely the cognitive, perceptual, organizational, social and cultural factors that influence the performance of forensic scientists as they draw conclusions from physical evidence and communicate their findings in the legal system."

Stolorow (2016) affirms that in response to the 2009 NAS report, the NIST and the U.S. DOJ signed a bilateral agency memorandum of understanding in March 2013, which specified the establishment of the OSAC model to develop standards and guidelines and promulgate implementation in all of the specific forensic science disciplines. At the time of the agreement, Stolorow (2016, page 101) says these consensus-based documentary standards and guidelines that will be developed and approved by OSAC "will be considered by crime laboratories as standard methods for specific analyses, potential discipline-specific standards for adoption as supplemental standards by accrediting bodies offering accreditation services to the forensic industry, officers of the court when evaluating processes employed and testimony given by forensic science experts, and by Congress and federal funding agencies in response to forensic science research priorities. The OSAC infrastructure will bring a uniform standards recognition platform to the community, enhance scientific rigor and increase communication among forensic scientists, research scientists, academicians, statisticians, attorneys, managers, quality assurance specialists and governmental entities."

As part of the Justice Department's efforts under the Task Force on Crime Reduction and Public Safety (Task Force), U.S. Attorney General Jeff Sessions in April 2017 announced a series of actions the department will take to advance forensic science and help combat the rise in violent crime. These actions are being undertaken on the expiration of the National Commission on Forensic Science (NCFS) and will increase the capacity of forensic science providers, improve the reliability of forensic analysis, and permit reporting of forensic results with greater specificity. The Task Force's Subcommittee on Forensics will spearhead the development of that strategic plan.

"The availability of prompt and accurate forensic science analysis to our law enforcement officers and prosecutors is critical to integrity in law enforcement, reducing violent crime and increasing public safety," Sessions said in a press release. "As we decide how to move forward, we bear in mind that the department is just one piece of the larger criminal justice system and that the vast majority of forensic science is practiced by state and local forensic laboratories and is used by state and local prosecutors. We applaud the professionalism of the National Commission on Forensic Science and look forward to building on the contributions it has made in this crucial field."

The DOJ says it will appoint a senior forensic advisor to interface with forensic science stakeholders and advise department leadership, as well as conduct a needs assessment of forensic science laboratories that examines workload, backlog, personnel, and equipment needs of public crime laboratories and the needs of academic and nontraditional forensic science practitioners, and issue a report to Congress. Additionally, the DOJ will seek public comment on how the department should move forward to strengthen the foundations of forensic science and improve the operations and capacity of forensic laboratories.

Stolorow (2016) is among those who hope to see OSAC drive change and improvement in the profession, including encouraging forensic practitioners to embrace this change and that all forensic analyses routinely employ quantification, uncertainty measurement and probabilistic modeling to the extent possible within each discipline. Additionally, Stolorow (2016) says the profession needs OSAC-approved standards and guidelines to be implemented in the practice of forensic science across all disciplines in addition to DNA, and that prosecutors, defense attorneys, and judges should use them in direct and cross-examinations of expert witnesses. And if that weren't already a dream come true for the field, Stolorow (2016) adds that the future should yield significant forensic science research that is well organized and well funded, with influence from OSAC to inform research priorities. Standards enforcement by accrediting bodies should also become "the rule rather than the exception," Stolorow (2016) notes.

The paradigm shift may take time and a few olive branches. Stolorow (2016, page 102) says that forensic scientists might still be nursing wounds inflicted by that 2009 NAS report "that calls into question his or her education and training, the predominance of law enforcement control and undue influence over the objective scientific decisions made by the forensic scientist in his or her analysis, conclusions, interpretation, report writing and expert testimony about the physical evidence he or she receives from the police. The report also opines that the analytical procedures, with the exception of forensic DNA testing, lacks sufficient scientific rigor underpinning the foundation of the science and lacks demonstrated validity and peer review to pass the test of reliability. The forensic scientist is also informed by the NRC that he or she fails to control for cognitive, contextual and confirmation bias in the laboratory processes that are the hallmark of his or her profession. If the initial reaction to the criticisms in the NRC report by the forensic science community seemed a bit defensive, I hope that scholars and stakeholders can appreciate the perception by many of the forensic science practitioners that the NRC report was unduly harsh in its overall assessment in 2009, whether that assessment was accurate or not."

Stolorow (2016, page 102) says that "a lot of improvement has been made by the entire forensic science profession since 2009 and that many practitioners have accepted the reality that they must embrace change. That is what good scientists do. If forensic science practitioners are going to demonstrate to the rest of the criminal justice community that they are truly good scientists, then it is my aspiration that the current progress in embracing change will continue into the foreseeable future."

To that end, the first-ever International Symposium on Forensic Science Error Management sponsored by NIST was held in July 2015 and attended by nearly 500 forensic practitioners, managers, lawyers, judges, academic researchers, psychologists, measurement scientists, and statisticians who gathered to examine the detection, measurement, and mitigation of errors in forensic science. As Stolorow (2016, page 102) points out, "Clearly, hundreds were willing to gather in recognition that forensic scientists do make errors, however infrequently, and to spend a week to examine ways to detect and manage errors in forensic science. Personally, I doubt that the concept to convene such a symposium would ever have been accepted by the forensic science community back in 2009."

Regarding requiring quantification, uncertainty measurement, and probabilistic modeling to the extent possible within each discipline, as suggested in the 2009 NAS report, Stolorow (2016) says that research projects are now underway in a number of forensic science disciplines to employ quantitative algorithms to objectify the data measurements of latent print minutiae and firearms and toolmark evidence striae, and employ probabilistic modeling to the correlation of patterns from evidence samples and known reference samples. Part of the effort comes from the new Forensic Science Center of Excellence, consisting of a consortium of universities led by Iowa State University in collaboration with Carnegie Mellon University, the University of California at Irvine, and the University of Virginia. Funded by the NIST, the center is tasked with improving the statistical foundation for pattern evidence (fingerprints, firearms, toolmarks, etc.) and digital evidence (computer, video, audio analyses, etc.), as well as developing education and training on probabilistic methods for practitioners and other affiliated stakeholders.

Also in the summer of 2014, NIST announced a competition to create a Forensic Science Center of Excellence to address pattern evidence and digital evidence, anticipating $4 million in annual funding over five years. Draft policy documents were announced in the fall of 2014, addressing topics as diverse as courtroom discovery and expert testimony, to defining forensic science and its service providers, to recommendations on accreditation and certification of medicolegal death investigation personnel. According to Butler (2015, page 13), "This work, which will begin at the awarded universities in mid-2015, will focus on developing probabilistic methods for dealing with pattern evidence and digital evidence and providing training materials with these new methods."

"Forensic science needs to base opinion on dependable, reliable scientific measurements," says NIST scientist John Butler, whom we first met in Chapter 2. "Many forensic disciplines need more research, and scientific measurements underpin what they are trying to do. I think we will get there but it is going to take time. NIST's Center of Excellence will look at pattern evidence in particular to bring more statistical firepower to these disciplines. We hope to bring statisticians to bear on the issue and provide data to bolster the underpinnings of how probabilistic measurements are made. A lot of times in forensic science you take a binary approach—it's either include or exclude an individual and it's very qualitative in terms of how you do that, and if it has been made by a human examiner, the more scientific rigor you have, the better you can prove your results. In order to do that you have to apply statistics and better probability like DNA provides, so we're trying to bring these other disciplines to a higher level of scientific rigor."

Analysts also must improve the language they use to convey their level of certainty, an issue that experts have addressed throughout this book. "The language that bench scientists use is very important," Butler says. "There is a level of education needed to get people to appreciate the fact when you say there is 'a reasonable degree of scientific certainty,' this statement can be viewed as proving that something must be in fact be true. What that means or does not mean, partly becomes a shield behind which people will hide. The challenge lies in the interface between the 'forensic' part and the 'science' part; in the legal arena, things are very binary—guilty or not guilty, and it's very final, very black and white. But for science, which works on a continuum, it is about thinking in terms of probabilities and statistics in a more quantitative fashion. So that interface and how you communicate across it, is key; lawyers and scientists speak a different language and to help that interface happen, you have to be able to get on the same page. By removing the 'degree of scientific certainty' phrase from the legal lingo, we have an improved, more accurate dialogue, and we hope to be able to move forward in some of this interface."

As Butler (2015, page 12) reports, "NIST has performed forensic science research in a number of areas over the past century. For several decades, NIJ supported NIST research efforts through interagency agreements with the NIST Office of Law Enforcement Standards (OLES). Since 2011, most funds to conduct forensic science research have come to NIST directly from Congress although some support from other agencies continues. As of early 2015, there were six primary focus areas for NIST intramural research in forensic science: ballistics and associated tool marks; digital and identification forensics; forensic genetics; toxins and drug analysis; trace evidence: and statistics. In addition, other agencies fund additional research at NIST in explosives detection, fingerprint analysis and fire research."

As Stolorow (2016, page 103) remarks, "Clearly, there has been tangible progress made through strong national leadership in the direction of improving the employment of quantification, uncertainty measurement and probabilistic models to the extent possible within forensic science disciplines."

Stolorow (2016, page 105) adds, "It is my aspiration that the combined critical mass of the two new national entities, OSAC and the National Commission on Forensic Science (NCFS), will bring sufficient attention to national forensic science research needs and provide real leverage to grab the attention of lawmakers. The objectives annunciated by both organizations include defining forensic science research priorities. It is hoped that the OSAC and the NCFS articulation of these forensic science research priorities will favorably influence legislators to increase funding for research significantly. At least a ten-fold increase in forensic science research funding would minimally improve the pace of strengthening the practice of forensic science but, ultimately, the effectiveness of this influence on supporting new legislation for research funding remains to be seen. One can remain hopeful."

Legal commentators have expressed hope that the NCFS can administer meaningful reform in an independent fashion. As Giannelli (2011a, page 57) observes, "Scientific values are often antithetical to law enforcement values—or at least frequently perceived to be so by prosecutors and police. In particular, the notion of transparency has repeatedly been trumped by an adversarial process that favors trial by ambush... The DOJ, the FBI Crime Laboratory, and some prosecutors have attempted to shape science by controlling the research agenda, hiding unwelcomed test results, attacking legitimate studies that were considered unfavorable, harassing scientists who disagreed with them, and 'spinning' these issues in the press."

Risinger (2010, page 9) comments that "The only solution the [NAS/NRC] Committee could envision is a substantial, well-funded research effort aimed at testing the claims of these areas across the whole range of issues that forensic practitioners currently claim to be able to resolve dependably, coupled with the hope that the results of such research will be incorporated into best-practice standards through laboratory accreditation and individual certification requirements operating upstream from the trial. In short, the problem children will be disciplined through research administered under the same reformed regime that will solve the problems of bad standards and lax practices in other more validated areas." He adds, "The NAS/NRC Committee clearly would like to see a forensic science world manifesting significant uniformity of high-quality practice, with results of well-validated processes uninfluenced by partisan considerations that are communicated to fact finders as neutrally as possible, without overclaiming or obfuscation. To make progress toward this clearly desirable but perhaps utopian vision, the Committee puts its faith in central command and control by a body committed to the best standards of modern science, or at any rate it recommends as close to such a model as it thought it could recommend with any chance of success, given the political realities of our federal system. It further places its faith in the power of accreditation of laboratories and certification of individual practitioners."

As the DOJ and NIST explained in a 2014 statement, "The National Commission on Forensic Science will work to improve the practice of forensic science by developing guidance and recommendations for the U.S. Attorney General on forensic specialties ranging from DNA analysis to firearms and toolmarks. Members of the commission are working to improve the practice of forensic science by developing guidance concerning the intersections between forensic science and the criminal justice system. The commission also will work to develop policy recommendations for the U.S. Attorney General, including uniform codes for professional responsibility and requirements for formal training and certification. The commission includes federal, state and local forensic science service providers; research scientists and academics; law enforcement officials; prosecutors, defense attorneys and judges; and other stakeholders from across the country. This breadth of experience and expertise reflects the many different entities that contribute to forensic science practice in the U.S. and will ensure these broad perspectives are represented on the commission and in its work" (https://www.justice.gov/opa/pr/us-departments-justice-and-commerce-name-experts-first-ever-national-commission-forensic).

Runkle (2016, page 76) identifies a wrinkle in the progress expected for the NCFS: "Despite the high hopes for the Commission, at its first public meeting in February 2014, several members commented that the appointment of the commission might be premature. That is, it is pointless to recommend requirements for accreditation, training and certification given the uncertain status of the sciences themselves. Why train forensic scientists to competently perform unreliable and invalid tests? These commissioners argued that an analysis of the underlying scientific and technical foundations for the forensic sciences should have precedence."

The NAS Committee's recommended reforms also included the establishment of a National Institute of Forensic Science (NIFS) and the subsequent removal of all American forensic science laboratories from law enforcement's administrative control. The road to this kind of oversight has been a long and winding one, fraught with politics, according to some forensic practitioners and commentators. Risinger (2010, page 10) confirms that such a proposal was originally suggested by Thompson (1974) and readdressed by Giannelli (1997), and adds, "The proposal is also undoubtedly wise, although in the end such a separation might be more formal than real."

Skepticism at the separation of forensic science from law enforcement persists. As Risinger (2010, page 11) comments, "I do not believe that conditions have changed sufficiently… for the accomplishment of this desirable result to have much of a chance. Laboratories have been intertwined with police organizations for too long to have the police organizations surrender control over them willingly. First, just on a level of pure bureaucratic power, organizations do not easily agree to give up significant centers of budget allocation, if for no other reason than that the bigger your budget is the more important and powerful you are. In addition, there is the natural fear that the new arrangements will change the relationship and the product in ways that law enforcement will not like—it may become less predictably supportive of the desires of law enforcement to have particular outcomes ratified. Whatever the reasons… few speaking for law enforcement agencies, prosecutorial agencies, forensic science organizations, or forensic science publications have supported either independence or the establishment of NIFS, and most that have spoken have opposed both."

Risinger (2010, page 12) adds, "Given the usual power in Congress of the law enforcement lobby and states' rights proponents in law enforcement matters, it does not seem to me that the independent agency called for—with its power to set national standards and then call for their implementation, and to influence that implementation through imposing conditions on federal aid to state forensic science laboratories—is likely to be adopted anytime soon. Furthermore, any hope of congressional action to coerce or encourage the establishment of independence of forensic labs from law enforcement control is also dead on arrival. Some narrow authority may be given to the NIST or some other existing federal agency, and some money for research on the problem children will almost certainly be forthcoming. But unless this research money is administered by an agency with strong science credentials, that develops both an understanding of the problems and a commitment to their solution, any 'honest broker' scientific research proposals coming from academia will almost certainly face stiff competition for the money with law-enforcement-sponsored, faux-research proposals of a kind that have been unfortunately common in the past, and which may suck up most of the money and generate mostly research pre-tailored to reaching results affirming the propriety of the status quo."

Koppl and Krane (2016, page 152) express concern that federal oversight of forensic science could create what they call "regulatory capture": "Any proposal to erect a regulatory body, whether at the federal or state level, comes with the risk that the regulatory body will be 'captured' by special interests. Regulatory and oversight bodies are supposed to constrain special interests and protect the general interest. When regulatory and oversight bodies instead serve special interests, these bodies have been 'captured.' Capture is the norm, unfortunately, which makes long-term beneficial change through oversight hard."

They add, "There is increasing agreement that institutional changes to forensic science in the United States are needed. Many observers have argued for sequential unmasking, 'independence' of crime labs from law enforcement, and a federal oversight body with broad regulatory authority. Proposals for change have tended to focus on hierarchical measures that minimize bias. There has been less emphasis on distributed measures and measures to leverage bias. We have emphasized these neglected approaches to bias in forensic science and called for the use of all four basic strategies for dealing with bias and error in forensic science: hierarchical measures that minimize bias, hierarchical measures that leverage bias, distributed measures that minimize bias, and distributed measures that leverage bias" (page 164).

Any additional layers of governmental oversight may run counter to the Constitution, some experts point out. "I am not involved in efforts to standardize, but you are bumping up against the Constitution in many ways," says Richard Saferstein, whom we first met in Chapter 1. "The power of policing resides with the states, not the federal government. I guess the only power the federal government can have over the states is monetary—telling them 'If you don't do it our way we won't give you grant money,' which it may come to, but I doubt it. Regarding nationalizing the crime lab, I think the outcome is probably very beneficial for the field but it probably won't be accomplished. My feeling is the best thing the feds can do is not bureaucratize the crime labs; all of the existing committees and subcommittees is mind-boggling. Look at the organizational charts they come out with! Instead, let's take all that money and put it into research. I really like what the NIJ is doing; I follow their reports and look at the grants they have given out and see what has come from those grants. I am a scientist and I feel that if we are going to improve the field, then we have got to do it through scientific research, not more bureaucracy. We must support individuals who conduct research, instead of investing more money to nationalize and separate crime labs."

Although separating forensic science from law enforcement may prove to be easier said than done, there are precedents for some of the other attempts at rehabilitation of forensic science. There have been previous attempts to establish oversight and kick-start improvements and quality assurance. Long before the NCFS, there was the Consortium of Forensic Science Organization (CFSO), which encouraged Congress to pass legislation directing NAS to create an independent needs assessment study of the various forensic disciplines. Using funding provided through the Science, State, Justice, Commerce, and Related Agencies Appropriations Act of 2006, this study eventually became the 2009 NAS report. The report triggered a number of hearings on Capitol Hill, including a March 10, 2009 hearing before the Subcommittee on Technology & Innovation Committee on Science and Technology in the House of Representatives. The hearing reviewed scientific and technical issues raised by the 2009 NAS report. This was followed eight days later by a hearing before the Committee on the Judiciary United States Senate. Other Senate hearings were held in May and September 2009. Other legislative action followed. On February 12, 2014, Sen. John D. Rockefeller IV (D-WVa) introduced the Forensic Science and Standards Act 2014 to establish a national program that would strengthen forensic science by promoting scientific research, establish science-based voluntary consensus standards and protocols across forensic science disciplines, and encourage the adoption of these standards. Rockefeller's bill never became law.

Gabel (2014, pages 312–314) refers to the recent past of forensic science reform as a "graveyard of good ideas," specifically referring to stalled and failed attempts at rehabilitation that have included the State and Local Criminal Forensic Laboratory Enhancement Act of 2009, a bill that never made it out of committee. Two years later, the Criminal Justice and Forensic Science Reform Act of 2011, which would have established an Office of Forensic Science within the DOJ, also died in committee. In 2012 and again in 2013, legislation to establish scientific standards and protocols across forensic disciplines was introduced; the Forensic Science and Standards Act of 2013 and its 2012 predecessor were intended to create a national forensic science research program to improve, expand, and coordinate Federal research in the forensic sciences and establish both a national forensic science coordinating office at the NIST and a forensic science advisory committee. As Gabel (2014, pages 312–314) explains, "Notwithstanding the failed 2012 Standards Act, the resurrected Standards Act is notable for its trailblazing approach to tackling forensic reform in a manner that prior legislation had not. The Act aims to fix forensic science by encouraging research, adopting standards, and creating accreditation requirements. The legislation, however, suffers from its corpulent proportions, despite its ambitious objectives. Aside from the historical failure rate of forensic reforms, the legislation is problematic because it would effectively birth a Lernaean Hydra with a multitude of agencies, committees, and other entities that border on redundancy and grandiosity. It would create a chaotic assemblage of organizations by establishing new entities under the auspices of the existing National Science Foundation (NSF) and NIST."

The Standards Act of 2013 never came to fruition and as Gabel (2014, page 315) notes, it became "another obituary in the history of forensic reform, likely doomed by a lack of political capital and a steep price tag."

Failed legislation could prompt the government to mandate standards, according to Gabel (2014), who explains that under *Gonzales v. Raich*, Congress has the power to regulate even noneconomic goods if it does so as part of a commercial regulatory scheme. As Gabel (2014, pages 316–317) notes further, "This could give Congress some latitude to regulate parts of the forensic science community. For example, Congress might choose to regulate instruments used in forensic science analysis, because it would have a rational basis for regulating their creation and use. But the power to regulate commerce would have its limits, especially related to research."

Congress could fund its own research, Gabel (2014, page 317) says, but "mandating the direction of university-level research likely would be beyond the scope of Congress's power, even if it were politically feasible. Congress is also limited either politically or constitutionally in what it can do to mandate what state and local courts admit as evidence. Even if Congress could significantly affect the landscape of the forensic science community through mandates, much of its effect would diminish if state and local courts did not adopt the same standards."

ADDRESSING BIAS, INCREASING RELIABILITY, AND FOSTERING INDEPENDENCE

Taking a dim view of the profession, Gabel (2014, pages 285–286) asserts, "American courts have improperly legitimized various forensic disciplines without subjecting them to the kind of scrutiny that would be required of novel scientific or technical evidence today. Courts accept the untested view that 'science,' such as fingerprinting and hair analysis, is generally accepted, science, and reliable. Such unsupported conclusions have lacked adequate scrutiny, whether from a scientific or a legal perspective ... Indeed, five years after the NAS Report, the so-called 'Path Forward' seems murky, and various political logjams have barricaded the road to reliability. I posit that reliability—the bedrock of forensic science—remains a fleeting notion, because efforts at reform have lacked coordination and implementation. The only way to adequately address the flaws brought to light through the NAS Report is to align the various stakeholders and make a concerted effort from all facets of forensic science, rather than waiting for guidance through a frustrated and exhausted legislative and judicial process."

The ability to make progress may lie with the ability to shore up forensic science and equip practitioners with the skills they need to identify sources of internal bias and external pressure from legal system stakeholders, and tools they need to conduct their analyses and interpretations accurately, in an environment that fosters as much independence as possible within current constructs.

Many forensic practitioners blame the adversarial legal system. "Science and the law always clash in an adversarial system," acknowledges George Sensabaugh, the forensic science educator whom we first met in Chapter 1. "People who get into the forensic science enterprise need to be aware of the context in which they work; they need to realize that the prosecution is going to try to embellish, to the extent that it can, the positive nature of whatever the evidentiary findings may be, and the defense is going to try to challenge the nature of those findings. That's our adversarial system in play, for better or for worse. A defense attorney told me years ago that his job is not to get the client off the hook but to make the prosecution prove its case. If the prosecution can't prove its case his client will get off the hook. That's a very straightforward way of looking at things and it's time we face that truth."

Sensabaugh continues, "It's also important to realize that more than 95 percent of cases are adjudicated by plea bargaining, so although we look upon one of the distinguishing characteristics one expects of being in forensic science is an appearance in court, the majority of the time whenever cases are being prosecuted, they don't ever go to court—the parties negotiate and come up with a plea arrangement. I think forensic scientists need to pay attention to writing really good reports before the bargaining process takes place so both sides have a full body of information—what is there in the scientific analyses to incorporate in the bargaining process. I have talked with some of my colleagues about this and they are so overburdened with casework that they just do the analyses as they can—if they know a case is going to court, it establishes the case as a particular priority and that moves it forward in the queue."

Forensic pathologist Cyril Wecht, MD, whom we first met in Chapter 3, says forensic science hasn't changed all that much, but the politics make it a new maze to navigate, especially for the uninitiated. "Forensic science and forensic pathology is not all that changed from how it was 50 years ago, but back then you didn't face the same kind of courtroom," he says. "Good or bad, what lawyers have come to learn is how to play the game. And forensic scientists are better equipped to handle it, the more they know it exists; the more experience you have had, the better you become and the more likely you are to succeed in the courtroom. The people under whom I trained were wonderful, but they had not confronted the kinds of things that now occur and the new dynamics in the courtroom."

"Medicine is fundamentally different from the law," says retired forensic pathologist Marcella Fierro, whom we first met in Chapter 2. "Medicine believes there is an absolute truth—that science can find an answer to many questions and that those answers do not lend themselves to debate. Science has settled them. Lawyers hope that through the adversarial system and the ensuing debate the truth will emerge. The approaches are different."

Fellow forensic pathologist Michael Baden says the autopsy will remain as it has but the stakes are higher and the politics are ever present in an adversarial system. "The traditional autopsy has been the same for the last 120 years," he says. "Unlike criminalistics and toxicology, which have made great advances in science and technique, the autopsy remains pretty standard throughout the world for the last 100 years or so, but what the medical examiner has to be careful about are the interpretations. Autopsies are straightforward but I've seen where people bend over too much to interpret the same findings because after all, now DNA is a new entrant into the autopsy room. DNA and future advances are important for identifying who the person is and also to help identify transfer between a perpetrator and a decedent, such as hairs and fibers. We have to learn how to do that properly and to hand it over to the crime lab and the crime lab takes over. We don't interpret those things; it is our job to collect them."

Baden continues, "I think what is very important and what is failing here is, initially when I started out, we would go to the scene of every homicide, the medical examiner would do the autopsy, and that was helpful. Things since then have progressed to the point that now there are non-physician techs who do a very good job but the autopsy starts at the scene and so I think it is important that medical examiners don't get divorced from the scene. Trained forensic pathologists know what to do during the autopsy and what we are going to look for—it all starts with the scene. In my day, all homicide scenes were visited by a physician trained to do scene work and then come directly into the autopsy room and do the autopsy; that can still be done with trained non-physicians but the scene has to be important and all I can see for the future is that medical examiners are going to continue to have difficulties with prosecutors. MEs learn at an early stage that if they go along with the prosecutor's theory of the case, they are not going to get fired. People such as Tom Noguchi, Cyril Wecht, Bernard Spitz, and myself, we have gotten into trouble because we said that we didn't agree with the prosecutor's version of things and then prosecutors can get medical examiners fired."

Baden points to wrongful convictions as an example of the politics that exist in the justice and medicolegal death investigation systems. "As we have seen in the last 15 years, in so many of the wrongful convictions cases, there has always been a medical examiner involved in those cases. And usually the ME has testified along with the theory of the prosecutor; then it turns out later that the prosecutor's theory was wrong but nobody gets punished. Rarely does a prosecutor not get re-elected when a prosecutor makes a decision that is wrong or when someone is wrongfully convicted and spends 20 years in prison for something they didn't do. No one gets punished for it—including medical examiners. If the ME goes along with the prosecutor even though it is a faulty case, he or she is not going to lose their job. But there's a tension that exists, especially in politically charged police-related cases, and MEs must hold fast onto their findings; if the bullet wound is through the back you have to say that even though the police's version is through the front."

As we saw in Chapter 2, forensic science is frequently vilified for the connection between the proximity to law enforcement and the margin for error related to potential for conflict of interest and examiner bias. Forensic science detractors have gotten much mileage out of the debate over undue influence by law enforcement and the assumption that forensic practitioners cannot perform independent work in a lab associated with a police agency.

James and Nordby (2003) acknowledge that "While crime laboratory scientists may pride themselves as being independent finders of fact, most operate under police jurisdiction or administration, and many scientists, perhaps unconsciously, develop the attitude that they work exclusively for the best interest of the police or the prosecutor. When emotions overcome reason, a zealous forensic scientist may intentionally or inadvertently deny real justice. Results are misinterpreted, or worse, falsified. Such flawed science may not be easy to spot, since it can only appear through the results of the scientific investigation. While no one can attain anything close to a perfect harmony of reason with emotion, forensic scientists at least have a duty to strike the best balance possible under life's most difficult circumstances. Of course, completely satisfying this duty remains both difficult and elusive."

In its Recommendation 4, the 2009 NAS report noted, "To improve the scientific bases of forensic science examinations and to maximize independence from or autonomy within the law enforcement community, Congress should authorize and appropriate incentive funds to the National Institute of Forensic Science (NIFS) for allocation to state and local jurisdictions for the purpose of removing all public forensic laboratories and facilities from the administrative control of law enforcement agencies or prosecutors' offices" (NAS, 2009, page 24).

In its Recommendation 5, the 2009 NAS report states that the "National Institute of Forensic Science (NIFS) should encourage research programs on human observer bias and sources of human error in forensic examinations. Such programs might include studies to determine the effects of contextual bias in forensic practice (e.g., studies to determine whether and to what extent the results of forensic analyses are influenced by knowledge regarding the background of the suspect and the investigator's theory of the case). In addition, research on sources of human error should be closely linked with research conducted to quantify and characterize the amount of error. Based on the results of these studies, and in consultation with its advisory board, NIFS should develop standard operating procedures (that will lay the foundation for model protocols) to minimize, to the greatest extent reasonably possible, potential bias and sources of human error in forensic practice. These standard operating procedures should apply to all forensic analyses that may be used in litigation" (NAS, 2009, page 24).

In its Recommendation 6, the 2009 NAS report says, "To facilitate the work of the National Institute of Forensic Science (NIFS), Congress should authorize and appropriate funds to NIFS to work with the National Institute of Standards and Technology (NIST), in conjunction with government laboratories, universities, and private laboratories, and in consultation with Scientific Working groups, to develop tools for advancing measurement, validation, reliability, information sharing, and proficiency testing in forensic science and to establish protocols for forensic examinations, methods, and practices. Standards should reflect best practices and serve as accreditation tools for laboratories and as guides for the education, training, and certification of professionals. Upon completion of its work, NIST and its partners should report findings and recommendations to NIFS for further dissemination and implementation" (NAS, 2009, page 24).

"One of the big problems with forensic science is its ideologies," says retired forensic science educator Jay Siegel. "Most of forensic science started in laboratories and many facilities are still police laboratories. One of the most important things that came out of the 2009 NAS report is recommendation four, which is to remove forensic science labs from police departments. These are science labs, police are not scientists and their cultures clash and budgetary issues arise and ethical issues arise and I think it is extremely important that forensic science labs become independent science laboratories. That is the case in some other countries, and it's going to be a very slow process here. I think there are some signs that a transition is taking place, and that's encouraging."

Not only should labs and examiners' offices be independent, but so too should the research that should be conducted. As the NAS report notes, "Scientific and medical assessment conducted in forensic investigations should be independent of law enforcement efforts either to prosecute criminal suspects or even to determine whether a criminal act has indeed been committed. Administratively, this means that forensic scientists should function independently of law enforcement administrators. The best science is conducted in a scientific setting as opposed to a law enforcement setting. Because forensic scientists often are driven in their work by a need to answer a particular question related to the issues of a particular case, they sometimes face pressure to sacrifice appropriate methodology for the sake of expediency" (NAS, 2009, page 23).

Cyril Wecht says, "We need total independence and severed ties with law enforcement agencies and prosecutors. If we push for this, more and more we will be improving the system and achieving the goal of objective medico-legal death investigations. We'll also be better equipped to answer the questions we are confronted with from families and courts and society overall. They are entitled to receive answers from us. We'll probably never reach 100 percent independence but we can certainly make significant strides in that direction."

"Removing law enforcement from the process isn't going to happen without funding to do that," says John Butler. "It won't magically happen otherwise. Our local lab here in Montgomery County, Maryland. is embedded in the same building as the police headquarters. So many labs are situated similarly, with an overall law enforcement structure that impedes acting as an independent agency. And even if you are an independent entity, you are still working closely with prosecutors, so that dynamic persists. Part of the fundamental challenge that exists with forensic science is that interface with the law and/or law enforcement, and so you can't separate it quickly. People will say, 'Just set up an independent lab,' but with private labs you can't always address all of the intricacies of the interface between law enforcement and the legal system and what the lab is trying to deliver in terms of services to provide data."

Butler continues, "As an illustration, when I was writing my last book I sat down for about an hour with six detectives, a prosecutor and the lab director, and we discussed lab reports and how they are actually used. Even if the lab is not connected to the police, how is the information in that lab report generated and being used? From the police standpoint, they told me they just want to know who the perpetrator was and whether or not they have the right guy. They frankly don't care about the details of the science. The prosecutor wants to know if she has the information she needs when going to court. So even if you have an independent lab, if you are contributing a report to this process, you need to know how the end user is going to use that data, and will they understand it and use it properly? That's when it becomes difficult to separate the physical lab even if you had it financially separated from law enforcement. That critical interface in terms of understanding that data and using that report properly is still going to be there. That's the challenge you face and always will. You can't ever fully pull that apart, even with plenty of funding."

Gabel (2014, page 292) emphasizes that "...forensic science disciplines lack significant peer-reviewed research of the scientific bases and validity studies that should support their methods. Fingerprint-matching techniques, for instance, lack sufficient data on the diagnosticity and reliability of even the most basic assumptions. For pattern-identification methods generally, research establishing the limits and measures of their performance is sorely needed. Although research in many disciplines would allow for more consistent, quantitative results, research culture has not found a foothold in forensic science. Without the requisite level of empiricism that grounds scientific endeavors, forensic science devolves into forensic art."

Houck 2006 (page 89) advocates moving research that has traditionally been conducted in police laboratories, which focuses on specific, case-related questions, to "the controlled environment of the academic laboratory. Such labs could investigate questions that clearly require more research. For example, recent legal challenges have called into question the long-held assumption of the absolute uniqueness of fingerprints, toolmarks, bite marks, bullet striations and handwriting matches."

As Gabel (2014, pages 292–293) asserts, "Despite the public desire for certainty and the legal requirement to prove guilt beyond a reasonable doubt, few forensic science methods have developed adequate measures of the accuracy of inferences made by forensic scientists. It seems to be common sense that every forensic technique should include the applicable level of uncertainty in the measurements that are made. Taken in isolation, the lack of scientifically acceptable standards for such a wide segment of forensic practices that continually calls itself a 'science' seems quixotic. The disconnect between forensic research and forensic practice occurred long ago and is the product of a criminal justice system that misplaces value in that gap. Many of the disciplines evolved solely for the purpose of solving crimes, and I hazard a guess that the inability to challenge forensic techniques' reliability due to the lack of solid research produces more convictions than acquittals. In the absence of validation studies, forensic techniques were initially applied to cases; once their application was established, the ongoing prosecutorial use of forensic techniques (and a good bit of judicial notice) continued unquestioned, and courts cemented their longevity."

Gabel (2014, pages 293–294) describes that "With a pile of cases to solve, research, repeatability and reliability assessments were—quite understandably—not crime labs' priority. Furthermore, implementing research and standards presents costs (in both workload and real dollars) that crime lab budgets simply cannot absorb. This steady progression to deem results acceptable, however, permitted forensic evidence development to continue unimpeded and elevated it to 'sure bet' status in criminal trials. Of course, some forensic evidence is more reliable than others, but that does not excuse a continued culture of 'because I said so' testimony that uses loaded terminology such as 'match,' 'positively' or 'to the exclusion of all others' without the proper considerations of validity and rarity found in other research sciences. This lack of a research-oriented culture in forensic evidence leads to errors in the way the evidence is used in prosecutions and presented in courts."

As we have seen, commentators assert that the lack of foundational research underlying forensic science disciplines contributes to the eventual errors in forensic testimony, such as exaggerating the inculpatory nature of the evidence by providing inaccurate or nonexistent statistics, and misstating the certainty of the results when the forensic technique, such as bitemark or fiber analysis, does not allow for it.

"Forensic science always has and probably always will have that human dynamic intertwined with the science," says John Butler. "Experts are currently discussing the best way to look at data and how to set up frameworks to minimize the human factor. We are examining how to set up analyses properly and implement them so that examiners are looking at the data at the right time in the right way and not be unduly influenced in some way."

To those who claim that forensic science is as bad as the 2009 NAS report purports, Butler says he shares an analogy between forensic science and math: "Basic math is two plus two equals four; algebra is two plus x equals four; and then you have calculus; part of the challenge that exists is I think basic math and algebra can be done very, very well. It's when you start getting into calculus that you have the challenges—either people aren't well enough trained to understand that, or the system isn't designed to cope with calculus because you are going to feed that into the legal community when lawyers and judges may need basic arithmetic and not going to handle integrals and derivatives of calculus.

You have excellent work done in labs at the basic math and algebra levels; where the challenges exist and where you hear the biggest problems are, is when you get a very complex DNA mixture, when you get a partial or latent print, you are in the calculus realm."

Butler continues, "Brandon Mayfield was a calculus-level problem attempted by the FBI. They should not have pushed to get a result. Evidence is the most intricate piece of the puzzle. Examiners are always comparing the sample to the reference piece in any aspect of forensic science but you don't have any control over the evidence sample, whether it is a partial print or a partial DNA profile or a fragment of a bullet. If you have compromised evidence or not fully realized or complete evidence, there's nothing you can do about that—it's what you are dealt. You are squarely in the calculus realm. The challenge is correct interpretation and assigning an accurate probability. The future of forensic science lies in how you translate that effectively to the court system to be able to use it appropriately. There is a significant margin for error when you are in the calculus realm. When you have a simple comparison you have a higher degree of confidence but when you have more challenging evidence, that's where you have the difficulties and the potential for errors."

In 2016, a number of researchers wrote a paper that may help close the book on bitemark evidence, long the poster child for questionable scientific merit in the eyes of many. As we have seen, legal commentators have pointed to a number of pattern-matching disciplines they say lack the scientific foundation needed to justify continuing admission as trial evidence. Saks et al. (2016) say that a likely next candidate for elimination is bitemark identification, pointing to the Texas Forensic Science Commission, which recently recommended a moratorium on the admission of bitemark expert testimony, and the California Supreme Court, which at the time of writing has a case before it that could "start a national dismantling of forensic odontology." As they explain further, "The rise and possible fall of bitemark identification evidence has broader implications—highlighting the weak scientific culture of forensic science and the law's difficulty in evaluating and responding to unreliable and unscientific evidence" (https://academic.oup.com/jlb/article/3/3/538/2544494/Forensic-bitemark-identification-weak-foundations).

Saks et al. (2016, page 541) add, "The claim of forensic dentists has been that they can accurately associate a bitemark to the one and only set of teeth in the world that could have produced the crime scene bitemark. However… no sound basis exists for believing that forensic dentists can perform such a feat. Despite the lack of empirical evidence to support its claims, to date no court in the United States has excluded such expert evidence for failing to meet the requisite legal standard for admission of expert testimony."

They continue, "Beliefs about the capacity of bitemark comparisons to accurately identify the source of a questioned bitemark have followed a trajectory from widespread skepticism through widespread credulity to a growing return to doubt. That growing doubt is based on the emerging realization that the field stands on a quite limited foundation of scientific fact, that there is 'a lack of valid evidence to support many of the assumptions and assertions made by forensic dentists during bitemark comparisons' (Pretty and Sweet, 2001) and that error rates by forensic dentists are perhaps the highest of any forensic identification specialty still being practiced. Bitemark testimony has been 'introduced in criminal trials without any meaningful scientific validation, determination of error rates, or reliability testing…' (NAS Report, 2009, pages 547–548)."

To restore credibility, Saks et al. (2016, page 567) suggest that "The scientific community must more carefully engage with the research foundations of forensics, and not just in landmark but in frequent national commissions; lawyers must aggressively brief challenges to foundations of forensic techniques; and judges must be far more willing to carefully examine forensic evidence before admitting it."

Experts insist that efforts are underway to improve reliability. As Butler (2015, page 4) states, "Many disciplines of forensic science, including DNA analysis, are undergoing change in the United States and around the world. New methods are being developed, validated, and put into use to help in criminal investigations. The validity and accuracy of older and even current methods are being challenged. New approaches for interpreting evidence via probabilistic modeling are being introduced. A better appreciation of difficulties that can exist for the field of forensic science is gained when the diverse cultures of scientific laboratories, law enforcement, and the legal community interact."

Butler (2015, page 5) points to the comments of Judge Harry Edwards, who co-chaired the NAS committee producing the 2009 report, who remarked, "... although there are many dedicated and skilled forensic professionals, the quality of practice in the forensic disciplines varies widely and the conclusions reached by forensic practitioners are not always reliable." Edwards adds that, "If courts blindly follow precedent that rests on unfounded scientific premises, this will lead to unjust results." Butler (2015) emphasizes that these comments "highlight an important challenge for forensic science that deals with a judicial system that is based on precedence (i.e., looking to the past) while attempting to embrace new discoveries and improvements (i.e., looking to the future)."

In order to establish improved policies, standardize and improve forensic practices, and fund research in forensic science, Butler (2015) reports that the White House Office of Science and Technology Policy (OSTP) coordinated the establishment of the Subcommittee on Forensic Science (SoFS) under the National Science and Technology Council (NSTC) to identify challenges and opportunities for addressing the 2009 NAS report recommendations.

Activities of the SoFS were coordinated through five interagency working groups (IWGs) that were each chartered with distinct objectives involving nearly 200 subject matter experts from 23 federal departments and agencies. As Butler (2015, page 7) notes, "Importantly, this effort also engaged, as advisory members, 49 individuals representing state and local forensic laboratories out of the recognition of the importance of drawing on the unique perspectives and input from the broader practitioner and criminal justice communities."

In May 2014, OSTP released a detailed report describing some of the activities and findings of the five SoFS IWGs, encompassing accreditation of forensic service providers, certification of forensic examiners, certification of medicolegal personnel, proficiency testing of forensic examiners, and a national code of ethics for forensic service providers. As Butler (2015, page 7) notes further, "Ideas and collective work generated out of the SoFS efforts have served as an important foundation for the work that is currently being carried out by the NCFS and OSAC, and many of the people involved in the SoFS are serving in these organizations."

In mid-September 2016, the President's Council of Advisors on Science and Technology (PCAST) recommended actions to strengthen forensic science and promote its more rigorous use in the courtroom. PCAST released its report, "Forensic Science in Criminal Courts: Ensuring Scientific Validity of Feature-Comparison Methods," which explored whether there are additional steps on the scientific side, beyond those already taken by the Administration in the aftermath of a highly critical 2009 National Research Council report on the state of the forensic sciences, that could help ensure the validity of forensic evidence used in the nation's legal system.

PCAST (2016) concluded that two important gaps warranted the group's attention: the need for clarity about the scientific standards for the validity and reliability of forensic methods, and the need to evaluate specific forensic methods to determine whether they have been scientifically established to be valid and reliable. The study aimed to help close these gaps for a number of forensic "feature-comparison" methods—specifically, methods for comparing DNA samples, bitemarks, latent fingerprints, firearm marks, footwear, and hair.

In the course of its year-long study, PCAST compiled and reviewed a set of more than 2000 papers from various sources, educated itself on factual matters relating to the interaction between science and the law, and obtained input from forensic scientists and practitioners, judges, prosecutors, defense attorneys, academic researchers, criminal-justice-reform advocates, and representatives of Federal agencies.

The report discusses the role of scientific validity within the legal system, explains the criteria by which the scientific validity of forensic methods can be judged, applies those criteria to the forensic feature-comparison methods mentioned above, and offers recommendations on Federal actions that could be taken to strengthen forensic science and promote its rigorous use in the courtroom. The recommendations—which are directed at the National Institutes of Standards and Technology (NIST), the White House Office of Science and Technology Policy (OSTP), the Federal Bureau of Investigation (FBI) Laboratory, the Attorney General, and the judiciary—include the following: NIST should perform regular evaluations of the scientific validity of current and newly developed forensic feature-matching technologies and should issue an annual public report on the results; NIST should take a leadership role in transforming three important feature-comparison methods—DNA analysis of complex mixtures, latent-fingerprint analysis, and firearms analysis—from currently subjective methods, with their heavy reliance on human judgment, into objective methods, in which standardized, quantifiable processes require little or no judgment; OSTP should coordinate the creation of a national forensic science research and development strategy; the FBI Laboratory should undertake a vigorous research program to improve forensic science, building on its recent important work on latent-fingerprint analysis; the Attorney General should direct attorneys appearing on behalf of the DOJ to ensure expert testimony in court about forensic feature-comparison methods meets the standards of scientific validity; the Attorney General should revise and reissue for public comment the DOJ proposed "Uniform Language for Testimony and Reports" and supporting documents to bring them into alignment with standards for scientific validity; and when deciding the admissibility of expert testimony, federal judges should take into account the appropriate scientific criteria for assessing scientific validity.

ENHANCING AND FACILITATING RESEARCH

Legal commentators have remarked upon a dearth of research in forensic science, attributed mostly to courts accepting most of the forensic identification techniques by virtue of early admissibility decisions. Giannelli (2011b) enumerates the reasons that may explain the lack of research in ensuing decades: "First, the early crime labs, as is still true today, were operational, not research, laboratories. Second, basic research can be both time-consuming and expensive, and the underfunding of crime laboratories has been chronic. Third, even if research was perceived to be desirable, these laboratories were ill-equipped to conduct it. Police officers, whose skills were developed through on-the-job training, staffed these labs. As would be expected, they were imbued with a police, not scientific, culture (https://business.highbeam.com/75261/article-1G1-250885611/forensic-science-why-no-research).

If the courts created the problem, Giannelli (2011b) says "The legal system shares responsibility for the lack of research. Experience gleaned from the DNA admissibility wars indicates that adversarial procedures sometimes do trigger research. Even the DNA proponents subsequently conceded that 'most would now agree that this extended debate has been good for the science. In contrast, there was little incentive for the government to sponsor research to validate the premises of forensic techniques that the courts had already accepted'" (https://business.highbeam.com/75261/article-1G1-250885611/forensic-science-why-no-research).

Writing further, Giannelli (2011b) says the lack of empirical research can be blamed on crime laboratories staffed by police officers with inadequate budgets and a lack of scientific training coupled with inadequacies in the legal system, which he says include "the lack of counsel, the failure to provide defense experts, and insufficient discovery." He adds, "In recent years, however, the reason for the lack of empirical research was simply a stubborn refusal to reconsider beliefs in light of credible challenges. This is the antithesis of the scientific method. As the NAS report noted, 'openness to new ideas, including criticism and refutation' is a fundamental principle of the scientific method. Instead of taking the lead in ensuring that the needed research was conducted, many forensic practitioners adopted a 'circle the wagons' mentality and attacked the critics. As a result, the opportunity for empirical research during the last decade was needlessly squandered."

One of the most notable areas addressed by both the 2009 NAS report and the 2014 progress report was forensic science research. It outlined federal funding for this research, including the $100 million-plus from the National Institute of Justice (NIJ) to fund more than 250 research and development projects related to forensic science, resulting in more than 600 scientific publications, presentations, and final technical reports listed in the National Criminal Justice Reference Service.

As we have seen earlier in this chapter, the failed Forensic Science and Standards Act of 2013 would have created a program that would have directed research efforts in the forensic sciences from a variety of federal groups. The legislation would have empowered NIST to develop a roadmap to achieve a unified federal research strategy that identifies and prioritizes research goals consistent with the 2009 NAS report. Additionally, according to Gabel (2014, pages 312–314), the Standards Act also would "provide NSF with a research grant program at an operating budget of $34 million for fiscal year 2014, increasing by $3 million each year until 2018. On top of the tremendous budget allocation, the most ambitious aspect of the Standards Act would be the creation of one or more new forensic science research centers under the auspices of the NSF. The Standards Act would establish the research center for four specific purposes: (1) to develop a plan to unify forensic research across federal agencies; (2) to 'build relationships between forensic science practitioners and members of the research community'; (3) to promote education of individuals with the aim of creating leaders in the forensic sciences; and (4) to disseminate their work."

From 2009 to 2014, a number of strides toward more and better research were taken despite legislative setbacks. In 2009 and 2010, NIJ issued a solicitation for applications for the funding of research projects to focus on expanding the scientific basis of forensic methods, developing quantifiable measures of the reliability and accuracy of forensic analyses, and developing an understanding of human factors that may affect forensic analyses—all concordant with a number of priorities identified by the 2009 NAS report. From 2011 to 2013, NIJ also issued two other core solicitations: one addressing basic scientific research (encompassing the physical, life, and cognitive sciences and is designed to increase knowledge underlying forensic science disciplines used in the criminal justice system), as well as applied research (addressing the development of highly discriminating, accurate, reliable, cost-effective, and rapid methods for identifying, analyzing, and interpreting physical evidence). Additionally, in 2013, the National Science Foundation (NSF) solicited proposals for research that addressed fundamental research questions with the potential to advance the forensic sciences. The research projects that NSF has been funding include studies on bias in lie detection, digital forensics, measurement science as it pertains to organic-compound standards setting, and skeletal biology. In recent years, the FBI Laboratory also has conducted research on friction ridge analysis, microbial forensics, the physical and chemical characteristics of improvised explosives, drug-facilitated sexual assault cases, and rapid DNA technology—resulting in a number of influential scientific publications. For example, the FBI Laboratory's research on friction ridge analysis resulted in two publications—"A Study of the Accuracy and Reliability of Forensic Latent Fingerprint Examiners" (*Proceedings of the National Academy of Sciences*, 2011) and "Repeatability and Reproducibility of Decisions by Latent Fingerprint Examiners" (*PLosOne*, 2012). Other significant publications on genetic markers for human identification as well as objective measurement techniques in firearm and toolmark analysis came out of NIST in 2013 and 2014.

The 2009 NAS report noted the need for the development of standards, guidelines, and best practices. In the years that followed, the interagency NSTC SoFS, established by OSTP, assessed a number of the challenges and opportunities facing the U.S. forensic science community and considered potential paths forward for a number of the issues raised by the NAS report. The Subcommittee's activities were coordinated through five IWGs that together involved the participation of 23 federal departments and agencies as well as state and local government partners. In 2014, OSTP was finalizing for public release a number of the Subcommittee's draft work products in the form of whitepapers on topics including accreditation, certification, professional ethics, proficiency testing, medicolegal death investigation, and standardization of reporting.

Work groups are considered to be an essential part of research; nonetheless, they came under fire in the 2009 NAS report, as Giannelli (2012) pointed out, adding that the report asserted there are no clear standards in place to determine who gains membership on standards-creating work groups (SWGs), and that neither SWGs nor their recommendations are mandated by any federal or state law or regulation. Not only are the SWG recommendations not enforceable, the report noted, but also it said that a number of SWG guidelines are too general and vague to be of any great practical use, and SWG committees have no way of knowing whether state or local agencies even endorse the standards. What's more, the report said that SWG committees do not attempt to measure the impact of their standards by formal study or survey.

According to the progress report (2014) in February 2013, DOJ and NIST announced a new initiative to accelerate efforts to strengthen forensic science through the development of improved standards. Under the initiative, discipline-specific Scientific Working Groups (SWGs), most of which were formerly overseen by DOJ components, will be reorganized and strengthened under NIST oversight.

In 2010 and 2011, NIJ and FBI created three new SWGs to develop and coordinate best practices in the areas of medicolegal death investigation, forensic toxicology, and disaster victim identification.

The Scientific Working Group for the Analysis of Seized Drugs (SWGDRUG), founded and funded by the DEA, developed a series of standards that establish a minimum basis of practice for the validation and sampling of seized drugs. Several of SWGDRUG's standards have been made into ASTM International Standards and are serving as guides for laboratories around the world. Since 2009, ASTM has revised or adopted standards relating to education and training (E2326), quality assurance (E2327), identification (E2329), sampling (E2548), validation (E2549), uncertainty (E2764), and clandestine laboratories (E2882).

In February 2012, the NIJ/NIST-led Expert Working Group on Human Factors in Latent Print Analysis released a report, "Latent Print Examination and Human Factors: Improving the Practice through a Systems Approach," with detailed recommendations for improving quality and reducing the risk of error in latent-print analysis and reporting. The publication includes a Latent Print Process Map that diagrams examiners' workflow to highlight points throughout the examination process where opportunities for error—as well as opportunities for preventing and correcting error—arise.

The NIJ/NIST-led Latent Print AFIS Interoperability Working Group has produced a number of publications to support state and local agencies in sharing fingerprint information across jurisdictions, including Writing Guidelines to Develop a Memorandum of Understanding for Interoperable Automated Fingerprint Identification Systems; Latent Interoperability Transmission Specification; and Markup Instructions for Extended Friction Ridge Features.

In April 2013, the NIJ/NIST-led Technical Working Group for Biological Evidence Preservation released The Biological Evidence Preservation Handbook: Best Practices for Evidence Handlers. This document provides best practices and guidance to ensure the integrity, prevent the loss, and reduce the premature destruction of biological evidence after collection through postconviction proceedings.

In June 2013, the NIJ/NIST-led Working Group on Forensic Science Laboratories created a Handbook for Facility Planning, Design, Construction and Relocation, a resource for laboratory directors, designers, consultants, and other stakeholders involved in the construction or major renovation of forensic laboratories.

In September 2013, the National Forensic Science Technology Center (NFSTC), a 501(c)(3) not-for-profit organization, collaborated with DOJ's Bureau of Justice Assistance (BJA), NIST, and NIJ to publish an updated edition of Crime Scene Investigation: A Guide for Law Enforcement, which provides crime scene response and prioritization guidelines, crime scene documentation and evaluation processes, and collection guidelines for specific evidence types.

The NIJ/NIST Working Group on Presenting Forensic Science Evidence Using Quantitative and Qualitative Terms (QQWG) is currently developing recommendations for reporting conclusions of forensic examinations, an important step in the process of standardizing and optimizing the presentation of quantitative and qualitative forensic science evidence to law enforcement and jurors.

In 2011, NIST conducted a review and evaluation of the accuracy of commercially available photo scales used in forensic laboratories and at crime scenes across the country. Photo scales are references used in the documentation of photographic evidence, allowing investigators to reconstruct the dimensional context of a scene. The study found a lack of consistency in product quality and accuracy and suggested pathways for establishing standards for forensic photo scales to help ensure accuracy and user confidence.

In 2013, OSTP created and filled the new position of Assistant Director for Forensic Science, under whose leadership—in consultation with NIST, DOJ, and NSF—OSTP has begun work toward the development of a National Research Strategy for Forensic Science. This ongoing effort aims to identify the most important knowledge gaps to help direct research efforts and priorities; coordinate and streamline research efforts across Federal funding entities; and foster collaboration between academic researchers and forensic practitioners. Strategies for achieving these goals include a thorough review and analysis of the current Federal forensic science research portfolio, including an analysis of the nearly 600 active federal research projects identified in 2012 by the Research, Development, Training and Education Interagency Working Group of the NSTC SoFS to identify gaps and overlap; the creation of one or more multidisciplinary forensic science research centers; and the use of incentive prizes to address specific challenges.

Also in 2013, to plan strategically for technological and research needs in the near and long term, the FBI Laboratory convened laboratory personnel to conduct a Gap Analysis and Prioritization Workshop, results of which were used by executive management for funding decisions and prioritization of research. Strengthening scientific capacity at the federal level was another goal alluded to by the 2014 progress report.

DOJ's Office of Justice Programs (OJP) established a Science Advisory Board comprising 18 highly regarded university-affiliated research scientists and practitioners. The NIJ Subcommittee of the Science Advisory Board has conducted a review of NIJ's physical science and technology portfolio and will review NIJ's forensic science program in 2014. NIJ has factored the Advisory Board's recommendations into the development of NIJ's research agenda, its engagement with the scientific community, and its dissemination of results to practitioners to enhance the impact of NIJ-funded research in the forensic science community.

In 2011, NIJ awarded a grant to RTI International (RTI) and its partners—Duquesne University, the University of North Texas Health Science Center, and Virginia Commonwealth University—to establish the Forensic Science Technology Center of Excellence (FTCoE). The FTCoE provides testing, evaluation, technology transition assistance, training and outreach, and other services for use by the forensic science community to help effectively transition emerging forensic technologies into the field. All of the Center's activities are designed to support activities that are intended for use by crime laboratories, forensic service providers (supporting criminal justice applications), law enforcement, and other criminal justice agencies to combat crime.

NIJ bolstered its peer-review process by instituting Standing Scientific Review Panels (SRPs), which have enhanced the quality and breadth of the NIJ grant-review process. In fiscal year 2012, NIJ invited SRP members to serve for two years with an option to serve for a third. NIJ plans to add new members each year so panelists serve overlapping three-year terms—an approach that will help maintain greater consistency from year to year. Additionally, a new scoring procedure used by the SRPs brings greater transparency to the peer-review process.

In 2012, the FBI Laboratory created a Research Review Team to enhance its evaluation of research project ideas, prioritize research, ensure suitable deliverables are established in research plans, encourage use of project managers to facilitate project efficiency, oversee financial and personnel obligations on research projects, and conduct frequent progress reviews of all research projects.

THE FORENSIC SCIENCE RESEARCH AGENDA

As we have seen, the 2009 NAS report was highly critical of the scientific foundations for several of the forensic disciplines, declaring that "Little rigorous systematic research has been done to validate the basic premises and techniques in a number of forensic science disciplines." and "...a statistical framework that allows quantitation... is greatly needed" (National Research Council, page 189).

In subsequent years since the report, a number of experts are making strides in advancing scientific thought in forensic science to address perennial, problematic issues. In May 2015, a workshop conducted at the American Association for the Advancement of Science (AAAS) and funded by the NIJ, the U.S. DOJ, and a number of other stakeholders assembled 17 experts in the experimental and behavioral sciences, law, policy, and government funding to address the need for a higher standard of forensic science research. A report titled "Forensic Science Research and Evaluation Workshop: A Discussion on the Fundamentals of Research Design and an Evaluation of Available Literature" summarized the presentations given at the workshop, and further established some of the key issues that face the forensic science community as it cultivates a research agenda moving forward (Bartick and Floyd, 2015).

As Bartick (2016a, page 1) observed, "With the foundations of forensic science under scrutiny, there is a general call to review the forensic science literature for strengths and weaknesses. This must be done by practitioners, and forensic scientist researchers in collaboration with academic scientists in traditional disciplines. Research articles determined to be sound science should be used to incorporate analytical methodology into standards for laboratory analysis. Currently, such standards are being addressed by the National Institute of Standards and Technology's (NIST) Organization of Scientific Area Committees (OSACs) and hopefully will be evidence-based. However, the ability of today's forensic scientists to properly evaluate the forensic literature has been called into question and a need to establish a research culture to 'place themselves on an appropriately secure foundation in the 21st century' has been postulated. This criticism relates to the training forensic scientists undergo. Typically, forensic science educational programs do not offer full courses or other opportunities for students to learn research methods in any depth. Statistics is not a requirement of the Forensic Science Education Programs Accreditation Commission (FEPAC) for a master's of forensic science graduate program. FEPAC requires a research project culminating in a report 'suitable for publication.' However, without the teaching of research methods, rigorous research is not possible. The master's level is typically the terminal degree for practitioners in the forensic sciences. Research training, extensive investigations, and publishing are required for PhD degrees and are key to the development of a research culture. In the U.S., only one recently established doctorate program currently offers a PhD in forensic science, a few universities offer interdisciplinary programs with a forensic science track, and a few programs confer PhD in forensic chemistry, forensic molecular biology, or forensic toxicology. Consequently, most practicing forensic scientists are neither equipped to evaluate the research papers of others, nor to conduct the quality of research that would be expected of an academic discipline."

Let's take a look at some of the research discussed at that 2015 workshop to illustrate the ongoing problem-solving since the 2009 NAS report.

Gatsonis (2016) emphasized that any examination of forensic science should start by recognizing its multidisciplinary nature, wherein the more advanced forensic disciplines draw methods and expertise from a variety of scientific disciplines. "For example, nuclear DNA and mitochondrial DNA analysis originated in molecular biology; and substance identification uses methods from analytical chemistry," said Gatsonis (2016, page 5). "Such forensic disciplines are generally based on solid scientific grounds because the validity of those methods has been established through past and ongoing research and development. If the analyses are executed according to the principles of science, they can be very reliable. As an example, when a sample is matched to an individual using DNA analysis, the analysis can also provide an estimate of the probability that the sample could have belonged to another individual. This is known as the random match probability and is typically very small."

Gatsonis (2016) enumerated the reasons why the science of DNA analysis rests on a solid foundation, including the extensive, peer-reviewed research behind the biological explanations for individual specific findings; the probabilities of false positives having been explored and quantified in some settings (even if only approximately); the laboratory procedures being well specified and subject to validation and proficiency testing; and the clear and repeatable standards for analysis, interpretation, and reporting. "In contrast to DNA analysis, when a fingerprint is declared a 'match' it is not yet feasible to estimate the probability that the print could belong to someone else (i.e., random match probability)," said Gatsonis (2016, page 5) "Just as concerning, examiners typically express their findings in a yes/no fashion, without reference to the error probabilities. Finally, the reproducibility of the results is different between these two types of analysis."

As we have seen, the NAS report's comment that "The level of scientific development and evaluation varies substantially among the forensic science disciplines...[w]ide variability exists across forensic science disciplines with regard to techniques, methodologies, reliability, error rates, reporting, underlying research, general acceptability, and the educational background of its practitioners" (NAS, 2009, page 5). The report calls for research to address issues of accuracy, reliability, and validity in the forensic science disciplines. In particular, the research needs include the following:

1. The conduct of studies establishing the scientific basis for demonstrating the validity of forensic methods.
2. The development and establishment of quantifiable measures of reliability and accuracy of forensic analyses. The corresponding studies should reflect as closely as possible the actual practice using realistic case scenarios and should develop estimates of performance measures that are averaged across a representative sample of forensic scientists and laboratories.
3. The development of quantifiable measures of uncertainty in the conclusions of forensic analyses.
4. The development of automated techniques capable of enhancing forensic technologies.
5. The conduct of studies of human observer bias and the sources of human error and contextual bias in forensic examinations.

Importantly, the NAS report stresses that research in the forensic sciences should be peer-reviewed and published in respected scientific journals.

Gatsonis (2016, page 6) reviewed the elements of an evaluation of the accuracy of forensic analyses, noting, "Understanding and quantifying statistical uncertainty and the magnitude of potential error in scientific results are fundamental objectives in the sciences, including the forensic sciences. For example, laboratory analyses are subject to measurement error (i.e., uncertainty about true quantity); fingerprint analyses can lead to false identification of individual prints because of observer error or low specimen quality; DNA analyses can lead to false identification of individuals because of contamination of samples or laboratory errors. Fuzzy use of language has been pervasive in discussions of errors and error rates in the forensic disciplines. In this section we describe basic concepts of the assessment of error in making the two common types of binary determinations in forensic analyses, individualization and classification. The former addresses the question of whether a piece of evidence can be attributed to a specific source. For example, was a particular fingerprint obtained from a specific individual? The latter addresses the question of whether a piece of evidence can be attributed to a class of sources. For example, was a piece of car paint obtained from a specific car model? At present, few forensic modalities have potential for addressing individualization questions but several of them have potential for addressing classification questions."

Gatsonis (2016) added that research on the accuracy and reliability of forensic modalities can benefit from paradigms developed in other branches of science, notably diagnostic medicine and clinical chemistry.

The impact that context and other cognitive factors have on human expert performance was addressed in the workshop by Dror (2016, page 53), who acknowledged, "With growing research and attention to the role of the human examiner, it is becoming very clear that bias and other cognitive issues are at the heart of forensic work. In addition to the cognitive research and literature which equivalently shows the effects of bias, the findings that human confirmation bias has contributed to forensic error and the National Academy of Sciences report have all further contributed to the transformation in the forensic sciences." Dror noted that with forensic scientists starting to receive education and training on cognitive issues, their comprehension is paving the way for further improvements in forensic science that address bias in crime scene investigations and bench analyses.

Dror (2016, page 53) gave the analogy of the misunderstanding of the work of crime scene investigators (CSIs): "The naïve view of CSIs is that they merely gather evidence from the crime scene for the forensic laboratory to examine. However, many decisions actually take place at the crime scene. CSIs have to determine where to look for evidence, whether what they find is actual data or noise, and then to decide whether evidence that they do find has sufficient information to justify sending it to the laboratory. All of these are more than mere technical collection of evidence, they are important decisions made at the crime scene, critical decisions, because they determine what evidence is collected, and what is not collected often is gone and cannot be retrieved later. Furthermore, CSIs also make clear evaluative decisions beyond those relevant to evidence collection. For example, they examine and determine bullet trajectories, analyze blood spatter patterns, and sometimes decide whether a crime has even been committed. The CSI work requires context so as to guide them in their work. However, contextual information can bias how they collect evidence, where they look for it, and their entire approach to a crime scene. For example, a detective briefing a CSI that they believe that the burglary is not real but an attempt at insurance fraud, or that the dead person did not really commit suicide but was murdered, affects how the CSI conducts their work. This is based on briefing, beliefs, that drive the CSI work prior to even arriving at the crime scene—i.e., it is not based on the actual crime scene. Similarly, investigating forensic evidence at a suspicious fire is biased if the examiner is first briefed that the owner of the property is in debt, has been unsuccessfully trying to sell the property and that they are going to get a very good payment from the fire insurance company. All of these, prior to seeing the burned property, bias the perception, interpretation and judgement of the investigator."

Potential bias in the forensic laboratories must also be addressed, according to Dror (2016, page 54), who explained, "When evidence arrives at the forensic laboratory, before it is even used for identification, it first has to be perceived. For example, a latent fingerprint mark consists of minutia (characteristics in the friction ridge flow, such as a bifurcation when it divides and separates into two). However, such analysis, the initial perception of the evidence is highly subjective and influence by a variety of cognitive factors. This is demonstrated by the variability among forensic examiners. The initial perception of the evidence is further influenced by other cognitive factors, such as the presence of another fingerprint for comparison. This is why it is critical to adopt procedures such as Linear Sequential Unmasking (LSU) which minimize cognitive biases."

Dror (2016, page 56) added that cognitive bias issues in the forensic laboratories also arise from the verification processes: "Issues around verification pertain to base-rate biases, where identifications are most often verified, thus causing an a priori expectation to verify (such cognitive issues also pertain to use of technology and database searches). Other issues pertain to the verification process not being blind, e.g., knowing who made the initial decision, what they based their decision on, etc. In fact, in many forensic laboratories, the examiners choose who will verify their work. There are other issues concerning what happens when an identification is not verified. All of these put the human examiner in the forensic laboratory in a cognitively problematic position, making it hard for them to achieve an independence of mind and make determinations based solely on the evidence."

Bias in forensic science research and literature must also be addressed, said Dror (2016, page 57) noting three main factors at play: "First, forensic science exists and operates within a non-scientific environment—what is probably even an anti-scientific adversarial legal system. Forensic science research and literature is often used in court, and that has impacted on what research is conducted, how it is conducted, and even if it is published. Second, much of the research and literature in forensic science has (and is) been produced retroactively to justify existing practices. Rather than doing the research and then devising practices based on research and data, what has transpired (and is transpiring) is the exact opposite. Forensic practices (for the most part) have developed basically without any research or data, these have been accepted by the courts, and have been practiced for decades. Then with the growing scrutiny and criticism of forensic practices, the forensic community has been working on producing and finding the research to support the existing practices. Thus, much of the research in forensic science has been motivated to underpin and justify the existing practices. This is, obviously, highly biased. This is further exacerbated by much of this research being led and conducted by the forensic examiners themselves, without proper input and guidance from non-interested parties. Furthermore, much of the literature and research is published (and reviewed) within the forensic community itself. Beyond the forensic community's perceived need and motivation to justify and underpin their existing practices (as well as defend itself from the criticism), the consequences of research findings that show major flaws in forensic work bias the way research is conducted, findings are interrupted, and the conclusions reached."

This is a major problem. Forensic research needs to be conducted "context free," that is, without the motivation to defend existing practices and fear from findings that show flaws in how forensic science is currently practiced and used in court. The literature created by forensic examiners to defend their ways has produced biased research and literature. Third, there is a basic lack of scientific culture in forensic science. In addition to the issues already stipulated above, there are further issues that pertain to the forensic community being open and transparent about what they do. For forensic research and literature to be done properly, forensic work needs to be documented, procedures and protocols should not be laboratory secrets, they (along with data) should be shared, and errors should be used for learning and improvement. These changes are not easy to make, but they (along with acknowledging limitations and uncertainties, and taking steps to minimize bias) are important in establishing a stronger scientific culture in forensic science. Without a research culture, much of the research and literature will suffer from bias.

The current state of the forensic science literature plays into the research agenda for the future by illustrating where gaps exist and exposing other weaknesses that need to be addressed in the desired culture of research for the field.

As Vosk (2016, page 60) notes, "The literature produced by the forensic sciences cannot be fully evaluated without considering the purpose of forensic science itself. Its sole reason for existing is to aid in the investigation and prosecution of crimes. The intended users of the work products of forensic science are, therefore, not just scientists, but, perhaps predominantly, laypeople who must be able to properly understand, apply, weigh and communicate them during the course of criminal investigations and legal proceedings. Accordingly, it is important that the literature produced by the forensic sciences not only be sound, but accessible to the law enforcement and legal professionals seeking to utilize forensic results. Moreover, it must be crafted with the expectation that it may be relied upon by lay jurors in determinations of guilt and innocence. Thus, to fully accomplish the mission for which forensic science was created, forensic literature must be sound and useful across four dimensions/contexts: scientific, investigative, legal and evidential."

The literature in any field can be susceptible to error and uncertainty, and Vosk (2016) enumerates five categories typically encountered in the forensic science literature: reporting of the error/uncertainty associated with methods/results; instruction on methods for determining error/uncertainty; explanation of theory underlying error/uncertainty; detailing of quality procedures; and policy discussions. Vosk (2016, page 61) explains that "No scientific method or result permits us to 'know' the truth of a particular proposition. The best that it can do is make it more or less likely. Measures of error and uncertainty provide the means by which the conclusions supported by a result can be understood and weighed."

As we have seen previously, terminology continues to vex the forensic science and medicolegal community. As Vosk (2016, page 61) observes, "A common problem encountered in the forensic literature is carelessness in the use of terminology. Concepts including error, error-rate and uncertainty are often ill defined and/or misused. For example, in the area of forensic measurements the terms error and uncertainty are often used interchangeably despite the fact that they represent completely distinct metrological concepts which convey different types of information about a measurement. As a result, authors commonly discuss and describe measurement error as if it were measurement uncertainty while being unaware of the full meaning of the former and the independent existence of the latter. This creates confusion which slows development of sound measures of error/uncertainty and undermines expert testimony relying upon these resources as their basis of knowledge."

Another shortcoming within the forensic literature according to Vosk (2016, page 61) is the mischaracterization of data and conclusions within technical papers by reported error/uncertainty: "The impacts of this are felt not just within forensic science but the courtroom where such materials are relied upon as evidence and undermine the fact-finding process. The origin of the problem is at least partly due to the fact that many subject matter experts tend to have little sophistication in experimental design and data analysis. Even when papers are submitted for peer review, the process typically relies upon reviewers with similar subject matter background and, therefore, deficits similar to those of the submitting authors. Thus, the same mischaracterizations can be found in peer reviewed as non-peer reviewed literature, albeit to a lesser extent. A possible way of addressing this situation is to encourage multi-disciplinary authorship, including both subject matter and error/uncertainty experts on publications, and, where journals are concerned, inclusion of error/uncertainty experts as reviewers prior to publication."

As Vosk (2016, page 62) says, "An area of concern not often appreciated in the evaluation of forensic science literature is the relationship between forensic science and the law itself. If forensic science is not understood by the legal professionals who work with it, the justice system will not be able to properly incorporate or have it considered. The inaccessibility of the forensic literature to many judges and lawyers, as well as lay jurors, subverts both pretrial decision-making and courtroom fact-finding processes by rendering many legal professionals and lay jurors unable to weigh claims contained within, or based upon, the literature in a manner consistent with the science therein. Rather, they are often forced to rely upon faith in the representations of a claimed expert or the acumen of legal professionals in establishing or destroying a witness's credibility when evaluating claims within or based upon the literature, neither of which may have anything to do with the scientific itself."

Vosk (2016, page 61) adds, "Although already good in some areas and improving in most others, as a whole, the forensic literature associated with error and uncertainty has not yet attained a level where it can be considered generally reliable. Nor can it be considered accessible to all those who must rely upon it. The suggestions offered herein address some of the underlying causes but not all. Use of non-peer reviewed publications as a means of self-marketing and special interest bias in the drafting of consensus standards and government forensic publications remain significant issues that must be addressed."

The NCFS identified two issues within the forensic science literature: It was unclear which literature citations were critical to support the foundation of a particular forensic science discipline, and some of the cited literature had not undergone a rigorous peer-review process.

Cole (2016, page 88) asserts that regarding the first issue, "There is a history of providing long bibliographies in support of the supposed scientific foundations of forensic disciplines. Closer inspection, in some cases, shows that the vast majority of the literature cited in these bibliographies is responsive to research questions that might be considered 'not foundational.' An example is latent print identification, for which bibliographies primarily supporting the non-foundational question of how friction ridge skin is formed were submitted in response to legal challenges to the validity of latent print analysis."

With regard to the second issue, Cole (2016) adds that "It has long been alleged that much crucial information about the forensic disciplines resides in trade journals and newsletters and that these publications fall somewhat short of the Platonic ideal of a peer-reviewed scientific journal, either by not engaging in peer review at all or, perhaps worse, by conducting a short of sham peer review with reviewers who either lacked scientific qualifications or who were interested in defending forensic science." There have long been claims that the forensic science journals were tainted by a guild mentality that may cause them to "avoid publishing anything that might reflect negatively on their field, thereby making forensic science journals forums for self-promotion rather than self-criticism."

This issue has been raised by Risinger and Saks (2003) who say they have examined reliability issues related to various forensic identification claims and identified several key issues: placing some propositions beyond the reach of empirical research; using research designs that cannot generate clear data on individual practitioner competence; manufacturing favorable test results; refusal to share data with researchers wishing to reanalyze the data; encouraging overstated interpretations of data in published research reports; making access to case data in FBI files contingent on accepting a member of the FBI as a coauthor; and burying unfavorable results in reports where they are least likely to be noticed, coupled with an unexplained disclaimer that the data cannot be used to infer the false-positive error rate they seem to indicate.

In a viewpoint document, "Establishing the Foundational Literature within the Forensic Science Disciplines," the Subcommittee on Scientific Inquiry and Research of the NCFS stated that "Scientific literature must be evaluated and be vetted through an objective and critical review process using tenets based on general scientific principles and practice. These tenets must be satisfied before any form of scientific literature is included in, and considered part of, a forensic discipline's scientific foundation."

The NCFS stated that "foundational scientific literature supportive of forensic practice" should meet a number of criteria: It should be subjected to independent and external peer review; it should be published in standard academic books and journals with ISBNs or ISSNs; the editors and editorial boards should be expert in the field; and the journals should have ethics and conflict of interest codes, be free searchable, and be indexed.

The NCFS also suggested that the following tenets of literature review should be considered in a critical review process that evaluates the merit of an individual article: Does the publication adhere to the guidelines stated in the NCFS viewpoint document "Scientific Literature in Support of Forensic Science and Practice"? Is the problem or hypothesis clearly stated? Is the scope of the article clearly stated as appropriate (article, case study, review, technical note, etc.)? Is the literature review current, thorough, and relevant to the problem being studied? Does this work fill a clear gap in the literature or is it confirmatory and/or incremental? Are the experimental procedures clear and complete such that the work could be easily reproduced? Are the experimental methods appropriate to the problem? Are the methods fully validated to the necessary level of rigor (fit for purpose)? Are the data analysis and statistical methodology appropriate for the problem, and explained clearly so it can be reproduced? Are the experimental results clearly and completely presented and discussed? Are omissions and limitations to the study discussed and explained? Are the results and conclusions reasonable and defensible based on the work and the supporting literature? Are the citations and references complete and accurate? Are the references original (primary) and not secondary? Are funding sources and other potential sources of conflict of interest clearly stated?

As Cole (2016, page 89) observes, "The NCFS suggests that forensic science literature more faithfully emulate the familiar mainstream scientific literature. No one could dispute that these criteria are useful minimum standards for a scientific literature. But will enforcement of these criteria allow us to trust the forensic science literature?"

The answer might be no, according to some commentators. Giannelli (2010, page 44) emphasizes that "Scientists with impeccable credentials should conduct the needed research. Moreover, they should be independent of law enforcement. The most thorough and well-reasoned reports in the field have come from impartial scientific investigations, most done by the NAS, including reports on voiceprints, DNA, polygraph, and bullet lead analysis. The process should also be transparent. Scientists are generally expected to exchange research data as well as unique research materials that are essential to the replication or extension of reported findings. The government has not only failed to conduct the needed research, it has thwarted efforts to do so. Indeed, conduct rivals that of some private corporations such as the tobacco industry—shaping the research agenda, limiting access to data, attacking experts who disagree with its positions, and 'spinning' negative reports. Currently, we have the worst of two possible worlds. Basic research in the forensic sciences is weak, and the only agency currently capable of funding research, the DOJ, is sabotaging efforts to conduct rigorous independent studies. The NAS report on forensic science provides a blueprint for rectifying this problem. Adoption of all recommendations would be the most important development in forensic science since the establishment of the crime laboratory in the mid-1920s."

As we saw in Chapter 2, scientific fraud in publishing—both within and outside of the forensic community—has made the headlines recently. As Cole (2016, page 90) notes, breaches in trust remind us that the scientific literature "does not serve as a seamless, always reliable conveyor of trustworthy information. Criticisms of the scientific literature and the peer review process that supposedly polices the integrity of most of it are so legion as to defy recitation. Most informed commentators today would view it as naïve to think of peer review as a powerful quality control mechanism rather than as 'just as a rough-and-ready preliminary filter.' ... High-profile frauds have continued to be exposed in natural science, medicine, and social science.... The retraction of scientific papers has become so common that the phenomenon has its own dedicated web site, and many disciplines and scientific institutions, including the National Science Foundation and American Association for the Advancement of Science, are concerned about crises of irreproducibility. The claims described above about lack of integrity in forensic peer review don't seem out of ordinary when considering scandals in mainstream scientific peer review."

Cole (2016, page 91) adds, "We should be cautious about assuming that the adoption of prevailing peer review and publication practices in mainstream science would be a panacea for whatever ills forensic science suffers. To be sure, the NCFS's suggestions should be uncontroversial, and the forensic science enterprise would probably benefit from trying to satisfy them. In concluding, I will offer some remarks that suggest that the process of generating trust in the forensic science literature may be more complicated than simply imitating the familiar attributes of mainstream scientific literature."

Cole (2016, page 92) reminds us that a very small percentage of forensic scientists actively engage in scientific discovery, so the forensic literature will reflect this fact: "We should expect a far greater portion to be engaged in relatively routine application of assays whose properties are relatively well understood. We should expect the needs that such groups have from 'the literature' to be quite different. And, finally we might expect there to be other small groups—case managers, laboratory directors, etc.—whose needs might be different still. In sum, we need to design a forensic literature that meets the needs of forensic scientists as we reasonably expect them to be in order to deliver forensic services. We do not want to design a forensic literature that merely imitates the mainstream scientific literature much of which is primarily oriented toward discovery science."

While it's true that not all forensic scientists will be adding to the knowledge base, the NCFS is trying to champion projects to facilitate more research into practice. On March 22, 2016, the NCFS voted to adopt its "Recommendations to the Attorney General to Fund Post-Doctoral Projects to Facilitate Translation for Research into Forensic Science Practice." In this document, the NCSF recommends that the DOJ develop and implement a grant program specifically directed toward funding multiyear postdoctoral fellowships (or the medicolegal equivalent) at federal, state, and local forensic science service providers (FSSPs) and forensic medicine service providers (FMSPs).

The NCFS states that one way to support advanced research at the postdoctoral level is to link cutting-edge science with current and future application needs and new directions in the forensic science community: "The NCFS believes that translational models must be developed to ensure that current research is integrated into forensic laboratories in a timely way that does not disrupt the workflow within them. Importantly, these models should also be directed toward integrating a research culture within the forensic sciences by creating a new path for research scientists that can lead to careers with FSSPs."

The goals of postdoctoral positions would be to attract early-career scientists to posts in which their research skills can be developed so as to benefit the individual awardee and facilitate scientific transfer from the academic environment to practice within forensic laboratories; incentivize the promotion and implementation of research within host organizations; publish original validated methodologies or results of forensic science community investigations; generate a cadre of scientifically trained investigators capable of establishing their own research programs in forensic science; and enhance communication between academia and forensic laboratories.

The NCFS says it believes that "bridging the existing gap between the academic research aspects of forensic science and the daily reality faced by practitioners in casework laboratories is vital to the scientific evolution of the profession. Bridging this divide presents an opportunity for nurturing the incorporation of promising research into forensic practice."

Regarding an implementation strategy, the NCFS says grants should be based on demonstrated partnerships between an academic institution and an FSSP or FMSP laboratory and linked to ongoing or recently completed NIJ research projects. The NCFS says the following criteria should be considered in the award of such grants: The principal investigator for the project should be the laboratory director, although the fellow may work directly with other laboratory staff on- or off-site at the laboratory director's discretion. The grant should emphasize a demonstrated partnership between an academic institution and the forensic laboratory. This would provide an academic environment for the trainee, who in turn would help forge closer bonds between academia and the laboratory. An academician may be a co-PI, but the intent of this program is to fund activities of the fellow in residence at a forensic laboratory. Salary and benefits should be commensurate with the needs of a postdoctoral fellow to work on-site at the forensic laboratory for two to three years. The grant should fund the cost of the project, including instrumentation as needed. The grants should be part of an integrated program in which the postdoctoral fellows interact with each other and meet on a regular basis for discussions, mentoring, and presentations. Proposed outcomes of the award should include publication of results of the projects in peer-reviewed journals, which promotes both the foundation of forensic sciences and the culture of publication in a forensic science laboratory, and is a necessary component for postdoctoral fellows' careers.

One of the more noteworthy developments within the realm of bolstering forensic science research is coming out of the American Association for the Advancement of Science (AAAS), which is conducting an analysis of the underlying scientific bases for the forensic tools and methods currently used in the criminal justice system. This project will evaluate the scientific underpinning of forensic practices, and, where these fall short, recommend a research agenda for the field.

Runkle (2016, page 76) reports that "Within months of the first Commission meeting, AAAS began an effort, funded by the Laura and John Arnold Foundation, responsive to the concerns raised regarding the state of the science. This project will evaluate the quality of the studies the forensic community relies on to support their practices and, where the scientific underpinning of these practices falls short, to recommend areas requiring further study. This gap analysis will produce a research agenda to serve as the basis for arriving at forensic methods that will inspire greater confidence in our criminal justice system. Although this analysis has been long needed, and many in the public and private sphere have urged its implementation, the AAAS project will be the first attempt to fill this void. At long last, there will be a rigorous evaluation of current forensic tools and methods, enabling justice to proceed as it should. Importantly, there will be a research agenda to guide scientists and funders."

As the AASS acknowledges, "For many years, there have been claims that the forensic sciences are neither valid nor reliable and may not meet the admissibility standards established by the U.S. Supreme Court in its 1993 Daubert ruling. The claims were underscored in a 2009 report of the National Research Council that found that forensic science as currently practiced has 'little systematic research to validate the discipline's basic premises and techniques.' This report does not, however, specify what in the literature supports current forensic practice and what does not, nor does it provide a research agenda for moving forward" (Runkle, 2016).

AAAS will fill this void by conducting a quality and gap analysis of 10 forensic disciplines. Working groups will be appointed for each forensic field, and an advisory committee will advise on every aspect of the overall project. As Runkle (2016, page 77) notes, "Recognizing that we anticipate that some forensic practitioners may 'push back' on any critiques of their work, so one forensic practitioner in the field under study will be included in each Working Group. The other Working Group members will be basic scientists or other technical experts appropriate to each forensic area, for example, physicists or statisticians."

Reports will be issued for each of the fields, indicating what research would strengthen the scientific foundation for that area. These project reports are expected to encourage basic research and contribute to improving the quality of forensic science used in the legal system. The project's impact will be transformational for the criminal justice system, enabling the public to have confidence that the ability to convict the guilty and exonerate the innocent is enhanced.

Although AAAS will evaluate all 10 of the forensic fields considered by the RDTE IWG, with the advice of the Advisory Committee, Runkle (2016) reports that three fields are being investigated in the first phase: fire investigation, firearms and toolmarks, and latent fingerprints. The work groups will attempt to answer a number of inquiries, including the following:

- *For fire investigation*: What literature exists that describes how basic science in the physics and chemistry of fires is translated into the practice of burn pattern analysis for practitioners? What is the literature that describes the key investigative issues that must be considered when performing burn pattern analysis and arson investigation at the crime scene? What literature exists that describes studies on understanding how cognitive bias may affect burn pattern analysis and arson investigations?
- *For firearms and toolmarks*: What literature documents the scientific domains used to inform the foundations of firearm/toolmark analysis? What research has been completed, if any, to determine the threshold for identification (individualization)? What studies have been performed to determine the error rates in firearm and toolmark analyses?
- *For latent fingerprints*: What scientific literature describes how distinct or similar fingerprints are across the overall population, related individuals, or identical twins? What scientific literature establishes the key sources of bias and characterizes the effectiveness or measures to mitigate the bias? What scientific literature characterizes the effect of analyst qualifications/experience on fingerprint matching accuracy?

According to Runkle (2016, page 78), "The recommendations emerging from this project promise to be transformative to the criminal justice system. Given the demand for this type of project from both public and private domains, along with the stature AAAS has in the scientific community and beyond, the reports coming forth from the project are likely to attract wide attention. AAAS views these reports as a way to encourage basic, traditional scientists to pursue the research topics raised in the reports and funding agencies to support these scientists. The reports will be a contribution to injecting a 'culture of science' into forensic research. The results of this project, scheduled to be completed in 2017, are expected to transform forensic science research and to improve the practice of forensic science, while boosting the public's confidence in the U.S. criminal justice system."

The AAAS project will add to the knowledge base already built by the various working groups in existence for the last decade following the 2009 NAS report. As Runkle (2016, page 75) notes, "The NAS report was a good start on improving forensic science and, coming from such a prestigious organization, has been widely quoted and influential. Nevertheless, in its overall critique of forensic science, it did not specifically point to the areas where the practices are supported by sound research and where they are not. And while it called for research from the 'scientific community,' it did not provide a research agenda to aid that community, including funding agencies."

In an effort to follow through on the NAS report, the NSTC Committee on Science established a SoFS in July 2009. SoFS' charter defines its purpose as advising and assisting the Executive Office of the President on policies, procedures and plans related to forensic science in criminal justice. SoFS members were told to emphasize "developing practical and timely approaches to enhancing the validity and reliability...in forensic science." Runkle (2016, page 75) reports that in May 2012, the SoFS charter was reauthorized and encouraged to "create a prioritized forensic science research agenda through a comprehensive gap analysis or other appropriate means."

SoFS appointed five IWGs. Among the IWGs, one—the Research, Development, Testing, and Evaluation IWG (RDTE IWG)—was tasked with addressing that "encouragement." RDTE IWG members realized they could create neither a gap analysis nor a research agenda without first ascertaining what literature already existed. Members drew up a set of questions for 10 forensic fields: bitemarks, bloodstain patterns, digital evidence, fiber evidence, fire investigation, firearms and toolmarks, footwear and tire tracks, hair evidence, latent fingerprints, and paints and coatings. The answers to these questions were deemed critical in determining whether or not a particular discipline was valid and reliable. The members sent the questions to relevant forensic entities representing these fields, asking them to identify books, articles, or other sources that supported the questions. The result of this effort, while not a gap analysis, was an important step on the way to that goal, providing future investigators with an annotated bibliography for each of the 10 fields. In May 2014, the NSTC issued a report—"Strengthening Forensic Science"—based on the conclusions reached by each of the five IWGs that together constituted the SoFS. The report stated that the RDTE IWG had "pursued the identification of foundational research that can be mapped to specific principles across the various disciplines of forensic science" (Runkle, 2016, page 75).

Other entities continue to address thorny topics in the profession. In early May 2016, NIST hosted a technical colloquium on a critical inquiry facing just about every branch of forensic science today—how should forensic examiners quantify the weight of evidence they find in a case? This was the first technical colloquium in the United States to focus specifically on this issue, and it generated a lively exchange of ideas. As forensic practitioners experience it daily, the weight-of-evidence question comes up whenever a forensic examiner assesses the likelihood that a piece of evidence left at a crime scene originated from a particular source. For example, a ballistics examiner compares a bullet found at a crime scene to a bullet that was test-fired from a suspect's gun. After comparing the surface patterns on the two bullets, the expert might testify in court on the likelihood that they were or were not fired from the same weapon. But how should the expert quantify that likelihood? How should they account for the possibility that the pattern on the bullet found at the scene was actually caused by a different but similar weapon? The chances might be extremely remote, but when a person's liberty hangs in the balance, quantifying the weight of evidence is a critical step toward a just outcome.

As we have seen, the need to quantify the weight of evidence was highlighted in the 2009 NAS report that urgently called for strengthening the practice of forensic science in the United States. NIST, along with the DOJ, is leading an effort to do just that. However, the best way to quantify the weight of evidence has been debated vehemently by experts with divergent and strongly held opinions on the subject, and the purpose of the colloquium, held at the NIST campus in Gaithersburg, Maryland, was to open a dialogue that might eventually lead to a consensus. Participants included forensic practitioners, forensic science researchers, and members of the legal and law enforcement communities.

Speaking at the colloquium, NIST's John Butler pointed to the culture clash that exists between science and the law, in that the legal community looks to the past (where precedence is desired), while the scientific community looks to the future (where evolving improvement is desired). Butler also acknowledged the tension between the two disciplines when the legal community wants finality and absolutes (guilty or not guilty court decisions), while the scientific community operates without certainty (rarely with probabilities of 0 or 1). Butler also spoke of the nomenclature-related challenges, where lawyers and scientists "often talk past each other because we do not appreciate a subtle or significant difference in the meaning of a word or phrase. A prime example of this is when 'validity' or 'validation' can mean something very different to lawyers than to scientists and forensic practitioners" (https://www.nist.gov/sites/default/files/documents/2016/12/07/02_butler_-_nist_quantifying_the_weight_of_evidence_-_may_2016.pdf).

Butler, who addressed the Jurisprudence Section at the 2015 meeting of the American Academy of Forensic Sciences (AAFS) with a presentation titled "Why DNA Interpretation Has Become More Challenging in Recent Years," shared his thoughts with the 2016 colloquium audience, explaining the five factors: more sensitive DNA test results; more touch evidence samples that are poor-quality, low-template, complex mixtures; more options exist for statistical approaches involving probabilistic genotyping software; many laboratories are not prepared to cope with complex mixtures; and more loci being added because of the large number of samples in DNA databases. Butler explained that forensic scientists are at the intersection of several key trends; the incredible success of DNA has led to more sensitive methods and more samples being provided, which has led to more complex mixtures that are pushing the boundaries of the current science. Additionally, statistical interpretation techniques have not kept pace with the methodology improvements, in that much of the forensic DNA community is effectively using a 1992 statistical tool (CPI) on twenty-first century data (Butler, 2016).

"We didn't want to direct the conversation, we just wanted to start it," says Elham Tabassi, an expert in fingerprint analysis and one of the NIST scientists who organized the event. "We wanted a free flow of ideas, and that definitely took place" (https://www.nist.gov/news-events/news/2016/06/how-quantify-weight-forensic-evidence-lively-debate).

"Published papers and rebuttals can go on forever," adds Reva Schwartz, another NIST scientist who organized the event. "But having so many people in the same room really moved the conversation forward" (https://www.nist.gov/news-events/news/2016/06/how-quantify-weight-forensic-evidence-lively-debate).

Among other things, participants discussed likelihood ratios, which have emerged as a leading method for quantifying the weight of evidence. Likelihood ratios compare the probabilities of two events—for instance, the probability of observing the features of a latent print left at a crime scene if the print was made by the suspect compared to the probability of observing those features if the print was made by some other, unknown, individual. A very high likelihood ratio indicates that the evidence is powerful; however, there is no firm consensus yet on how exactly to calculate a likelihood ratio, or even if that is the best approach to quantifying the weight of evidence.

"I think it's fair to say that there were intense, though always respectful, discussions on quantifying the weight of evidence using likelihood ratios, including their limitations and different statistical approaches to implementing them" (https://www.nist.gov/news-events/news/2016/06/how-quantify-weight-forensic-evidence-lively-debate), Tabassi says.

One of the problems, she notes, is that certain words mean different things to different people, and an important next step will be to settle on common language. Schwartz and Tabassi plan to publish a technical review of the colloquium as well as establish an online forum where the conversation can continue. At the time of writing, the next installment of this colloquium was planned for the summer of 2017.

So much of the dialogue centers on achieving more and improved information of value, and Tjin-A-Tsoi (2013) says that forensic laboratories can increase the value of the data they provide in at least three ways. The first is by increasing reliability by strengthening objectivity and scientific underpinning. The second is by providing more information at "activity" level (such as information that reveals how traces fit together in larger patterns of crime-related activity). Finally, laboratories can enhance the information they offer by developing tools and methods that bring to light traces that have hitherto been unavailable because they are imperceptible to the human senses. End users also are pushing forensic practitioners to deliver their results more expediently, and going forward, forensic entities will need to address the backlog issue, improve process management, and create new, faster technologies.

Concepts that have worked in the corporate world, such as the methodology known as Lean Six Sigma, may be considered for the forensic entity. As Tjin-A-Tsoi (2013, page 15) observes, "Historically, the field of forensic science is a collection of communities of craftsmen and highly educated experts in a large number of different fields. Forensic laboratories often contain many different forensic disciplines and sometimes tend to resemble a collection of fiefdoms. Deep interdisciplinary cooperation is relatively rare, and individualism is an often-dysfunctional part of the culture. Practitioners in the field of forensic science are highly committed, closely focused on the content and quality of their work and, in general, not particularly interested in process management, efficiency, delivery times, costs or other matters of this nature. Because of this, process optimization has been somewhat neglected, resulting in practices that are often less efficient than they should be. By applying modern process redesign methods, spectacular progress can be made toward faster delivery times, higher productivity and lower costs. Process redesign can also help with backlog reduction. Many of these methods are data-driven and quantitative, which means that natural scientists and engineers can relate to the methodology."

TECHNICAL MERIT STANDARDS

In June 2016, the NCFS made to the U.S. Attorney General a number of recommendations regarding technical merit standards. The first recommendation was that NIST should establish an in-house entity with the capacity to conduct independent scientific evaluations of the technical merit of test methods and practices used in forensic science disciplines.

As the 2009 NAS report noted, there exists "substantial evidence indicating that the level of scientific development and evaluation varies substantially among the forensic science disciplines" and that a "body of research is required to establish the limits and measures of performance and to address the impact of sources of variability and potential bias" (NAS, 2009, page 7). As the NCFS points out, currently, no independent national scientific entity or organization has been charged with the independent evaluation of technical merit studies for forensic science test methods, and adds, "In order to ensure that the evaluations of forensic science tests, methods and practices are rigorous, reliable, uniform, consistent, fair, and impartial, it is critical that a single independent scientific agency be responsible for this work. NIST is an independent science agency and has the intellectual resources to assemble the necessary knowledge base. However, NCFS recognizes that NIST is a non-regulatory agency and is not recommending that NIST's function here will be regulatory in nature" (https://www.justice.gov/ncfs/file/865156/download).

A second recommendation from NCFS was that the results of the evaluations will be issued by NIST as publicly available resource documents: "NIST's evaluation may include but is not limited to: research performed by other agencies and laboratories, its own intramural research program, or research studies documented in already published scientific literature. NIST should initially begin its work by piloting three resource documents to establish their design and requirements. The release of these documents should be broadly disseminated in the scientific and criminal justice communities and accompanied by judicial trainings" (NCFS, n.d.b).

While NIST may have a centralized evaluative role, the NCFS encourages universities, scientific agencies, and other research entities (e.g., the Statistical and Applied Mathematical Sciences Institute [SAMSI] and the Center for Statistics and Applications in Forensic Evidence [CSAFE]) to conduct research investigating the technical merit of forensic science disciplines. NIST will evaluate these data, reports, and studies generated by this robust and diverse scientific research community. The resulting resource documents will be continually updated as the state of the science develops. Centralizing the evaluative role will facilitate the development of a knowledge base at NIST that will build over time.

A third recommendation from NCFS is that the OSAC for Forensic Science leadership, the Forensic Science Standards Board (FSSB), should commit to placing consensus documentary standards on the OSAC Registry of Approved Standards for only those forensic science test methods and practices where technical merit has been established by NIST, or in the interim, established by an independent scientific body. An example of an interim independent scientific body could be an OSAC created Technical Merit Resource Committee composed of measurement scientists and statisticians appointed by NIST and tasked with the evaluation of technical merit.

As the NCFS states, "All three recommendations are consistent with NIST's mission, statutory function, and delegated responsibilities in the Memorandum of Understanding. These three recommendations are founded on the principle that forensic science tests, methods and practices should be subject to independent scientific evaluation before they are used in judicial proceedings. The vision and hope of the NCFS is that NIST will develop resource documents for all forensic science disciplines, but that process will take time. In the interim, proponents of a forensic science test method or practice can seek technical merit evaluation from another independent scientific body, such as a technical merit resource committee within OSAC" (NCFS, n.d.b).

Even as the community figures out its research infrastructure, a number of interesting developments are taking place. In the 2015 report, "The Impact of Forensic Science Research and Development," the NIJ noted, "Forensic science R&D in the 1980s laid the groundwork for advances in the 1990s and early 2000s that had a profound impact on crime laboratories. Although the scientific advances, particularly the growth of DNA testing, provided more effective tools for analyzing evidence and identifying perpetrators, they also led to a dramatic increase in the demand for lab services. By the late 1990s and through the 2000s, demand outstripped the ability of the labs to respond quickly and efficiently. Today, scientists and technicians at forensic labs are under relentless pressure to produce results faster and at lower cost" (NIJ, 2015).

NIJ employs a two-pronged approach to supporting forensic labs. In the short term, NIJ awards grants to labs that cover the increasing costs of processing cases, assist in DNA backlog reduction, and support ongoing efforts to adopt more advanced instrumentation and analytical methods. In the long term, NIJ awards grants to scientists to conduct research, both basic and applied, that can lead to methods, techniques, and technology that will advance forensic science and, ultimately, public safety and justice.

As the NIJ (2015, page 4) explains, "Innovation is an essential way to assist crime labs. For example, high-tech robotic workstations can now process large numbers of DNA samples simultaneously, allowing crime labs to work more efficiently. NIJ-supported research helped in the development of fully automated systems that amplify DNA from small samples to determine a person's genetic profile. The workstations not only make labs more efficient but also lower the cost of DNA processing. NIJ is also funding several projects that seek to apply more sophisticated methods to detect and analyze evidence. Examining evidence for trace amounts of blood or other biological material is time consuming for law enforcement and crime lab personnel, and it requires techniques that can compromise or destroy evidence. One NIJ-funded project involves developing a camera with multispectral and fluorescence imaging capabilities to detect and identify fingerprints, body fluids, stains and other residues at crime scenes. Such imaging technology would make it easier for investigators to find and process evidence while minimizing evidence contamination. Researchers working on another NIJ-supported project are developing methods that will allow investigators to identify the body fluids in a stain without destroying any of the stained material. Researchers are also exploring how to use one sample to determine multiple pieces of information, such as body fluid type and genetic information associated with identity."

The NIJ (2015) adds, "The growing demands for evidence processing in recent years have clearly shown that labs must move to more efficient and sophisticated methods and procedures. Scientific and technological advances made possible through strong support for research will be essential to ensuring that crime labs keep pace with increasing demand."

An NIJ grant was the genesis of the research conducted by John M. Butler and was part of the beginning of the evolution of DNA testing with a forensic science application. Butler, who is special assistant to the director for forensic science in the NIST's Special Programs Office, says that the $70,000 NIJ grant awarded to the University of Virginia (UVA) in 1993 launched his journey into forensic science.

But an interest in solving mysteries dates back to Butler's childhood. "When I was a kid I read Sherlock Holmes and Encyclopedia Brown stories that ignited my imagination," says Butler, who even penned a NIST internal communications (March 10, 2016) called "Sherlock Holmes and Me" that alluded to his interest in all things forensic.

"I was in seventh grade when I first got interested in both science and law," Butler recalls. "I had a biology teacher my freshman year of high school when I was 14 who really turned me on to getting excited about science. One of the neatest experiences I have had in my life was about eight years ago when I had a chance to return to my hometown in Missouri where I grew up and give my biology teacher one of the books I had written. I signed it for him and thanked him for inspiring me to get into science. I am grateful for the good experiences with science that I had as a teenager, and I have always been interested in learning. I have read thousands of books over the course of my life. I love reading and have always been that way. It's the search for knowledge and trying to gain more information and that's why I love living in the information age where there is so much to learn. I love the research aspect to all of this and I have always loved solving puzzles—Rubik's cube came out in seventh grade and learned to solve it, as I have always enjoyed solving puzzles."

Butler used these skills to tackle one of the most significant challenges related to capillary electrophoresis (CE) to speed up and automate DNA testing of short tandem repeats (STRs). As Butler explains in an NIJ interview, analytical chemists Ralph Allen at UVA and Bruce McCord at the FBI Academy's Forensic Science Research and Training Center in Quantico, Virginia, were conducting research on CE in 1993 when they recruited Butler, who had just completed his first year of graduate coursework at UVA, and began working at the FBI Laboratory. "The FBI supplied the instruments and the samples. I was the labor force in developing new methods involving CE. Little did I know that my work in this NIJ–UVA–FBI experiment would help pioneer the DNA analysis technique that is used worldwide today," Butler says.

He continues, "While working in Quantico, I volunteered to help on another project, which was looking for a rapid method to accurately determine the amount of DNA sample to put into mitochondrial DNA (mtDNA) sequencing reactions. I was able to use my CE instrument to actively analyze mtDNA polymerase chain reaction (PCR) products. Our team collaborated with the FBI's Forensic Science Research Unit, and by the end of that first summer, our hard work had paid off: We had a working method for extracting, amplifying and sequencing mtDNA from human hair."

That same year, Butler was developing new methods and exploring optimal conditions for rapid CE separation of STR markers, and published his first paper in 1994. Butler presented his research findings and reviewed the mtDNA quantitation technique he had developed in Quantico at the annual meeting of the American Academy of Forensic Sciences. "What really got everyone's attention was that, using the CE method, I performed the world's fastest separation of an STR allelic ladder at the time—a mere five minutes. This was revolutionary because the separation method used at that time (slab gel electrophoresis) was labor-intensive, was not automated and provided poorly quantifiable results in two to three hours."

Butler continued his graduate research and in 1995, discovered that Applied Biosystems, a primary supplier of forensic DNA reagents and instrumentation, was about to release a new CE instrument and STR kits. He notes, "My graduate work—and that initial NIJ research grant—helped pioneer the technique that soon became the primary workhorse for DNA testing worldwide" (https://nij.gov/journals/276/Pages/butler.aspx).

Butler says that over the years, NIJ funding has continued to make his research possible. "After I served as a National Research Council postdoctoral fellow at NIST and the Armed Forces DNA Identification Laboratory (AFDIL), an NIJ grant took me to the West Coast. Chris Becker, the president and CEO of a start-up company named GeneTrace Systems, Inc., based in Menlo Park, California, recruited me to work on rapid analysis of STRs using time-of-flight mass spectrometry. The NIJ-funded work involved collaborating with the California Department of Justice, then located across the San Francisco Bay in Berkeley. I visited the department, which helped me better understand the challenges facing forensic laboratories and thus ensure that the DNA methods I developed would improve the capabilities of crime-solving laboratories. When GeneTrace Systems decided to no longer pursue forensic DNA analysis, NIJ funding once again made it possible for me to change coasts. I returned to NIST to continue with my forensic science interests. Annual funding provided through an interagency agreement between NIJ and NIST's Office of Law Enforcement Standards helped us create a world-class research group during the first decade of the 21st century. Throughout my career, NIJ funding has allowed me to conduct meaningful research, write books that have influenced the field, and interact with the scientific and legal communities. Hopefully, the funds that NIJ has invested in me have made, and will continue to make, a difference for good."

Butler received his bachelor of science degree in chemistry from Brigham Young University in 1992 and his doctorate degree in chemistry in 1995 from the University of Virginia. In the fall of 1995, Butler joined NIST as a postdoctoral fellow. He spent two years in the commercial sector, working for Gene Trace Systems between 1997 and 1999, and then returned to NIST as a fellow and group leader of the Applied Genetics Group in the Biochemical Science Division.

Butler has authored a number of seminal textbooks, including *Fundamentals of Forensic DNA Typing* in 2009 and *Advanced Topics in Forensic DNA Typing: Methodology* in 2011. His papers have resonated in the field as well. According to Science Watch (2011), Butler's 2003 *Journal of Forensic Sciences* article, "The Development of Reduced Size STR Amplicons as Tools for Analysis of Degraded DNA," has been cited more than 100 times, ranking it among the field's top-five most cited since 2001.

Butler credits chemistry as being at the heart of everything he has been able to accomplish in his career. "Chemistry helps you think critically and analytically, to question everything and to have the desire to learn. I attended Brigham Young University as an undergraduate and instead of studying biology I studied chemistry. Even though I loved biology more, I saw that the chemistry program was more rigorous and I became interested in how you get information out of instruments and how you learn from that data. As an example, the problem I have with just a general forensic science degree is in many cases you are just giving information, you are not teaching people how to design an experiment and how to think critically about whatever tests they are conducting."

Butler continues, "When I got to graduate school I studied analytical chemistry. I still had the desire to study biology and conduct DNA work, so that led to the connection between analytical chemistry and biology for DNA measurements. My dissertation was on measuring DNA separations and measuring DNA with capillary electrophoresis which is the technique used worldwide, so I was the first person back in the early 1990s to actually do separation of DNA and type the DNA molecule for forensic purposes with the technique now that is used everywhere."

As a pioneer in DNA, Butler says he derives great satisfaction from seeing what he helped develop grow in its impact on science. "It has been a lot of fun to see and it motivates me to keep working, keep learning and keep trying to share knowledge," Butler says. "Part of that also comes from my background, my family and growing up on a farm. I've always had the desire to help other people, caring and serving others. I relish the opportunity to help other people and work for the betterment of society."

Butler has used that desire to serve others in his work as vice chair of the NCFS, a federal advisory committee to the DOJ that is working to improve the interface between science and the law. Butler also has written 5 textbooks defining the field of forensic DNA analysis, published more than 150 peer-reviewed articles and invited book chapters, and presented 300-plus invited talks and training workshops.

"People either have jobs or they have careers," says Butler, when describing his work ethic. "Some people just have a job they go to with the one goal of bringing home a paycheck. I see my work as a career that I will enjoy long term, and I believe that if you can enjoy going to work and then enjoy going home, you're probably a happy person. I feel like I am very blessed in that regard—I have a great family that I enjoy going home to at night and I also love my job and I can't wait to get to work. It's not a job to me, it's a career and a chance to make a difference and to serve others and to have a positive impact on society."

Butler says the most successful practitioners demonstrate a constant curiosity, something that can be nurtured in students when coursework is structured to promote critical thinking skills and foster an innate interest in continual learning. "We need people to dig deeper and really understand what they are learning from the educational system," Butler says. "We need more statistical analysis and statistics training, designing experiments; digging deeper and really thinking about the problem at hand is very important."

Butler says that scientists must engage fully with their colleagues in forensic science. In a recent NIJ interview, Butler comments, "I've learned many things over the last 20 years. One of the most important is that to fully understand the problems that need to be solved, you must visit forensic laboratories and speak with the scientists about challenges they face. It is always best to understand the problem before producing a meaningless solution, which can sometimes happen with undirected research efforts. Once you complete your research, conduct training workshops in the laboratories and online to help translate research results into practice. Regular communication between researchers and practitioners is essential to move fields forward" (https://nij.gov/journals/276/Pages/butler.aspx).

Butler also advises that graduate students seize every opportunity they can to jump-start their research experience early. In the NIJ interview, Butler explains, "I would encourage university professors to give graduate students an opportunity to present their work at major conferences and help prepare them to succeed. As for students, collect and read everything available in the scientific literature about the problems you are trying to solve. Then write, rewrite and rewrite again until you can produce polished publications. The currency of scientific research is getting your results published in a peer-reviewed journal. I have found that ideas for new research projects come as you pay attention to details in the articles you read, especially if you are reading more broadly than just in your area of focus. As Isaac Newton famously shared with a colleague, 'If I have seen further it is by standing on the shoulders of giants.' Innovative research ideas come from connecting dots that, in many cases, earlier scientific research has already defined. Knowing the literature in your field and in complementary ones helps you move your field forward. Perhaps one day, future researchers will view your work as a 'giant,' from which they will be able to see further" (https://nij.gov/journals/276/Pages/butler.aspx).

RESEARCH FUNDING

As the 2009 NAS report notes, "Student research and exposure to research is a critical component of an appropriate forensic science education. Research funding supports both faculty and graduate student research. Funding also supports the acquisition and maintenance of equipment and major research instrumentation and laboratory renovation" (NAS, 2009, page 230).

As noted in Chapter 2, the level of funding for forensic science research programs is seen by many observers as inadequate; in order for universities to run graduate-level programs in the science, research dollars must be made available. However, the amounts of such R&D funds available to support forensic science at the NIJ are small and are all but nonexistent from the NSF, and other funding sources, the NAS report notes, adding, "The lack of research funding has discouraged universities in the United States from developing research-based forensic degree programs, which leads to limited opportunities to attract graduate students into such programs. Only a few universities offer PhD-level education and research opportunities in forensic science, and these are chemistry or biology programs with a forensic science focus. Most graduate programs in forensic science are master's programs, where financial support for graduate study is limited. In addition, the lack of research funds means that universities are unlikely to develop research programs in forensic science. This lack of funding discourages top scientists from exploring the many scientific issues in the forensic science disciplines. This has become a vicious cycle during which the lack of funding keeps top scientists away and their unavailability discourages funding agencies from investing in forensic science research. Traditional funding agencies have never had a mission to support forensic science research" (NAS, 2009, page 230).

According to the NIJ's 2014 annual report, the most current data available at the time of writing, NIJ has provided more than $125 million since 2009 to fund more than 300 research and development projects related to forensic science, resulting in more than 600 scientific publications, presentations, and reports.

In 2014, NIJ further strengthened its commitment to forensic science research and development by issuing a solicitation to laboratories to conduct research studies designed to produce practical knowledge to improve the examination of physical evidence in forensic science laboratories. Through this solicitation, NIJ will inform best practices by evaluating existing laboratory protocols, developing validated methods that can be replicated by other laboratories—making a direct and immediate impact on laboratory efficiency—and assisting in the development of policy decisions.

Nearly all forensic science research funds are channeled through DOJ. NIJ and the FBI are the two primary federal sources of funding for forensic science research. NIJ provides the bulk of funds for research; the BJS 2002 census found that of the 12 percent of laboratories that had resources dedicated to research, the primary source of funding for this research was NIJ.

According to the 2009 NAS report, "There are several explanations for the relative lack of funding for basic and applied research in the forensic science disciplines. First, forensic practice was started in, and has grown out of, the criminal justice and law enforcement systems. Many forensic science techniques were developed to aid in the investigatory phase of law enforcement and then were adapted to the role of aiding in prosecution by providing courtroom testimony. Thus, forensic practitioners who work in public crime laboratories often are seen as part of the prosecution team, not as part of the scientific enterprise. Second, some of the forensic science disciplines rely on an apprenticeship model for training, rather than on codifying their methods in a scientific framework. Third, federal agencies that fund scientific work, such as the National Science Foundation, the National Institutes of Health, and the Department of Defense, generally have not considered forensic science as part of the science base they need to support. It has been only in recent years that the National Institute of Justice has taken interest in funding forensic science research, but the majority of these funds have been awarded to reduce case backlogs, especially for cases that involve the analysis of DNA" (NAS, 2009, page 187).

The 2016 U.S. federal research budget was about $84 billion, according to Mervis (2016), who reports the leader in research money is the National Institutes of Health (NIH) at $32 billion, followed by NASA at $19 billion, then the NSF at $7.5 billion total budget. As Bartick (2016b, page 96) observes, "The only federal agency whose mandated mission includes funding research in the forensic sciences is the Department of Justice (DOJ), National Institute of Justice (NIJ), Office of Investigative and Forensic Sciences (OIFS). NIJ currently has a forensic science research budget of about $30 million for FY 2016, up from $22 in 2015. This budget is less than 0.1 percent of the NIH 2016 budget. NIJ was off the radar in the report by *Science*. The bottom line is, that with this comparatively low funding, it makes it difficult to carry out the recommendations to improve the rigor and amount of forensic science research that was recommended in the National Research Council (NRC) report of 2009."

An update on NIJ funding was provided in the 2015 report, "Support for Forensic Science Research: Improving the Scientific Role of the National Institute of Justice," which was requested by the Committee on Strengthening Forensic Science at the NIJ and the National Research Council. This report follows the two prior National Research Council reports: the 2009 report, "Strengthening Forensic Science in the United States: A Path Forward," and the 2010 report, "Strengthening the National Institute of Justice." The first report raised concerns about the location of a research institute for forensic science within

DOJ, while the latter report made recommendations for improving the scientific independence and transparency of NIJ's research program while remaining within DOJ. As the 2015 report notes, "The debate still continues on the appropriate location for a research institute for forensic science in the United States, and this committee did not take a position on that issue because of the narrowness of its charge" (Committee on Strengthening Forensic Science at the National Institute of Justice, National Research Council, 2015). The report summarized that "The need to improve the scientific basis for some forensic disciplines is high: because of the volume of forensic transactions processed annually in the United States, even the smallest of error rates can have great consequences and erode the public's confidence in a fair and credible criminal justice system. Given NIJ's mission to serve state and local law enforcement as well as its ties to the forensic science research and practitioner communities, the agency has a unique and critical role to play in efforts to advance forensic science research" (National Academies of Sciences, Engineering and Medicine, 2015).

The 2015 report said that "NIJ has made some very useful changes to its process for soliciting and awarding research grants, thereby improving the agency's scientific capability. These improvements include: making its processes to identify the needs of forensic science practitioners more transparent; increasing the level of autonomy and independence for its scientific peer-review process; obtaining final sign-off authority for its research awards; expanding the size of its research and development portfolio across forensic science disciplines; expanding outreach and dissemination to the practice and research communities; attracting new investigators to forensic science research; increasing the number of graduate student fellowships; and formalizing partnerships with other federal agencies involved I forensic science research, including NIST, the FBI Laboratory, DFSC, and the Bureau of Alcohol, Tobacco, Firearms and Explosives. Taken together, these efforts have restored authority that is appropriate for a science agency and addressed some previous concerns about NIJ's independence and contributed to the building of a research infrastructure necessary to develop and sustain research that advances forensic science methods."

Bartick (2016b, page 97) says that "NIJ's ability to improve forensic science research in the foreseeable future will be constrained without adequate support from federal policy makers across both the executive and legislative branches. Support from DOJ leadership is particularly essential, given that NIJ's placement within the department has been perceived as a potential source of conflict of interest."

But the 2015 NRC report is more optimistic, stating, "Assuming these recommendations are fully implemented and any barriers overcome, this committee believes NIJ has the potential to lead forensic science research across the federal government, a role with clear and striking consequences for the criminal justice system" (National Academies of Sciences, Engineering and Medicine, 2015).

Bartick and Floyd (2015)'s take on the 2015 NRC report is that "NIJ is doing well under the circumstances. However, a real boost is needed in financial support to place the agency in a position to carry out their mission. We researchers, with an interest to work toward enhancing the rigor of forensic science, hope that this will play out."

Other agencies have responded to the siren call of the 2009 NAS report to support forensic science research. One of them is the NSF, which has exhibited a strong interest to include forensic science research as a funding imperative. A 2013 "Dear Colleague" letter from the NSF solicited forensic science research and education proposals, including the aforementioned workshop on forensic science literature. And as we have seen, the NIST has been internally involved with forensic science for some time with a current budget of $7 million for its projects. In 2013, the DOJ, partnering with NIST, established the NCFS, and additionally, NIST has a strong oversight managing role of the OSACs, which have taken over the former role of SWGs. As Bartick (2016b, page 98) notes, "The OSACs have reviewed the SWG guidelines and are now setting the standard analytical methods for the forensic disciplines. Recommended research and development needs are now coming forth. However, no funding commitment toward OSAC requested research has come through the federal legislature as yet. NIST is also the sponsor for the Forensic Science Center of Excellence Program, The Center for Statistics and Applications in Forensic Evidence (CSAFE) has been awarded and is a consortium led by the University of Iowa and is tasked with focusing on pattern and digital evidence with a total award of $4 million for five years to be extended depending on the success."

As Bartick (2016b, page 98) observes, "With a very good U.S. scientific research budget in 2016, comparatively, the direct forensic science research needs are getting little attention. If the needs recommended by the NRC 2009 report are to come to fruition, a much greater commitment is necessary."

Gabel (2014, pages 319–320) explains that tying federal funding to the adoption of standards is a less direct method to create effective national forensic standards and that "a program that tied federal funds to state participation would be a constitutionally viable option to encourage states to adopt national forensic standards. Because tying federal funding to national forensic standards might be constitutionally permissible does not mean that it is the best or easiest method for encouraging their adoption. There are also practical challenges, such as getting states to act and securing a source of funding."

Gabel (2014, pages 321–322) says that considering economic conditions and approaches to federal spending, identifying significant sources of funds to support a national forensic standards program would be challenging: "Arguments for such a program should include both any cost savings and any economic stimulus such a program would create."

Commentators point to previous attempts to secure adequate funding as a means of learning from past mistakes regarding funding levels and funding administration. Congress has already tied federal funds to some forensic science initiatives, the most visible being the Paul Coverdell National Forensic Sciences Act, which awarded grants to states and units of local government to help improve the quality and timeliness of forensic science and medical examiner services. As Gabel (2014, pages 321–322) explains, "The Coverdell grant program has faced two problems that any national forensics standards program would need to overcome. The first is its total funding level, which would need to be significantly higher than the Coverdell program's $33 million high point to initiate and ultimately maintain a national forensic standards program. The second problem is the Coverdell system's administration. An Innocence Project report found enough significant problems with the program's administration to call into question whether it even ensured that the law's most basic requirements were being followed. Again, history does not bode well for establishing a federal forensic agency that has authority over nonfederal forensic stakeholders."

THE SEARCH FOR STANDARDS AND CREATING A CULTURE OF SCIENCE

The NAS Committee seemed to be optimistic about what it characterized as the "self-correcting nature of science": "The methods and culture of scientific research enable it to be a self-correcting enterprise. Because researchers are, by definition, creating new understanding, they must be as cautious as possible before asserting a new 'truth.' Also, because researchers are working at a frontier, few others may have the knowledge to catch and correct any errors they make. Thus, science has had to develop means of revisiting provisional results and revealing errors before they are widely used. The processes of peer review, publication, collegial interactions (e.g., sharing at conferences), and the involvement of graduate students (who are expected to question as they learn) all support this need. Science is characterized also by a culture that encourages and rewards critical questioning of past results and of colleagues. Most technologies benefit from a solid research foundation in academia and ample opportunity for peer-to-peer stimulation and critical assessment, review and critique through conferences, seminars, publishing, and more. These elements provide a rich set of paths through which new ideas and skepticism can travel and opportunities for scientists to step away from their day-to-day work and take a longer-term view. The scientific culture encourages cautious, precise statements and discourages statements that go beyond established facts; it is acceptable for colleagues to challenge one another, even if the challenger is more junior. The forensic science disciplines will profit enormously by full adoption of this scientific culture" (NAS, 2009, page 125).

The 2009 NAS report emphasized the need for better research to establish limits and measures of performance: "A body of research is required to establish the limits and measures of performance and to address the impact of sources of variability and potential bias. Such research is sorely needed, but it seems to be lacking in most of the forensic disciplines that rely on subjective assessments of matching characteristics. These disciplines need to develop rigorous protocols to guide these subjective interpretations and pursue equally rigorous research and evaluation programs. The development of such research programs can benefit significantly from other areas, notably from the large body of research on the evaluation of observer performance in diagnostic medicine and from the findings of cognitive psychology on the potential for bias and error in human observers" (NAS, 2009, page 8).

The 2009 NAS report continues, "Some forensic science disciplines are supported by little rigorous systematic research to validate the discipline's basic premises and techniques. There is no evident reason why such research cannot be conducted. Much more federal funding is needed to support research in the forensic science disciplines and forensic pathology in universities and private laboratories committed to such work. The forensic science and medical examiner communities will be improved by opportunities to collaborate with the broader science and engineering communities. In particular, there is an urgent need for collaborative efforts to develop new technical methods or provide in-depth grounding for advances developed in the forensic science disciplines; provide an interface between the forensic science and medical examiner communities and basic sciences; and create fertile ground for discourse among the communities. NIFS should recommend, implement, and guide strategies for supporting such initiatives" (NAS, 2009, page 22).

Recommendation 3 in the 2009 NAS report states, "Research is needed to address issues of accuracy, reliability, and validity in the forensic science disciplines" (NAS, 2009, pages 22–23). The NAS report further recommended that the NIFS should competitively fund peer-reviewed research in the following areas:

- Studies establishing the scientific bases demonstrating the validity of forensic methods.
- The development and establishment of quantifiable measures of the reliability and accuracy of forensic analyses. Studies of the reliability and accuracy of forensic techniques should reflect actual practice on realistic case scenarios, averaged across a representative sample of forensic scientists and laboratories. Studies also should establish the limits of reliability and accuracy that analytic methods can be expected to achieve as the conditions of forensic evidence vary. The research by which measures of reliability and accuracy are determined should be peer-reviewed and published in respected scientific journals.

- The development of quantifiable measures of uncertainty in the conclusions of forensic analyses.
- Automated techniques capable of enhancing forensic technologies.

To answer questions regarding the reliability and accuracy of a forensic analysis, the research needs to distinguish between average performance (achieved across individual practitioners and laboratories) and individual performance (achieved by the specific practitioner and laboratory). Whether a forensic procedure is sufficient under the rules of evidence governing criminal and civil litigation raises difficult legal issues that are outside the realm of scientific inquiry.

In a 2011 paper, respected thought leaders Jennifer L. Mnookin, Simon A. Cole, Itiel E. Dror, Barry A. J. Fisher, Max M. Houck, Keith Inman, David H. Kaye, Jonathan J. Koehler, Glenn Langenburg, D. Michael Risinger, Norah Rudin, Jay Siegel, and David A. Stoney established the call for a culture of research and emphasized, "In our collective opinion, the pattern identification disciplines, as well as other forms of forensic science evidence, must be placed on a more rigorous scientific foundation. More generally, we believe that a significant culture shift is required: Forensic science needs to focus more on science than on law, to shift from a quasi-adversarial perspective to a research orientation. In short, we call for the development and instantiation of what we will term a research culture within forensic science" (Mnookin et al. 2011).

Mnookin et al. (2011, page 725) echo numerous other papers and commentaries by stating, "We all firmly agree that the traditional forensic sciences in general, and the pattern identification disciplines, such as fingerprint, firearm, toolmark, and handwriting identification evidence in particular, do not currently possess—and absolutely must develop—a well-established scientific foundation. This can only be accomplished through the development of a research culture that permeates the entire field of forensic science. A research culture, we argue, must be grounded in the values of empiricism, transparency, and a commitment to an ongoing critical perspective. The forensic science disciplines need to substantially increase their commitment to evidence from empirical research as the basis for their conclusions. Sound research, rather than experience, training, and longstanding use, must become the central method by which assertions are justified."

Mnookin et al. (2011) add, "In our collective opinion, the pattern identification disciplines, as well as other forms of forensic science evidence, must be placed on a more rigorous scientific foundation. More generally, we believe that a significant culture shift is required: Forensic science needs to focus more on science than on law, to shift from a quasi-adversarial perspective to a research orientation."

They say that a research culture would "affect how evidence is understood, change analysts' relationship to empirical data, and alter how evidence is reported," and acknowledge that while change does not come easily, "this transition is both necessary and, while difficult, genuinely feasible" (Mnookin et al. 2011, page 731).

Many have levied the charge that certain forensic science disciplines are supported by inadequate empirical data that do not justify the claims that analysts frequently make. While some commentators acknowledge that "experience, training, and longstanding investigatory and legal use can be sources of legitimate knowledge for pattern identification analysts," Mnookin et al. (2011, page 736) also recognize that "experience and training can give examiners, from a subjective point of view, sincere and deeply held confidence about their ability to do what they claim to do. But we do not believe that experience and training alone can validate universalist claims, such as the claim that latent fingerprint identification experts can individualize the source of a print to the exclusion of all other possibilities, or the claim that document examiners' experience enables them to assess the entire range of differences between two handwriting exemplars that can still be consistent with authorship by the same hand."

Instead, a research agenda for the forensic sciences should be driven by the unresolved issues and unanswered questions that persist, such as the capabilities and limitations of any particular pattern discipline; how often pattern identification analysts make mistakes, what triggers these errors, and what circumstances tend to increase the risk of error; and how prevalent is the effect of cognitive bias on the activity of forensic examiners, among many other queries. While research continues to emerge, Mnookin et al. (2011, page 737) say that "as of yet, the research basis that would permit a satisfying scientific answer to any of the above questions does not exist." Practitioners and commentators alike point to a lack of published scientific research and an even bigger dearth of resources and funding on the part of government agencies or research organizations in order to support such endeavors.

One might expect that in the aftermath of the 2009 NAS report, the call for research would become more urgent, but the process is fraught with challenges, including defining that research culture to mean "a culture in which the question of the relationship between research-based knowledge and laboratory practices is both foregrounded and central," according to Mnookin et al. (2011, page 740) who add, "We mean a culture in which these questions are answered by reference to data, to published studies, and to publicly accessible materials, rather than primarily by reference to experience or craft knowledge, or simply assumed to be true because they have long been assumed to be true."

Mnookin et al. (2011, page 753) describe what they call a "core constellations of values" that are necessary for a well-functioning research culture in any discipline: empiricism, transparency, and an ongoing critical perspective. They add that "a sign of a mature discipline with a well-entrenched research culture is a willingness to engage respectfully with opposing viewpoints; it is a commitment to focusing on the merits of proposed theories, the adequacies of research methodologies, and the assessments of the data rather than resorting to inflated rhetoric or personal attacks. Forensic scientists have sometimes found it too easy to respond with a personal attack instead of substantive assessment of critics' arguments. ... In a research culture, participants should, ideally, learn from disagreements rather than fear them. ... The development of a research culture in these areas still has a long way to go. When accused of being insufficiently research-based, or insufficiently linked to academia, practitioners in the pattern identification fields have sometimes responded by invoking the scientific foundations articulated by the pioneers of their fields. Whatever the qualifications of these early practitioners, in a healthy research culture, the scientific bona fides of a profession would be unlikely to depend on these pioneers of the distant past."

Unlike some commentators who have been derisive in their observations, Mnookin et al. (2011, page 758) are pushing for a research agenda that does not point assign blame. They also emphasize that the current lack of a research culture "is not forensic scientists' fault. The two most significant causes are a dearth of funding and the fact that prosecutors, investigators, and the courts are the primary clients of forensic science. Until recently, very little federal grant money was available for non-DNA forensic science research. This lack of funding, combined with the general paucity of resources in triage-driven, overworked laboratories, made research an exceedingly unlikely central priority. In addition, few practitioners had the background skills to develop substantial research programs even if the institutional climate had supported it."

Instead of being actively involved in research for which they are unprepared, Mnookin et al. (2011, page 760) expect practitioners, especially those in the pattern and impression evidence, to "become more sophisticated in thinking about data and the legitimacy of inference. Expecting most practicing pattern analysts to become PhD-level researchers is not realistic, nor is it even a good idea. If, however, practitioners at all levels operated within a research culture, they would hone their critical thinking skills and regularly question what basis supports their claim to knowledge, both in an individual case, and more broadly in a given discipline. Moreover, while all laboratory personnel need not, and indeed should not, be researchers themselves, it would not be unrealistic to require certain key personnel—perhaps the lead technical worker in a unit, and whoever is authorized to approve standard operating procedures—to have some minimum research qualification and experience."

Mnookin et al. (2011, page 764) enumerate the barriers to creating a research culture in forensic science, including inadequate funding of applied research projects, as well as a lack of participation from university-based researchers from a variety of fields. They explain, "We strongly believe that forensic science would benefit from the emergence of a cohort of individuals with the skills and the background to operate both in the academic research community and in the world of practitioners. Currently, in the pattern identification field, the number of practicing analysts with a PhD in any discipline is quite small indeed. (This is in stark contrast to a number of other forensic fields, including DNA analysis and toxicology, in which a significant number of analysts hold PhDs.) The majority of forensic practitioners in pattern identification need not—and should not—pursue PhDs. But if some relatively small fraction of practitioners were full citizens of both the world of research and the world of practice, it would offer enormously beneficial spillover effects. These practitioner-researcher hybrids could wear two hats by being true insiders in both communities. They would be valuable translators, mediators, and educators in both domains. They could both convey to fellow practitioners the need for a research-based approach and contribute to ensuring that research focuses on areas of genuine and important concern to practitioners."

Another critical step for creating and nurturing a research culture, according to Mnookin et al. (2011, page 764), is the creation of research-based forensic science programs within academic institutions: "While two-hat experts with a PhD in a substantive non-forensic field along with practical forensic experience can be key mediators between a research culture and forensic practice, research programs also have a place within forensic science departments. Academic forensic research programs will not generate a research culture in the forensic industry, but a small number of excellent research-oriented graduate programs in forensic science could help promulgate a research culture and could also produce valuable research."

STATISTICS IN FORENSIC SCIENCE REFORM

So as we have seen, research and technical standards are going to be the backbone of a reformed forensic science enterprise in the United States. There's every indication that statistics could be an important part of that future infrastructure.

The American Statistical Association (ASA) took a particular interest in forensic science following the 2009 NAS report, with the ASA board of directors voting in 2010 to endorse its recommendations. In a formal statement, the ASA board recognized the pivotal role of forensic science in the judicial system and cited the value of statistical methods and research to improve forensic methods. Noting that statisticians have played an important role in the constructive criticism of current forensic science practices, the

ASA board said they can continue to play an important role in the reforms urged by the NAS. As the board noted, "Statisticians can make vital contributions toward establishing measurement protocols, quantifying uncertainty, designing experiments for testing new protocols or methodologies, and analyzing data from such experiments" (ASA, n.d.).

The ASA board noted that sound statistical practices are essential for the proposed institute to achieve its mission; examples of such practices include the assessment of current and newly developed forensic practices using properly designed experiments and data analytic methods; the use of statistical methods based on established principles and procedures for the analysis of data, including estimated error rates; the review, in mainstream scientific journals, of novel methods (beyond variants of established methods) developed for the analysis of data; the employment of modern statistical quality control and quality assurance procedures to assure that measurements, procedures, and testimony are of high quality; the application of proficiency tests that employ accepted statistical designs, and, whenever possible, are double blind to avoid potential biases; and the availability of all expert reports to interested parties and the provision of sufficient supporting data and information to permit independent review.

Also in 2014, ASA made recommendations to the NCFS, observing that, "Too often, forensic science is seen as a collection of techniques used to analyze and compare samples, rather than as a scientific discipline. This problem goes beyond perception; there is a need to build up a coherent logical and scientific framework for the forensic science disciplines. The field has seen progress, including some administrative steps to address the problem. Indeed, among the latter, the creation of NCFS is a notable accomplishment. Nevertheless, progress in forensic science reform is slower than many would like and much work remains to be done. While forensic science-related 'miscarriages of justice' may be relatively rare, they are very serious, and we should work to prevent them by increasing the use of sound scientific methods" (ASA, 2014).

To address these issues, ASA outlined four steps to be taken in parallel to enhance scientific thinking to benefit the practice of forensic science. The first recommendation, "ensure uniform use of the scientific method throughout the forensic sciences," moves decision-making in forensic science from heuristics (based on examiner training and experience) to data-based procedures (based on objective gathering of data at key process points). As ASA notes, "Forensic science must utilize rigorous scientific methods, especially in the development of methods based on measured data to support the decisions made during forensic evidence examinations and the conduct of well-designed and executed experiments, both to improve and to validate forensic analysis procedures. Both phases require extensive statistical expertise working alongside subject-area expertise from the earliest stages; bringing statisticians into the process any later than that greatly limits the value that they can contribute with often damaging consequences (irrelevant or unusable data, poorly defined or invalid process, etc.) Principles of good experimental design (e.g., replication, blocking, randomization, blinding) ensure the soundness of the results and avoid the criticisms associated with poor designs" (ASA, 2014).

ASA's second recommendation, "insist on rigorous documentation of protocols," speaks to careful documentation of the processes used in each forensic science discipline as a critical first step for quality control and for process improvement. As the ASA states, "It is also necessary to implement safeguards to ensure established protocols and procedures are followed. Systematic documentation of forensic science processes provides a natural way to identify points where variability may arise among examiners or among laboratories, thereby enabling scientific studies where appropriate. Such studies might, for example, focus on characterizing and continually improving the practice of forensic science.

Consistent documentation is also helpful in standardizing procedures, and is essential for later review, both internal and external ... Once the process has been well defined and appropriate standards have been developed, mechanisms must be established to enforce the adherence of these standards, as well as to continually update them as more data and better procedures are identified through regular process monitoring" (ASA, 2014).

Regarding ASA's third recommendation, "encourage a culture of openness to consulting outside experts," the organization notes, "Science advances most rapidly by professional exchange of ideas, so this culture should be encouraged, particularly as some outside scientists may have expertise not readily available in-house. Cooperative centers and research grant programs could facilitate such interactions" (ASA, 2014).

ASA's fourth recommendation, "establish a foundation in logic, decision theory and statistical reasoning in educational and training programs for forensic science," speaks to the need for a "common decision framework across the forensic sciences and encourages contributions toward problem solutions from all forensic fields." As the ASA explains, "Educational programs in forensic science have consisted largely of courses focused on individual techniques (arson, handwriting analysis, latent print analysis, toolmarks and firearms, computer forensics, etc.). This approach fails to emphasize the common elements of quantitative logic, deductive reasoning, and statistical thinking, all of which are essential ingredients in making inferences from forensic evidence, but which are, under current educational systems, either poorly understood or, at best, under-appreciated. While some educational institutions are working on revised curricula, all forensic science programs should teach such a scientific underpinning, including quantitative logic and deductive reasoning, appreciation for and recognition of situations where uncertainty exists, and methods of understanding how to quantify and interpret measures of uncertainty" (ASA, 2014).

Another organization keenly interested in offering its expertise to the NCFS and staking a claim in forensic science reform following the 2009 NAS report seems to be the American Chemical Society (ACS), one of the largest professional organizations in the United States. In its "Position Statement on Forensic Science," the ACS notes, "Physical evidence presented in courts is frequently analyzed using forensic science techniques. The credibility of the legal system critically depends on forensic tests that are consistent and scientifically valid, witnesses who are certified and recognized as forensic experts, and laboratories that are accredited by an appropriate governing agency" (ACS, n.d.).

In its position statement, ACS asks policymakers to support forensic science reform through the following general and specific recommendations:

1. Strengthen scientific rigor within the forensics culture and expand and integrate forensic science research with the larger scientific community.
    a. Consult scientists, law enforcement, and legal professionals to identify forensic science research priorities.
    b. Establish federal funding opportunities to support forensic science research and graduate education by both the existing scientific community and newly trained forensic scientists.
    c. Support collaboration and communication between scientists performing basic and applied research relevant to forensic science and forensic science practitioners.
    d. Establish a structure for forensic case reports that is rooted in the scientific method.
    e. Ensure the independence of the forensic science community from law enforcement.

  f. Optimize the federal government's support of forensic science research by coordinating efforts across agencies.
  g. Promote forums for communication of advances in forensic science at technical research conferences and in peer-reviewed journals.
2. Quantitatively assess and improve the accuracy of forensic analytical methods.
  a. Support work to quantify the reliability and accuracy of existing methods based on scientifically rigorous criteria.
  b. Research and quantify sources and effects of human error and automate forensic tests where appropriate.
  c. Develop and certify analytical techniques and standards appropriate for forensic applications.
3. Monitor and ensure the quality of forensic science education and practice.
  a. Use congressional authority over available grant funding to promote forensic science research.
  b. Mandate rigorous accreditation of laboratories, certification of scientists, and other forensic science practitioners, and establish ethical standards.
  c. Develop a new quality control framework to strengthen and supplement existing requirements for accreditation, regular inspections, and enforcement procedures.
  d. Provide education for law practitioners, scholars, and judges in forensic science methods and practice.
  e. Provide training for forensic scientists in law enforcement, evidence collection, and the law as these all pertain to the practice of forensic science.
  f. Develop outreach programs for the public that highlight the capabilities, limitations, and potential of forensic science.
4. Address challenges for using forensic science when responding to homeland security crises.
  a. Train forensic scientists for potential roles in an emergency.
  b. Establish rules for sharing security-sensitive findings with the wider research community.

In 2014, the ASA's Ad Hoc Advisory Committee on Forensic Science also sent a letter to the NCFS, which stated in part, "We at the ASA commend the creation of the National Commission on Forensic Science and offer to support your important work in any way we can. A prominent theme within 'Strengthening Forensic Science' is the need to undergird the science in the forensic science disciplines. We are convinced statistical scientists can be helpful in this regard" (ACS, n.d.).

EDUCATION AND TRAINING

As we saw in Chapters 3 and 4, education and training is a cornerstone of professional development of forensic practitioners and is essential to the field's future.

Tjin-A-Tsoi (2013) points to the collision of two factors—forensic investigations are becoming increasingly important and "mission critical" to customers, as well as forensic science is becoming more complicated and difficult to understand for the layman—as constituting one of the fundamental challenges of the field: "For almost everyone, a suspect's confession is much easier to understand than, for example, the evidential value of a complex chemical analysis. Nevertheless, the latter may provide a much higher evidential value. Furthermore, using forensic investigations correctly, in a non-biased way, and interpreting results as intended, is not as easy as it may seem. All this points to a growing need for training and education. This applies not only to forensic investigators, but even more so to the users of forensic information. This is largely due to a change in the whole process of criminal investigation. In a sense, the role forensics plays is similar to automation in factories: it 'technologizes' the production process in criminal investigations. In manufacturing, the nature of the 'human factor' has changed. Manual labor has been partially replaced by technology (machines) and knowledge workers (who design, create, and program the machines). Similarly, traditional labor-intensive investigative methods are being replaced or complemented by forensic science and technology. But this means that all the stakeholders in this process need to be trained to deal with this new situation. Police officers, prosecutors, and judges, for instance, need to know how to use forensics properly: they need to ask the right questions, and they need to interpret forensic results correctly" (Tjin-A-Tsoi, 2013).

At the federal level, the 2014 progress report issued by the White House noted a number of developments. NIJ funded an NIJ-Forensic Sciences Foundation Grant Program, which provides research grants to students at colleges and universities that are accredited by the Forensic Science Education Programs Accreditation Commission for projects that contribute to improving the analysis of forensic evidence and/or understanding forensic science. NIJ also provides grants through NIJ's Graduate Research Fellowship (GRF) program, which provides assistance to universities for dissertation research support to outstanding doctoral students undertaking independent research on issues related to crime and justice. NIJ has recently expanded the GRF to provide support across a wider range of social, physical, and forensic sciences. In addition, NIJ restarted its visiting scholar program, through which it hosts forensics scholars from other institutions.

"The fundamental dilemma of the educational process in the forensic science area is that is that we want our forensic scientists to be scientists," says forensic science educator George Sensabaugh. "They need to be able to recognize questions that they potentially might be able to address through scientific investigation and analysis and be able to present those in a meaningful way in whatever forum is appropriate. The pressures within the field are not always consonant with that objective; one such long-standing pressure comes from the prosecutor and the defense counsel who want the scientific analyses to take them in a particular direction, and sometimes they are only providing the lab with the information that will further their case—they will leave out information that might be relevant to doing analyses in a particular case."

Sensabaugh continues, "The other pressure from crime labs themselves to some extent becoming increasingly factory-oriented. We're moving toward analysis and interpretation that is automated—evidence comes in and is put on a production line. At the end of the process, reports are automatically written and reviewed by individuals but sometimes the reports are reviewed independently of the context of the case. Therefore, what laboratory managers are looking for are people who can conduct analyses accurately but not always from the standpoint of asking the scientific questions about what they are doing, and this is a larger problem. My concern is that at some point in the not-too-distant future, is that human judgment is removed entirely. Currently, almost all manufacturing operations can be done robotically, and even medical diagnoses may get to the point where physicians base their diagnoses on computer-calculated algorithms with probabilities attached to each diagnosis. This approach will certainly standardize diagnosis but it also takes individuals' expert insights out of the picture. Does it benefit us to train people and emphasize the scientific role of the actual 'doing' of science when they are going to be conducting analyses more by rote? That's a dilemma for which I don't have an answer."

Regardless, Sensabaugh has offered his opinions on the future of forensic science and its educational agenda. In a November 7, 2012 lecture to the attendees of the California Association of Criminalists (CAC), "The Challenge of Academic Forensic Science: Past, Present and Future," Sensabaugh emphasized that an academic presence is an important component in establishing the legitimacy of forensic science. As we saw in Chapter 1, Sensabaugh was a student of Kirk's school of thinking and he says Kirk's vision of making forensic science more scientific instead of technical is a tenet to pursue for the future. But knowing the politics of academia, Sensabaugh says it is not enough to serve the interests of forensic science and the criminal justice stakeholders; the academic program must be sustainable, establish its relevance, maintain cross-disciplinary relationships, be competitive for extramural support and funding, and nurture its existing critical mass without being perceived as a drain on the system's fiscal lifeblood.

Sensabaugh says the academic challenges abound, including solidifying scientific contributions, training competent professionals, and boosting critical research that will benefit the various forensic disciplines. These challenges don't exist in a vacuum, Sensabaugh notes, pointing to the tumultuous last 50 years of change that has propelled forensic science ahead in terms of technological advances, computational power, statistical evolution, and revolutionary chemical analyses, and simultaneously holding it back through increased scrutiny and criticism, plus escalating regulatory pressures, protocol-driven analyses, silos of expertise, and diminished input into investigations.

Taking all of these factors into consideration, Sensabaugh asserts that academic programs that serve the profession must also equip the professional to cope with the realities of the world. To that end, qualities of integrity, respect, and competence must be cultivated throughout the curriculum. Critical thinking skills must be developed and honed, and there must be continued emphasis in forensic education and training that scientific truths are universal, not skewed for the prosecution or for the defense, Sensabaugh says. "Crime labs will play an increasingly important part in the criminal justice enterprise and to that extent should be better resourced. Crime labs must adopt a culture that for each case integrates the contributions of the different specializations."

For the future, Sensabaugh hopes for a forensic science enterprise that will be strong enough to weather the onslaught of technology, the dying off of some types of expertise, and the fall-out from aforementioned trends impacting the field. Sensabaugh quips regarding protocol-driven analyses, the downside to that is that "If you are a hammer, everything looks like a nail." Additionally, he sees a time in the very near future when technology could trump human analyses. Quality improvement, accreditation, and certification will be key, as educators team up with employers to prepare the next generations of forensic scientists.

Most importantly, Sensabaugh says, the field will need to solidify its scientific foundations as the field continues to "ride the coattails of the DNA revolution." Taking a cue from the 2009 NAS report, Sensabaugh says the future will be all about addressing the deficits of pattern evidence and resolving claims of uniqueness, and hopes that answers to these questions will be provided by genetics, chemistry, and statistics. "We must collaborate with academics in relevant disciplinary areas to establish a better scientific foundation for all domains of forensic science so we can identify the limits of when solid science merges into speculation," he says. "We must enhance the credibility of the field, address our mistakes and uncertainties, and take a hard look at malfeasance on the part of practitioners. There also must be an acknowledgement that flaws in the legal system contribute to erroneous convictions but that forensic science often takes the fall for it. I think forensic science takes the hit because it is discrete and identifiable whereas the criminal justice system is compound and diffuse, making it difficult to pinpoint a source of error."

More than five years after he delivered that presentation to the CAC, Sensabaugh says his thoughts hold up over time, and adds, "I think the main challenge to forensic science education and to forensic research is properly preparing students for rigorous careers. And as part of that training, we must consider research to be an important component.

Research entails defining a problem, developing approaches to address the problem, and then following through with conducting the appropriate analyses or testing to get an answer to the problem posed originally. That's analogous to each case posing unique and distinctive challenges subject to scientific examination using logic and the tools of science. But if one is going to do that in an academic setting, it really needs to be a setting where research is highly valued. I have had the good fortune to be in the UC system and have spent my entire academic career at Berkeley, so I could maintain that education agenda. Some forensic science academic programs don't have that research infrastructure that enables them to maintain that critical agenda and to be able to maintain a laboratory and secure research funding. Establishing a research culture is the academic cultural context for forensic science education for the future."

It's a future belonging to the next generation of scientists, says Sensabaugh: "Most academics have a useful life, and those who are at the end of their careers need to step aside so younger people can assume their place in the field, since the future is theirs," he says. "I can talk to the younger generation of scientists to tell them where I think academic issues in general may be wandering off the mark or where we are losing sight of some of the goals in forensic science, but the next generation has to define what it wants the field to be because they are the ones who are going to live in it."

What the future of forensic science will hold is anyone's guess, but the boundaries will continue to be tested and pushed, and expectations of science will need to be managed, Sensabaugh says. "Will forensic science ever reach its limits? Not as long as the science keeps progressing and the research keeps pace. A prominent molecular biologist at UC Berkeley stated some 50 years ago that all the basics of biology already had been discovered and now it's just a matter of filling in the gaps. He was wrong. I have faith that as long as people continue to ask questions about the world in which we live, that new tools will be developed that will enable us to see things that we had not seen before, or see things in different ways, and that people will be asking different sets of questions and those questions will then shape what we know at any point in time and that will continue for future generations."

As we have seen, research may only be limited by funding, and not the imagination of future scientists. "I think if more funding becomes available to do more aggressive kinds of research, certainly there is no lack of interesting problems out there to be solved," Sensabaugh says. "Part of what I think the forensic community has to do is establish research collaborations with innovators who are employing new technologies. For example, there was an article in *Science* about the divide involving ancient DNA, including a commentary on how most work on ancient DNA is being done in Europe because the EU governments are funding that kind of research, whereas it's not considered to be a research priority in the U.S.—that area of research has gone abroad because the money is abroad. Research on the developmental biology of fingerprint formation might be able to get funded but you would have to pitch it in the form of a developmental biology argument and show that it has some pertinence to fundamental biology. Other forms of impression evidence, firearms or toolmarks—probably the NIJ has to throw money at it. There also must be an appreciation that science tends to go in fits and starts and sometimes there are steps backwards and no great progress is made until something happens and progress can break through. Our funding agencies seem more directed toward the utilitarian nature of science than just doing something for the sake of doing it even though there is ample demonstration that doing it because the question is interesting and could yield benefits far beyond what could have been anticipated."

Sensabaugh says that forensic science research must operate more like the no-fatality highway safety approach: "If we want safer highways, we need to build a research infrastructure with the funding that supports long-term goals. Most operational crime labs lack this infrastructure; the case load is all they can deal with. I fear this kind of research infrastructure exists in only the largest crime labs because they can absorb the cost of a scientist who is only working on a particular research problem and their caseload can be carried by the rest of the group. In the academic sector, we cannot do science with short-term funding. Grants that are only a year or two in duration can't support a graduate student; in public health or science, most people have successions of grants so they have that commitment for five years, the duration of the average PhD program. If you have that kind of funding you can take on students, but if not, you can't."

Sensabaugh isn't alone in the quest for a better education system to serve the U.S. forensic enterprise.

As an educator, Jay A. Siegel has unleashed thousands of forensic students onto the world, extending his reach further by authoring several textbooks in the field. That he has prepared a generation or two of individuals for the rigors of forensic science work is among some of his more modest accomplishments compared to the contributions he also has made to championing the profession later in life.

Chemistry was Siegel's science-related siren song into the profession. "Chemistry, along with physics and biology, has always interested me," says Siegel, adding "My high school chemistry teacher really lit the fire for me." Siegel continues, "My mother was a nurse who wanted me to become a medical doctor, so I was on the pre-med track, applying to medical school my junior year and being accepted by a few programs. At the time I still felt my calling was education, and specifically chemistry education. I was going to be a chemist and teach others what I loved so much; I felt I was good at it and enjoyed it immensely. Chemistry was rewarding, and I thought it was a great profession that was helpful to the public. I pursued a PhD in chemistry with the thought that I would get into some university and teach."

Life has a funny way of interrupting the best laid plans, however. "Along the way I was ABD—all but dissertation," Siegel says with a chuckle. "My coursework and exams were finished and I was writing my dissertation when one day an FBI questioned documents examiner came onto campus at George Washington. He was there to teach a continuing education class on how handwriting comparison was done and documents were prepared. I thought, 'What the heck,' I'll sit in on it because it was open to anyone. I took the course and I thought, 'This stuff is really interesting.' At that time questioned documents weren't considered all that scientific, but still, I thought this type of analysis was fascinating."

Siegel continues, "I sort of filed it away. When I was finishing my PhD I started to look for a job and one of my professors who knew I took this questioned documents course and had an interest in all of this, knew a director at a local crime lab in Virginia, which just happened to be the Virginia Bureau of Forensic Sciences. This professor advised me to look into whether or not there were any jobs and investigate how one broke into this field. So I met with this lab director who was an ex FBI agent, and he and I hit it off immediately. He said he had an opening for a drug chemist—an analytical chemist who knows how to analyze heroin, cocaine, marijuana, PCP, those types of drugs. I had the analytical background and got the job. I started testifying in court quite a bit and was thrilled with this experience I was afforded."

"Around the same time I had been teaching a course at night part-time on basic chemistry for nurses at a local nursing school," Siegel recalls. "I loved teaching and I thought, 'I have got to combine this.' After three years at the Virginia crime lab, I wanted to move on. By then I was married and my wife wanted to get out of Washington, D.C., so I applied for a job in Denver at the Colorado Bureau of Investigations. They needed a forensic chemist and I was interested in that position. However, one of the people who interviewed me for that job was chair of the chemistry department at Metropolitan State College. They were trying to launch a forensic science program but they didn't have a faculty person to do so. They were looking for someone with teaching experience and some interest in forensic science, so I took that opportunity. I worked there for three years and then a position opened up at Michigan State; my wife was a graduate of Michigan State and was happy to move back there. It was the most established forensic science program in the country and their director was retiring after 40 years. I took that position and thought, 'I will stay here for a few years and see what happens,' and I was actually there for 25 years."

Now retired, Siegel last served as a professor and the director of the Forensic and Investigative Sciences Program at Indiana University–Purdue University in Indianapolis.

"I moved to Indianapolis so I could take a job starting a forensic science program at Indiana University, and looking back at my career, I'd say I had always been sort of an evangelist about forensic science and starting new programs. I also helped launch two forensic science programs in Australia—one at the University of Technology in Sydney and the other in Western Australia in Perth. I was always interested in starting forensic science programs and developing educational programs, and it was that course in questioned documents that opened up the world of forensic science to me—I had no idea it even existed until then."

Besides a home in the classroom, Siegel has testified as an expert witness more than 200 times in seven states, as well as in federal and military courts. He also has found time to write those aforementioned textbooks and served as editor in chief of the *Encyclopedia of Forensic Sciences.*

"I really enjoy writing," Siegel says, "whether it's book chapters for other authors or serving as editor of that encyclopedia. Elsevier wanted me to write a textbook, so I got together with my friend Max Houck over a beer at an American Academy of Forensic Sciences meeting and we discussed writing it our way—we wanted to write a book for people who needed a solid background in forensic science, so we wrote *Fundamentals of Forensic Science* for college students and that got followed up by another textbook for another publisher for the high school level, *Forensic Science: The Basics.* I enjoy sharing my knowledge with others. I was also editor of a book in advanced-level forensic chemistry where I gathered 12 authors to write various chapters. It just came out and I think it's the best thing I have been associated with in my career. Writing has been very rewarding for me."

Siegel has been active in a number of industry associations, including being a Fellow with the AAFS, where he was awarded the Paul Kirk Award for outstanding service to the Criminalistics section in 2005. He is also a member of the ACS, the Midwest Association of Forensic Scientists, and the Forensic Science Society (United Kingdom). He is a member of the International Association for Identification and an academic affiliate member of the American Society of Crime Lab Directors (ASCLD).

"In my retirement I have given up a lot of the things I used to do and I swore I would no longer be involved in education," says Siegel, "however, Georgia Tech has been talking with me about teaching an undergraduate forensics class. I have no interest in serving with the National Commission on Forensic Science, and I go to AAFS meetings to show my face and sell my books and to see a lot of friends there, but the politics of forensic science is for younger people. I have a few writing projects and I am doing some consulting on criminal cases right now but the difference is, when you are retired you can do things on your schedule and not someone else's, and that's been enjoyable. My wife says I am not retired at all," Siegel says with a laugh, but adds, "I am busy doing what I want to do."

When asked about a lasting legacy, Siegel points to the accomplishment of being named a distinguished fellow by the AAFS in 2009 for his work in education. "For better or worse, I have been in forensic science education my whole career and that is what my legacy is going to be, I think," he says. "I have been recognized as a distinguished alumna for my publishing efforts, and with my name on textbooks I will go on beyond my tenure as a professor and forensic scientist. What I'd like to be known for is my efforts in improving forensic science education."

Siegel continues, "What I have enjoyed the most in my life was teaching and working with my students, as well as conducting research supported by various grants. Working with students is why I got into academia in the first place."

PRIVATIZATION AS A RESPONSE TO FORENSIC SCIENCE ISSUES

Sometimes the best of intentions can't get the job done, and more definitive action is required, especially for something as hardwired as law enforcement's marriage to forensic science. A radical approach to the challenges faced by forensic science was implemented a few years ago in the United Kingdom. As we have seen, there have been a number of British scientists who have made significant contributions to the formation and advancement of forensic science. But in 2012, the United Kingdom took what some experts believe is a giant step backward when it decided to privatize its forensic science operations.

Mcandrew (2012, page 42) concedes that "Given the recent global recession, many national governments have been forced to implement austerity measures, and the forensic science industry has not been immune to such changes. Proposals to privatize some or all aspects of forensic science services have been bantered about for decades, but the recent economic climate has brought this idea back to the forefront of public debates. Although privatization has been shown to have many benefits in the provision of other goods and services, the idea of privatizing forensic services has been harshly criticized by scholars and practitioners." Mcandrew (2012) adds that despite criticisms through the lens of economics, and arguments offered regarding why market approaches in forensic science may be more successful than might have originally been imagined under certain conditions, recognition of those economic forces and reaction by forensic laboratories to address inefficiencies may provide the effective delivery of forensic services that forestalls privatization efforts.

The closure of the United Kingdom's Forensic Science Service (FSS)—a UK government-owned company that provides forensic services to the police and government agencies of England and Wales—"will lead to an increase in miscarriages of justice," according to three-quarters of the UK forensic scientists who responded to a New Scientist survey (Geddes, 2012). The surveyed UK forensic scientists also said they believed that that moving to private and in-house police labs will reduce impartiality in interpretation, and therefore accuracy, of evidence. Geddes (2012) adds that "The survey also raises fresh questions about issues of bias in forensic science, with nearly one-third of respondents admitting they sometimes feel pressured to produce a particular result, while three-quarters say they sometimes have insufficient time to evaluate cases."

The closure was prompted by a shrinking forensic science market that caused the FSS to lose between £1 million and £2 million a month, according to some reports (Geddes, 2012). William Thompson, of the University of California at Irvine, was quoted by Geddes (2012) as observing, "At a time when the deficiencies in forensic science are increasingly apparent, to lose one of the major research institutes is not just a loss for Britain, it's a loss for the entire world."

Geddes (2012) quotes Peter Gill, former senior scientist at the FSS, as remarking, "This survey is important because this is the only hard evidence we have on what is really happening (in labs). There has been a problem with obtaining information from the scientists because they are prohibited from expressing opinions in public."

The survey found 92.3 percent of respondents thought the impact of the closure on criminal justice would be mostly negative, while 76.4 percent thought it would lead to an increase in miscarriages of justice. When asked about the effect of switching forensic work to private and in-house police labs, 70.3 percent agreed or strongly agreed that this would reduce impartiality in the interpretation of evidence, while 64.7 percent said it would make it harder for scientists to accurately interpret evidence. The survey also found that 28.6 percent of respondents sometimes or always feel pressured to produce a particular result, while 75.4 percent say they have insufficient time to evaluate a case properly; 83.6 percent believed the issue would worsen over the next five years.

As Geddes (2012) observes, "All together, this suggests a real need for measures to reduce bias in UK labs and raise standards of forensic science as a whole, regardless of the decision to close the FSS. Eighty-one percent of respondents felt that more independent research is needed to overcome current weaknesses in forensic science in the UK—something many feel will now no longer get done."

Several decades ago, Rodger (1991, page 167) observed, "Privatization of forensic science may be right. Reasons for privatization may be identified in expected improvements in areas of efficiency, economy and so on, but the bottom line in all the calculations ... must always be to the benefit of the court of law and the pursuit of justice ... Fundamental to the concept of privatization is the pursuit of efficiency."

And that means cost effectiveness. As Rodger (1991, page 167) notes further, "It is certainly the case that cost is more and more a determining criterion in crime investigation and it is clearly proper to demonstrate management efficiency. There is a strong school of thought these days which considers that the way to demonstrate management efficiency is to call in management consultancy. With all due respect to management consultancy, predetermined off-the-shelf management packages suitable for the office and the factory will have their relevance, but they tend to assume we're in the business of manufacturing something. We must ensure that we adopt the management package to meet the requirements of forensic science rather than adopt the forensic science to suit the requirements of the management package. Terminology abounds with strategy statements, performance targets, output measure, resource implications. Forensic science is not a production line, where effectiveness and efficiency of the operation can be directly related to the number of sausages, cars, computers produced divided by the number of people on the payroll."

Rodger (1991, page 168) says that performance indicators cannot be allowed to obfuscate the real business at hand, but it is a reality that the definition of performance indicators for forensic science are comparative statistics on which performance or expected results are measured against a benchmark such as last year's case figures. Rodger adds that these figures assessing the efficiency and effectiveness of the organization are "utter rubbish" and that "The day any forensic science laboratory believes that its effectiveness is demonstrated in terms of the number of cases processed per scientist is the day that laboratory loses any genuine claim to the title 'forensic'" (page 168).

Maguire et al. (2012) acknowledge that "Budgets for forensic science laboratories have always been meager relative to the caseload demands on their services, but the pressure to do more with less has been growing at a more rapid pace recently for laboratories around the world. Much of this pressure is related to the stress on government budgets from global recession. During any fiscal crisis, governments look to areas in which public budgets can cut costs to move toward greater fiscal responsibility; in the most recent global recession those cuts, some draconian, have affected forensic science laboratories with some notable reductions in force. Rather than passively await the decisions of officials from outside the laboratory environment, laboratories may have a greater hand in their destiny through preemptive action before unwanted changes are thrust upon them. To do so it is essential that laboratory directors have a firm grasp on foundational economic realities. With that knowledge, directors can begin to use those realities to increase cost-effectiveness while maintaining efficiency. In many situations the optimal response may be to make cross-jurisdictional agreements to insource or outsource casework. In other situations, the response may lead to reorganizing existing or opening new facilities to spread a heavy caseload among multiple laboratories for a more effective division of services. In some circumstances a private sector solution may be optimal as excess caseloads are outsourced to private laboratories or entire investigative areas diverted to the for-profit market."

Concerns regarding the efficacy and quality of forensic examinations for criminal trials in Britain following the 2012 closure of the FSS and outsourcing to private firms prompted the National Audit Office (NAO) to conduct an investigation. The study was commissioned by the House of Commons Science and Technology Select Committee (CSTSC), which has long criticized the government for scrapping the FSS without considering the implications of privatization. Following the release of the NAO's scathing report, the CSTSC warned that the government was sacrificing forensic science services the state depends on to keep costs low.

The Home Office's 2014 report cited a number of key issues, including the lack of data on the overall size of the forensics market and the proportion of this delivered in-house by police force laboratories; the lack of consistent accounting practices across police forces in England and Wales, making it challenging to get a complete picture of forensics expenditure; and the lack of an official strategy to ensure the forensic market is in good health, both in the short and long term.

The Home Office's 2014 report noted that, "The data available publicly on forensics spending is limited. The information that is available is incomplete, inconsistent and/or difficult to access." It also observed that, "The forensic science regulator has no statutory powers to enforce compliance with quality standards. The regulator sets the standards that all suppliers of forensic services should meet, both public and private, but it has no statutory powers to ensure laboratories are compliant with those standards." Making matters worse, the Home Office also said that it "has not produced a strategy for forensics" and that "There is limited data available publicly on forensics spending. This data is incomplete, inconsistent and difficult to access."

What's notable about the situation in the United Kingdom is how closely it parallels the United States in some key deficits, such as research. For example, the FSS, the largest publisher of peer-reviewed research in forensic science in the United Kingdom, over a 10-year period only equaled the research produced by the chemistry department of the University of Strathclyde in just one year. A survey by the aforementioned university examined 35 universities that teach forensic science and showed that almost half of them had never published a single peer-reviewed paper during the period surveyed, and the average rate of publication was two papers per decade. It's a vivid picture of the dramatic differences between research in the forensic world compared to the general scientific world.

According to Fraser (2011), "In addition to funding, a systematic and effective research program in forensic science will require the closely structured and mature collaboration between academic institutions, forensic science providers, the police service and others in the criminal justice system. This situation does not exist at present in England and Wales. Academic institutions cannot be engaged due to lack of funding and neither the forensic science providers nor the police service have demonstrated sufficient understanding of research programs of this type. It is difficult to imagine that the research situation will be improved by the loss of the FSS or their replacement by a privatized organization. Without funding sources and effective collaborations with academic institutions it seems likely that future research in a private market will focus on short term economic benefits for the individual companies" (House of Commons Science and Technology Committee, 2011).

Fraser (2011) adds that closure of the FSS "is an undesirable outcome that will impact adversely on criminal justice" and may trigger a number of unfavorable outcomes such as fragmentation of evidence when multiple providers are used; poor communication between users and providers; reduced information sharing between providers and the police service; and less development of effective working practices. Fraser (2011) adds, "The market appears to be extremely fragile, uncertain and immature. It is essential that strategic capacity and a capability to provide forensic services are maintained but it is unclear at this stage how this is to be established. The significance of a wholly privatized forensic market for criminal justice and how this will develop in economic and scientific terms is impossible to predict" (House of Commons Science and Technology Committee, 2011).

Gabel (2014, pages 350–351) observes, "... the United States could still achieve a program comparable to that in the United Kingdom by utilizing existing frameworks to create research partnerships. The United Kingdom's forensic science program, once a predominantly public entity, thrived after the government released control in favor of the competition and cost effectiveness that come with private markets. Although many fought back, arguing that closing FSS favored saving money at the expense of quality, data suggests that is not the case. It is doubtful that research partnerships might ultimately privatize the U.S. system of forensic science (or at least decouple crime labs from law enforcement agencies). After all, the United Kingdom is far smaller, with fewer jurisdictions and less crime. Moreover, similar privatization in the U.S. prison system has been widely criticized. Finally, the U.K. system could be characterized as capitalism all dressed up: it requires much more than a new dress and some shoes. To decrease costs while improving quality standards, as the United Kingdom did, the traditional idea behind capitalism—privatizing industry to increase competition—would probably require significant government regulation."

Back in the States, Richard Saferstein alludes to our own political woes. "In this current political landscape, I believe that who is in the White House and in Congress is key to the future of forensic science," he says. "I believe we are going through a political tug-of-war, with and the Republicans being more anti-regulation and the Democrats supporting additional regulation. I don't want to take sides but I predict if the Republicans win the White House, organizations such as the National Commission on Forensic Science and OSAC are going to disappear. In my opinion, OSAC is an attempt at over-regulating the field. Don't get me wrong, it's backed by good intentions, but I really believe that the money would be better spent in research. We are running into Constitutional issues here; say we come up with some sort of platform to standardize the field—how is the federal government going to impose that upon the states? Look at what happened with Obamacare, for example. I'm sure many of the states would resist imposition, on the part of the federal government, on the inner workings of the state crime labs, rightly or wrongly. As contrast it's interesting to look at what is happening in the U.S. as opposed to what took place in Britain, which has pretty much done away with government intervention in forensic science. They have privatized their whole system and have gone in a totally opposite direction than the U.S. It's curious, this strong contrast between the U.S. and Britain."

LIKELIHOOD OF PROGRESS IN THE FUTURE

The tug-of-war that Saferstein mentions is evident in the reaction to that 2009 NAS report. As Kaye (2010) points out, the report was issued a year after the beginning of a serious recession, when competing interests and other legislative priorities were vying for attention from lawmakers: "As lobbying from the Innocence Project (in favor of NFIS), the National Association of District Attorneys (against it), the American Society of Crime Laboratory Directors (against it) and other organizations continues, the prospects for a well-funded, centralized forensic science agency to promote research and regulation seem remote. The recommendation to move laboratories out from under the administrative control of police agencies also is unlikely to be widely adopted. A more likely outcome at the legislative level is an increase in appropriations for forensic science research, upgrades to laboratories, mandatory accreditation, and improved training—things that all interested parties support."

As Gabel (2014, page 351) notes, "Taking steps toward establishing a privatized (and thus, competitive) forensics industry—coupled with quality regulation and government funding—would promote the use of cost-efficient procedures that produce valid, reliable, and accurate results."

That criminalist Paul Kirk would address a fugue state in forensic science decades earlier may not bode well for the field currently: "Is it not time to make a serious effort to define a goal, so that we may all talk about the same thing and move in similar directions, in order that the field will command greater respect, and generate more pride in its accomplishments?" (Kirk 1963, page 238)

As Miranda (2015, page 147) notes, "We need to be certain that the path charted is truly forward and not simply more complex for its own sake. The NAS report has value—not simply because its authors are learned or experienced, but because there is actual truth in it. We can embrace the uncomfortable truths and assertively resist the errors in it, calling them what they are."

And as Butler (2015) observes, "... a great deal of activity has occurred in an effort to strengthen forensic science disciplines since the NRC report was published more than six years ago. However, there is still much to be done, and more progress has been made on some of the NRC recommendations than on others. The National Commission on Forensic Science and the Organization of Scientific Area Committees are beginning to take action on policy and practice issues, respectively. Progress is being made on many fronts by various stakeholders in the forensic science community. To meet the many needs for strengthening all of the forensic disciplines in the future, increased research funding and focused efforts will continue to be crucial. A commitment to make appropriate changes will need to come from laboratory management and staff. Embracing change will be possible as communication improves among the many stakeholders who create and use forensic services."

Gabel (2014, pages 351–352) advocates research over federal oversight, asserting, "Evidence admissibility is largely dependent on implementing and enforcing comparable standards, which should be achieved for the entire forensic process, from crime scene to courtroom. Yet, consistency and predictability across the forensic nervous system are few and far between. Ultimately, we can do better. Establishing a federal entity to oversee reforms in forensic science attempts to accomplish too much in a sector that remains fragmented and impervious to change. Research partnerships between crime labs and universities, on the other hand, will improve lab efficiency, foster communication between labs, and unify oversight. Improving crime labs would directly correlate to keeping innocent defendants out of jail, and in some cases, alive. Research partnerships should prioritize the NAS report recommendations to streamline, simplify, and accelerate forensic reform. Only when all crime labs speak the same language, use the same methodologies and protocols and embrace the science component of their name will forensic science be better. Reforming forensics is no small task. It will take cooperation from scientists, lawyers, judges, and policymakers—but it can be done."

The experts interviewed for this book vary in their levels of confidence that the critical issues in forensic science will be addressed adequately in the future.

One expert who believes progress is being made is retired forensic pathologist Marcella Fierro. "The National Commission on Forensic Science is setting standards to take forensic sciences out of the back room, making clear that labs and medical examiner offices should be accredited, ensure that practitioners are trained and certified, that the degree to which sciences can be interpreted is buttressed by science. Interested parties are now aware of the issues. That was a first step. The second step is working on the issues and the third is taking the information from the second step and implementing it nationally."

Regarding the next generations of forensic practitioners, Fierro says, "Forensic pathology is a wonderful way to take the science and curiosity and caring of medicine and apply it to public health and the courts. In addition to working on individual cases it is also the practice of population medicine. It is not all just dead bodies. Forensic pathologists are the generators and keeper of health data—identifying unsafe products that have resulted in death, occupational hazards, occupational disease etc. Who first recognized the opiate use crisis? We did. Who developed the data supporting the use of seatbelt? We did. Who rang the alarm for hantavirus? We did. Read the Poisoner's Handbook by Deborah Blum to see how forensic pathology contributed to the public health and wellbeing of citizens. The NYC office complied unassailable statistics that changed the public health. No one else did. It is a great career. I can honestly say that I never went home from work not thinking that as a physician I did something of value that day."

Saferstein says the future will come down to bolstering the field with the requisite research and standards. "I have read synopses of the (2009 NAS) report and my feeling is there were some points that were justifiable," he says. "But I think it all comes back to research, and that's key for the future. There were areas that the NAS report pointed out that were weak and very much out of line with objective elements of science, and rightly so. I think what has to be done for future improvement is developing systems of verification. I like what the fingerprint industry has done with AFIS for verification; that to me is the key, particularly in areas that are very subjective, such as pattern analysis. I think the community must develop a system of verification like the fingerprint discipline has done by having a second analyst look at the material and verifying the results of the first analyst."

Saferstein continues, "The future will continue to evolve. Who would have ever thought DNA would be as important and strategic to the field as it has become? Someone like Paul Kirk might have never been able to imagine something like that. I'm not sure what the next major advancement would be, but I'm certain something exciting is on the horizon. For me, a foray into forensic biometrics is on tap for the next edition of my textbook. I think it behooves all of us to pay attention to how the field is moving forward and advancing. We have an obligation to our field to stay current. It raises everyone's game."

Cyril Wecht concurs that education and training, credentialing, and certification might help address deficiencies in forensic science. "It will not eliminate all of the perceived problems with concerns such as bias, because after all, we are not machines, but it can help. I still criticize the government for the lack of funding and follow-up on some of the more important recommendations in the (2009 NAS) report, and have a long way to go to make good on those recommendations. More attention needs to be paid to the field in order to continually improve the level of education and training that scientists receive, as well as putting into action the recommendations in the (2009 NAS) report."

Jay Siegel says the future rests on funding and appropriations and calls this the "critical piece" of the puzzle. "We had funding from Congress for the committee that produced that 2009 report, and the National Commission on Forensic Science is receiving shoestring funding, but key to our future viability is federal financial support. If we cannot get money from Congress to implement these recommendations and research, then nothing is going to happen. Money must come from Congress but the problem is that despite some federal laboratories, the majority of crime labs are state-based and as such, they each have their own rules. This has been one of the more significant problems in the field—we have no national umbrella to oversee and organize all of it. The NAS committee's very first recommendation was to call for a national institute of forensic science that would provide a conduit for funding and also help everyone get organized but that was dead on arrival in Congress. You don't ask to create new agencies with these reports, but hopefully something will come of these efforts nonetheless. We know we have supporters in Congress, but whether we can get them to coalesce around these improvement efforts remains to be seen. We need grant money to conduct research, we need funding for the education of forensic scientists, for lab modernization, for standards development, and for forensic pathology education and training, which is in a sorry state. There is a whole litany of issues that needs to be funded and that funding needs to come from the federal government. Congress thinks the government is already too big and no one wants to spend any money, let alone spend money on forensic science."

Siegel says he advocates an emphasis on master's and doctorate-level programs for the future. "During the last few years I was working with master's degree students, our introductory course 'textbook' was the 2009 NAS report; we dissected the findings and the recommendations, using them as a jumping off point to discuss the issues facing forensic science. The problem was, there wasn't any science in the course, just a discussion of the problems in forensic science. However, it's unfair to let people into our field and into an adversarial legal system without making certain they understand and the main issues. Even before the report, I always tried to drum into my students that they must be a neutral person in an adversarial system and that is very hard to do. I also tell them they must speak for the science, as science can't always speak for itself. They must be able to explain in scientific terms what the evidence tells them. I remind them that the science is everything, and to resist the politics and pressure that go along with it. So I was coloring outside the lines before the lines were drawn, but especially since the report came out. It gave me a vehicle to develop a graduate program, and even now in the undergraduate program, that explores elements of big-picture issues—although the undergraduate program is usually so jammed up with science, forensic science, investigations, law, that there's not much room for getting in-depth exploration in these areas."

Siegel adds, "I believe that the days of bachelor's degrees in forensic science are numbered; if it were up to me, I would go to a master's program and doctorate program only immediately. I think a student would be better served by getting a strong chemistry, biology and math background, and then apply it in a master's or doctorate program in forensic science. Based on my 35 years of being an educator, I think that's the best approach for students, instead of trying to give them an applied degree with all the chemistry, physics and biology in an undergraduate program. I think that process is very slowly happening but it's very difficult. I think the future of forensic science ought to be at the graduate level. I think the move ought to be toward graduate work in forensic science where there is room in the curriculum for discussion of these important non-science issues, because students will be getting most of their forensic science and basic science at the undergraduate level. People are starting to see how many problems there are in this field and a lot of that attention has got to be in the form of research, and that's best done at the graduate level."

Siegel says the field is departing from the notion that forensic science is a mere offshoot of criminal justice, a trend that will continue in the future as it addresses claims that it is not scientific. "As I always told my students, there is no such thing as forensic science; we beg, borrow and steal whatever we need from other disciplines of science," he says. "DNA typing didn't arise from forensic science, it came from recombinant science conducted in medical research labs. Drug analysis didn't arise from forensic science, it came from analytical chemistry. So with the exception of fingerprints, firearms, toolmarks and questioned documents, which only have a context in forensic science, we are awaiting new developments in science so that we can cherry-pick which ones will help us advance what we do. The current revolution in computers, imaging and robotics will help us increase efficiencies in crime scene investigation and forensic analysis; we may not yet know exactly how they will be adopted, but then again, in 1980, we didn't know anything about DNA typing either. So those advances offer encouragement that forensic science will progress and will become more and more of its own science, but also still use the best of what exists in the larger scientific world."

"I am optimistic about the future in that regard," Siegel continues. "The field shows a willingness to appropriate what is needed from other scientific developments to see how they will help in forensic science. Imaging has become so important; maybe it will be key to fingerprint and firearm and any microscopic comparison because the computers can see things in fine detail that we cannot see and make connections that we can't. Those are important things as long as we don't lose sight of the fact that it's the scientists who have to make the determinations, not the machines. This is why polygraphs have never really been accepted as real because you don't want the machine doing the jury's job of determining guilt or innocence or trying to determine if someone is lying or not. That is still the purview of the jury. So we have to be careful about forensic science getting disconnected from its scientists; we have to ensure the scientists make the ultimate determinations and not the machines."

Man *versus* machine just might turn into man *and* machine in the future, but right now, experts say it's got to be the right balance. In terms of how man and machine might continue to push the boundaries of science and forensic science, John Butler says, "I think sometimes you don't know what you don't know yet, and that's the challenge we face in science. I believe the future will be all about how analysts interpret evidence. It's not just the data that you collect and the measurements that you make, but the meaning of the data. In many regards we are reaching our limits with DNA because if you get a small amount of DNA you collect from something, was that transferred there from something else? From someone being there before the crime happened, was that transfer because someone then touched something else and you get secondary and tertiary transfer where you are essentially contaminate a sample? Just because you can detect DNA doesn't mean it is probative or useful in that case, and so that is really where the boundary lies. We must know the meaning of the source and the activity level of something—the hierarchy of propositions—what does the DNA really mean, more than just simply having it. Greater sensitivity in the techniques we use adds to the complexity of the result which means the interpretation is actually more challenging, not easier. There is always a balance and a fundamental rule in analytical chemistry is that as you drive sensitivity in any technique, you are then going to compromise specificity. We want to make sure we are at an appropriate level of specificity measurement and the interpretation of that measurement in order to get the best result from the analysis. It goes beyond just instrument or technique, it's the fundamental thinking about interpretation, which is key for the future of forensic science."

REFERENCES

American Chemical Society (ACS) (n.d.). Position Statement on Forensic Science. Accessible at https://www.acs.org/content/acs/en/policy/publicpolicies/promote/forensic-science.html

American Statistical Association (ASA) (n.d.). American Statistical Association Supports Major Reforms of the Nation's Forensic Science System (press release). May 3, 2010. Accessible at http://www.prweb.com/releases/2010/05/prweb3943104.htm

American Statistical Association. Recommendations for the National Commission on Forensic Science from the ASA Ad Hoc Advisory Committee on Forensic Statistics. 2014.

Bartick EG. Overview. In: Forensic Science Research and Evaluation Workshop: A Discussion on the Fundamentals of Research Design and an Evaluation of Available Literature. National Institute of Justice. May 6, 2016a.

Bartick EG. Government's Role in Funding Scientific Research. In: Forensic Science Research and Evaluation Workshop: A Discussion on the Fundamentals of Research Design and an Evaluation of Available Literature. National Institute of Justice. May 6, 2016b.

Bartick EG and Floyd MA. National Institute of Justice. Forensic Science Research and Evaluation Workshop: A Discussion on the Fundamentals of Research Design and an Evaluation of Available Literature. May 26–27, 2015 Washington, D.C.. Accessible at https://www.ncjrs.gov/pdffiles1/nij/250088.pdf

Bell S. *Crime and Circumstance: Investigating the History of Forensic Science*. Prager. Westport, CT. 2008.

Butler JM. U.S. initiatives to strengthen forensic science & international standards in forensic DNA. New trends in forensic science genetics. *Forensic Science International: Genetics*. Vol. 18, Pages 4–20. September 2015.

Butler J. Perspectives and Challenges from NIST Involvement in Forensic Science. From: Technical Conference on Quantifying the Weight of Forensic Evidence: Online Proceedings. May 5, 2016. Accessible at http://biometrics.nist.gov/cs_links/ibpc2016/tc/presentations/Day1/02_Butler%20-%20NIST%20Quantifying%20the%20Weight%20of%20Evidence%20-%20May%202016.pdf

Cole SA. How Do We Trust the Scientific Literature? In: Forensic Science Research and Evaluation Workshop: A Discussion on the Fundamentals of Research Design and an Evaluation of Available Literature. National Institute of Justice. May 6, 2016.

Committee on Strengthening Forensic Science at the National Institute of Justice, National Research Council. Support for Forensic Science Research: Improving the Scientific Role of the National Institute of Justice. Washington, DC: The National Academies Press. 2015.

Dror I. Recognition and Mitigation of Cognitive Bias in Forensic Science: From Crime Scene Investigation to Forensic Research and Literature. In: Forensic Science Research and Evaluation Workshop: A Discussion on the Fundamentals of Research Design and an Evaluation of Available Literature. National Institute of Justice. May 6, 2016.

Dror IE and Stoel RD. Cognitive Forensics: Human Cognition, Contextual Information and Bias. In: *Encyclopedia of Criminology and Criminal Justice*. Springer, New York. Pages 353–363. 2014.

Fraser J. Forensic Science Service: Written evidence submitted by the University of Strathclyde. February 22, 2011. Accessible at http://www.publications.parliament.uk/pa/cm201011/cmselect/cmsctech/writev/forensic/m91.htm

Gabel JD. Realizing reliability in forensic science from the ground up. *104 J Crim L & Criminology 283*. 2014. Accessible at http://scholarlycommons.law.northwestern.edu/jclc/vol104/iss2/2

Gatsonis C. Plenary I: The Status of Research in the Forensic Sciences. In: Forensic Science Research and Evaluation Workshop: A Discussion on the Fundamentals of Research Design and an Evaluation of Available Literature. National Institute of Justice. May 6, 2016.

Geddes L. Forensic failure: 'Miscarriages of justice will occur'. *New Scientist*. 2012. Accessible at https://www.newscientist.com/article/mg21328514-600-forensic-failure-miscarriages-of-justice-will-occur/

Giannelli PC. Daubert and Forensic Science: The Pitfalls of Law Enforcement Control of Scientific Research. U. Ill. L. Rev. 53. 2011a.

Giannelli PC. Forensic Science: Why No Research? Case Research Paper Series in Legal Studies Working Paper. September 2011b. Accessible at http://ssrn.com/abstract=1924429

Giannelli PC. The Abuse of Scientific Evidence in Criminal Cases: The Need for Independent Crime Laboratories. 4 VA. J. SOC. POL'Y & L. 439. 1997.

Houck M. Intellectual infrastructure: A modest critique of forensic science. *Science and Justice Journal*. Vol. 53, No. 1. Page 1. March 2013. http://www.scienceandjusticejournal.com/article/S1355-0306(13)00002-6/abstract

Houck MM. *CSI: Reality. Scientific American*. Page 89. 2006.

Houck MM. Overview. In: *Professional Issues in Forensic Science*. Elsevier. Page xxi. 2015.

House of Commons Science and Technology Committee. The Forensic Science Service. Seventh Report of Session 2010–12. 2011. Accessible at https://www.publications.parliament.uk/pa/cm201012/cmselect/cmsctech/855/855.pdf

James SH and Nordby JJ. *Forensic Science: An Introduction to Scientific and Investigative Techniques*. CRC Press, Boca Raton, FL. 2003.

Kaye DH. The Good, the Bad, and the Ugly: The NRC Report on Strengthening Forensic Science in America, 50 Sci. & Just. 8; 2010.

Kirk PL. The ontogeny of criminalistics. *Journal Criminal Law, Criminology and Police Science* Vol. 54. Pages 235–238. 1963.

Koppl R and Krane D. Blinding as a Solution to Bias. In: *Minimizing and Leveraging Bias in Forensic Science*. Elsevier. 2016.

Maguire C, Houck MM, Williams R and Speaker PJ. Efficiency and the Cost-Effective Delivery of Forensic Science Services: Insourcing, Outsourcing, and Privatization. Forensic Science Policy and Management. Pages 62–69. October 24, 2012. Accessible at http://www.tandfonline.com/doi/full/10.1080/19409044.2012.734546?src=recsys

Mcandrew W. Is privatization inevitable for forensic science laboratories? *Forensic Science Policy & Management*. Vol. 3, No. 1. Pages 42–52. 2012. Accessible at https://www.researchgate.net/publication/271991843_Is_Privatization_Inevitable_for_Forensic_Science_Laboratories

Mervis J. Research agencies revel in final 2016 budget. *Science*. Vol. 351, No. 6268. Pages 10–11. January 2016.

Miranda DM. *Evidence Found: An Approach to Crime Scene Investigation*. Elsevier Academic Press, London. Page 147. 2015.

Mnookin J, Cole S, Dror I, Fisher BAJ, Houck MM, Inman K, Kaye D, Koehler J, Langenburg G, Risinger M, Rudin N, Siegel J and Stoney D. The need for a research culture in the forensic sciences. *UCLA Law Review*. 58. Pages 725–779. 2011.

National Academies of Sciences, Engineering and Medicine. Support for Forensic Science Research: Improving the Scientific Role of the National Instiute of Justice. Committee on Strengthening Forensic Science at the National Instiute of Justice. Washington, D.C. 2015.

National Commission on Forensic Science (NCFS) (n.d.a). Recommendations to the Attorney General to Fund Post-Doctoral Projects to Facilitate Translation for Research into Forensic Science Practice. March 22, 2016.

National Commission on Forensic Science (NCFS) (n.d.b). Recommendation to the Attorney General: Technical Merit Evaluation of Forensic Science Methods and Practices. June 7, 2016.

National Commission on Forensic Science (NCFS) (n.d.c). Establishing the Foundational Literature within the Forensic Science Disciplines. Accessible at https://www.justice.gov/ncfs/file/795341/download

National Institute of Justice. Forensic Science Research and Evaluation Workshop: A Discussion on the Fundamentals of Research Design and an Evaluation of Available Literature. Edward G. Bartick and McKenzie A. Floyd, Eds. May 6, 2016.

National Institute of Justice. The Impact of Forensic Science Research and Development. April 2015.

National Institute of Justice. Annual Report 2014.

National Institute of Justice. NIJ Funding: Supporting emerging scientists, building our future. *NIJ Journal* No. 276. January 2016.

National Research Council. Strengthening Forensic Science in the United States: A Path Forward. Washington, DC: The National Academies Press, 2009.

National Science Foundation. Dear Colleague Letter: Forensic Science. http://www.nsf.gov/pubs/2013/nsf13120/nsf13120.jsp

President's Council of Advisors on Science and Technology PCAST Releases Report on Forensic Science in Criminal Courts. September 20, 2016.

Pretty IA and Sweet D. The Scientific Basis for Human Bitemark Analyses: A Critical Review. 41 Sci and J. 85. 2001.

Risinger DM. The NAS/NRC Report on Forensic Science: A Path Forward Fraught with *Pitfalls. Utah* L. Rev. 225. 2010.

Risinger D and Saks MJ. A house with no foundation. *Issues in Science and Technology*. Vol. 20, No. 1. Pages 35–39. 2003.

Rodger WJ. Privatization of forensic science: Policy options in forensic science-relevance to privatization. *JFSS*. Vol. 31, No. 2.Pages 167–172. 1991.

Runkle D. A Quality and Gap Analysis: An AAAS Forensic Science Literature Project. In: Forensic Science Research and Evaluation Workshop: A Discussion on the Fundamentals of Research Design and an Evaluation of Available Literature. National Institute of Justice. May 6, 2016.

Saks MJ, Albright T and Bohan TL et al. Forensic bitemark identification: Weak foundations, exaggerated claims. *Journal of Law and the Biosciences*. Pages 1–38. 2016.

Science Watch. Best Evidence: NIST's John M. Butler on Advances in Forensics. September 2011.

Simoncelli T. Rigor in forensic science. In: *Blinding as a Solution to Bias: Strengthening Biomedical Science, Forensic Science, and Law*. Academic Press. Pages 129–131. 2017.

Stolorow M. Looking to the Future of Forensic Science Impacted by OSAC Standards Activities. In: Forensic Science Research and Evaluation Workshop: A Discussion on the Fundamentals of Research Design and an Evaluation of Available Literature. National Institute of Justice. May 6, 2016.

Thompson MA. Bias and quality control in forensic science: A cause for concern. *Journal of Forensic Science*. Vol. 19. Pages 504, 512. 1974.

Tjin-A-Tsoi TBPM. Trends, Challenges and Strategy in the Forensic Science Sector. March 2013. Accessible at https://www.nist.gov/sites/default/files/documents/oles/trends-challenges-and-strategy-in-the-forensic-science-sector-march-2013-_tcm120-494231.pdf

Vosk T. Treatment of Error and Uncertainty in the Literature: A Source of Enlightenment and Confusion. In: Forensic Science Research and Evaluation Workshop: A Discussion on the Fundamentals of Research Design and an Evaluation of Available Literature. National Institute of Justice. May 6, 2016.

White House's Office of Science and Technology Policy Strengthening Forensic Science: A Progress Report. February 2014. Accessible at https://www.whitehouse.gov/sites/default/files/microsites/ostp/forensicscience_progressreport_feb-2014.pdf

Index

For Product Safety Concerns and Information please contact our EU
representative GPSR@taylorandfrancis.com
Taylor & Francis Verlag GmbH, Kaufingerstraße 24, 80331 München, Germany

www.ingramcontent.com/pod-product-compliance
Ingram Content Group UK Ltd.
Pitfield, Milton Keynes, MK11 3LW, UK
UKHW050756180926
475701UK00007B/1086
* 9 7 8 0 3 6 7 7 8 4 0 0 3 *